Published by

Adonis & Abbey Publishers Ltd
P.O. Box 43418
London
SE11 4XZ
Tel: + 44 845 388 7248
Website: http://www.adonis-abbey.com
Email: editor@adonis-abbey.com

Nigeria
Adonis & Abbey Publishing Company
P.O. Box 10546 Abuja,
Nigeria
Tel: +234 816 5970458

First Edition, August 2012

British Library Cataloguing-in-Publication Data
A catalogue record for this book is available from the British Library

ISBN: 9781909112018

Printed and bound in Great Britain

RE-NEGOTIATING THE NIGERIA-NATION

ESSAYS ON STATE, GOVERNANCE AND DEVELOPMENT

JIDEOFOR ADIBE

Adonis & Abbey
Publishers Ltd

TABLE OF CONTENT

SECTION ONE: PERSONALITIES IN HISTORY

SECTION THREE: THE ECONOMY

SECTION FIVE: BELIEF SYSTEMS, IDEAS AND IDEATIONS

PREFACE

Re-negotiating the Nigeria-Nation is a collection of articles published variously in my weekly columns in two leading national newspapers in Nigeria - the *Daily Independent* and the Daily *Trust*.

The idea to maintain a weekly column in a Nigerian newspaper came sometime in 2008, when, after some twenty years of living outside the shores of the country, I began making serious arrangements to return home. Like most Nigerian professionals in the Diaspora, there really comes a time when the motivation to keep living 'abroad' simply dries up and home – meaning the country of one's birth - begins to hold a magnetic attraction despite the persistence of the challenges that helped to prolong one's self-imposed exile. Though I had continued to write about the conditions at home since I left the country in August 1988, I felt that a regular weekly column would force me into greater commitment to following the developments at home.

Through a friend, Ugochukwu Ejinkeonye, a writer, blogger and columnist, who was then a member of the editorial board of the *Daily Independent*, the management of the newspaper discussed my interest and decided to put me on a six-month trial before a column was eventually assigned to me. I remain deeply appreciate of this gesture which was to launch me into being a newspaper columnist in Nigeria.

In August 2010 I decided to do a one-month 'sabbatical' with the Daily Trust in Abuja. It was my first time ever of visiting Abuja and I simply fell in love with the city. While on the 'sabbatical' I began writing for the paper and was subsequently offered a column in the newspaper.   I was subsequently appointed a Member of the paper's Editorial Board and 'promoted' to a Back Page Columnist shortly after I relocated to the country in March 2011. I remain most grateful to the Chief Executive/ Chairman of the paper's Editorial Board Mannir Dan Ali, the Acting Editor Suleiman Bisalla and Opinions Editor Ibrahim Auduson for the opportunity and support. I am equally grateful to the other members of the paper's Editorial Board for vigorous exchanges at the Board's weekly meetings which I have continued to find highly stimulating and a good opportunity to learn. Many of the articles in this collection benefited from the robust exchanges in these meetings.

I am equally grateful to the readers, in particular the regular readers of my works who often keep faith by writing, texting or calling to commend or critique each output. These comments have proved extremely useful in helping me strive to become better with each work.

It is often said that journalism is history written in a hurry. I am not sure if column writing fits into that genre. As an academic, I try my best, with each piece, to embed it in sober research. Despite this, any errors of facts and interpretations in any of articles are mine, and are regretted.

With a collection of articles written over a number of years, there is often a challenge of how to arrange them to give the work both coherence and a narrative logic. I have chosen to arrange this into five sections around issues on – Personalities; Nation-building, Elections and the Contest for Power at the Federal Level; Units of the Nation- State, the Economy and Belief systems, Ideas and Ideations and Nigeria and the Rest of the World. Obviously there are overlaps and some of the articles could fit into more than one section.

Even after the articles have been grouped into these five sections, there is an additional challenge of how to arrange the articles within each section: should they be arranged according to date of publication or according to thematic relatedness? I opted for the latter but decided to put at the end of each article the date of publication to help contextualize the discussion.

This collection is not only meant to show my thoughts on some of the issues that drive Nigeria's politics and society but is also meant to be a modest contribution to the country's marketplace of ideas – a key infrastructure that underpins the country's democracy project.

Jideofor Adibe
Abuja, August 2012

SECTION 1
PERSONALITIES IN HISTORY

CHAPTER 1

WHY WE SHOULD RALLY BEHIND LAWAN FAROUK

I do not approve of corruption and do not mean it should be condoned. However while I concede that some of the allegations against Lawan Farouk, the four-time Member of the House of Representatives from Kano State are weighty, I will argue that we should 'tactically forgive' or overlook his alleged crimes and indiscretions . I shall elaborate on this later.

To recap, the Lawan-led ad hoc committee on fuel subsidies uncovered monumental illegal payments to oil companies and marketers to the tune of $6 billion. According to the committee's findings, 17 marketers did not obtain FOREX but claimed to have imported petroleum products, 15 marketers obtained FOREX but did not import petroleum products, 71 oil marketers were recommended to face probe and refund N230.1 billion while 18 oil marketers committed other infractions. The report also revealed that N127.8bn, split in tranches of N999 million, was paid 128 times to "unknown entities" within 24hours while some 15 purported fuel importers collected $337,842,663 in 2010 without importing any fuel!

Nigerians, who were heralded into the New Year with news of the removal of subsidies on petroleum products, were furious and wanted heads to roll. The government was hesitant in implementing the recommendations of the Committee amid pressure from the media, civil society groups and some legislators. Then out of the blues came what looked like a fight-back by what one newspaper called "oil thieves": Malam Lawan, who had become a folk hero of sorts following the damning revelations against the subsidy cabal, was alleged to have demanded the sum of $3m from Femi Otedola, for his companies Zenon Oil and African Petroleum to be taken off the list of erring marketers. It was alleged that there are both video and audio recording of him accepting a bribe of $620,000 as part payment of the $3m demanded.

Both Otedola and Lawan had their versions of events. And each version had holes that ought to be seriously interrogated. What seemed fairly established is that money changed hands.

Ian Fleming's James Bond novel, *Goldfinger* (1959), has a line that is very apt in this situation: The principal character in the novel Auric Goldfinger told James Bond: "'Mr Bond, they have a saying in Chicago:

'Once is happenstance, twice is coincidence, the third time it's enemy action.'"

How many times has the hunter become the hunted whenever there is a probe in which the high and the mighty are implicated? I can count at least four in recent times - more than the three the gangsters in the Chicago of the 1920s and 1930s would require to conclude it was an enemy action:

First, in 2008 following claims that the country spent $16 billion on an Integrated Power Project to enable it achieve 10,000 megawatts of electricity by 2007, a House of Representatives' Committee headed by Godwin Ndudi Elumelu was mandated to investigate why so much money was spent without any noticeable improvement in electricity supply. The Committee indicted past leaders, ministers, government officials and many high-profile personalities. Suddenly the report got rubbished when Elumelu and others were arraigned for allegedly stealing N5.4bn meant for the Rural Electrification Agency.

Second, on October 12 2011 Senator Bukola Saraki, former Governor of Kwara State moved a motion for the investigation of the Fuel Subsidy Management fund. He noted that while the sum of N240bn was budgeted in 2011 for fuel subsidy by the end of August 2011 N931bn had been spent on fuel subsidies. Saraki's motion was to unleash a number of events that led to the naming and shaming of the fuel subsidy cabal. His motion also probably influenced the House of Representatives' decision to set up a committee to probe the fuel subsidy regime. However, not long after these events Saraki became a marked man. He was questioned by the Special Fraud Unit (SFU) of the Nigeria Police Force (NPF) over N8.5 billion loan granted by the defunct Intercontinental Bank Plc to some companies he is alleged to be a shareholder.

Third, there was also the Capital Markets probe chaired by Herman Hembe, who accused Ms Arunma Oteh, the then Director-General of the Securities and Exchange Commission of sundry financial improprieties including spending N42.5m to procure three Toyota vehicles without a tender's board meeting in breach of the Public Procurement Act 2007 and of spending N850,000 on food in just one day and N85,000 on another day. Ms Oteh in turn alleged she was being unfairly treated by the Hembe Committee because she had refused to accede to their demand for a bribe of N44m. She also accused him of collecting an estacode and a business class ticket to attend an emerging market conference in the Dominican Republic without actually attending the conference or returning the money. The EFCC has since filed charges against Hembe and his deputy Ifeanyi Azubogu on the last allegation and the case is still in court.

There are at least three threads that run through the above instances. One, is the ease with which the hunter is turned into the hunted. Two, is that in each instance the law enforcement agencies are quick to swoop on the crusader as soon as there are allegations of malfeasance against him while they pretend to be deaf, dumb and blind at the revelations of the criminal wrong doings of the filthy rich, the powerful and the well-connected. Three, the pattern of a fight-back tends to be the same: raise questions about the character of the main crusader and then use the law enforcement agencies to utterly discredit and humiliate the person and by so doing raise questions about the integrity of the crusade.

My personal opinion is that unless the dark forces that are holding the country hostage are unmasked and neutralized nothing will ever come out of any probe. In fact their tactic ensures that anyone appointed to probe anything in which these dark forces have interest, will be forced to do deals with them or risk being rubbished because as they would say in my village, there is hardly anyone you go digging into his/her anus without encountering some faeces. The bribery allegations against Lawan - which are admittedly serious – appear to be a mere subplot in a complex story whose storyline is still unfolding to the rest of us but completely known to the dark forces that control this country. For this, I believe that 'dealing' with Farouk now is less urgent than unmasking and neutralising these dark forces. There is also a need to unearth the system dynamics that often turn otherwise good and principled people into compromised individuals. Additionally, the more Farouk is rubbished – rightly or wrongly – the more the integrity of the report produced by his committee is called into question. And this is exactly what those dark forces want.

There are several instances in our daily life in which the crimes of an individual are tactically overlooked in order not to allow such to get in the way of accomplishing a higher objective. For instance the government uses that principle to turn suspected criminals into State witnesses or in the granting of amnesty such as happened with the Niger Delta militants.

Chinua Achebe vividly illustrated this principle of 'tactical forgiveness' in his novel No Longer At Ease (1960). In the book, the main character Obi Okonkwo was an upright and principled man who was never swayed by prevailing norms and practices. For instance when he was sent to London by his village to go and study Law so he would come back and handle their land cases, he chose instead to follow his heart and read English. At a reception by his village to welcome him from England he attended the event wearing a simple shirt when he knew the expectations were for him to wear the best suit in town. He also addressed them in the 'is' and 'was' type of English when he knew the expectation was for him to bamboozle them with the 'English that fills the mouth'. Though he was sponsored by his village to study in England, he refused to use his position in the civil service to influence the recruitment of members of his town or ethnic group into the service, regarding such as nepotism. Above all he married the woman he loved – an 'osu' (an untouchable) even though he knew such was an abomination by his people. A man with such a profile as Obi Okonkwo was the least you would expect to take bribe. Yet he did, overwhelmed by systemic pressures to do so and was caught the first time he tried it!

Despite being a huge disappointment to his kinsmen, his town union decided to rally behind him because he was their only 'eye' so to say in that scheme of things. Though Farouk has not been found guilty, there is a need to rally behind him and pretend that he was either framed up or a mere victim of system dynamics which has a way of swallowing those that want to rapidly change the way it works. After the oil thieves have been dealt with, we can then call Malam Farouk aside and then demand explanations for what really happened between him and Otedola.

Daily Trust, 21 June 2012

CHAPTER 2

BETWEEN AZAZI AND HIS CRITICS

Reports that the National Security Adviser General Andrew Owoeye Azazi blamed the PDP's zoning and power rotation arrangements for the increased spate of violence in the country have generated intense media interest. Speaking at the recently concluded South-South Economic Summit in Asaba, Delta State, and General Azazi was quoted by the Vanguard of April 30 2012 as saying: "The issue of violence did not increase in Nigeria until when there was a declaration by the current President that he was going to contest. PDP got it wrong from the beginning. The party started by saying Mr. A can rule, and Mr. B cannot rule, according to PDP conventions, rules and regulations and not according to the Constitution. That created the climate for what is happening. Is it possible that somebody was thinking that only Mr. A could win, and if he did not win, he could cause a problem in the society?"

By appearing to imply that the PDP is anti-democratic and that its zoning and power rotation policies are unconstittutional and a trigger for the spate of violence in the country, Azazi unwittingly handed an ammunition to PDP's opponents. And as should be expected, the party was livid for the General's wild gaffe. The Publicity Secretary of the party Chief Olisa Metu was quoted by the same Vanguard as retorting: "Appointees of government should navigate only on the terrain where their authority would not be humbled by superior knowledge so as to avoid attracting undeserving and unnecessary ill-feelings for their principal." Several members of the party have called for the General's sack.

But how true is it that Azazi attacked the PDP?

Though a literal reading of the text would seem to suggest that he blamed the PDP's zoning and power rotation policy for the spate of violence in the country, I honestly don't believe it was what he meant to convey. My personal opinion from reading the 'offensive' statements attributed to him is that he was probably trying to ingratiate himself to the President by using innuendos to defend him from his apparent weak handling of the Boko Haram challenge. He sought to do this by buying into one of the conspiracy theories popular in the South, namely that Northern politicians are using Boko Haram to make the country ungovernable for Jonathan because he is an ethnic minority from the South and a Christian. A corollary of this 'theory' is that the North feels it is their 'birthright' or 'turn' to rule, and because they lost to Jonathan, who is one of their own, they decided to make the country 'ungovernable' for him. Like every conspiracy theory, there are fragments of 'evidence' that could be doctored to support a position that had been adopted apriori. In this case the evidence was former Vice President Alhaji Atiku Abubakar's quote of Franz Fanon (JF Kennnedy also made a variant of this quote) that those 'who make peaceful change impossible make violent change inevitable' during the acrimonious PDP primaries in late 2010. There was also Buhari's call on his supporters to defend their votes. As politicians are wont to do all over the world, these remarks were abstracted from their contexts, turned on their heads and politicised – despite the fact that a UPN-leaning newspaper repeatedly published the same quote by Atiku after the 1983 presidential elections won by the NPN. There were also several politicians from the South who used even stronger language than Buhari did to urge their supporters to defend their votes. As mentioned earlier, it is in the nature of politics that gaffes by political opponents are maximally exploited for political mileage just as statements by opponents could be taken out of context to achieve the same purpose. This is precisely what politicians mean when they urge their colleagues not 'to play politics' with an issue. Several statements by President Jonathan have also been taken out of context and politicised by his political opponents – such as when he said he was probably not the most qualified to be President but that God knew why He chose him for the job. His opponents quickly twisted this to imply that he had admitted that he was not qualified to be the President.

It is important to underline that it is not only people from the South that have conspiracy theories about Boko Haram. Many Northerners have their own conspiracy theories about the sect. One of the popular ones is that Boko Haram is actually a creation of the presidency to make the North or Islam look bad and by so doing help the President to mobilise Christian and Southern support. Honestly these set of 'theories' are just what they are – mere 'conspiracy theories' - that is a belief that important events are driven by secret plots that are generally unknown to the public.

Whaever may be General Azazi's motive in making the 'offensive statements credited to him, it is possible to interrogate the factual correctness or otherwise of some of his assertions.

'PDP got it wrong from the beginning. The party started by saying Mr. A can rule, and Mr. B cannot rule....' General Azazi was factually wrong for implying that the PDP introduced zoning and power rotation arrangement in the country. The truth is that this was an initiative of the defunct NPN even though the principle behind it had been embraced by all the major political parties in the country even before independence.

"The issue of violence did not increase in Nigeria until when there was a declaration by the current President that he was going to contest." General Azazi was also wrong when he created the impression that there is a causal relationship or association between zoning and power rotation on the one hand and violence on the other.If such a relationship or association existed, then the NPN's zoning and power rotation arrangements would have also led to violence. Also Boko Haram began its violence in January 2010 – before Jonathan even became the Acting President – when it killed four persons in an attack at Dala Alemderi Ward in Maiduguri metropolis as the beginning of a series of reprisal attacks for the extra judicial killing of its leader Mohammed Yusuf following a clampdown on the sect authorized by the late Yaradua in 2009.

It cannot of course be ruled out that some people in the North were aggrieved by the fallout from the contentious PDP's presidential primaries. In Nigeria's peculiar manner of sharing privileges, the Yorubas are believed to control the corporate economy, the Igbos the commercial economy while the North holds political power. Certainly there may be those who feel that with the presidency going to a Southern Christian, the North's lever in ensuring that it is not dominated has been removed. In Nigeria's political parlance, such people feel the North has become 'marginalised' – just as the Igbos, Yorubas and virtually every ethnic group in the country have their own tales of exclusion and marginalisation. In essence, feelings of exclusion and cries of marginalisation are part of Nigeria's political culture and therefore cannot, on their own, be triggers of violence.

If, as I have argued earlier, General Azazi probably merely set out to use innuendo to absolve the President from any incompetence in handling the current security challenges, it is obvious he did not succeed. If anything his effort boomeranged. More importantly by dabbling into high octave politics, General Azazi brings into focus his performance as the National Security Adviser. Given the security situation in the country, it is unlikely many Nigerians will score him high.

There are a few important revelations about President Jonathan from the 'Azazigate'. When asked about the 'offensive' statements credited to Azazi, Jonathan was quoted by ThisDay of April 29 2012 as saying: "I read in the newspapers some journalists quoting the national security adviser. Until I read the script myself and listen to him, I cannot properly react to his statement...One thing I do know, like philosophers will say, human beings disagree because people use different words to mean the same thing and use one word to mean different things."[emphasis, mine].

Three important revelations are emphasised here: One is that the President actually reads newspapers – not many leaders do as they rely on a 'summary of what the papers say' written by their aides. Two, is that even though he does not look it, it is possible that the President is enamoured by philosophical reflections – going by his reference to what philosophers say in the quote attributed to him. Three, is that the incident has generated the first quotable quote from the President: '...human beings disagree because people use different words to mean the same thing and use one word to mean different things'. The late chief Awolowo once complained that our leaders – or their speech writers- are incapable of articulating 'quotable quotes'. Apart from Buhari's remarkable "this generation of Nigerians and indeed future generations have no other country than Nigeria. We shall remain here and salvage it together", is there any quotable quote that can be readily associated with any of our past Presidents or Heads of State?

Daily Trust, 3 May 2012

CHAPTER 3

NGOZI'S BID FOR WORLD BANK PRESIDENCY

The recent nomination of Dr Ngozi Okonjo-Iweala by South Africa, Nigeria and Angola for the World Bank presidency has been generating intense conversations internationally and among Nigerians. 'Auntie' Ngozi, whose candidacy has been endorsed by the African Union, faces two other challengers – the US nominee, Jim Yong Kim, a Korean-American and the 17th President of Dartmouth College, and José Antonio Ocampo Gaviria, a Professor at Columbia University, who was nominated by Brazil.

It must be conceded that there is a high degree of ambivalence in conversations about Dr Okonjo Iweala. Here is a woman who is very admired for her superior education (Harvard, MIT), simplicity, non-intimidating presence, poise and the way she appears completely unfazed by her career accomplishments. Yet, her career accomplishments at the World Bank, a reason many admire her, is equally a major reason why she is intensely distrusted, if not disliked, by some constituencies. Ngozi spent most of her working life in the World Bank, whose (and its institution, the IMF's) brand of economics is deeply distrusted by many Nigerians, especially after the sad experiences of the structural adjustment programmes of the 1980s and 1990s, which were supported by the two Bretton Woods institutions.

Those who distrust her from this plank often feel vindicated by the rather tactless invitation of Christine Lagarde, the French Managing Director of the IMF, who visited the country from December 19-20 2011. Barely two weeks after her visit, the government ambushed Nigerians with the announcement that subsidies on premium petroleum products had been removed, effective from January 1 2012. Dr Okonjo-Iweala was thought to have facilitated Mademoiselle Lagarde's visit.

Apart from the civil society groups who see her as an agent of Western imperialism (largely on account of her long association with the World Bank), there is also a strong suspicion that many of her cabinet colleagues privately envy or loathe her designation as 'Co-ordinating Minister of the Economy' – the first among equals who must vet their projects and budgets. Ngozi is also apparently not liked in the National Assemblies where it is thought that her insistence on budget cuts do not go well with many legislators. She is equally thought not to be on the good books of several contractors who feel she is unduly plugging avenues of private accumulation. Her greatest supporter however seems to be the President who has continued to give her political cover.

The bid to lead the World Bank

Despite the ambivalence about Ngozi – a personality that is admired but whose competence is derived from a highly distrusted institution - the key questions around her bid to lead the World Bank are: is she really qualified for the job? Are there any benefits for the country if she succeeds in her bid? And what are her chances of clinching the job?

To answer the first question requires knowing the pedigree of the 11 Presidents the World Bank has had so far. Starting from the first President of the Bank, Eugene Isaac Meyer, an American financier, publisher of the Washington Post and Head of War Finance Corporation under Woodrow Wilson, the expectation has been that any boss of the World Bank must be someone versed in financial matters and with the experience of working in government and managing complex institutions. Contrary to what many people believe, you do not need to be an economist to lead institutions like the World Bank or the IMF. Christine Lagarde, the current Managing Director of the IMF is a lawyer and a significant number of the past presidents of the World Bank were also lawyers with financial sector experience. Ngozi has a PhD in Regional Economic Development from MIT. She had been Vice President and Corporate Secretary of the World Bank Group and later Managing Director of the Bank. She had variously been Nigeria's Finance Minister, Foreign Affairs Minister and currently Finance Minister and Co-ordinating Minister of the Economy. She was among those touted as possible replacement for former World Bank President Paul Dundes Wolfowitz, a political scientist, who was President of the Bank from 2005-2007.

Based on the requirements of the job, there is no doubt that Ngozi is eminently qualified. Some have included as her advantage her 21 years experience in the Bank. The truth is that this is not an obvious advantage. It in fact remains a controversial issue in the appointment of people to head complex institutions like universities and big businesses whether it is better to elevate someone from within the organisation or to get an outisder. Though elevating someone who knows how the system works removes substantially the need for a learning curve, some feel it is often more difficult for an insider promoted to head big organisations to carry out needed reforms. This thinking is probably the reason why of all the

11 Presidents of the World Bank so far, none has been from the career ladder in the Bank.

Some have asked, how, what appears to be the pursuit of personal glory by Dr Okonjo-Iweala, could benefit the country. Those who expect that as President of the World Bank Nigerians will be given preferential treatment when they apply for jobs at the Bank or that she could influence more of the Bank's projects to be sited in the country, will be disappointed. The World Bank is not like Nigeria or most African States where the President's word is virtually law and State Governors could direct state universities to be located in their village. The critical benefit for the country will be its 'hurrah effect' – the feel good factor of knowing that one of our own is out there mixing it up with the top dogs of the world. Ngozi's appointment will also be a PR coup for the country, an inestimable investment in the quest to re-brand the country. Her appointment will equally be a big boost to the Jonathan administration in the eyes of the inernational community – for pulling off what will be regarded as a diplomatic coup. Even the mere fact that she is seen as the African candidate is already a sort of victory for an assumed shuttle diplomacy of the Jonathan administration.

On face value 'Auntie' Ngozi's chances are not enormous because of the unwritten rule that the Presidency of the Bank should go to the US while the Managing Director of the IMF should be reserved to the Europeans. That arrangement had its roots in the balance of power configuration in July 1944 when 730 delegates from all the 44 Allied nations gathered at the Mount Washington Hotel in Bretton Woods, New Hampshire, United States, for the United Nations Monetary and Financial Conference. Among the outcomes of that conference was the establishment of both the IMF and the World Bank in 1945. Though the world has changed remarkably since the 1940s, both America and Europe have clung stubbornly to the system of power configuration of that gone era. It is likely that in nominating Jim Yong Kim, a Korean American who emigrated to the US when he was just five years old as the US candidate, President Obam hoped to meet half-way those who wanted people from the emerging economies to be given a chance and those who believe it is an American birth right. This sense of entitlement will be the greatest structural threat to 'Auntie' Ngozi's bid despite formal promises that the selecton will be based on merit. In selecting the next person to head the World Bank, America has 15% voting right and could count on European support. Nigeria has less than one percent voting right.

Despite the obvious structural and inherent constraints to her candidacy, I believe that Ngozi has two critical advantages in her favour:

she is the only female candidate and will most likely bring to bear on her candidacy and on the interviewing panel that power of female enchantment. Ngozi also has history on her side. When Emeka Anyaoku became the third Secretary-General of the Commonwealth Secretariat on July 1 1990, not only was he the first African to hold the post but also the first to be selected from a career in the Secretariat. In the same vein, when Kofi Annan became the seventh Secretary General of the United Nations on January 1 1997, not only was he the first Black African to hold the position (yes, his predecessor Boutros Boutros Ghali was also an African, albeit a 'White' one), but also the first person with an extensive career in the United Nations to be so appointed. If Ngozi gets the job, not only will she be the first African and first woman to hold the position but also the first person who had an extensive career in the Bank to to be appointed to head it.

Daily Trust, 29 Mar 2012

CHAPTER 4

SHEGUN AGANGA: TEN MONTHS AFTER

Finance Minister Segun Aganga is a very brilliant man. You do not become a managing director of Goldman Sachs, a leading investment banker in the world, for being stupid.

And for a Blackman to have become so in the United Kingdom – an essentially White world - meant there must have been one or two things going for him besides his obvious academic brilliance. When he was appointed Finance Minister, some Diaspora Nigerians proudly appropriated him as representing their 'constituency' in the government. But has Dr Aganga, managing director in hedge funds at Goldman Sachs since 2003 until he was appointed Finance Minister, really delivered?

Several observations could be made:

One, in our type of countries, where the institutions are weak and the wishes of the man of power are virtually law, it will be unfair to completely blame any Finance Minister for the failings of the economy. For Dr Aganga who was appointed Finance Minister on the eve of an election year in which the President is also a candidate, assessing his performance becomes even more complicated since political considerations are often the dominant considerations in policy-making and execution in an election year. My personal opinion is that the legacy of Dr Aganga, an expert in wealth management, may well be tied to the fate of the National Sovereign Wealth Fund, which has his finger prints all over it.

Two, while Dr Aganga can be excused for any non-performance of the economy, it is possible to assess the extent to which he has brought the 'x-factor' to governance – positive intangibles that reflect his long years of sojourn in Europe and from being a director of a major investment bank. My strong feeling here is that he takes criticisms of the economy by top politicians and public figures as a direct attack on his competence and consequently reacts inappropriately. A case in point was when former Vice President repeatedly expressed concerns about the direction of the economy, in particular over the regime's accumulation of huge loans and depletion of both foreign reserves and the Excess Crude Account. There is no doubt that Atiku's concerns about the economy were, as should be expected of any presidential candidate, tainted with politics. Unusual for a Finance Minister, Dr Aganga jumped into the fray and warned Atiku, a politician, not to 'play politics' with the economy. In

31

our political tradition, a Minister is considered too junior to take a direct shot at a presidential candidate, especially a credible one who had been a former Vice President of the country. Dr Aganga further told Atiku that the 'economy is too technical for some people to understand' (*ThisDay*, November 25, 2010). In countries like the USA, this statement would have opened him up to charges of 'elitism' - of talking down to people.

Three, ironically while Dr Aganga believes that the 'economy is too technical for some people to understand', some economists hold a similar 'disdainful' view of him on grounds that he is not a macroeconomist, has not published any paper on Nigerian economy and has questionable understanding of how Nigeria works, having been living abroad for too long. I have several times found myself playing the role of Dr Agang's unofficial spokesman, especially among economists - not because he is a fellow Diasporan but more because I have tremendous respect for what he has accomplished at a personal level and also believe that with his exposure he will be able to attract competencies that will complement his own skills. Dr Aganga graduated in 1980 with a First Class Honours in Financial Accounting from the University of Ibadan and subsequently did post graduate studies at Oxford University, UK.

Four, with the lull in political activities following the end of the primaries, it may perhaps be germane to have honest discussion about the direction of the economy. Besides the undeniable depletion in foreign reserves and excess crude accounts, there are other worrying statistics: The *Vanguard* of July 20 2010 reported that the federal government raised alarm over the increasing rate of unemployment in the country which official figures said was at 19.47% (some say the real figure is likely to be around 40-50%). On November 5, 2010, the *Nigerian Tribune* reported that the "World Economic Forum (WEF) has slammed Nigeria over alleged poor governance and inadequate infrastructure financing" and downgraded the country to 127 out of 139 countries. In the 2010 Human Development Report compiled by the United Nations Development Programme (UNDP), Nigeria was grouped among the 41 countries considered to have the "least human development". According to the Report, Nigeria's wealth —as defined by gross domestic product per head—has slipped. The GDP per head in Nigeria was given as a mere 1,224 dollars, compared to 9,812 dollars in South Africa, 1,628 dollars in Kenya and 2,197 dollars in Cameroon. On life expectancy, the Report said that in 2010 Nigeria's life expectancy was 48.4 years on average below that of Ghana (57.1.), Cameroon (51.7), Benin Republic (62.3) and Uganda (54.1). Meanwhile a list released by Transparency International on October 26, 2010 showed that Nigeria has fallen four steps (from 121 position in 2008 to 130 in 2009 to 134 in 2010). Again in October 2010, it was reported that Nigeria slipped from 35th to 40th position in the Mo Ibrahim good governance ranking of 53 countries in Africa. Similarly a survey conducted as part of its membership operational audit in January 2010 by the Manufacturers Association of Nigeria, showed that 839 manufacturing companies closed shop in 2009 as a result of harsh operating environment. . With these statistics – and politics aside - it is difficult for any patriotic Nigerian not to be concerned.

Five, with due respect, I disagree with the Finance Minister that expressing what I will regard as robust concerns about the direction of the economy amounts to deliberately talking down the economy. I am uncomfortable with some of the language used by the Minister in replying to critics, including his use of innuendo to suggest that Professor Chukwuma Soludo, former Governor of the Central Bank, should be in jail- apparently for his rather ill-advised harsh criticisms of the direction of the economy in the media. In the 'marketplace of ideas' theory of democracy, it is generally believed that "the best of truth is the power of the thought to get itself accepted in the competition of the market". And this implies looking beyond the messenger - even if his ideas offend, shock or infuriate - to interrogate his message and accommodate those that are useful. It is precisely this capacity to look beyond a repugnant messenger and to accommodate uncomfortable criticisms that separates mature democracies from banana republics.

Daily Trust, 27 January 2011

CHAPTER 5

ADAMS OSHIOMHOLE: A LABOUR ACTIVIST AS GOVERNOR

The recent threat by the Edo State Governor 'Comrade' Adams Oshiomhole to arrest Chief Anthony Anenih, the former Chairman of the Board of Trustees of the PDP, made headlines. Oshiomhole was quoted as saying: "Whether Anenih likes it or not, I am the chief security officer of Edo State. I can restrict his movement in this state if he becomes a security risk. I can arrest him, prosecute him and have him jailed"(Daily Sun online January 24, 2010).

The context of Oshiomhole's threat is the battle for the soul of Edo state, which, Chief Anenih, also known as "Mr Fix it", had long regarded as his fiefdom. It is thought that Oshiomhole exploited the schism between Anenih and his former political godson Professor Osunbor who was declared the winner of the 2007 poll by INEC. Apparently Oshiomhole promised to be a more loyal political godson than Osunbor in exchange for Anenih's support during Oshiomhole's protracted legal battle to unseat the law professor from the Edo Government House. Oshiomhole was reported to have publicly feted Anenih as a father figure to him and had in numerous public fora poured effusive encomiums on the political godfather while the alliance lasted. However as often happens between political godfathers and godsons, the unholy alliance began to unravel as soon as power was won and consolidated. As the former allies fell out, the 23 January 2010 re-run elections of the Etsako central constituency of the Edo State House of Assembly became an opportunity to determine who is really in control of the soul of Edo politics.

While I am not a fan of Anenih's politics, I equally believe that so-called political godsons who obviously exploit the political godfathers to gain power only to start demonising them once they have won and consolidated power, are not often sufficiently told their 'sins' to their face. There is something morally wrong in the present trend whereby some relatively weak power hawks willingly enter into an unholy alliance with some powerbrokers only to double-cross their benefactors and camouflage their deceit by unnecessary moral grandstanding. To constantly demonise the political godfathers while exonerating, or even lionising their political godsons, is akin to blaming only the perpetrator of a 419 scam while treating the victim as innocent. Just as both the perpetrator and victim of a 419 scam knew they were involved in a shady

34

deal, so does a political godson often know that his adopted political godfather can deliver power to him only by using unconventional methods. Where is the honour in double-crossing the devil after using the same devil to achieve your goal of capturing power? It is unacceptable to assume the moral high ground when the devil wants to fight back because anyone who wants to go to equity must go with clean hands.

Apart from being unimpressed with Oshiomhole's grandstanding, there are also concerns about the implications of his threat for our young democracy. In his threat, Oshiomhole was implicitly telling us that as the Chief security officer of Edo state he has the judiciary in his pockets and even knows the type of punishment that will be meted to those convicted by the courts. In more mature democracies such as the US and the UK, it is extremely difficult for public officials to even bring libel actions against the press or anyone for fear that such could 'chill' free speech and undermine democracy. In free speech jurisprudence, Oshiomhole's threat to Anenih is a greater danger to democracy than the threat of using libel action to 'chill' criticisms of a public official.

Though Oshiomhole impressed many people as President of the Nigerian Labour Congress, history teaches us that some of the most famous labour leaders of the past few decades failed woefully as political leaders. This should be a source of concern to Oshiomhole. Consider for instance the cases of Lech Walesa of Poland and Frederick Chiluba of Zambia – two of the most celebrated labour leaders of the last 40 years.

Lech Walesa was in 1980 the leader of the occupational strikes held in Lenin Shipyard in Gdansk, Poland, where he had been employed as an electrician since 1970. The strike committee legalised itself into National Coordination Committee of Solidarmosc Free Trade Union, otherwise known as Solidarity, with Walesa as the Chairman. He won the Nobel Peace Prize in 1983 and in 1990 decided to cash his fame by contesting the presidential election in Poland. He won the election but quickly found there was a world of difference between being a labour leader and being President as the goodwill he accumulated as labour leader was squandered in no time. He was for instance notorious for changing his cabinet every year in what he termed 'revolution from the top'. He lost re-election in 1995, and when he tried running again in 2000, he got less than one percent of the votes cast.

Consider again Frederick Chiluba of Zambia. After being expelled in his second year in secondary school for his political activities, the pint-sized rabble-rouser developed a passion for trade unionism while working as a bus driver. He later joined the National Union of Building from where became the chairman of the Zambia Congress of Trade Unions. In

1981, President Kenneth Kaunda detained Chiluba and several leaders of ZCTU for calling a wild strike that paralysed most of the Zambian economy. In 1991 he won the country's multi-party presidential election as the candidate of the Movement for Multiparty Democracy (MMD), defeating long-time President Kenneth Kaunda. He was re-elected in 1996.

Like Walesa, Chiluba failed as President of Zambia to replicate his successes as a labour leader. He was rather infamous for his Machiavellian tendencies such as amending the country's constitution in order to stop citizens with foreign parentage from standing for the presidency of the country – a move that was aimed at stopping Kaunda from running against him at the 1996 presidential elections (he was himself to face charges that his real father was from Zaire). President Chiluba did very little to stop the escalating crime and poverty in his country and instead tried to amend the constitution to elongate his tenure. On 4 May 2007 a London high court judge Peter Smith accused him of shamelessly defrauding his people and flaunting his wealth with an expensive wardrobe of "stupendous proportions". His eventual acquittal from these charges triggered protests across Zambia, especially among leading NGOs in the country. So much for a once popular labour leader!

While it may be too early to judge the performance of Adams Oshiomhole as Governor, it is obvious that when the balance sheet of his administration is drawn up, channeling scarce state resources to defeat an ageing political godfather will hardly count as an 'achievement'. And if Oshiomhole, who, so to say, is carrying the banner of the 'progressives', the 'radical press' and the 'usual suspects' fails as Governor, it would accentuate the usual derisory dismissal of these groups by traditional politicians with smiles of superior wisdom, and of course that cliché: talk is cheap.

Daily Trust, 4 February 2010

CHAPTER 6

AS SOYINKA JOINS PARTISAN POLITICS

T he recent news that Wole Soyinka has decided to join partisan politics made headlines. The Nobel laureate, who was elected unopposed as chairman of the Democratic Front for a Peoples Federation (DFPF), also disclosed that the aim of the new party, which was initially denied registration in 2002, was to "sanitize and transform Nigeria's nationhood into a democratic sanctuary for all her citizens".

Soyinka's decision to embrace partisan politics raises a number of pertinent issues:

One, the new party raises a vital question of unity among the 'progressives', as it will now seem that virtually everyone of those often labelled by the press as 'progressive' – the late Gani Fawehinmi, Femi Falana, Pat Utomi, Balarabe Musa, Arthur Nwankwo etc. – is now the chairman (or is it the owner?) of a political party. This trend must be dispiriting for those hoping that the ascendancy of the 'progressives' in Nigerian politics will provide a genuine alternative to the current form of politics, which is often characterised by acrimony and disunity among the contending elites in their quest for power and lucre. If every 'progressive' must 'own' a political party -none of the founding chairman of these parties has ever stepped down or been voted out of office - it raises legitimate questions about the democratic credentials of the leaders of the 'progressive' camp.

While it is legitimate to criticise our traditional politicians who too often bombard the public space with the fallouts of their acrimonious intra-elite feuds for power and money, it is equally imperative that those who position themselves, or are seen as the alternatives to the traditional politicians, are very sensitive to the implications of their political conduct. For instance as the clamour for an alternative to the existing political order continues to get louder, with some even calling for a revolution, it could be legitimate to interrogate the implications of the tendency for each 'progressive' with a name recognition to carve out his own political fiefdom rather than work in concert with others for democracy and national unity - should they come to power.

Two, no one can ever accuse the highly revered Soyinka of 'mee-tooism', so it can be averred that it is unlikely that he decided to found his own party simply because other 'progressives' are doing so. Soyinka had already become an icon even before he was awarded the Nobel Prize in literature so he hardly needs a platform to engage in the political process. We must therefore believe Soyinka, who is affectionately called the Kongi, when he said the new party was founded to "sanitize and transform Nigeria's nationhood into a democratic sanctuary for all her citizens". He gave us a further insight into the rationale for founding the party: "The DFPF for now is disinterested in the overall national scene. But after taking control in one state, one council, one ward, would begin to reach out through example to others, gradually evolving a civic rule that governs and performs through mutual collaboration"(Next online, September 25, 2010). While this objective appears laudable, it is not without problems. Do the extant laws governing the formation of political parties permit a party to emerge with the sole aim of winning power in just one state – even if it was meant to use that state as a model? How logical is it for a political party which has a national chairman and other officers from other parts of the federation to proclaim that it is disinterested in the national scene and will want to win power in just one state? What will be the criteria for deciding which state to target?

Three, the respected Kongi also implied that membership of the new political party will not be open; saying that certain category of politicians who cross carpet from the existing political parties will not be accepted. This again raises the question of whether the DFPF - which by the way sounds more like a liberation movement than a political party - intends to be a political party or just a cause group. A political party, as opposed to a cause group, actively canvasses for support and membership with the aim of winning political power. It can be inferred that a political party, which from inception erects hurdles on membership contradicts the notion of political parties as they are traditionally known.

Four, it remains unclear how the DFPF will help the presidential aspirations of Nuhu Ribadu who has over the years cultivated the support and friendship of Soyinka and a faction of the civil society that is allied to him. Mallam Ribadu has since declared that he will seek to realise his presidential ambition under the Action Congress of Nigeria. With many Nigerians seeing Ribadu as a sort of Soyinka's protégé, wouldn't it have been more beneficial to Mallam Ribadu's ambition if Soyinka had embraced the ACN rather than seeking to found his own party? There are fears that the mileage that Ribadu might have hoped to earn from his carefully cultivated association with Soyinka and his associates may be diluted with Soyinka's chairmanship of the DFPF.

Five, Soyinka's entry into partisan politics could re-open the old debate about activist creative writers in politics. Activist creative writers such as our own Kongi, Ngugi wa Thiongo of Kenya and Bate Besong of

Cameroon, are often said to operate like house flies that settle on the wounds of society. They are perhaps the people that Camilo José Cela, the Spanish winner of the Nobel Prize in Literature in 1989 had in mind when he said a writer is necessarily a denunciation of the time in which he or she lives. One of the defining features of activist creative writers is their tendency to use the protest format, which includes the deployment of combat language that is couched in anger, invectives and bitterness to engage the political process. Most mean well. However they often open themselves up to charges of naivety, if not dismissed with a wave of the hand as 'political paper weights' by traditional politicians because their premises and approaches are often so divorced from reality that even in a free and fair election they will pose no threat to the existing political order. Therefore while we will remain grateful to Soyinka for his life-long commitment to the struggle for justice, not to talk of his gift of quotable quotes, we must use the opportunity of his foray into partisan politics to interrogate the whole notion of 'progressivism'. Who is a progressive? Does 'progressive' politics really exist in Nigeria, and if so, what is the character of its current form? Do 'progressives' really want power or are they simply enamoured by protest politics? Can Nigerian 'progressives' provide a genuine alternative to the current political order?

Soyinka is a man who is much respected, if not idolised by most people who can string words together. Therefore as he dabbles into partisan politics with his full creative weight, questions are bound to arise, for which many of us will respectfully demand answers.

Daily Trust, 29 September 2010

CHAPTER 7

ATTAHIRU JEGA AND THE SEARCH FOR A NIGERIAN HERO

Nigerians seem to be in constant search for public heroes - competent little messiahs who will not hesitate to put their conscience above their life or subordinate self to the common good despite temptations and inconveniences of doing so. Our constant search for heroes could itself be a subconscious rejection of our present crop of leaders and their desiderata for our predicaments. Whether this search is predicated on forlorn hope or merely an apologia for our inertia is another thing. What seems a constant in our recent history however is that virtually every publicly anointed messiah had turned out an ordinary mortal lacking any form of Midas touch. Our hopes have consequently always been betrayed.

Will Professor Attahiru Jega turn out to be any different? Is the problem with our choice of anointed heroes or with our expectations?

Since his nomination to replace Professor Maurice Iwu as chairman of the Independent National Electoral Commission (INEC), most commentators have eulogised the choice, saying it was an indication that President Jonathan truly wants to give the country a credible election as he promised. Professor Jega's appointment and the commentaries that followed raise a number of important issues:

One, those placing their faith on Professor Jega as the new 'Messiah' point to his 'intimidating academic credentials', and his activist record as President of ASUU in the 1990s. The problem however is that 'intimidating academic credentials' have never been sufficient to a hero make out of any of our past electoral umpires. It could in fact be argued that all the previous chairmen of INEC and its precursors – starting from Eyo Esua (1960-1966) to Maurice Iwu (2005-2010) had paraded 'intimidating academic credentials'. Yet the elections they conducted were mired in controversies. True, Jega is a professor of political science. But so too were Eme Awa (1987-1989) and Humphrey Nwosu (1989-1993).

Similarly having a respected activist background has never been a guarantee of success in policy-making roles. Professor Iwu, who by a common agreement was a failure in the post, was also an activist: he was reportedly the secretary of ASUU at UNN and at one point the body's national Vice Chairman. In fact two of the most successful labour leaders in the last 50 years – Frank Chiluba of Zambia and Lech Walesa of

Poland- were unable to replicate their successes as labour leaders when they became the president of their countries.

The above is not to take anything away from the impressive personal credentials of Professor Jega but to draw attention to the fact that his professional accomplishments and personal attributes have to interact with a number of environmental variables to determine whether he will make a success of his job or not.

Two, some dissenters to the eulogies that followed Jega's nomination point out that he had a chummy relationship with Professor Maurice Iwu, the umpire that many Nigerians love to hate. It was for instance alleged that when Jega was President of ASUU, Iwu was his deputy and that when Iwu became INEC chairman; Jega became a consultant to the electoral body. The alleged chummy relationship, even if true, is however insufficient to tell us how Jega would perform as INEC chairman, as Iwu would have contested and won the post of ASUU Vice Chairman in his own right, not as a joint ticket with Jega. Also implying that Jega did wrong by accepting a consultancy position from Iwu would be stretching logic to its elastic limit - unless of course it can be proved he was not qualified for any job he did, or that his appointment did not follow due process or that he was paid more than his peers doing similar jobs. Similarly implying he was complicit in the failings of INEC because he was an external consultant to the body is to turn reason on its head. Since when have external consultants started taking blames for the failures or successes of organisations they consult for? How many external consultants are blamed or praised for the failings or successes of government agencies and even international bodies like UN, World Bank and the IMF?

What is often left out in the commentaries that followed Jega's appointment is the impact of system dynamics – the ability of a system to change someone, not just for the worse, but also sometimes for the better. We have seen otherwise good men with the best intention who became negatively transformed by the system just as we have also seen dodgy characters who got radicalised by the system. A good example of the latter is Dr Chris Ngige when he was Governor of Anambra state.

Three, commentators have also criticised the nomination of Jega for not following the recommendations of the Uwais Report on electoral reform, especially on the removal of the power to appoint INEC chairman from the President. I believe the tendency to see the recommendations of the Uwais panel as the magic elixir that will fix the problems with our elections is exaggerated. For instance while removing the power to appoint the chairman of INEC from the president could make a difference in countries where the institutions are strong, it is not certain it will have the same effect in our type of societies. Can an independently appointed INEC chairman really disobey a strong-willed President in the mould of Obasanjo who got his way with even non-PDP governors despite not appointing them (at least in theory)? Besides, how does the removal of the power of the President to appoint the chairman cushion the umpire from other sources of pressure such as politicians, traditional rulers and one's ethnic or religious groups?

Four, Jega is unlikely to 'succeed' – if by this we mean conducting an election that will be acceptable to the generality of Nigerians - for the simple fact that the odds are stacked against him. In an environment of excruciating poverty and where political office is the quickest avenue for material accumulation, the quest for political offices is understandably anarchical, a do-or-die affair. Unfortunately as INEC chairman, Jega's remit will be to conduct elections, not to fight illiteracy, poverty or change the attractiveness of political offices that are partly responsible for elections' endemically contentious nature. Also does Jega have the remit to deal with some of the deliberate chaos unleashed by politicians to maximise the chances of their purveyors being 'settled'? Does Jega have enough time to fix the sham that is the current voters' register?

Five, there is an erroneous belief that if we fix elections, then the 'dividends of democracy' will be felt in our pockets. The truth is that the link between democracy and economic progress is at best controversial. It is for instance thought that 'enlightened autocracies' are better able to marshal the resources necessary to promote economic development than are democracies, and that certain levels of economic development and literacy are necessary for democracy to take hold and flourish in a country. This should of course not be misconstrued as an argument for 'enlightened autocracy' because despite the propensity of democracy in our type of society to unleash fissiparous tendencies, it offers the best hope of long-run material well being predicated on individual freedom. As Albert Einstein would say: "Everything that is really great and inspiring is created by the individual who can labour in freedom."

Daily Trust, 24 Jun 2010

CHAPTER 8

WAS JEGA'S APPOINTMENT AS INEC CHAIRMAN A MISTAKE?

Since the appointment of Professor Attahiru Jega as INEC Chairman, there has been a certain euphoria that at long last 'a Daniel has come to judgment'. The former Vice Chancellor of Bayero University Kano has variously been feted as 'a man of integrity', 'incorruptible' and 'an activist' who is unlikely to compromise his position. His recent demand for N74 billion for a new voters' register, in a manner of take-it-or-leave-it, is however rightly raising furores:

One, beyond the hype, there is a legitimate question of whether Jega is really suitable for the job. His claim to fame lies principally in his being an 'activist' and leading the Academic Staff Union of Universities (ASUU) through a successful nationwide strike during the regime of Ibrahim Babangida. While no one will deny that Jega was successful as ASUU president and is deservedly respected as an honest man, there is however a whole world of difference between being an agitator and being an administrator. It is actually axiomatic that most 'social critics', 'activists' and labour leaders are poor administrators and rarely make good leaders. For instance two of the most famous labour leaders of the last 50 years – Frederick Chiluba of Zambia and Lech Walesa of Poland - failed as president of their respective countries. Nearer home, while Balarabe Musa, a radical activist, was unable to deal pragmatically with an NPN-dominated House of Assembly as Governor of Kaduna State during the Second Republic and was subsequently impeached, Peter Obi, a relatively honest businessman, has been able to govern Anambra state with a State House of Assembly in which his APGA party has virtually no representation. In this sense, being an 'activist' could actually be an albatross in performing the job of INEC chairman because while 'activists' and 'social critics' tend to be good with logic and in identifying the ills of a system, they are often less endowed with the acumen of how to fix the problems they are clever at identifying.

Two, though Jega was Vice Chancellor of Bayero University Kano when he was appointed INEC chairman, it is debatable whether his brief tenure in that position gave him sufficient administrative experience to run an agency as complex as INEC. There is often an unfortunate tendency in our country to appoint people with long academic qualifications but little administrative experience into management positions that they are practically unprepared for. It is for instance not uncommon to appoint a Professor who had never managed a N5 million budget in his life or knew what balance sheet means to head an agency whose budget runs into billions of Naira. Often forgotten is that being a Professor or a PhD is a very theoretical enterprise that has very little bearing to cognate experience even in one's field of specialisation. I would have preferred that the euphoria that surrounded the appointment of Jega was based on his achievements as the chairman or director of an organisation similar in complexity or in its budget as INEC.

Three, the issues surrounding Professor Jega's demand for N74 billion raise a vital question of whether we would perhaps have been better off appointing as INEC chairman someone who had cognate experience in a senior position at INEC. One of our banes as a country is the lack of policy continuity. We have been told that since 2008 Iwu's INEC maintained a policy of 'continuous voter registration', which was reportedly in place in all the headquarters of the local governments in Nigeria. We were also told that just before Iwu was sent on disengagement leave that INEC had concluded plans to detail their staff to various markets to register voters and help in voter education. Additionally, we are aware that Iwu's INEC had held regular seminars, retreats and consultations with civil societies and had also set up elaborate staff training and development programme, including the establishment of the Electoral Institute in 2005. The impression one got from Jega's demand was that nothing was available on the ground - with Iwu's voter register said to have only ten percent reliability. Even if we discount for Iwu's tendency to sound very re-assuring only to disappoint big time and his inappropriate emotional intelligence in the face of criticisms, one gets the impression that INEC under him invested well in staff training and development. Would someone with relevant experience of working in INEC have found a way of continuing from where Iwu stopped at less cost? It is germane to note that before he was sent on retirement leave, Iwu had even rolled out a time table for the conduct of the elections in January 2011, with rumours that he was asking for N5 billion to 'clean up the voters' register'. True, Iwu might have had an ulterior motive with that move, but it is baffling at the innuendo suggesting that all the money ploughed into INEC under its previous bosses had been wasted. This tends to be a typical 'academic outsider's' reflex.

Five, there are concerns that Jega may be buckling under the pressure of high expectations, and therefore looking for alibi in the self knowledge that he is unlikely meet those public expectations. This could be gleaned from the threats he had been unleashing on us recently: he asked for N74 billion Naira before August 11 or he would not guarantee free and fair elections; he had indirectly suggested postponing the elections because the recent amendments to the Electoral Act had put tremendous pressure on INEC; he also wants due process requirements in procurement to be by-passed for INEC to enable it meet the deadline. If all these are conceded, what stops Jega from waking up on the eve of the election with a demand for N200 trillion Naira to re-equip the Nigerian police - or he cannot guarantee us free and fair elections?

Six, perhaps the burden of expectations on Professor Jega could be lightened if we begin an honest discussion of the benchmarks for assessing our own 'free and fair' election. For instance, in the US which has been a democracy for donkey years, there are still vociferous problems with voter registration and voting irregularities. In the last presidential elections in the USA for instance, ACCORN, a community organizing group thought to be sympathetic to Obama, was accused by the Republican National Committee of generating phoney voter registration cards in at least eight states. In the UK, which is one of the oldest democracies in the world, many people who turned out to vote at the last election could not do so because of long queues or unavailability of voting materials. However, despite these shortcomings, the elections in these countries are usually regarded as 'free and fair'. What will be the benchmarks for our own 'free and fair' elections?

Seven, there is an inherent danger in acceding to all of Jega's requests under an implied notion of emergency because virtually all other sectors of our political economy are equally under such emergency – from healthcare, electricity and roads to transport. I am not necessarily arguing that Jega's request should not be attended to, but using a sort of blackmail to preclude debates and discussions on these could legitimately trigger agitations from other agencies and sectors of the economy, on how much they must be given before they can do their job.

It is part of the Nigerian condition that our yesterday has a way of being better than our today. Otherwise who will ever think that in less than two months of being INEC Chairman, Jega seems to be already making Maurice Iwu to look good?

The article was completed before the Senate passed the sum of N89.5 billion for the new voters' register and conduct of the 2011 elections on Tuesday, August 10, 2010.

Daily Trust 11 August 2010

CHAPTER 9

ANAMBRA STATE GOVERNORSHIP RACE: SHOULD NGIGE RUN AGAIN?

Some 50 candidates have reportedly indicated their interest in running to become Governor of Anambra state in 2010. Obviously, for some of the candidates, to be 'also-ran' is all they need, either to massage their ego, position themselves, or get a slice of the funds made available to political parties by INEC.

One name however that cannot be brushed aside in the discussion of who occupies the Government House at Awka, come next year, is Dr Chris Ngige, former Governor of the state. For those of us who appropriated him as a metaphor for courage and good governance in Anambra state, there are legitimate concerns over the implications of his candidacy – win or lose- for the Ngige myth.

One, is a concern over what Americans would often term 'the second term curse' – a tendency for an otherwise popular leader to be tarred and diminished by scandals or bad luck in his second term in office. In the USA for instance, of the three presidents that won re-election since 1974 when Richard Nixon resigned in disgrace amid the Watergate scandal – Ronald Reagan, Bill Clinton and George W Bush - none escaped the 'second term curse'. Ronald Reagan was diminished in his second term over revelations that the regime sold weapons to Iran and illegally diverted the profits to the contras, a rebel group fighting the Sandinista government in Nicaragua. Bill Clinton's second term in office was marred by revelations of illicit sex liaisons between him and former White House intern, Monica Lewinsky, which subsequently led to his impeachment by the House of Representatives in December 1998. George W Bush finished his second term in office as one of the most unpopular American presidents in history, as he left behind a bankrupt economy to Americans. Other second term American presidents had similar 'curses': Woodrow Wilson for instance suffered a stroke and saw his dream of the League of Nations rejected during his second term in office while James Madison's second term saw the British burn the White House. Nearer home, the myth of Obasanjo as an austere and incorruptible man was pooh-poohed during his second term in office.

Though Nigeria is not quite the USA and Ngige did not actually complete his first term, there is a sense in which his running for the office and winning will mean a second term in office with the possibility of a 'second term curse' unravelling the Ngige myth.

Two, Anambra state does not have a tradition of giving any of its governors a second term. This cultural aversion to the creation of a political monarch is a challenge for both Ngige and Peter Obi. Ngige faces additional challenge in this regard if the rumour that he is planning to tap Emeka Etiaba, son of the current deputy governor of the state, as his running mate, turns out to be true because the Igbos deeply abhor dynasties. If Ngige and Emeka Etiaba were to run together, would the ticket be able to simultaneously break the jinx of 'no second term' political culture in the state, and the Igbos' distaste for dynasties?

Three, the context, which helped to make Ngige a hero has changed. Ngige became a hero against the backdrop of a David fighting the goliaths – the political godfathers whom Aso Rock was allegedly protecting. This context meant that the cleverness of any move by Ngige was exaggerated. There was also a convergence between the sympathy reserved for the underdog, the exaggerated cleverness of every move made by Ngige as he fought for his political survival, and of course some concrete achievements as Governor. Were Ngige to win in 2010, this important context of a victim would not be there.

Another important context that would be missing was the extremely poor performance of the preceding Dr Mbadinuju administration, which correspondingly lowered the bar of public expectation. Were Ngige to win in 2010, the bar of public expectation will have changed so drastically because Governor Obi not only kept up with Ngige's signature road construction and timely payment of salaries, but will also leave behind a huge moral capital. Despite his own shortcomings as a politician, Obi's critics quickly concede to him prudence, good manners and self-discipline (including the extremely rare feat of not being a womaniser despite being a Governor and a man of immense personal wealth!). It is my belief that Obi will end up being most remembered in the state for the moral capital he will leave behind rather than for any concrete achievement. Can Governor Ngige live up to this moral capital?

Four, is the challenge of which political platform Ngige will use to run. If the current speculation that he will run on the platform of AC turned out to be true, then there are historical problems to contend with. As the AC increasingly becomes a reincarnation of the AD, (itself a reincarnation of Awo's UPN), the party will, in Igboland, unconsciously re-awaken the internalised fallouts from the ageless rivalries between the late Dr Nnamdi Azikiwe and the late Chief Awolowo, which have continued to define the political relation between the Igbos and the Yorubas. This relation, which is seeped in deep distrust, makes it almost impossible for any party thought to be an Igbo or Yoruba-dominated party to win any election in the west or east respectively. In its current configuration, it will be a miracle for the AC to win any election in Igboland just as it will be for PPA or APGA to win in Yorubaland, even if they were to field Governor Fashola of Lagos state as their candidate.

Five, there is a belief that Ngige as Governor has made his signature achievements – with road construction and timely payment of salaries. It is often argued that people have signature achievements, or *magnum opus,* which they will find hard to replicate or surpass. This is usually epitomised in the dictum that a sequel rarely lives up to the original or to the expectations of the audience: Can Chinua Achebe for instance ever write another novel to equal or surpass the popularity of *Things Fall Apart?*

Obviously there are many people who would love to retain Dr Chris Ngige as a metaphor for performance, a mythical figure who could have transformed Anambra state into an E*l Dorado* were he allowed to complete even a first term in office. Unfortunately an Ngige candidacy – wins or lose - will have grave implications for this myth. If I were Dr Ngige, I would opt to run for the Senate rather than seek to be Governor again. In that way, I would at least convince myself that I have moved on.

Daily Indpendent, 14 May, 2009

CHAPTER 10

AUNTIE DORA: THE RESIGNATION OF A MINISTER

The recent announcement by Professor Dora Akunyili that she was resigning as Minister of Information and would contest the Anambra Central Senatorial seat under the All Progressive Grand Alliance (APGA), has generated several headlines and commentaries. Dora Akunyili (DA), affectionately called 'Auntie Dora' by her admirers, said she was quitting the Jonathan Goodluck administration to "join my Governor, Mr. Peter Obi, who is doing a great job" in the building of Anambra State as an APGA Senator.

Several issues are raised by Professor Akunyili's resignation, and declaration for APGA.

One, is the question of her relationship with APGA, the PDP and even President Goodluck Jonathan. It will for instance be interesting to know how long DA has been a closet member of APGA, given allegations by supporters of Chukwuma Soludo, the former CBN Governor, that she played an unspecified role in the defeat of their candidate during the last governorship election in Anambra State. There are also questions about APGA's relationship with the PDP, given that the President was apparently privy to Dora's closet membership of APGA, and that Peter Obi is one of the Governors that have purportedly endorsed Jonathan's candidacy for the 2011 presidential election.

Two, DA's formal declaration of intent to run for a Senate seat under APGA also has implications for Peter's public persona. If it turns out that there was a *quid pro quo* between DA and Governor Peter Obi and that a Senate seat is a 'thank you' for helping him win the last Governorship election in Anambra State, then Peter Obi's image will suffer, because, his greatest asset, in my opinion, has been the 'moral capital' he is perceived to have brought to governance. DA's image will equally suffer as it will accentuate allegations by her critics that she is an 'egomaniacal opportunist', willing to do anything for power.

Even more challenging for Peter Obi, will be how to help DA achieve her ambition without alienating APGA's long-time members who may also be nursing the same ambition. For instance Chief George Ozodinobi, a foundation member of APGA, and the first federal legislator on the platform of the party (2003- 2007) who had already indicated interest in running for Senate in the same Anambra Central constituency, has reportedly accused DA of trying to 'reap where she did not sow'.

Both 'auntie' Dora and Governor Peter Obi will also have to confront a 'zoning' challenge. For instance DA comes from the same ward as both Governor Peter Obi and the party's national chairman, Chief Victor Umeh. Additionally, Mrs Uche Ekwunife, currently a Member of the House of Representatives under PDP but seeking for re-election under APGA, is also from the same constituency. The issues of zoning and potential allegations of domination are therefore likely to become extra hurdles standing between DA and her senatorial ambition.

Three, there is a very strong feeling that the presidency did not manage Dora's resignation and decampment to APGA well. Even if the presidency had deliberately created the circumstances that forced her to resign, wouldn't it have been better to persuade her to 'hibernate' and delay the announcement until at least after the presidential primaries? On the other hand, if truly DA felt like leaving and the presidency was unable to convince her to hang on for a little while, why was she not fired to blunt any political damage such an announcement will do to the government? The truth is that by announcing her resignation so close to the primaries, DA – whether seen as an opportunist or a woman of courage – seems to have passed a strong, two-in-one vote of no confidence on both the government of President Jonathan and his party, the PDP. Given that DA jumped ship just before the regime of the late Umaru Yaradua finally crumbled, many are wondering if she had seen anything ominous about the Jonathan regime and had decided to leave before the house tumbles.

Four, it is tempting to speculate on the political fate of DA if she either fails to win APGA's nomination or is defeated in the election proper. Will she still remain a loyal APGA member or will she once again jump ship to where opportunities appear more promising? There are speculations that DA's main reason for joining APGA is to position herself to run for the Governorship in 2014 – after allegedly lobbying and failing to get the PDP to make her the 'consensus' candidate in the last Governorship election. There is certainly nothing wrong with ambitions. However when ambition for power seems too vaulting, it also becomes repulsing. One of the dangers of being in the public glare for too long is the risk that one will suddenly start internalising and believing the hype of invincibility from supporters - making it easy to lose a sense of proportion about one's real political weight.

Five, DA's brand of politics – fiery and courageous if you are on her side, or opportunistic and egoistical with a love of drama if you are on the side of her critics – brings back the old question of women in politics Does politics masculinise women or is it only women of a certain masculine disposition that can get involved in politics and rise to the top? This question is vital because one of the feminist arguments for why more women should get involved in politics is women's alleged ability to humanise power by bringing their supposed natural compassion and gentleness to bear in what is otherwise a dog-eat-dog game. Unfortunately it will seem that only a few women are truly able to bring their supposed natural sense of motherly love and compassion into politics. And 'auntie' Dora does not seem to be among such few women.

Six, it is tempting to suspect that DA is being set up for the Ikemba and Soludo treatments. In the 1983 elections in the Second Republic, Chief Emeka Ojukwu, the Ikemba of Nnewi, who had a year earlier returned from exile in Ivory Coast to a reception by an unprecedented mammoth crowd, was lured to contest for Senate only for his party, the NPN, to allegedly work clandestinely for his defeat and demystification. In the same vein, after failing to be re-appointed as the CBN Governor, Professor Soludo was apparently lured into contesting the Anambra State Governorship election only for his party to allegedly work surreptitiously for his defeat. There is a strong suspicion that DA is being set up for a similar treatment. And like Ikemba and Soludo, 'auntie' Dora appears happy to swallow the bait.

Daily Trust, 23 December 2010

CHAPTER 11

BETWEEN NGIGE AND AKUNYILI

Anambra State has always been politically challenging, especially in the current political dispensation. In this sense, the controversial outcome of the April 9 National Assembly elections, which pitted former Governor Chris Ngige against former Information Minister Dora Akunyili in a dog fight essentially means that the State has once again managed to live up to its political notoriety.

At issue in the Ngige and Akunyili imbroglio is who represents the Anambra Central Senatorial district. After the election, the 'original' Returning Officer Alex Anene alleged that results from some areas were 'mutilated' and that he was being intimidated and financially induced by the State Government, which supports Professor Akunyili, to announce the 'falsified' results. Claiming that his life was in danger, Mr Anene 'vamoosed' only to re-appear after the Resident Electoral Commissioner for the State Professor Chukwuemeka Onukaogu had appointed his re-placement, Professor Esimole, who, almost immediately announced that the election between the two titans was inconclusive.Several issues surround the election:

The April 9 Anambra Central Senatorial election was essentially a continuation of the bitterly fought February 2010 Governorship election in the State. In that election, Dora Akunyili, a PDP member and Information Minister at the time, was accused of playing uncertain roles in the outcome of that election, which favoured Governor Peter Obi, an APGA candidate, and which the likes of Andy Uba had described as 'technical rigging'. Akunyili's traducers claimed she went into an unholy alliance with Governor Obi in which she would help Peter Obi to win a re-election in return for the Governor ensuring that she succeeds him in 2014. When Akunyili resigned as Information Minister to run for a senate seat under APGA, the conspiracy theorists claimed vindication, especially given the manner in which she emerged as APGA candidate. Her emergence as the APGA candidate quickly coalesced the 'aggrieved' forces from the 2010 Governorship election just as it seemed to energise Governor Obi into proving that his declaration as the winner of the 2010 election was not a fluke.

Two, in presenting their sides of the story both Ngige and Akunyili have understandably sought to assume the moral high grounds. But there is nothing in their antecedents to suggest that they are incapable of lying.

cheating or manipulating the political process. Ngige, we all know, admitted that he went to Okija shrine with his political godfather Chris Uba to swear an oath of allegiance to him. In the same vein, Professor Akunyili, despite her carefully cultivated image of a courageous woman, seems to be driven by blind ambition. While at NAFDAC for instance, she was said to have lobbied every 'lobbyable' to be made a Minister (the late Adedibu claimed she also lobbied him to lobby the late Yaradua on her behalf). She was also accused of lobbying the PDP to make her the 'consensus' candidate in the 2010 Governorship election in Anambra State – an accusation she never denied. Other positions she was said to have intensely lobbied for included being made INEC Chair Person and being a running mate to one of the presidential aspirants in the PDP. I am personally wary of people with vaulting ambition for as the Roman historian Sallust would say: "It is the nature of ambition to make men liars and cheats, and hide the truth in their breasts, and show, like jugglers, another thing in their mouths: to cut all friendships and enmities to the measure of their interest, and to make a good countenance without the help of a good will.". Therefore to get to the truth of what really happened in the senatorial election, we must look beyond the attempts by these two actors to play the ostrich and look at the stakes in the election and the interests of the various gladiators, including Governor Peter Obi. The actors' public personas should count for nothing here.

Three, the 'original' Returning Officer for the senatorial zone Alex Anene, together with the other officials of INEC in the State, including the Resident Electoral Commissioner Professor Chukwuemeka Onukaogu, must convince INEC beyond any reasonable doubt that they were not captives of any of the forces with vested interests in the outcome of the contest. There are several questions that beggar answers here: Though later news reports that two gun men 'ransacked various offices' at the Nnamdi Azikiwe University in search of Mr Anene after he announced the results would seem to corroborate his story that his life was in danger (which in turn could justify his going underground), we need to know what measures he took to intimate his superiors at INEC of his fears. The REC for Anambra State too has questions to answer: When Anene went into hiding, what measures did he take to find him? Did he offer him public assurances of protection before appointing his replacement? And did the newly appointed Returning Officer carry out any investigations before concluding that the elections were 'inconclusive' or was he merely appointed to act out a script, which Anene refused to act?

It should be recalled that in the 2009 re-run Governorship election in Ekiti State, the state's REC Mrs Ayoka Adebayo also went into hiding, claiming, as Mr Anene did, that she was being pressured to announce results that her conscience would not permit her to announce. No one was appointed to replace her and even her letter of resignation from her hiding place was rejected. Coincidentally Professor Akunyili was part of a joint press conference called by then Inspector of Police Michael Okiro and then INEC Chairman Maurice Iwu in which Mrs Adebayo was given an ultimatum to report herself or face harsh consequences. Why was Anene not publicly assured of his safety or declared wanted as happened in Ekiti to 'smoke' him out of his hiding place?

Four, while I commend Professor Jega's decision to set up a committee to probe what really happened in that Senatorial election, I would have preferred he did not make this statement attributed to him when he called a press conference on the issue: "The Registration Officer absconded only to reappear after the Resident Electoral Commissioner had appointed his replacement who had declared the election inconclusive." (Vanguard April 14, 2011). The judgmental tone of the statement could be misconstrued as bias.

Five, though under the law, only an election tribunal or court of law can overturn the declaration of Ngige as the Senator elect, findings from the committee will impact on the current battle between the duo in the court of public opinion. This battle will in turn affect the legitimacy or otherwise of the declaration of Ngige as the Senator elect.

The rehabilitation of the 'professorate class'

One of the fallouts from the current election cycle could well be the rehabilitation of the 'professorate class'. Jega used many Professors as Returning and Collation officers in the state. If the subtext was to show that men of integrity were used to oversee the elections, then an association between being a professor and having integrity may have been unwittingly created. Will this boost interest in academics?

Daily Trust, 21 April 2011

CHAPTER 12

BETWEEN NGIGE, OBI AND SOLUDO

As the dust generated by the recent PDP ward congress in Anambra state and the subsequent emergence of Professor Chukwuma Soludo as the party's flag bearer for the February 2010 elections settles, it is tempting to speculate on how the campaign will turn out. Which of the candidates is best positioned to create a new narrative that will harness the current individual achievements of the people into an imagined community to which all the citizens will proudly tap into, and gratefully subordinate themselves to? What qualities and baggage do these candidates bring to the table?

If the election does take place, it will be safe to assume that based on current political configuration, and barring a re-enactment of the Ifeanyi Ararume scenario in Imo state, it will be a-three horse race between Dr Chris Ngige, Governor Peter Obi and Chukwuma Soludo, the immediate past governor of the Central Bank of Nigeria.

Dr Chris Ngige

Whatever his critics may say, Dr Chris Ngige was perhaps the first Governor of the state to pay workers salary on time and construct roads on a scale never seen before in the state. It is generally believed that after Ngige, it will be really difficult for any Governor of the state to use insufficient receipts from the Federation Account to justify non-performance or to owe teachers and other state government functionaries their salary for months. However, while Ngige remains popular in the state, his candidacy is likely to face a number of challenges:

One, the context, which helped to make Ngige a hero, has changed. Ngige became a hero in the context of a David fighting several goliaths (the political godfathers whom Aso Rock was allegedly protecting). This context exaggerated the cleverness of his moves, including probably his accomplishments. In the 2010 election, the compassion reserved for an underdog will not be there. It will simply be Dr Ngige and other candidates selling themselves to the electorate. Governor Obi for instance claims he has outperformed Ngige in his signature road construction and timely payment of salaries. Similarly, despite the current tsunami in the banking sector, even Professor Soludo's most ardent critics concede he is competent and very likely to 'deliver' transformational change, if elected.

It is believed that the entrance of Soludo into the race will affect the perception of competence for both Ngige and Peter Obi.

Two, Ngige's political platform, the AC, could be an albatross. As the AC increasingly becomes a reincarnation of the AD, (itself a reincarnation of Awo's UPN), the party will, in Igboland, unconsciously re-awaken the internalised fallouts from the ageless rivalries between the late Dr Nnamdi Azikiwe and the late Chief Awolowo, which have continued to define the political relations between the Igbos and the Yorubas. This relation, which is sipped in deep distrust, makes it almost impossible for any party thought to be an Igbo or Yoruba-dominated party to win any election in west or east of the country respectively.

Three, Ngige's three-year battle with his 'godfather' Chris Uba, (including his kidnapping, tales of Okija shrine and the associated mayhem), was associated with one of the most divisive and chaotic periods in the politics of the state. Many voters who want a new beginning for the state are likely to worry whether an Ngige victory will not reactivate the fissiparous tendencies in the state and the attendant waves of violence.

Four, there are also many who still see Ngige as basically a shady character who made a pact with the devil at an Okija shrine in order to gain power. It is instructive to note that Senator Emma Anosike, one of Ngige's most ardent supporters in the 2007 elections, is now Soludo's running mate.

Governor Peter Obi

Governor Peter Obi has been a darling of the radical press and Internet bloggers, partly because of the long and arduous struggle he waged against Dr Chris Ngige and his political godfather, Chris Ubah, to actualise a mandate he won at the polls in 2003, but which was stolen from him. Many agree he is genuinely committed to the state, and is doing his level best – though some of the achievements he claims remain contentious. He also has the support of the Ikemba of Nnewi, Dim Chukwuemeka Odumegwu Ojukwu, though it remains debatable how much this could help him electorally. Against all odds, Obi emerged the consensus candidate of APGA – a feat that will only cement his image as a cat with more than nine lives.

Despite the above, and in spite of the power of incumbency, Obi's candidacy faces major challenges:

One, many see him as a highly divisive figure, whose tendency to present himself as a saint and the rest as villains (or after the state's treasury) made it impossible for him to calm nerves and lower the state's political temperature. Rather than be a unifying symbol, critics say he worsened the situation by introducing religion into the politics of the state and by being at war with virtually everyone, including the deputy governor, Dame Virgy Etiabam. Critics also accuse his regime of having the largest number of resignations of key state functionaries in the history of the state and say it is a conclusive evidence of his lack of skills in managing people. Additionally, they say that under his watch, Anambra state became both the crime and kidnap capital of the country. The critics equally argue that Obi is incapable of unifying the state, formulating a big visionary idea or generating a big narrative to which many stakeholders in the sate will willingly subordinate themselves.

Two, Obi's greatest asset – his 'saintly' image of a prudent and incorruptible Governor - took a bartering recently by the still unexplained N250m in cash intercepted in an official car in the Governor's convoy, heading to his house in Lagos - on a Sunday, earlier this year. It is very likely that his opponents will make a huge political capital out of this during the elections.

Three, Obi is also accused of being selfish, and of wanting to be the only star in the firmament. He is for instance accused of missing many opportunities to form a grand political alliance with Orji Kalu's PPA, which would have made APGA (or the alliance) the party to beat in the state. His critics similarly accuse him of failing to make efforts to unite his bitterly divided APGA until the last minute when it dawned on him that he might not have a platform to run for re-election.

Professor Chukwuma Soludo

Professor Chukwuma Charles Soludo is perhaps one of the best-known names in Nigeria today, largely because of the gusto with which he carried the bank consolidation exercise. Though some are beginning to question whether the consolidation was as successful as it was made out to be following the recent revelations of non-performing loans, his supporters argue that under him Nigerian banks became the fastest growing in Africa, expanding globally into 21 countries, with asset growth of approximately 277 per cent and a 42 per cent increase in employment in the sector as at March 2009. Soludo's supporters argue that without his consolidation exercise (which turned 89 relatively weak banks into 25 mega banks), and his vision in building up a huge foreign reserve of about $53billion at the time of peak oil prices (when many governors were calling for it to be shared out), the impact of the global economic meltdown on the country would have been much more calamitous. Soludo's supporters exonerate him from the current crisis in the banking sector, arguing that banks across the world have been facing difficulties since the financial crisis began, not just Nigerian banks (Iceland for instance lost all of its banks within two weeks of the global financial crisis). They equally deny that Soludo had a 'cosy' relationship with bank chief executives and was lax in his oversight functions, arguing that he in fact sacked some bank executives - Mrs Joy Udensi Ifegwu, chairman of Citizens Bank, and Adebisi Omoyeni, Group Managing Director of Wema Bank – on poor governance grounds. Soludo's supporters equally claim that he was seriously addressing some of the issues being raised by the new CBN governor but was doing so discreetly in order not to panic the financial system which was at risk from a global loss of confidence in banking and financial services.

Soludo is also often accused of arrogance, though his supporters swear that he is a humble and compassionate man, and that what is often mistaken as arrogance is his supreme self-confidence, charisma and decisiveness. Whatever may be the true situation, it is likely that his opponents will try to make a political capital out of it. Despite the hurdles facing Soludo, there are certain things that seem to favour him in the race:

One, he is generally seen as someone who likes to dream big and accomplish big. At the CBN, he embarked on consolidation when few gave the exercise any chance of success. Already he is talking of making Anambra state another Dubai and Taiwan – something that is likely to resonate well in a state that likes to believe it is populated by geniuses and daring entrepreneurs.

Two, while Ngige and Obi appear to be divisive figures and are closely associated with the politics of infamy, kidnapping, and high crime rate in the state, even Soludo's critics concede he has good people's skills and knows when to pick his fights. He is for instance one of the few members of the Obasanjo kitchen cabinet to retain the support of the Yar'Adua regime. His supporters believe he has the charisma to deliver a grand vision that will inspire order and end the chaotic and fractious nature of Anambra politics.

Three, the political history of Anambra state also favours Soludo. No Governor from the state has ever been given a second term in office – something that could work against both Peter Obi and Dr Ngige. Similarly all who have contested and won elections in the state - from Jim Nwobodo to Dr Mbadinuju, Peter Obi, Dr Ngige and even Chief Andy Uba - have been 'dark horses', who appeared to emerge from nowhere only few months to the election. No one who has announced his candidacy more than a few months to the actual election in the state has ever won the contest. If this trend continues, Soludo will be the prime beneficiary, just as he is likely to benefit from the determination of the PDP to win the state.

Daily Independent, 18 January 2010

CHAPTER 13

DOES PETER OBI REALLY DESERVE OUR SYMPATHY?

The moves by the Anambra State House of Assembly to impeach Governor Peter Obi have recently dominated the news. The fact that the impeachment moves came on the heels of President Obasanjo's state visit have led some to point accusing fingers to Abuja – despite denials and moves by the president's men to show that the contrary is the case. The impeachment moves have also evoked many emotions – not necessarily on whether the allegations made against the embattled governor are true or not, but that the good people of Anambra state deserve a breathing space.

The emotions are understandable. Anambra state has hardly known peace under any 'democratic' dispensation (or more correctly under any plural political competitive environment). The history of 'wahala' politics in the state pre-dates the coming of the current Republic. It was for instance a key feature in the Jim Nwobodo regime (1979-1983), where he virtually waged battle and succeeded in forcing out all known political figures from the state NPP in a bid to become the only star in the state's political firmament. Jim's Vanguard also routinelybattled the Vice President, Dr Alex Ekwueme, whose Man Friday, Senator N.N Anah, vowed, and did in fact return fire for fire. When Chukwuemeka Odumegwu Ojukwu returned from exile and allied himself with the NPN and the tempestuous Dr Chuba Okadigbo, the political temperature in the state became considerably raised, with Jim's Vanguard routinely slugging it out with the Ikemba Front.

Yes, the above was in the old Anambra state, one may argue, but as they say, it is the same sugar, just another day. Fast-forward to 1999. Shortly after the inauguration of the current Republic in May 1999, the new state governor, Dr Chinweroke Mbadinuju began his own macabre hide-and-seek dance with one 'Sir' Emeka Offor, said to be his political godfather. Anambra state was turned into a theatre of the absurd, with the highly inept Dr Mbadinuju funnelling all the state resources into his private battles for survival while salaries were unpaid, and schools were on indefinite strike. No one could rein in Dr Mbadnuju - who conveniently masked his mischief and incompetence with a religious façade while the state regressed and was being underdeveloped under his watch. The self-styled 'Sir' Emeka Offor was also a law unto himself and no one seemed able to call him to order – not Abuja, where he obviously enjoyed unfettered access to those that matter, not the love of the collective good of the Igbos who were being set back by those shenanigans, not the fear of sanction by his Oraifite community because he felt he had grown bigger than his town.

In 2003, a realignment of political forces at Abuja resonated very powerfully at Anambra state, throwing up a new political god-father, 'Sir' Chris Uba, and a new political godson, Dr Chris Ngige, whose battles are too well known to be recounted here. I am among those who felt that Peter Obi could have, (after fighting for the mandate for about a year) dropped his protracted legal battle to reclaim a mandate he was thought to have won at the polls – for the greater good of the people of Anambra state. History is in fact replete with people who have subordinated their individual ambitions and rights to the collective good. Justice – the act of determining rights and assigning rewards or punishments - must never be confused with rights – what someone is entitled to, or feels entitled to morally and legally. While justice is communal in character, rights are usually individualistic. Peter Obi's protracted legal battle was waged on the grounds of the search for justice – rather than for rights (it is really no one's rights to be a governor). But in doing so he forgot the communal nature of justice, which could have been an auto-restraining factor in this quest, and which would have forewarned him when to give it all up – especially given what Anambra state was going through, and had been through, under the highly incompetent Dr Mbadinuju.

In many parts of the world, elected presidents and prime ministers sometimes willingly step down from a position they had worked hard to get to when they feel that their actions, or sometimes even the actions of their subordinates, have threatened the common good. Some refuse to pursue the quest for justice to the point where the common good will be threatened.

A good example is Al Gore, often described as "the man who used to be the next president of the United States". Many people still believe he was robbed of victory in 2000. But he knew when to stop the quest for justice for the greater good of the community. He had to throw in the towel and send a congratulatory message to President Bush shortly after the recounting of the votes in Florida to avoid a protracted legal challenge that would further polarize Americans and rubbish the country more in the eyes of the world. He accepted his fate with certain equanimity, saying: "I wanted it, and it was not to be". Today he has built sufficient political capital, in part by the dignified way he accepted his fate, that no one will begrudge him if he chooses to cash this accumulated political capital in 2008. Peter Obi similarly had a good opportunity to accumulate a huge political capital had he been a little more gracious in his pursuit of justice, had he not mistaken justice for rights or vengeance, and had he been a little more discerning to find he was merely a pawn in a bigger political chessboard in the state.

His obsession with reclaiming his mandate via a three year legal battle also made him oblivious of the fact that his party, APGA, was disorganised, was from all indications not ready to rule, and had only two members in the House of Assembly. This was the kind of situation where a more discerning person, knowing the nature of Nigerian politics, and knowing the fate of Balarabe Musa as a PRP Governor in an NPN-dominated Kaduna House of Assembly in the 1980s, could have cautioned himself that the mandate, if actualised under the circumstances, could be a poisoned chalice. I was particularly miffed that he was still fighting for the mandate even when there was only one year left of it and the people of Anambra state seemed to have happily moved on under Ngige. Given the fact that the learning curve for posts like governorship could stretch to 18 months, and that Peter Obi was never known to have worked in the state's public sector to properly understand the nuances and dynamics of running the state, his regime, coming at the time it did, was bound to be seen as retrogression. I believe this was why he was routinely accused of non-performance. Things necessarily had to stop or slow down for him to find his rhythm, learn the job, get used to the office and its politics and articulate his own vision based on actually existing realities (as opposed to campaign promises that tend to be theoretical and platitudinous).

No one will take away some of the personal achievements of Peter Obi, including his board memberships and chairmanship of many high-profile companies, and the fact that he comes across as a decent man – despite his reported wealth. The argument however is that he could have built more political capital for himself by knowing when what was a fight for justice mutated into an unbridled struggle to realise a personal ambition. At this point, a number of people stopped seeing any altruism, any consideration of the interests of the people of the state in the whole quest to actualise the mandate.

It is true that Dr Ngige's performance may have been exaggerated but in a state where, even under Governor Jim Nwobodo's old Anambra state, newspapers carried such headlines as "Teachers to Smile" (because their salaries were being paid), his ability to pay teachers' salary as, and when due, was a huge achievement (Dr Mbadinuju owed them arrears of over six months, and schools were closed for over a year). Dr Ngige was also credited with repairing and maintaining roads – again something people of the state do not usually expect from their governor. The fact is that perception of competence, even when there is not much to show for it on the ground, is salutary to development. Today Nelson Mandela is regarded as one of the greatest living moral authorities – and rightly so. But try to pin down his concrete achievements and you will run into problems because Mandela's legacy is intangible – a hope for white and black South Africans. For Dr Chris Ngige, he seemed to give hope to the saying that 'it shall be well with us' (now conveniently mocked by some journalists). This hope was the reason why Abuja could not use the State House of Assembly to remove him, why the various inanities of 'Sir' Chris Uba failed, and why Abuja could not create the conditions that would enable it create a state of emergency. Dr Chris Ngige, despite his obvious weaknesses spoke the language of the people, and in time, could become one of the rallying points of Igbo renaissance. Again, whatever name we may call members of the Anambra state House of Assembly today, let us remember that they stood solidly behind Dr Ngige – despite pressures from known quarters. They refused to play ball with forces that were more powerful than Ngige, and which could feather their nests far better than Ngige could.

Whatever goes around comes around. Whatever one sows one reaps - one way or the other. It will be absurd and hypocritical for a man to hire a prostitute and at the same time be complaining that he is not getting true love. When the late Dr Chuba Okadigbo connived and plotted in the removal of a fellow Igbo, Evans Enwerem, as president of the Senate, he was unwittingly laying the foundation for his own removal through the same process of intrigue because as they say, a coup begets a coup. Should we now rally to save Peter Obi – on the arguments that the good people of Anambra state have suffered enough – when he did not show the same consideration in his protracted quest to 'reclaim his mandate'? I do not think it is any use dismissing the legislators as rascals. The governor should be made to reply to the allegations against him – some of them quite serious. Our emphasis should be in ensuring that due process is followed and that the legislators are not being teleguided from somewhere by the hands of Esau.

Beyond the fate of Peter Obi are a number of fundamental questions thrown up by the recurrent troubles in Anambra state, which have implications for the Igbos and the Igbo nation.

a) There is an urgent need for the Igbos to put their house in order if they want to be taken serious by other ethnic nationalities in the country. Granting that some of the recent travails of the state seem teleguided from Abuja using some Igbo rascals as fronts, it may also be pertinent to pose the question of whether a President of Igbo extraction could have been capable of teleguiding such mayhems in say Yorubaland or Hausa/Fulani land. These days, commentaries on Anambra politics have become a convenient mask to poke fun on the Igbos and deride their obvious individual achievements in many fields. To paraphrase a Ghanaian academic, someone may have helped to inflict the tragicomedy in Anambra state, but the ultimate responsibility to fix the problem, and refuse that it will happen again, is that of the Igbos.

b) The willingness of the Igbos to be used to destabilise and destroy their common good has also implications for the group's position in the competition for the scarce socioeconomic resources in the country, including power at the highest level. This is because politics, in its crude form as practised in Nigeria and other developing countries, is essentially about who gets what, when and how? In this, the doctrine of the three Cs - Conspiracy, Consciousness and Cohesion, plays a determining role in the ability of the various contending groups to position themselves, filibuster, manoeuvre and decoy - without taking their eyes away from their critical objectives in the political processes and engagements. Unfortunately, the Igbo nation - as opposed to Igbo individuals - is terribly deficient in the 3cs, without which it is difficult for any group to maximise its gains from a political process.

c) The troubles in Anambra also bring up the need for the Igbos to make collective effort to develop Igboland, rather than seeing the homeland only as a place for retirement. This lack of a long-term vision for the area is perhaps one of the reasons why, with the possible exception of Enugu, all other Igbo cities - Onitsha, Aba, Awka etc are virtually 'failed' cities, incapable of attracting other non-Igbos to create the kind of competitive cosmopolitan environment where the Igbos thrive best. If the Igbos could develop and make their cities habitable as they contribute in making other parts of the federation, it will also be much easier to engender the kind of pride and consciousness that is currently lacking, and which will make it difficult for brigands to be used to subvert the common good. This I think should be the priority of

Ohanaeze rather than the current embarrassment that it is (witness its support for a third term for Obasanjo at a time the same organisation was canvassing for a president of Igbo extraction).

d) The imbroglio in Anambra state equally raises a more fundamental question about the nature of our federalism. Federalism is a system in which the various federating units are each, within a sphere, independent and co-ordinate. Agreed that the atomistic nature of the federating units and the central government's control of the key petroleum resources have made our system more of a unitary state in federal clothing, but the current environment where governors live in fear of an imperial president does not bode well for either federalism or democracy. It is a system that must not be allowed to continue. Unfortunately the governors who should be co-ordinating to collectively resist the imperial president are busy competing to be in his good books. Again, one of Peter Obi's consolations in his largely self-inflicted travail was that the President had asked him to face his job. But as some will say, his travails may well be his comeuppance for subordinating the common good to his selfish ambition.

Daily Trust, *28* **August, 2010**

CHAPTER 14

GOVERNOR PETER OBI AND THE SECOND TERM PROJECT

Governor Peter Obi of Anambra state appears to be many things to many people. For some, his long and arduous struggle to actualise a mandate he won at the polls in 2003, but which was stolen from him, defined him as a tenacious man, who knew how to use the law to get what he believes is rightly his. Obi's apparent doggedness, his courage to look the political godfathers in the eyes, his impeachment and reinstatement, his survival in an opposition-dominated state legislature, have won him grudging respect, even applause, especially from the radical press and Internet bloggers. But what are Obi's realistic chances of winning a second term in 2010?

Anambra state has so far no history of re-electing any of its Governors to a second term in office. One of the explanations for this is that the state has a high churn rate of excellence. There appears to be an unwritten rule that given the rapid rate at which the state produces great achievers in all fields, an incumbent of a top political position will get just one term to enable others to take their own 'turn'. This perhaps also explains why dynastic politics is deeply abhorred in the state. Even the shelf life of political godfathers in the state does not last longer than the equivalent of one term in office for a Governor. Can Peter Obi break this jinx?

Apart from the above peculiar character of the state, Governor Peter Obi faces other equally important hurdles.

One major hurdle is the Ngige factor. Governor Obi appears not to fully understand why Chris Ngige is so popular in Anambra state. He seems to believe, rather naively, that Ngige's popularity is based only on the roads he built. The truth is that besides road construction, Ngige's brief regime was the first time in the history of the state that civil servants, teachers and pensioners were not only paid regularly but also paid on time. Given the extremely low bar of public expectation, which the preceding inept regime of Dr Mbadinuju bequeathed to the state, it was easy for Ngige to be seen as an overachiever and a metaphor that contradicted the reasons given by previous regimes for non-performance.

The Ngige myth also benefited from the menacing activities of political godfathers in the state. He won national sympathy when he became the first sitting Governor in the country's political history to be abducted, with Aso Rock clearly fingered in that unholy act, which was also interpreted as a collective insult on the Igbos. Ngige's struggles for personal survival became therefore appropriated as Igbo resistance of the alleged Obasanjo-masterminded onslaught in the state. Even the highly revered Chinua Achebe turned down an award of GCFR by the Obasanjo regime, saying he was appalled by the brazenness of the thugs ravaging the state and "the silence, if not connivance, of the Presidency." There are many who still see Obi as an instrument used by Aso Rock to defeat that perceived Igbo resistance.

The Ngige myth was such that even the shady way he became Governor was turned to his advantage. Instead of an unreliable character who made a pact with the devil at an Okija shrine in order to gain power, Ngige was successfully re-invented as an astute man who deceived the political godfathers into believing he was making a pact with them only to double cross them in the interest of the state (according to Ngige he had his chaplets in his pocket when he was taken to the Okija shrine to swear an oath of allegiance to Chris Uba, and had obtained the permission of a priest before going there).

Despite his iconic status in the state, it will be naïve of Ngige to believe he will have a smooth ride to the Government House at Awka. As the experience of Winston Churchill who became hugely popular for leading Britain to victory against the Axis powers during the Second World War but paradoxically lost the 1945 elections showed, being popular does not necessarily mean that such popularity could be easily converted into electoral assets.

Another hurdle facing Governor Obi is that while few people doubt that he is prudent with the state's resources, many also feel uncomfortable with his apparent personalisation of the state's politics. For instance Obi appears to wrongly believe he was elected on his own merit rather than riding to the Government House at Awka on the coattail of Ikemba Nnewi and the APGA he led. He also seems to wrongly believe that people will look at what he believes he has accomplished in the state and re-elect him on those bases. Politics is a team sport in which the perception of a party often translates into the electoral fortunes or misfortunes of the party members. Obi seems to wrongly believe that calls for him to make APGA the party to beat in the state meant calls for state resources to be shared. When political scientists say there are no saints in politics, they generally mean that the struggle for state power is characterised by so much high-wire intrigues and horse-trading that it is unlikely that anyone will win or retain power without having indulged in such shenanigans. In this sense therefore, projecting the persona of a saint while tainting the rest as vultures comes across as hypocrisy, even selfishness.

However crude it may sound, people and corporations that support candidates for political offices anywhere in the world expect to be 'rewarded'. This is what Harold Lasswell, the late American political scientist and communication theorist meant when he argued that politics is simply the art of "who gets what, when and how" Has anyone wondered why the composition of a cabinet is a closely watched event in any political clime?

It certainly does not say very well of Governor Peter Obi that APGA, his party, is virtually non-existent in Anambra state. The result of the recent two bye-elections in the state, generally believed to be free and fair, and won by the PDP, should be a wake up call for the Governor.

It was a delight travelling through my town of Ozubulu, Ekwusigo LGA of Anamra state, during a recent visit to Nigeria, to see some street lights mounted in a section of the town (and some were actually working!). I was equally impressed by Governor Obi's original idea of making town unions an informal fourth tier of the government because historically town unions have been reliable agents of development among the Igbos. Though Governor Obi does not seem to have done badly in some areas of governance, including road construction, there remains a certain detachment to his regime, with some of his achievements being actually credited to Ngige. It will be a mistake for the Governor to believe that this alienation from his regime is propaganda by his political opponents. In politics, the powerful and the potentially powerful groups mediate between the people and the government, and help to shape the way any regime is perceived. Perception is everything in politics. It will seem that at the moment Governor Obi may not be winning the perception battle

---

Daily Independent, 16 **April, 2009**

CHAPTER 15

DR EGWU'S EDUCATION ROADMAP

Minister of Education Dr Sam Egwu deserves commendation for the roadmap for the Nigerian education sector, which he presented recently to the National Stakeholders' Forum. No one doubts that the country's education sector is in a sorry state, and deserves urgent fixing. The quality of education has declined so much that many of the graduates produced by the nation's tertiary institutions are simply unemployable. Teachers' morale is also at an all-time low, and like most civil servants, they have to moonlight in order to survive. The sector remains grossly under-funded and basic school necessities like laboratories and well-equipped libraries are simply not there. Lecturers in universities and other tertiary institutions are routinely accused of corruption and such unprofessional conducts like trading sex and money for marks. Dr Egwu's education roadmap is therefore timely.

There are four components of this roadmap: Access and Equity, Quality Assurance, Technical and Vocational Education and Training and Funding. The document outlines improvement and turn-around strategies for each of the sub sectors of education namely basic, post-basic and tertiary. It acknowledges it was not the first serious attempt to reform the sector but that the elephant in the room with past efforts has been with implementation. For this, the roadmap rightly places a lot of emphasis on implementation.

While unveiling the plan the Minister was quoted as saying that the "process of charting the roadmap began with a comprehensive review of previous efforts undertaken by past administrations in order to learn from them... I believe in building upon what is already in place without reinventing the wheel. Let me take this opportunity to commend the efforts of my predecessors as we found extensive documentation of all their hard work and efforts." (This Day, March 31 2009).

It is very refreshing to see a Minister depart from the usual tendency to demonise one's predecessor in office. We are much more used to a Minister or Governor announcing his or her arrival in office with a concomitant dismantling of the programmes initiated by his or her predecessor. Too often the incumbent acts as if his or her reputation would be enhanced only by undermining the reputation and programmes of his/her predecessor in office. When was the last time we heard a government official say a positive thing about his or her predecessor?

Despite the apparent deliberateness with which the roadmap was formulated, and its departure from the 'pull-down-my-predecessor' syndrome, the roadmap faces a number of big hurdles – some from its design and others from environmental factors.

One, at the level of vision, the roadmap seems to divorce the problems in the education sector from the general problems of underdevelopment. Some of the problems it correctly identified with the sector such as funding, access and quality are in fact symptoms of an underdeveloped economy, not the underlying causes of the problems with the education sector. It is unlikely that the reform will succeed in isolation of the other sectors of the economy to which the education sector is linked. How for instance can quality be improved if wage levels in the sector are insufficient for the educators to live on such that moonlighting is generally accepted as a necessary supplement? Or how can you create enthusiasm among pupils if they necessarily have to spend most of their time outside school helping out with the family's petty trading? How can you encourage effective learning and studentship in tertiary institutions if there are armies of unemployed and underemployed graduates roaming the streets, forlorn, and uninspiring to any one?

Two, at the level of design, the roadmap plans to use a 'representative' sample of schools and institutions across the country as demonstration projects. The assumption here is that what works in the representative sample will also work in similar schools and institutions across the country. Unfortunately this assumption could be erroneous because of the likely biases in the selection of the samples, including the need to 'reflect the federal character'. This is likely to be compounded by problems posed by the differences in social, class, cultural, spatial and historical access to education among the different geographical areas of the country. Will the performance of samples from say Ikoyi, Lagos, and highbrow areas in say Abuja be representative of the likely performance of schools, say in remote rural areas of the country?

Three, while presenting the roadmap, the Minister was also quoted as saying: "I have proposed reinstating an assessment at the end of the sixth year so as not to pass students on who have not mastered the requisite basic skills at the primary level."

According to him, the total dependence on continuous assessment to promote pupils "is not helping us. It only helps to produce more illiterates." The Minister's stance on this unfortunately appears to be a retrogressive step that could end up undermining some of the objectives of the roadmap. Obviously if examinations were to be a good way of producing excellence, then the quality of our higher education, where examination is more of a way of life, wouldn't be in such a parlous state. The world is increasingly moving away from the era where children are made to repeat classes because they failed examinations or judged too harshly by examinations. Continuous assessment ensures that children's various abilities are encouraged rather than condemned and that they are allowed to develop according to their various rhythms without being made to feel inferior to their faster-paced age mates.

Four, omitted in the reform is the unnecessarily long number of years spent in pursuing some degree and diploma programmes in Nigeria. Why should it take six years to produce a law graduate and five years to produce an engineering graduate in Nigeria while it takes only three years or less to produce similar graduates in most other countries? What is the sub-text here? That Nigerians are slow learners? Unfortunately in an increasingly competitive international labour market where age is a big issue, Nigerian graduates are being unnecessarily disadvantaged. The roadmap should in fact have considered the introduction of conversion programmes as we have in many countries. In the UK for instance, a non-graduate in law who wants to become a lawyer can opt to do a one year conversion programme in law and will be deemed to have satisfied the academic stage of legal training if he successfully completes such a programme. In Nigeria such a graduate will be required to spend another four to five years.

Given the above therefore, while the roadmap is a bold step, what the country perhaps needs is a re-invention of its education system.

Daily Independent, 9 April 2009

CHAPTER 16

GOVERNOR MARTIN ELECHI:
FATHER-FIGURE OR SOFT DESPOT?

Governor Martin Nwancho Elechi, 70, can rightly claim to be one of the fathers of Ebonyi State, having led the Ebonyi State Movement in a decade-long campaign for the creation of the state. A 1966 first class honours graduate in economics, Chief Elechi had held many prominent political positions at a time some of his current political opponents were perhaps still wearing diapers. For instance between 1970 and 1975, he was variously Commissioner for Lands, Survey and Urban Development; Commissioner for Trade and Industry; and Commissioner for Works and Housing in the defunct East Central State (from where the current five states in the South East were carved out). Chief Elechi, a member of the 1977/1978 Constituent Assembly, also served as the executive secretary of the National Party of Nigeria (NPN) between 1980 and 1982. It was perhaps in recognition of his role as one of the founding fathers of Ebonyi State that his predecessor in office, Dr Sam Egwu, allegedly facilitated his emergence as the Governor of the State in 2007.

Several observations could be made about Governor Elechi especially in relation to his political opponents.

One, Chief Elechi was already on the other side of 60 when he became Governor, making him one of the oldest Governors in the current political dispensation. Given his age and political pedigree, there is often a temptation in such a situation for one to see himself as a patriarch, the grandfather who had seen it all. The flip side to a patriarch being actively involved in politics is that he is bound to feel insulted because politics is a contact sport in which the players psychologically prepare themselves to throw more punches than they get. How will the father-figure feel when people who were still running around stark naked when he had already become famous began to throw the inevitable punches?

Two, flowing from a patriarchal disposition is a certain messianic complex. This is a feeling that one is a sort of saviour to a people and that such people should demonstrate sufficient gratitude to the messiah at all times and on all issues. Chief Elechi is said to routinely threaten either to quit as Governor or not to present himself for re-election. For instance in an 'Open letter to Governor Martin Elechi' by Senator Emmanuel Onwe dated November 6, 2010 and published on the website, www nigeriavillagesquare.com, Dr Onwe alleged that in a meeting Governor

Elechi held with a few selected members of the Ikwo PDP executives on 23rd October 2010, he threatened to "withdraw from re-contesting the gubernatorial election in the event that an Ikwo man (read Senator Emmanuel Onwe) proceeds to run for the senatorial election in Ebonyi Central". He was also quoted by the Vanguard of January 24, 2011 as threatening that "if the results [of the last PDP primaries in the state] were tampered with at any level, he would severe himself from the governance of the state...."

Three, what is often difficult to reconcile is Chief Elechi's tendency to threaten to withdraw from his messiah role and an apparent jittery from legitimate opposition moves to unseat him. In politics the opposition is there to keep the incumbents on their toes, not to laud them. While the mature democracies recognize that a vibrant opposition is necessary both for the defence and the expansion of the democratic space, in our type of society what we often find is a tendency to co-opt, blackmail or muzzle the opposition, short-changing the citizens in the process. In the last PDP primaries for instance Governor Elechi, who is the campaign coordinator of the Jonathan/Sambo Campaign Organisation in the South East was among the overzealous Governor- supporters of the President who forbade members of their state legislature from meeting Alhaji Atiku Abubakar, who was then Jonathan's rival for the PDP presidential ticket. The caption of the story in the Sun of October 26, 2010 was telling enough: "Don't Come to S'east, Gov. Elechi tells PDP presidential aspirants". Again in the run-up to President Jonathan's visit to the State last February, Chief Elechi also alleged that the opposition parties were hatching a "plot to throw sachet water and other items on him at the Abakaliki Township Stadium, just to discredit him and make him look unpopular before the President... If they try it, security operatives will subdue them. They should not blame us for our actions." (National Mirror [online], February 22, 2011)

Four, even more worrying for our democracy is Chief Elechi's 'ban' on ANPP from holding its national rally in the State (the rally held anyway). In an advertorial published in the Daily Trust of Thursday March 3, 2011, Chief Elechi gave reasons for the measure. These included that after the 2007 elections, in which Dr Ogbonnaya Onu, the current national chairman of the ANPP was also a candidate, the party embarked on protracted legal challenge of his emergence as the Governor even though it "had no structures on ground, did not campaign and were therefore not prepared for elections." Chief Elechi also alleged that the new project of the ANPP in the state is "to bring down the current administration by making Ebonyi State ungovernable through total breakdown of law and order in the state to force the federal government to declare a state of emergency and to make the forthcoming elections visibly riotous and totally lacking in credibility." The Governor further argued that "Abakaliki is a small provincial capital struggling to measure to the status of a state capital. The facilities available there have always proven inadequate for state functions despite our efforts to expand the scope of facilities there". Based on this, Chief Elechi concluded that Dr Onu's decision to "impose the national rally of his party on such an innocuous and inadequate state capital has sinister motives".

With all due respect, I find the reasons advanced for the 'ban' on the ANPP's rally rather petty and unbecoming of an elder statesman. This should however not be misconstrued as a defence of Dr Onu on any of the issues raised against him. What I find objectionable is that the entire advertorial was about Dr Onu and issues related to the conduct of the 2007 Governorship elections in the state. Is Dr Onu who is merely the national chairman of the ANPP now synonymous with the party such that his perceived political sins should be visited on the party? There is equally an ooze of hypocrisy in some of the reasons given. For instance if the facilities in Abakaliki are too meagre for a national campaign rally, how come the Governor had no qualms using the same facilities to host the president's whistling campaign visit and even had to urge people in the state to turn out in their numbers to demonstrate their support for the political aspirations of the president? Unfortunately Governor Elechi is not alone in this worrying tendency of trying to thrust a dagger into the heart and soul of our democracy project.

Daily Trust, 10 March, 2011

CHAPTER 17

BABANGIDA, FEDERALISM, AND 2011

Former military president General Ibrahim Babangida is reportedly consulting widely on whether to join the 2011 presidential race. Speaking in Abeokuta on April 1, 2010, as chairman of Governor Gbenga Daniel's birthday lecture series, Babangida was said to have recommended 'true federalism' as the recipe for the country's intractable political problems. The Vanguard (online) of 1 April 2011 further quoted him as saying: "Some people have tagged me an advocate of confederalism. True federalism is the issue for this country. We have lived together for 50 years and there are issues that must be addressed."

There are several observations about Babangida's recommendation of 'true federalism', and his putative presidential ambition:

One, federalism as a political system in which sovereignty is constitutionally divided between a central governing authority and the constituent units (states, local governments or provinces), rests not only on the federating units having enough political autonomy to preserve their local peculiarities but also sufficient financial autarky to ensure that their independence is not compromised. The current 36-state system for instance clearly undermines the principle behind the adoption of federalism in the country because with the possible exception of Lagos and the old Kano state, virtually all the states in the country are dependent on allocations from the federal government for their economic survival. This means that starting from the creation of the 12-state structure by Gowon in 1967, Nigeria has been a unitary state in a federal clothing – a matter which was not helped by military rule and its associated centralised command structure of rule. Though Babangida's prescription of 'true federalism' could be a panacea for many of the country's problems, its effectuation would involve a number of very tough decisions, including re-organising the current 36 state structure into about six to make each unit financially viable and reduce the cost of government. Does Babangida have what it takes to enforce such a tough but very necessary action?

Two, despite his shortcomings and army of very vocal critics, Babangida remains one of the very few Nigerians who feel truly comfortable in the company of other Nigerians, irrespective of their ethnic origin or religion. In a fractious and polarised country, where an increasing number of citizens are challenging the basis and viability of the Nigeria project, individuals who enjoy legitimacy from across the main fault lines, will be looked upon by many, including foreign friends of the country, to play a leading role in preventing the country from falling over the precipice.

In addition to transcending ethnic and religious divide, no leader has perhaps humanised power or retained personal followership outside of office, more than the gap-toothed General. Some 17 years after he stepped aside from power, you still find influential individuals from all over the country who proudly call themselves 'Babangida boys'. It is simplistic to believe that all his loyalists are people who benefitted materially from him when he was in power. A friend, who is now late, once told me of his encounter with Babangida when the latter was the Head of State. The friend was in the VIP lounge at the Murtala Mohammed airport when suddenly Babangida had to pass by to go and board a flight. On sighting him, Babangida left his security details, walked up to him, called him by his name, shook his hands, and asked about his elder brother. In a country where every penny whistle wants to be called a trumpet and political leaders take it as an insult if you fail to treat them as deities, gestures like that often win people's hearts. In this respect, Babangida could be said to be one of the few Nigerian leaders whose humanity was not destroyed by the trappings of power, and this could well be the basis of his appeal to many people. It was said that even as Head of State Babangida still remembered to call or send birthday cards to his friends. If you have had a friend who became even a Local Government councillor or came into sudden wealth, you will better appreciate what power or money is capable of doing to otherwise good people, or how difficult it is for most people to manage success.

Three, while Babangida's personal qualities will guarantee him substantial support from across the country's main fault lines, they are likely to become an albatross when it comes to restructuring the country for 'true federalism'. Restructuring the country for true federalism would involve taking on the powerful political class – governors, senators, ministers and other political gladiators and wannabes who are likely to fight to preserve their privileges. With Babangida's reputation for cherishing friendship and not wanting to hurt the feelings of his friends, it is doubtful if he will be able to take such a tough action that will be hugely unpopular with his political associates. In contrast to Obasanjo or Buhari who are very decisive with a single-minded devotion to any cause they believe in, Babangida seems to rely on cunning to achieve his objectives. As military president for instance, his strategy was a combination of co-optation ('settlement'), going on a charm offensive and allying with different groups to achieve a particular objective and then moving out of the alliance as quickly as the goal was achieved.

Four, though Buhari has the requisite toughness and decisiveness necessary to restructure the country, he lacks the acceptance that Babangida enjoys from across the ethnic and religious divides. As Head of State for instance, Buhari committed a mortal sin of constituting a Supreme Military Council of 19, with 12 of these coming from the North, and 11 of them being Muslims. He also chose as his deputy, Tunde Idiagbon, a fellow Northerner and Muslim. This lack of sensitivity to the country's main fault lines means that he remains deeply distrusted in the South and by non-Muslims. In fact even before he was overthrown in 1985, his regime was openly derided in the South as either 'the military wing of the NPN' or 'the armed faction of the Kaduna mafia'. He is therefore unlikely to be a viable presidential candidate on any party platform or a unifying factor in this moment in our political evolution. Chief Obafemi Awolowo committed the same grievous error in 1979 when he chose Philip Umeadi, a Christian Igbo, to be his running mate. If reports that Buhari is set to choose Tinubu, a fellow Muslim, as his running mate, is true, then it becomes questionable how much he understands the sensibility of the country he once led and aspires to lead again. Though Abiola won with a Muslim-Muslim ticket, I remain unconvinced that the regime would have been a success if the mandate was actualised, given the depth of the religious chasm in the country.

Five, it will be almost impossible to find an ideal leader for Nigeria in 2011– someone who will combine the best attributes of Obasanjo, Buhari, and Babangida with Nuhu Ribadu's passion for the job. The ideal leader, just like the ideal man or woman, is perfectly academic. In the end we will have to settle for a leader, who, like the rest of us, is not perfect, but who hopefully possesses some abilities to make a difference. Babangida may not possess all the qualities needed in our president at this historical moment, but he certainly possesses some critical ones. The crucial question for me is whether his personal qualities will facilitate or militate against his own definition of the primary task at hand, which is restructuring the country for 'true federalism'.

Daily Trust, 8 April 2010

CHAPTER 18

BABANGIDA WAS WRONG TO APOLOGISE FOR
'JUNE 12'

Former military Head of State Ibrahim Babangida has reportedly apologised for annulling the June 12, 1993 elections, won by the late Moshood Abiola. He has variously been quoted as saying that he conducted the 'best election' in the country and would take responsibility for the annulment, which he implied was an error he regretted. He was quoted by the Tribune (online) of 16 August 2010 as saying that politicians from the South-West, where the late Chief Abiola came from, "had forgiven him after apologising on the issue." Former Oyo State Deputy Governor, Hazeem Gbolarumi, who is a leader of one of Babangida's campaign groups, also apologised to Nigerians on behalf of the Minna General.

I will argue that the apology, rather than mollify his traducers, compounds Babangida's problems:

One, by admitting the annulment was a mistake, and using innuendos and body language to apologise without giving reasons for the annulment, Babangida concedes the argument to his critics that it was something done on a whim or out of malice. One would have expected Babangida to articulate a cogent explanation for the annulment, and defend it forcefully if he believes in it, so that his argument would, in the marketplace of political ideas, compete with the notions of 'justice' and 'democracy' under which the campaign against the annulment was waged. There were several rumours on why the election was annulled - that Abiola was an agent of foreign powers and for that reasons the military government was uncomfortable handing over power to him, that Abiola was a serial sponsor of coups and because of that some military boys felt such a person would only inherit power over their dead bodies, and that as a close friend of the military top brass, they knew him better than other Nigerians and would not trust him with the leadership of this country. By apologising the way he did, we have not become wiser on the reasons for the annulment and he has unwittingly strengthened the argument of some of his critics that he tries to please everyone. Effective governance is not a popularity contest and shouldn't be because some tough decisions necessarily have to be taken by leaders. Rather than the 'forgiveness' he craves by his apology, it will in fact only increase the sense of triumphalism by his opponents, who had defeated him on the issue and forced him to 'step aside'. Had Babangida forcefully defended his conviction – if the annulment was done out of conviction – he would probably have been able to convince some people that it was a decision taken in the national interest based on the evidence available to him at the time.

Two, by apologising the way he did, or giving the impression that he was pressurised into annulling the election, his stature as a leader is diminished rather than enhanced. Besides, in litigious countries such as the USA and UK, such forms of apology could lead to a floodgate of compensatory law suits. For instance as unpopular as the Iraq War was, especially when the search for the so called Weapons of Mass Destruction that was a trigger for the war turned out negative, the two architects of the war, George W Bush and Tony Blair, have stood their ground that they acted in good faith on the basis of intelligence available to them at that time. True, there are circumstances in which apologies by leaders could be a show of humility and strength but rarely in matters of critical state policies such as cancelling an election in which people have invested fortunes and time.

Three, the events triggered by June 12 show that power is rarely handed over to anyone on a platter of gold. It is to the eternal credit of a faction of the Yoruba elite that they were able to lead and sustain a campaign to re-claim what they felt was theirs. Before Abiola and June 12, there had been coups and counter-coups in this country and nothing happened. Politicians invested huge resources in organising political parties or running and winning primaries only for these parties to be banned – and nothing happened. But when it came to June 12, a faction of the Yoruba elite, which was Conscious, Cohesive and Conspiratorial led other Nigerians in successfully resisting it by virtually making the country ungovernable. Not even the appointment of Shonekan, a Yoruba, could mollify them. In this sense, it is wrong for anyone to say they conceded power to the South or the Yorubas. The truth is that a faction of the Yoruba elite staked an overwhelming claim for their 'right', and the only way at that time for the country to move forward was to appease them by having another Yoruba run a civilian administration in lieu of Abiola.

Four, the successful struggle over June 12, has an important ramification for the current controversy over the PDP's zoning arrangement, namely that power is rarely handed over to any one on a platter of gold. In democratic dispensations, it means staking a powerful claim to what you believe is your 'right' and making your ideas supporting the claim dominant in the marketplace of political ideas.

In this sense, power could be likened to a crown jewel thrown into a furnace of fire while zoning could be equated to an agreement on the order in which contenders will be allowed to wear this crown jewel. If it comes to the turn of Mr X, it will be up to Mr X to stake such a powerful claim to his 'right' that others will be forced to respect it. If it comes to a person's turn to wear the crown jewel, and the person is unable to retrieve it from the furnace, it means he has not staked a powerful enough claim for his right or shown sufficient preparedness for it and should therefore really not complain if he is bypassed. It is in the nature of power that even if it is agreed and pasted on billboards throughout a country, that say in 2011, it will be the turn of Mr Y to wear the crown jewel, there will always be others who will come forward to stake counter claims. The fate of Mr Y will therefore depend on his preparedness and how forcefully he stakes his claim for his entitlement. The struggle for power is not for the lily-livered.

Five, it is surprising that the Igbos who are supposed to be the beautiful brides in the ongoing controversy over zoning (it is the only group in the three geopolitical zones of the political south not to have produced a president in the current dispensation) do not seem to appreciate they have a bargaining chip. This immediately raises the question of whether the group has a faction of its elites, close to state power, who are Cohesive, Conscious and Conspiratorial enough to set the agenda and fight for the group's interest? Even Governors Peter Obi of Anambra State and Sullivan Chime of Enugu State - the two Igbo leaders who are arguably the best positioned to play critical roles in this dispensation and benefit from the process- seem not to even know that history is beckoning on them.

Dialy Trust, 26 August 2010

CHAPTER 19

BETWEEN OTEH AND HEMBE

The salacious revelations at the probe of the Securities and Exchange Commission by the Capital Markets Committee of the House of Representatives provided Nigerians with the sort of infotainment that draw and addict some people to the tabloids. While in countries like the UK and the US celebrity indiscretions and sexual escapades of otherwise dour-looking and family values-touting politicians form the fulcrums of this sadistic form of entertainment, in our dear country, where adultery is no one's business and promiscuity by the political class is seen as heroic or evidence of one's virility, rapacious raid on public funds and being silly enough not to cover one's tracks very well are the gravamen of this infotainment. Which is why the several probes by the House of Representatives centre on public officials being 'named and shamed' for dipping their fingers, often all ten of the fingers at a go, in the cookie jars they were supposed to husband.

It all started with the Chairman of the House Committee on Capital Market and other Institutions Herman Hembe who, using mostly innuendos, accused Ms Arunma Oteh, the Director-General of the Securities and Exchange Commission, of not being above board. Among the sundry allegations against Ms Oteh were that the SEC approved the sum of N66.1m to rent an official apartment for her in Maitama after she had spent N30m on hotel accommodation in eight months. She was also accused of spending N42.5m to procure three Toyota vehicles without a tender's board meeting in breach of the Public Procurement Act 2007 and of spending N850, 000 on food in just one day and N85,000 on another day. I didn't watch the televised proceedings at the lower chamber but media reports suggested Ms Oteh felt cowed and boxed into a corner. When she appeared at the House the following day, she had re-grouped and decided to go on the offensive.

Unlike Hembe, her allegations of corruption against the Committee chairman were bare-knuckled, if not desperate. She claimed she was being persecuted for her stance on corruption, rehashing the riposte: "I was told upon my appointment that whenever you try to fight corruption, corruption will fight you back." With this, it became a competitive narrative of who, between Ms Oteh and Hembe, was fighting corruption and who was trying to profit from it. Ms Oteh inferred she was being unfairly treated by the Hembe Committee because she had refused to play ball. "In asking the SEC to contribute N39m for this public hearing, don't you think that you are undermining your capacity to carry out your duties?" she reportedly asked the chairman. She also alleged that 24 hours before the hearing started on Wednesday March 14, 2012, Hembe had demanded N5m from her. "I question the ability of the chairman to carry out a credible hearing. The reason I say I doubt his credibility is that in October last year, the SEC paid you estacode and a business class ticket to an emerging market conference in Dominican Republic. Please tell Nigerians whether you actually went there and please also tell the Nigerian people if you didn't go, or you actually returned the money", she was quoted by the Leadership of March 20 2012 as saying.

There are obvious holes in the accusations and defences by the two. If Ms Oteh spent N850,000 a day or N30m in a hotel accommodation in eight months, what is the comparative expenditure of equivalent officials lodged in a hotel during that period for us to judge the extent of her extravagance? Granted, spending such amounts of money on accommodation and feeding may sound huge, even obscene to some of us, there must be a benchmark for comparing these expenditures or the laws they broke, if these were not meant to play to the gallery. Similarly the defence by Hembe that after 'collecting' the estacode to travel to the Dominican, he got up to Texas but did not attend the conference because he was advised it was already winding down reminded one of Bill Clinton's answer when he was asked if he ever smoked marijuana when he was running for the presidency. Bill Clinton claimed he smoked but did not inhale. Hembe's explanation of the incident honestly was silly, but even sillier was Ms Oteh's opportunistic use of the issue as a tool of counter attack. If she was truly being harassed because she was 'fighting corruption' why did it take her some six months to realise that Hembe did not travel to the Dominican Republic for the conference and even then only after she was put on the spot for apparent financial indiscretion? I think it is important to establish whether Ms Oteh offered the trip to the conference in the Dominican Republic as a financial inducement to Hembe or whether the latter indeed demanded for it. It is also important to establish whether it is legal or conventional for the SEC to sponsor members of the legislature to such conferences and if so, the amount of estacode such would normally attract.

What came out of the way Ms Oteh came swinging wild counter punches is that the way top officials react under pressure is also an index of leadership. Whether we call it being calm under pressure or emotional intelligence, as Thucydides, the Greek historian would say, nothing impresses people more than self restraint. Obviously restraint does not mean one cannot defend oneself vigorously. More savvy people would probably have maintained a dignified ambience even if they felt unfairly persecuted. And if Ms Oteh really wanted to also rubbish Hembe wouldn't it have been more effective if such had been leaked to the press? By counter-punching the way she did, she gave the impression her allegations were afterthoughts or that at best she and Hembe were accomplices in crime. With Hembe rightly stepping down as the Chairman of the Capital Markets committee following her allegations of corruption against him, a question is immediately raised on whether Ms Oteh has enough moral capital to continue as the DG of SEC while the allegations against her are being investigated by both the ad hoc committee of the House and possibly by the EFCC and ICPC.

On a broader scale, the spat between Hembe and Ms Oteh underlies the uneasy relationship between accomplished professionals and politicians, especially members of the legislatures who have an oversight functions over MDAs, which are often manned by experienced professionals. While the politicians, many of whom are less accomplished professionals than the Ministers or Director-Generals they supervise tend to be conscious of the fact that they are elected representatives of the people, there is a feeling that some of the professionals feel irritated at being summoned on a 'whim' to be 'humiliated' or for their professional accomplishments to be rubbished. This could probably explain why quite a number of the professionals summoned by both chambers, especially the lower chamber, try as much as possible to shun such invitations. Hembe, a lawyer from Benue State is just 36. On the other hand, Ms Oteh, from Abia State, made First Class Honours in computer science from the University of Nigeria Nsukka and also holds a Master degree in Business Administration from Harvard Business School. Her CV also indicated that she had worked in various multilateral institutions including the Harvard Institute for International Development and Centre Point Investments Limited of Nigeria. In 1992, she joined the African Development Bank where she rose to become the Vice President for Corporate Management in 2006. She became Director General of the SEC in January 2010.

Another pertinent issue from the Hembe-Oteh spat is the question of whether televised public hearings are geared only for infotainment and the accompanying media trial or for real fact finding. While televising such probes may be aimed at showcasing transparency, the accompanying media and public trial may actually negate the real aim of such probes and in certain instances could lead to playing to the gallery or being overtly defensive. Moreover since a camera cannot capture any choreographed underlying processes of a probe it means that the fact that a proceeding is televised does not necessarily mean that it is transparent. As a matter of fact televised images could be used to legitimate a lie.

Additionally it will also be necessary to interrogate the usefulness of these probes and what they have actually achieved on the ground. We have had so many of such probes – power sector probes, the pensions probe, the probe about the location of GSM base stations by operators, the probe of subsidy payments on premium petroleum products and so on and so forth. Am I the only one who cannot see what these probes have accomplished apart from the momentary fury and sound that they provide?

Daily Trust, 22 March 2012

CHAPTER 20

BUHARI'S QUEST FOR A SECOND CHANCE

There is something about Muhammadu Buhari that seems to appeal to many Nigerians. This, perhaps, has something to do with the persona he projects onto the public space – the image of an honest and self-disciplined man. This public identity appears to be reinforced by his slender tall frame, simple sartorial taste and unsmiling demeanour.

As military Head of State, Buhari is credited with one of the most patriotic sentiments ever uttered by any Nigerian Head of State. On coming to power on December 31, 1983, via a military coup, he made a clarion call for unity and patriotism, declaring that "this generation of Nigerians and indeed future generations have no other country than Nigeria. We shall remain here and salvage it together." This invocation of nationalism was later captured in a biopic in which the character Andrew was caricatured for cowardly seeking to 'check out' of the country instead of staying behind to help salvage it from its numerous challenges. The Andrew jingle was a big boost to Buhari's image as a patriot. On March 20, 1984, the Buhari regime launched what it called 'War Against Indiscipline' (WAI), which was to come in phases, with the first phase emphasising a queue culture. The initial successes of WAI, coupled with the wide disenchantment with the overthrown political class, added another fillip to Buhari's (and Idiagbon's) already growing images as sort of junior messiahs. Though the goodwill was squandered in less than one year of coming to power, (even the regime's signature WAI had begun to lose steam by the time the second phase was launched), there are still many Nigerians who believe that Buhari would have fixed many of the problems in the country if he had not been toppled by Babangida in August 1985. The unsmiling retired General apparently believes so too, for he contested for the presidency in 1983 and 2003 on the platform of ANPP. From all indications, he will do so again in 2011 under the banner of Congress for Progressive Change – a political party he registered late last year.

Buhari's quest for a second chance to run the affairs of the country however raises a number of issues:

One, despite a near consensus that he is an honest man, some of Buhari's political mistakes as Head of State will most likely continue to haunt him and stand on the way between him and his ambition. As Head of State for instance, Buhari committed the mortal political sin of constituting a Supreme Military Council (SMC) of 19, with 12 of these coming from the North, and 11 of them being Muslims. He also chose Tunde Idiagbon, a fellow Northerner and Muslim, as his deputy. It was the first time in our political history that the two highest offices in the land would come from the same political region and religion. This apparent ignorance or lack of sensitivity (or both) of the country's main fault lines means that Buhari remains deeply distrusted in the political South and by non-Muslims.

While everyone makes mistakes, what has been surprising to many political observers is that Buhari does not seem to have made any conscious effort to show that some of the things that happened when he was Head of State were honest mistakes – despite the fact that ethnic/religious watchers capitalised on these to engineer a legitimacy crisis that paved the way for Babangida to ease him out in August 1985. For instance Buhari appeared not to understand that the prolonged media speculations that he was working to pick Bola Tinubu, a fellow Muslim, as his running mate, was only reinforcing a certain stereotype of him, which would do him no good, especially in the political South, and among non-Muslims. Buhari also seems not to have worked on his body language, which continues to suggest some unease in the company of Nigerians from other sections of the country.

It is instructive that the late Chief Obafemi Awolowo, a man who is well respected for his intelligence and self-discipline, committed the same grievous political error in 1979 when he chose Philip Umeadi, a Christian Igbo, to be his running mate. It is true that Abiola won in June 1993 with a Muslim-Muslim ticket. I remain however unconvinced that the regime would have been a success if the mandate was actualised, given the depth of the religious chasm in the country.

Two, it is also not exactly clear whether Buhari really wants to win political power in the current civilian dispensation or is merely enamoured by protest politics. It is axiomatic that you first need to win or capture power before you can use it to transform the society. Does Buhari really believe that his political party - registered only in late 2009 and without clear structures on the ground or sources of funds to effectively compete in the elections - will be able to supplant the existing political parties, whatever their shortcomings? One would have expected a politician really interested in becoming the President of the country to fight from a party with a realistic chance of winning at the polls. In this context, it was surprising that in the reported merger/coalition talks between his newly formed party and AC, Buhari was giving conditions as if he was doing AC favours rather than the other way round.

Three, there are also legitimate questions about why Buhari wants to be a civilian President. Some cynics have averred that Buhari and Babangida are in the race simply out of 'me-tooism' – because another former military Head of State, Olusegun Obasanjo, also ruled as a civilian President. The argument here is that the candidacies of Buhari and Babangida are no more than a continuation of the inter-Generals' feuds that led to coups and counter coups during our prolonged experience with military rule.   Other critics blame it on boredom among the retired Generals.

Whatever may be their real (as opposed to their declared reasons) for joining the presidential race, I do not subscribe to the view that they should be banned from contesting on the grounds of their perceived misdeeds while in office – unless of course they are disqualified by the Electoral Act. In fact those hiding under various banners to agitate for the banning of some candidates from running – including Buhari and Babangida - are greater threats to our democracy than these candidates because of the illogic in trying to use a combination of anarchical means and hypocritical grand-standing to purportedly defend the democratic space.

While I believe that Buhari and others should enjoy the same rights all of us have - to vote and be voted for - we need to sharpen our interrogation of their reasons for wanting the highest office in the land, which they had already enjoyed the privilege of occupying before. For Buhari, his manifesto has never been more than a populist rhetoric about the need to fight corruption and indiscipline. While these two malaises are admittedly pervasive in our society, they are in fact mere symptoms of a larger problem, rather than the causes of our current challenges.   In this respect, candidate Buhari needs to develop a coherent and feasible manifesto that will pose and answer the 'what', 'how' 'when' and 'why' questions around the issues of our federalism, the appropriate number of federating units, fiscal federalism, economy, security, unemployment and education. He also needs to convince his supporters that he is really in this race to win and not for another consolation prize of 'also ran'.

Daily Trust, 30 July 2010

CHAPTER 21

DECONSTRUCTING UMARU YAR'ADUA

Umaru Yar'Adua remains largely unknown despite occupying the most powerful position in Nigeria in the last two years. Relatively obscure before Obasanjo catapulted him into that position, his taciturn nature has led to several speculations about him and his idiosyncrasies. Who is really Umaru Yar'Adua? Is he an intensely insecure and diffident man as he sometimes comes across, or a very deep, thoughtful but simple Fulani man who has very little appetite for the flamboyant life style of his predecessor - as some of his supporters claim? Is the office of the presidency just too big for him or is he just a Fabianist, a slow starter, who believes in investing as much time as possible in planning and strategising before executing? Is Yar'Adua really a servant-leader, someone who was reluctantly thrust into the position he now occupies or a manipulative power hawk, who read Obasanjo very well and aptly positioned himself for the position he got?

A recent article by Nasir el Rufai, entitled "Umaru Yar`Adua: Great Expectation, Disappointing Outcome", and published on a number of websites recently could perhaps help to provide answers to the above questions. The former boss of the Federal Capital Territory tells us he has known Umaru Yar'Adua since 1972 and had played some key roles in making him president after he was drafted to fly the PDP flag. El Rufai, who has been declared wanted by the Economic and Financial Crimes Commission for alleged large scale corruption, also claims to have played a crucial role in reviewing drafts of the inaugural speech delivered by the president elect on May 29, 2007.

It is possible that el Rufai's article was spurred by a certain need to fight back a man he felt he contributed in making the President but who chose to keep mute, if not silently connived, in his perceived persecution by the EFCC. But what can we learn about Umaru Yar'Adua from el Rufai's article – regardless of the author's motive?

One, is a possibility that Yar'Adua could surprise everyone by suddenly over-performing expectations. Currently nicknamed "Baba Go Slow" for his lacklustre performance, el Rufai concedes that after eight months of similar non-performance as Governor of Katsina state, things had suddenly picked up. He admitted that though Yar'Adua inherited "an empty treasury, a bloated civil service, huge pension arrears, and many construction projects" that were abandoned halfway, he was to prove his critics wrong because within two years, "the books had been balanced", and "Katsina State Government cleared the pension arrears, reconciled domestic debts, and began the completion of abandoned projects." El Rufai also concedes that though Yar'Adua's achievements as Governor were mixed, what "is not in dispute was that the quality of schools and hospital buildings, urban and rural roads and fertilizer distribution system improved dramatically under his watch." Coming from an aggrieved enemy of the regime, this acknowledgement of competence could be a source of hope for Nigerians frustrated at the president's snail pace of governance. The flipside to this however is that Yar'Adua's supporters could also use it to canvass for a second term for him, claiming that he had merely used his first term in office to plan and strategise, and would use his second term to execute his policies.

Two, though Yar'Adua sometimes comes across as an insecure and diffident man, passages from el Rufai's article suggest the opposite. For instance el Rufai narrates that in May 2007, he received a letter from the President-elect asking him to send the names and resumes of three people to be appointed into 'senior government positions'. Obviously el Rufai read more to the letter, so rather than send the nomination to Yar'Adua, he requested a meeting with the President elect to "ascertain what positions he had in mind." Yar'Adua told him he had written a similar letter to "every State Governor or PDP Chairman as appropriate as he intended to nominate Ministers, Ambassadors and Chairmen of Statutory Corporations from the list." An obviously disappointed and deflated el Rufai, who perhaps expected a slot in the regime, then concluded that that "distributive state-of-mind was the first sign for me that Yar'Adua was not on the right track. I suggested that if he chose his cabinet that way, he would end up with 'not the best people'. He listened and thanked me for my views, but explained that his election was made possible by State Governors and PDP leaders and his first priority was to keep them on his side, for the time being."

That Yar'Adua may not be easily swayed by opinions once he has made up his mind could also be illustrated by his refusal to exercise his prerogative of mercy on Amina Lawal, an unmarried woman from Bakori who was sentenced to death by stoning by a Sharia court for adultery – despite the strong international condemnation the case attracted. Luckily the Court of Appeal quashed the case. Katsina was the fifth Northern state to introduce the controversial Sharia Law in 2000.

Three, contrary to the image of a reluctant President, Yar'Adua could in fact be a power hawk. From Rufai's article we see a man who actively sought and plotted for power. He was Katsina State Secretary of SDP and a member of the party's National Caucus. Though he contested the

Governorship of Katsina State in 1991and lost, his ambition for power did not die with that defeat. He positioned himself and was nominated to run again in 1999, and won. Even after he was hospitalised for six months in Germany in 2001 for renal failure, he returned, not to retire from politics, but to resume as Governor. He also quickly arranged for the Deputy Governor, Tukur Jikamshi, who became the Acting Governor in his absence, to be impeached on grounds of abuse of state resources but perhaps to prevent a potential challenger in the 2003 election, which he also won. These are hardly the moves of someone who does not hunger for power.

The story of how he emerged as the PDP's presidential candidate also suggests a man who had cleverly studied Obasanjo and plotted ways of warming himself to him and the then power establishment at Abuja. El Rufai tells us that around 2002 Yar'Adua claimed "to have had a very vivid dream that he will be elected president to succeed President Obasanjo in the near future". Apparently Yar'Adua's strategy of actualising that dream included giving unalloyed support to Obasanjo's policies while distancing himself from the Ota farmer. Here he seems to believe the cliché that familiarity breeds contempt and revelled in the friends-winning formula of projecting a persona of an "undemanding, simple and humble" Governor. But while keeping a distance from Obasanjo, he directed his Katsina caucus group, the K-34, to fully support Obasanjo and his policies – at a time when Obasanjo had become a pariah in the North. He also directed all Katsina State representatives in the National Assembly to support the "proposed Constitutional Amendment and expelled Aminu Bello Masari from K-34 for non-compliance with his wishes."

What could therefore be surmised from Rufai's article is that Yar'Adua could be a determined but foxy politician, whose political skills may be underrated – pretty much the same way some had underrated Obasanjo to their peril.

Daily Independent, June 18, 2009

CHAPTER 22

GOVERNOR FASHOLA AND THE NUDE DANCERS

The recent report that the Lagos state government had shut down four strip clubs around Opebi Street and Allen Avenue in Lagos made headlines and elicited naughty guffaws from people as such stories are wont to do. According to the report, the Lagos State Environmental and Special Offences Monitoring Unit, which sacked the clubs, whisked off 33 of the nude dancers and two of their managers. Governor Fashola, a man many of us admire, was apparently forced to act following the protest of religious leaders at the increasing number of strip tease and nude clubs in the city. Cardinal Anthony Okogie, the Catholic Archbishop of Lagos, was quoted as saying that the rapid increase in the number of nude clubs was a sign that evil had descended on the city and asked the Governor to sack the clubs.

While the Lagos State Government has the right to take measures that it believes will preserve the public good, there is a feeling that the issues involved with strip and nude clubs are not as simple as presented by religious leaders. In a secular, plural and democratic society, an issue like this, however morally repugnant one feels about it, deserves at least a public discussion - as done in many of the countries we often look up to as models of democracy and freedom.

Several arguments used to justify a clampdown on sexually explicit expressions in public places:

One, is the morality argument. Traditionally states have always felt a need to suppress or at least strongly regulate sexually explicit expressions in order to maintain 'morality' and 'standards of decency'. The primary concern of the moralists appears to be that sexually explicit expressions could undermine moral values and the institution of marriage. The British lawyer, judge and jurist, Lord Devlin, articulated this view in his book, *The Enforcement of Morals* (1965). Lord Devlin argued that since a shared set of basic moral values is essential to a society, public authorities are justified in protecting the society against attacks on these values - such as mounted by pornography and nude dancing.

Opponents of a clampdown however counter that in a plural society, any consensus or 'moral glue' regarding sexual attitudes has either disappeared or is rapidly disappearing. In other words, they posit that the argument that nude dancing will endanger morals is untenable in a society where the notion of sexual morality is increasingly becoming contentious.

Opponents of a clampdown also contend that the 'enforcement of morality' argument neglects the 'moral autonomy' of individuals, namely that it is up to individuals, not the state, to make their own moral decisions on whether they should go and patronise nude clubs or not. They equally argue that a clampdown disrespects the fundamental right of nude dancers over their bodies, especially in a secluded area where people are not forced to watch.

Two, nude dancing has also been criticised from a feminist perspective. The argument here is that permitting sexually explicit expressions such as nude dancing or pornography would amount to a damaging attack on the dignity of womanhood. It is also argued that sexually explicit expressions often have a coded ideological message, namely that the woman is a mere object of gratification.

Supporters of nude dancing however counter that if explicit sexual expressions embody a 'political message' as contended by feminists, then it will be wrong for the state to suppress it since such ideological expressions, as unpalatable as they may appear to some, are contributions to the marketplace of ideas that enrich democracy.

Three, critics of nude dancing equally argue that the images people are exposed to bear a causal relationship to their behaviour, implying that permitting nude dancing and strip tease clubs would encourage promiscuity or aggression towards women in the society. Those against a clampdown however rebut this, arguing that if this line of reasoning is stretched, it would also mean banning many films and TV shows as well as sports that depict violence such as boxing and wrestling, since they would apparently also promote violence in the society. They further argue that the offence nude dancing may cause to some is sometimes misconstrued to be a damage it will do.

Additionally, opponents of a ban accuse the state of 'selective justice'. They argue that the wide availability of pornography on the internet and semi pornography magazines as well as the ubiquity of pop videos featuring scantily dressed females and male dancers show that the society is quite thoroughly saturated with sexuality in a commodified form. So, why pick on nude dance clubs, they argued?

In the US, court decisions on nude dancing tend to be contentious, especially when presented as an artistic expression that deserves a First Amendment protection. For instance in September 2008, a judge in Des Moines, Iowa, USA, ruled in favour of a nude dancing club owner charged with violating Iowa's indecent exposure law. The case concerned a 17-year-old niece of the local Sherriff, Steven MacDonald, who danced nude at a club. The club owner, Clarence Judy, was charged with violating Iowa's public indecent exposure law. Judy's lawyer contended that: "Dance has been considered one of the arts as is sculpture, painting and anything else like that. What Clarence has is a club where people can come and perform." The judge ruled that prosecutors failed to prove that the strip club does not qualify as a theatre because Iowa law allows nudity at theatres, museums and other venues devoted to the arts or theatrical performances. The judge further argued: "Given the First Amendment implications of a statute that may limit expression, it is not the role of the Court to judge the taste or quality of the art represented at Shotgun Geniez when determining whether or not it is a theatre."

Even when the courts have ruled in favour of local obscenity or indecency laws, it has often been split decisions. In 2000 for instance, the Supreme Court ruled by 6-3 to broaden the authority of the state of Pennsylvania to regulate sexually expressive conduct. At issue in the case was an ordinance from the city of Erie, Pennsylvania, banning public nudity and requiring dancers in adult clubs to don at least pasties and a G-string before appearing on stage. In 1998, Pennsylvania's top court struck down the ordinance, rejecting the city's argument that the nude dancing ban was justified to combat crime. The Supreme Court reversed that decision in March 2000. In criticising the Supreme Court ruling, *The New York Times* argued: "Dancing in the nude, like other forms of dance, is an expressive activity that conveys a distinct artistic message warranting free-speech protection."

The above would suggest that in a plural society such as Lagos, banning nude dancing on the say-so of religious leaders, however much we respect them, could amount to imposing a particular form of morality on all. The clampdown could also possibly infringe on the rights of the nude dancers and the club owners.

Sahara Reporters 14 January 2010

CHAPTER 23

JEROME OPUTA UDOJI: THE EXIT OF A TITAN

He was perhaps best known for the 'Udoji Award' of the mid 1970s, when many public servants received huge salary increases and were also paid lump sums in arrears, following a lopsided implementation of the recommendations of the Public Service Review Commission set up by the Federal Government in 1972, which he chaired. Jerome Udoji's date of birth was not recorded. What was however certain was that he started formal education in 1917. Udoji thought that because the missionaries took early interest in him, that he must have started school as young as three. His children estimated that he was born in 1912. My own estimate is that he was probably born in 1910.

Udoji commanded respect both nationally and internationally as an honest, disciplined and intellectually alert public administrator and private sector operator. In our town, Ozubulu in Ekwusigo Local Government Area, he was virtually deified as an influential wise patriarch whose counsel or intervention was constantly sought by both the lowly and the mighty on virtually any issue under the sun. He abhorred all forms of exhibitionism and would sternly discourage such from any one close to him.

It was an honour for me, when in 1987, Udoji formally engaged me as research assistant in the preparation of his memoirs, *Under Three Masters* (1995, Ibadan, Spectrum). Though I left the country for further studies the following year, I continued to be involved with the memoirs, including reading and commenting on several of the drafts. We got along so well that he gave me an unfettered access to his speeches and correspondences. I was later to select, arrange, edit and publish some of these as, *Which Way Nigeria?: Selected Speeches of Chief J.O. Udoji* (2000, Ibadan, Spectrum).

Udoji trained as a teacher at St Charles Teacher Training College, Onitsha, graduating in the late 1920s. He later moved to the West where he first taught at Ibadan Grammar School before moving to Abeokuta Grammar School between 1940 and1941. At that time, the respected Reverend I.O. Ransome Kuti, (Fela's father), was the principal of the school. While at Abeokuta and as part of his contribution to the war effort, Udoji joined the Abeokuta Special Constables and quickly rose to be the commander. This was to be a turning point in his career because the European Superintendent of Police at Abeokuta at that time, after watching one of his parades, took special interest in him and eventually convinced him to leave teaching for the colonial civil service. In 1944, Udoji left for further studies in England, graduating in Law from Cambridge University in 1948. He left Nigeria in the same ship as Chief Obafemi Awolowo.

On his return from England, Udoji joined the Colonial Administrative Service and rose to become, in 1959, the Chief Secretary to the Premier of the Eastern Region, Dr Michael Okpara, as well as Head of the Region's civil service, and Secretary to the Executive Council. He remained in that position until the coup of 1966.

When Ojukwu was appointed administrator of the Eastern Region following the coup, Udoji felt so hounded that he had to resign his appointment. At the outbreak of the civil war, Udoji felt shadowed by the Ojukwu regime and escaped, eventually taking up job in Kenya as a Consultant to the Ford Foundation on Public Administration. He remained in that position until he was appointed Chairman of the Public Service Review Commission by the Gowon regime in 1972.

Knowing how disappointed Udoji was at the way he felt Ojukwu had mistreated him, from about 2002, I began moves to publicly reconcile the two. I had met Ikemba in 1988 at the Enugu home of the social critic and publisher, Chief Arthur Nwankwo. At that time Babangida was dribbling the political class with the promise of an impending transition to civilian rule and Ikemba was toying with the idea of starting a party he called the Populist Party of Nigeria. I was later sent by Ikemba and Chief Nwankwo, along with two others, (Comrade Kalu and Dr Dike) to 'represent the Igbos' at the first anniversary of Awolowo's death in 1988. We were asked to make discreet contacts with prominent Awoists to start the process of a 'handshake across the Niger.' I didn't want Udoji, a man I adored, to continue to carry that bitter disappointment with Ikemba, whom I also respected. I considered it an honour that I was able to persuade Udoji on the need for public reconciliation with Ikemba, though our plan was eventually torpedoed by ill health.

After his chairmanship of the Public Service Review Commission, Udoji became active in the private sector. He was at a time Chairman of the Manufacturers' Association of Nigeria and President of the Nigerian Stock Exchange. In fact, between 1974 and 1993, he was either the chairman or on the board of at least 13 major corporations, including the Nigerian Tobacco Company, RT Briscoe, Michellin and Nigerian International Bank. Udoji was the first Nigerian to be appointed Chairman of a multinational corporation in Nigeria and his success in that position opened the way to other Nigerians: Christopher Abebe in UAC,

Michael Omolayole in Lever Brothers, Gamaliel Onosode in Cadbury and Jamodu in PZ.

A deeply religious and energetic man with strong convictions, Udoji abhorred injustice in any form and would not hesitate to get involved if he felt a 'voiceless' person was being maltreated. He rested in the Lord on April 2, 2010 and will be buried on Friday, May 214 The vacuum he left will be difficult to fill, especially in our town, Ozubulu

Madam Angelina Nwokolo, 1910-2010

For as long as I have known her, she was simply 'Mama Nnukwu' (Grandma). I lived with her eldest son, Sunday, and his family, while a primary school pupil at Onitsha in the 1970s. She treated me like one of her grandchildren and I would often spend holidays with her sons, in turns.

Mama Nnukwu was a conflict-avoiding, unassuming and generous woman. Though she had been wheel chair-bound for some years, her faculties never deserted her. When I visited in April 2009, she had no difficulty recognising me. I had joked that I visited because I was missing her famous bitter leaf soup. She laughed, and called one of her daughters to bring out the necessary condiments for her to prepare the soup for me. I spoke with her again on the phone about two weeks before her transition. She sounded strong, and asked when I planned to return again. Mama Nnukwu transited to the Lord on April 10, 2010 and would be buried on May 14, 2010. She will be greatly missed

'Babangida, Federalism and 2011'

I regret that the above article (published by the *Daily Independent*, *The Guardian* and several websites), gave an erroneous impression that I was promoting Babangida's purported presidential ambition. That was not the intention of the article at all. My style has always been to acknowledge someone's strengths before disagreeing with the person, or to point out a person's weaknesses before eulogising him/her. In the Babangida article, I started by acknowledging his skills in networking across the country's main fault lines before arguing that even this key personal attribute would hinder rather than facilitate the pursuit of his stated goal of restructuring the country for true federalism. I regret any wrong impression created by the article.

CHAPTER 24

JONATHAN AND THE IGBO QUESTION

The Igbos, grudgingly respected for their entrepreneurial skills, are often derided for their perceived lack of unity and ability to articulate and doggedly defend their common interests. This perception, often exaggerated, or deliberately aimed at subtly disparaging them, feeds into an existential lacuna of patriotic elites, who are Conscious, Cohesive and Conspiratorial, and who enjoy universal legitimacy in Igboland such that they can set and defend the group's interest.

In the post-Biafran war era, perhaps nothing challenges the ability of the Igbos to articulate, defend and build the necessary alliances that will ensure the protection of their interests more than the current debate on PDP zoning and President Jonathan's candidacy in the 2011 presidential elections. In the current politics of PDP's zoning arrangement, it could be argued that the strategic interest of each geopolitical zone ought to be defending its chances of producing the president of this country. In this sense, the politics of zoning and the candidacy of President Goodluck Ebele Jonathan (GEJ) raise a number of significant issues for the Igbos of the South East political zone.

One, while it is true that ethnic/zonal politics and the subsequent arithmetic of 'my turn' which it purveys is a crude method of leadership recruitment, the Igbos do not gain any respect or advantage by feigning disinterest in the ethno-regional identity of whoever emerges president of the country when others are playing the game. If it does not really matter who governs, why is power sharing agreement often at the centre of civil conflicts in Africa? Why did an overwhelming majority of Blacks and Africans enthusiastically support the candidacy of Barrack Obama during the last presidential election in the USA? Not to have a strong voice in this ethno-regional politics is in fact to facilitate its own marginalisation and drift towards being an ethnic minority in the country.

Two, the Igbos have been in the forefront of the industry of complaints against marginalisation in the distribution of political appointments and relative absence of federal presence in their area. They have also for years been calling for a president of Igbo extraction. This means that there has been a latent articulation of Igbo interest even before the current politics of zoning began. This raises the question of which side, in the current divide between those for and those against a Jonathan candidacy, best allies with the articulated Igbo interests? My personal opinion is that a Jonathan candidacy, in the current politics of zoning, strongly conflicts with Igbos' own interest because they are the only major ethnic group which has not produced an elected president of this country, and 2015 is their best chance of doing so.

Three, one of the arguments used to sell GEJ's candidacy to the Igbos is that he is one of their own. Dr Wolfe Obianime, President of the Ijaw National Congress (INC), was reported by the Tribune (online) of September 6, 2010 as telling the 16th annual convention of the World Igbo Congress (WIC) in Philadelphia, USA: "I do not need to bait the Igbo people, Goodluck Jonathan is from the eastern region... his name is Goodluck Ebele Azikiwe Jonathan. So why must he bribe his brothers to get what he wants?" This line of reasoning, however, appears to be mere gimmickry, if not mischievous, because those who divided the country into six geopolitical zones for convenience had a reason for treating the South South and the South East as separate political entities. Similarly, canvassing Igbo support for Jonathan on the basis of old regional solidarity is misleading. It is in fact tantamount to asking Anambra State to concede its rights, such as allocation from the Federation Account, to either Imo, Ebonyi or Abia State because they were all carved out from the defunct East Central State. It is in fact possible to turn this argument around by asking why President Jonathan cannot give up his candidacy in 2011 to help the Igbos actualise their own quest for a president of Igbo extraction by 2015.

Four, it has also been argued that because of the civil war and the complicated relationship it created between the Igbos and the other ethnic groups in the country, the Igbos are better off at this time supporting an Ebele or Emeka from the South South than one from the South East. This argument is, however, not only defeatist but also amounts to persuading the Igbos to accept that they are second class citizens. Was Obama not also told that it was too early for a Blackman to aspire to become president of the USA? It could in fact be argued that the PDP's zoning arrangement, as imperfect as it is, presents perhaps the best opportunity for a president of Igbo extraction in 2015.

Five, efforts to sell GEJ to the Igbos are contradicted by the apparent discrimination against the Igbos in his presidency. For instance, under Jonathan, no Igbo person holds any of the six Class A ministerial appointments in his cabinet – despite being a major ethnic group occupying one of the six geopolitical zones. Similarly, the Igbos have been losing the key public offices they held under the Obasanjo regime without a commensurate appointment into positions of similar significance. Instances here include governorship of the Central Bank (lost under Yar'adua) and chairmanship of INEC (lost under GEJ). The argument here is not about retaining incompetent Igbos in their positions but ensuring that the delicate political balancing in appointments is maintained. For instance, in the recent shake-up of the service chiefs, the Igbos were again clearly short-changed as they lost two key positions - that of Chief of Defence Staff formerly held by Air Marshal Paul Dike, and the Inspector General of Police held by Ogbonna Onovo. In return, an Igbo, Major-General Onyeabo Azubuike Ihejirika, was appointed Chief of Army Staff (COAS). There have been efforts, apparently by the president's men, to play up the appointment of Ihejirika as the first time since the end of the war that an Igbo man would be appointed COAS. However, such playing to the gallery is not only patronising but also disingenuous as it amounts to persuading the Igbos that losing two key positions and getting one in return is in their best interest, or that the post of Chief of Army Staff is enough consolation for their right to aspire to be president of this country by 2015.

In conclusion, few people doubt that the 'hurrah effect' of having one of their own as president of this country in 2015 is one of the surest ways for the Igbos to end their perceived marginalisation and drift towards being an ethnic minority group. However, since power is rarely handed to any one on a platter of gold, the time for them to start laying an overwhelming claim for this entitlement is now. And they must lay such claims without sentiments or apologies.

Daily Trust, 15 September 2010

CHAPTER 25

JONATHAN, BABANGIDA AND THE SWORD OF DAMOCLES

In the *Sword of Damocles*, the Roman politician and philosopher Cicero tells the story of Dionysius II, a king who ruled Syracuse in the fourth century BCE. Briefly Damocles was a courtier in the palace of Dionysius II, and like any good praise singer, constantly flattered the king with unparalleled grovelling. One day the king asked Damocles if he would like to swap places with him – just for a day - to see what it was like to be a king. An excited Damocles gladly agreed and roles were switched. However towards the end of his one-day reign, while seated at dinner, Damocles looked up and saw a heavy sword suspended directly over his head, hanging by a hair. In panic, he fled the court and banished all thoughts of power from his mind.

In popular culture, the *Sword of Damocles* is often used to illustrate the perils of being in power or a sense of foreboding. True, Damocles might have been naïve about how a ruler could use the power of incumbency to 'deal decisively' with the source of that sword but the moral remains relevant: long knives are daily out for the man of power. Unlike Damocles however, most fight back, not run away. There are usually three possibilities: a truce (usually resulting in what is in Africa often euphemistically called 'government of national unity'), the man of power is dethroned (usually not without a bloody fight) or the opposition is mercilessly crushed.

How do President Jonathan Goodluck and Babangida come into this?

Ever since Jonathan became the substantive President on May 6, 2010, it will seem that his body language has been indicating that he may contest for the Presidency in 2011, triggering a foreboding of the implications of his decision to contest or not contest for the country. At issue is the PDP's zoning arrangement, which President Jonathan obviously benefited from. Some have argued that it would amount to betrayal for the arrangement to be jettisoned mid-way after one section of the country has benefited from it and the North is yet to 'complete its turn'. Former Head of State, Ibrahim Babangda, has thrown his hat into the ring in support that the zoning agreement must be respected. Not only has he emphatically stated that he would run for the presidency, he has also, in what would appear to be a coded defiance, made it known he would not step down for any one. He went a step further by becoming one of the arrowheads of the Northern Elders Forum, which met recently in a media show of Northern solidarity. The group insisted that the zoning arrangement must be respected.

Several issues are raised in what now appears to be veiled jabs between the Babangida camp and the presidency.

One, the camp of Jonathan has been apparently responding to the 'Babangida challenge'. It is possible that recent reports that the federal government has set up a committee to review the Okigbo Report, (which allegedly recommended that Babangida should be prosecuted for purportedly mismanaging $12.4 billion in a Dedicated and Special Accounts while he was in office) is part of the weapons in the armoury of the President's camp. If this is so, then no one knows how this will pan out because no living Nigerian Head of State has ever been probed. Even Abacha, long presented as the poster boy of public corruption in Nigeria, especially under the Obasanjo regime, was quickly absolved of the charge by a cream of Northern leaders that included Buhari and Babangida. It is therefore likely that if Babangida is probed, it could be politicised and trigger calls for all past leaders of the country, including possibly Jonathan himself, to be equally probed.

Two, it will be counter-productive if Babangida hopes that President Jonathan will be intimidated by his being one of the arrowheads of Northern solidarity via the Northern Elders Forum. Unlike Damocles, modern president are aware of how to employ the power of incumbency to try to neutralise potential threats. If anything, the stance of the Northern Elders Forum could harden Jonathan and compel him to contest, as he may not want to be seen as succumbing to intimidation. Even if Jonathan decides not to contest, he could be forced to get his own pound of flesh by mobilising to ensure that none of the arrowheads of the Forum succeeds him - pretty much the same way Obasanjo successfully prevented Atiku from succeeding him.

More importantly, Babangida, who has always been very good in networking across the country's main fault lines, risks being diminished by his open identification with a sectional project. Despite his faults, very few people can accuse him of being an ethnic chauvinist. Now by appearing to use primordial identities to mobilise support, he risks acquiring an ethnic toga, which will in turn alienate his supporters from other sections of the country. Babangida could easily have avoided this by championing a national movement of people advocating for the respect of PDP zoning (as a matter of principle) – after all they are many non-Northerners who have also been calling on President Jonathan to respect the PDP's zoning arrangement by not contesting in 2011. The fight for the validation of Abiola's mandate by NADECO and others was for instance done in the name of 'fight for democracy' – even though many people believed it was essentially a Yoruba project. Similarly, when former Vice President Atiku opposed Obasanjo's plan to elongate his tenure, he did so in the name of respecting our constitution and protecting our democracy – not that such would cheat the North, even though this could well be the sub-text of his opposition.

Three, in what is thought to be a veiled reference to Babangida and the meeting of the Northern Elders' Forum, President Jonathan, in far away Canada, was recently quoted as saying that Nigeria is a country peopled by ethnic bigots "who reach out to their narrow cleavages when they cannot compete," (ThisDay online, June 26, 2010). President Jonathan was right. That ethnicity exists only in the context of the struggle for scarce socio-economic resources has long been recognised by political scientists. But much as the President was right, he was wrong to make the statement primarily because it is considered improper for a President to criticise his or her country when abroad. Additionally, that sentence could play into the hands of those trying to use ethnic sentiments to mobilise support (all politicians are of course guilty of this) if it is interpreted to mean that the President has accused a section of the country of being afraid to compete. This could possibly throw us back to the era in which our politicians freely used intemperate language. For instance, reacting to the purported statement by President Jonathan, elder statesman and former presidential adviser to President Shehu Shagari, Tanko Yakassai, was quoted as saying that "the Northern Elders Forum should be congratulated because in whatever they did, all the ethnic tribes of the north like the Kanuri, Nupe, Gwari, Fulani and Hausas were usually accommodated... This is unlike what is happening in Jonathan's Ijaw National Congress where the Ibibio, Urhobos and others are not accommodated," (ThisDay online, June 26, 2010).

What appears certain in the veiled battle of wits between the camps of President Jonathan and that of Babangida is that come 2011 – or even before it – something or someone will eventually give in.

CHAPTER 26

MARKETING JONATHAN'S PROBABLE PRESIDENTIAL CANDIDACY

The anticipated presidential candidacy of Goodluck Ebele Jonathan (GEJ) has become a big business trapped in high wire politics and intrigues. The *Daily Trust* (online) of August 28, 2010, reported that the Goodluck Support Group (GSP) co-ordinates over 1,027 other groups who are "calling and begging" President Goodluck Jonathan to run in the 2011 election. The paper also reports that GSP runs a pro-Jonathan newspaper called *Goodluck News*, and that one of the headlines in its maiden edition was the supposed divine proclamation: "God will not forgive Jonathan if he does not contest".

Though fortune hunting inevitably plays a role in the support and opposition to the anticipated candidacy of GEJ, a deconstruction of the arguments of the contending groups will seem to suggest that they have helped to infuse vibrancy in our marketplace of political ideas. And if unfettered competition in the bourse of political ideas is the hub of democracy, then the anticipated candidacy may have in fact helped to advance our democracy project. Just as war is said to be a continuation of diplomacy by other means, threats of secession or Armageddon frequently deployed in the support and opposition to GEJ's probable candidacy should be seen as part of an aggressive political marketing.

It is possible to identify at least six dominant arguments and the groups thought to be purveying them:

One, there has been an increasing tendency by Igbo supporters of GEJ to market him as one of their own by emphasising his Ibo name of 'Ebele' and nickname of 'Azikiwe' and the fact that his wife, Patience, who is from Okirika, is Ibo-speaking. This form of marketing is perhaps meant to mollify the Igbos who are opposed to his candidacy on the ground that it would be inimical to the campaign to produce a President of Igbo extraction by 2015.

A variant of this marketing strategy is an argument that GEJ comes from Bayelsa state, which was part of the old Eastern Region, dominated by the Igbos. The argument here is that support for GEJ will not only be a show of old regional solidarity but could also help in healing the rift between the minorities of the old Eastern Region and the Igbos which was thought to have been partly caused by the altercation between Professor Eya Ita and Dr Nnamdi Azikiwe in 1952. Some purveyors of this viewpoint argue that it is better to adopt GEJ as an Igbo and then present a checklist of Igbo interests he must protect in exchange for Igbo support. Others want a firm promise from him that he will in fact help to ensure that a President of Igbo extraction will emerge in 2015.

Two, a pro-Jonathan argument, often linked to people from the South-South, is that they produce the bulk of the nation's wealth, and therefore should be allowed to produce the nation's president as a reward. In this line of reasoning, Jonathan is thought to be under tremendous pressure to run from those who believe a refusal to run would mean 'throwing away' their golden opportunity. But this argument has been challenged on grounds that every part of the country, contrary to the common belief, actually brings something to the table: the North, it is argued, is undoubtedly the nation's food basked, the South East its commercial nerve and the South West its corporate soul. Opponents equally argue that before the first oil boom in 1973, wealth from other parts of the country had been used to develop many of the cities in the South South.

A variant of the resource owner argument used by the pro GEJ groups is that conceding the Presidency to the South South would help to mollify the militants in the zone. Opponents of this however counter that such a 'reward' to militants could incentivise other geopolitical zones to tacitly nurture militants as bargaining chips.

Three, a pro-Jonathan argument linked to some Northern youths is that despite the fact that the North has ruled the country longer than any other zone in the country; the region remains the poorest and the most disadvantaged in critical human development indices in the country. For this group therefore support for Jonathan is a protest against the Northern political leaders for supposedly betraying the region by their purported selfishness. Some groups also argue that support for GEJ will be an appropriate reward for South South's historical political support for the North. Opponents however counter that the North has already paid back for this support by an early 'liberation' of the area during the Nigerian civil war.

Four, a pro-GEJ argument that is sometimes linked to the South West is the use of various arguments to discredit or ridicule the PDP's zoning arrangement - such as arguing that it is unconstitutional, anti-meritocracy, or not meant to be permanent, or meant to be among the six geopolitical zones rather than between North and South. Opponents however counter that many of the anti zoning elements from this zone are only trying to play smart because they have taken their 'turn' and now shudder at the prospect of having to wait for 40 years before having another shot at the presidency

Five, GEJ has also been marketed on the basis of performance. Supporters for instance argue that queues at petrol stations have disappeared, and that there has also been a noticeable improvement in power supply since GEJ became the President. Supporters also play up the recent promise by GEJ that the problem of epileptic power supply would be solved by December 2012. Critics are however not convinced. They challenge GEJ's track records, accusing him of both incompetence and profligacy, including the depletion of the country's foreign reserves and inability to arrest pervasive insecurity in the country.

Six, in addition to the main contending arguments, the expected GEJ's candidacy has also been marketed and contested around such latent polarities and solidarities as Middle Belt versus core North, Christian versus Moslems, Igbos versus Ibos and North versus South East. Overall, the arguments for, and against a GEJ candidacy is being fought aggressively but decently – as ought to be in a democracy. There is no unanimity of opinions within any ethnic group or geopolitical group – which could mean we are coming of age as a democracy.

In all these, the President has maintained such a studied silence that no one can say with certainty what his thoughts are on his probable candidacy. Opinions also are sharply divided on whether his silence is political smartness or cowardice.

Daily Trust, 1 September 2010

CHAPTER 27

JONATHAN AND THE CRISIS OF THE NATION-STATE

Just when Nigerians were beginning to bask in the euphoria of a possible dawn of a new era following the relative success of the National Assembly elections on April 9, the aftermath of the presidential polls that followed a week later is turning out to be a killjoy. While Nigerians were at least initially unanimous about the freeness and fairness of the National Assembly polls, primordial binoculars appear to determine one's assessment of the conduct of the April 16 presidential polls. There also appears to be a re-assessment of the April 9 National Assembly polls, with some now saying that the exercise appeared credible only because the bar of public expectations was extremely low after the false start of April 2, when Jega had to abort the elections mid way.

My personal opinion is that the acrimonies and violence that followed the presidential polls in some parts of the North are reflective of the crisis in our nation- building project. There are several salient issues here:

One, there appears to be a strong desire among Nigerians, including by the apparent beneficiaries from the current system, for the country to get its act together. This was clearly reflected in the eagerness with which most Nigerians supported Professor Jega's seemingly unending demands for money and time as his conditions for offering credible elections. Paradoxically while most Nigerians appear eager to see the country move forward, they equally appear to fear that doing the right thing to help the country achieve that goal will dislodge them from their 'economy of affection' – their succour and comfort zone, which is often driven by irrational sentiments.

Two, with official results giving a landslide victory to President Goodluck Jonathan, a key challenge for him is to recognise the dimensions and manifestations of this crisis of the nation state, and how this was impacted upon by the zoning controversy and the violence that followed his victory in some parts of the North. True, even in the best of times the country always seems to hang on the precipice - partly because of the politicisation of the fault lines of region, ethnicity and religion. For President Jonathan therefore his ability to dowse the current tension will depend on the extent to which he can skilfully apply wisdom, political bargaining and a combination of carrots and sticks to renew the faith of the aggrieved actors in the Nigeria project

In trying to lower the current political temperature, the first thing to eschew is a sense of triumphalism and the use of intemperate language. In this sense, suggestions that people like IBB and Atiku should be sanctioned by the PDP for alleged anti party activities – apparently for facilitating a failed merger plan between ACN and CPC could only fuel the crisis. In the same vein, calls by the President of the Christian Association of Nigeria, Pastor Ayo Oritsejafor for Buhari, a former Head of State with a sort of cult political following in the North to be arrested (for allegedly instigating the post election violence in parts of the North) is myopic, if not sycophantic and irresponsible. My personal opinion is that the President needs to engage the opposition figures, especially Mohammed Buhari and the Ciroma group. He needs to tap into his famed humility to listen to their grouse and engage them honestly.

Three, in the short-to- medium terms, Jonathan needs to re-invent his public persona in such a way that he will be a more inspiring figure for people across the major fault lines. True, his 'guy-next-door image' and being apparently unfazed by the trappings of power are assets. But he needs top-ups. I would love to see the President develop some springs in his footsteps, wear less of the Ijaw fedora cap and occasionally appear for press conferences in jeans trousers with his sleeves rolled up. These symbolic shifts in his public persona will help to rupture his current deep association with ethnic and regional enclaves and make him more of a national icon. It will also help if the President can distant himself from some of his supporters who became extremely polarising figures before, during and after the campaigns in an apparent bid to ingratiate themselves to the presidency.

Four, it is also important that the President appreciates that the current crisis of the nation state, though dangerously exacerbated by the zoning controversy and the aftermath of the presidential elections, has overwhelming economic undertones. Poverty, unfulfilled economic aspirations as well as general underdevelopment and the pervasive scarcity of the socioeconomic values that it engenders, increase the attractions of the 'economy of affection' as a comfort zone. The President can attack the economic basis of this crisis of the nation state by articulating a quickly realisable economic vision, with an accompanying roadmap. Since governance is a continuous process and the President has indicated he will leave office by 2015, I will prefer to see him focus on no more than two key issues, say electricity generation and fighting general insecurity in the country. If the President can leave a lasting legacy in these two key areas, he will have written his name in gold in the annals of our political history and in our nation-building project.

Daily Trust, 25 April 2011

CHAPTER 28

THE CAMPAIGN STRATEGIES OF JONATHAN AND ATIKU

Is the PDP primaries draw near, it may be worth reviewing some of the campaign strategies deployed by the two main candidates for the PDP ticket – President Goodluck Jonathan and Atiku Abubakar. How have these Campaigns sought to market their principals? How do they define their rival? And what are their strategies for damage control?

Marketing their Principals

From the time he formally declared his interest in the 2011 presidential race, the Goodluck Ebele Jonathan (GEJ) Campaign has built the thrust of its political marketing on a 'moving train' narrative - basically that every one is queuing up to join its bandwagon. It constantly rolls out a wave of endorsements, some apparently contrived, to support this story line. Jonathan is also marketed as being divinely ordained to rule - and therefore likely bring good luck to Nigerians, if elected.

The Atiku Campaign Organisation tries to reap political capital out of the fact that its principal developed a policy document as early as 2006 by marketing it as evidence of thorough preparedness for the job. Consequently Atiku, through his Campaign, regularly throws a debating challenge to Jonathan in apparent bid to showcase his preparedness for the job, and Jonathan's apparent unpreparedness for it.

In addition to marketing their candidates on substantive issues, the Campaigns also engage in nuanced marketing of certain intangible attributes of their principals. For instance the Atiku Campaign appears to play up two main posters – one in which he is wearing the traditional ''Hausa *babariga* and 'Hausa cap' – apparently to appeal to his Northern constituency and another in which he is attired in suit and tie – apparently to showcase him as corporate person who is not clannishly tied to any ethnic group. This is perhaps to use innuendo to define Jonathan, who almost always wears 'Ijaw hat' as a regional/ethnic candidate with limited exposure. The Jonathan Campaign on the other hand tries to exploit some appurtenances of office – such as playing up a telephone call made by President Obama to President Jonathan for his handling of the crisis in Ivory Coast. The aim is to make him look like a statesman who is respected by other world leaders.

Defining their opponent

Campaigns usually try to aggressively negatively define their opponents through simple words/phrases in a bid to put such candidates on the defensive. For instance in the last presidential election in the USA, Obama constantly reminded voters that a vote for his rival, John McCain, would be 'four more years' for the then hugely unpopular George W Bush. The Jonathan Campaign has sought to define Atiku by almost always wrapping 'corruption' or 'desperate for power' in most messages it sends out about Atiku.

Though the Atiku Campaign has been attacking Jonathan's economic policies repeatedly, it has so far not tried hard enough to wrap these criticisms around such simple negative defining words/phrases as 'incompetence' or 'not to be trusted.'

Exploiting gaffes

It is not abnormal for campaigns to go into scaremongering by exploiting gaffes or even mischievously quoting an opponent out of context. For instance the Atiku Campaign maximally exploited Jonathan's ill-advised hasty exoneration of MEND during the October 1 bombing in Abuja. The Atiku Campaign also came up with advertorials which tried to exploit the statement credited to President Jonathan where he allegedly threatened PDP Governors that if they failed to support his candidacy, he would not go down alone.

The GEJ Campaign similarly exploited the statement made by Atiku during a stakeholders' conference on December 15, 2010 where he quoted Frantz Fanon's warning that those who make peaceful change impossible make violent change inevitable. The Jonathan Campaign deliberately omitted the part of the speech where Atiku said that such a violent change was not what the country needed at this time, and instead twisted the message to imply that he was preaching violence. After the 1983 election, one of the newspapers supporting the late Obafemi Awolowo, who was then challenging the results of the election, constantly carried on its front page window the same quote by Fanon without anyone trying to make a political capital out of it.

Damage Control

In campaigns, mistakes are inevitable just as embarrassing documents docking up are always a given. Most campaigns have damage control strategies for such eventualities. For instance following the successful exploitation of the gaffes committed by President Jonathan in response to the October 1 bombing incident, and Henry Orkah's interview with *Al Jazeera*, the GEJ Campaign first sought to discredit the interview by raising doubts about whether the person who granted the interview was actually Orkah. It also attacked *Al Jazeera's* motives in conducting the 'fake' interview. However after Orkah repeated the same interview to several media houses, including the *Financial Times* of London, the GEJ Campaign shifted strategy and began labelling him a serial liar.

In a recent PDP NEC meeting, Jonathan reportedly suffered a humiliating defeat when the Governors allegedly rejected his preference that the presidential primary should come ahead of other primaries. To blunt the impact of that defeat, his Campaign cleverly orchestrated the President's endorsement by 21 PDP Governors – despite the fact that nearly all of the said Governors had previously endorsed him, some more than once. The Campaign also began rolling out a wave of other endorsements, some apparently contrived, to blunt the impact of that humiliation.

The Atiku Campaign on its own responded to the exploitation of their principal's quote of Frantz Fanon by the Jonathan Campaign by buying advertorials in newspapers and highlighting the part of the speech where Atiku said that violent change 'is not what the country needs now' (but which the Jonathan Campaign deliberately left out). Their aim was to show that the quote attributed to Atiku was taken out of context. It also went on offensive by taking issues with Jonathan over a document which claimed that a Presidential Task Force set up in 2006 by then President Obasanjo had found Jonathan guilty of false declaration of assets. By so doing, it succeeded in forcing the GEJ Campaign on the defensive on another front.

Recently the Atiku Campaign admitted that it circulated a 'rigging roadmap', which it said was authored by the Jonathan Campaign. The Jonathan Campaign first claimed the document was "a badly cloned version of its working document", then denied any association with it and finally went on the offensive accusing Atiku of desperation and of trying to blackmail the President. For both Campaigns, their damage control strategies appear to be to defend and attack from another front.

Daily Trust 20 December 2010

CHAPTER 29

THE RE-INVENTION OF GOODLUCK JONATHAN

Omething is happening imperceptibly to our President, Goodluck Ebele Jonathan (GEJ). Shortly after he assembled a new cabinet following the April 2011 general elections, it seems there has been a gradual but deliberate abandonment of the public persona which GEJ used to good effect when, as Vice President, a cabal within the presidency sought to prevent him from being sworn in as the Acting President. GEJ's pre-April 2011 persona was that of a gentle, if diffident man, who would readily give a sympathetic ear to any argument and does not mind changing his mind several times on the same issue. This persona ironically made him come across to many people as a very humble and unassuming gentleman, who saw the office of president as a burden bestowed on him by destiny, which he was struggling with difficulty to carry, and relying on his name of 'Goodluck' to help him carry it. I believe this persona of an uncomplicated guy- next- door who was in dire need of protection from the more sophisticated Goliaths in the political arena, was a key reason why many people during the PDP's presidential primaries and the April 2011 elections axiomatically declared him a good man, a sort of a biblical David chosen by God to take the country forward at this moment in our political history. It would also seem that for most of the Governors, GEJ's special appeal during this period was the same public persona of a diffident and malleable man who could be easily swayed. That type of person, they must have reasoned, was someone they could do business with because they could always convince him with a 'superior argument' rather than Atiku, who could be too 'politically smart' to be swayed or Buhari who could remove the immunity clause in the constitution and herd as many of them as possible into jail for any infraction.

GEJ's pre-April 2011 public persona was solidified with his rather touching story of how he grew up and went to school without shoes. That public persona resonated well with many ordinary Nigerians making it extremely difficult for the proponents of zoning to turn him into an odious figure. In fact, my belief is that were GEJ a little more self-assured or strongly opinionated on anything during the hotly contested PDP presidential primaries it would have been much easier to demonise him and the zoning argument would perhaps have achieved a different outcome.

I believe the abandonment of GEJ's pre-April 2011 public persona became pronounced during the Justice Salami-Justice Katsina Alu saga. It will be recalled that in August 2011 the Nigerian Judicial Council suspended Justice Ayo Salami from office with immediate effect following his alleged disregard of the Council's directive to tender apologies to the NJC and to the then Chief Justice of Nigeria (CJN), Justice Aloysius Katsina-Alu, with whom he had been involved in an altercation bordering on allegations of corruption and influencing election tribunal proceedings. The NJC had recommended the compulsory retirement of Justice Salami for misconduct. Despite the hoopla in the media against the NJC's decision, the 'normally' indecisive President acted decisively, quickly accepted the recommendation of the NJC and refused to bulge despite the media campaign.

There was equally the case of the President's proposal for a- single term tenure for the President and Governors. Just when everyone thought he had quietly allowed the idea to die a natural death in the face of an overwhelming popular opposition, the President later declared that the idea was still alive and that contrary to media reports that the single term tenure proposal was for six years, it was actually for seven! He has stuck to his gun on the issue, insisting that the opponents of the idea had misunderstood his intentions.

The government's proposal for the removal of subsidies on petroleum products has followed the same emerging trend. Rather than recoil from a fight as people feel the pre-April 2011 GEJ would do, he has stuck to his gun, feeding into the impression that he is now being re-invented as a man of conviction, who will hold onto his belief, no matter the level of opposition. The emerging new GEJ, who will quietly but firmly defy pressures, reached a crescendo during the just concluded PDP gubernatorial primaries in Bayelsa State, the President's home State. Though the PDP has continued to deny it, the general belief is that GEJ is behind the decision to disqualify Sylva Timipre from contesting for the PDP gubernatorial primaries because of his alleged political sin of campaigning against his being made the Acting President when the late Yaradua had become very ill and a cabal within his government held the country hostage. The significant thing here however is not that the President was opposed to Timipre's candidacy but that he remained adamant in his opposition despite the reported interventions of the South South Governors, the Governors' Forum and other eminent Nigerians that reportedly included former President Shehu Shagari and former Head of State Yakubu Gowon. Also though there was a court order (or 'motion on notice', depending on which side you are in the confusion), the PDP went ahead to hold the nomination – despite popular anger that the party was flouting a court order. The new GEJ, as if to damn the pressures, quickly congratulated the party for doing a 'good job' of conducting the primaries.

The new GEJ also showed in the way Mrs Farida Waziri was sacked as the Chairman of the EFCC. The issue here is not just the sacking but the manner in which it was done decisively. He sacked her just before he left for France, ensuring that the news would still be 'hot' in the media by the time he would be meeting with his French hosts. The art of 'making a statement' by finding a major scapegoat in the anti-corruption war just before a foreign trip was perfected by the wily Obasanjo who would often use such to demonstrate to his foreign audience that his regime was serious in fighting corruption in the country.

I believe the putative re-invention of the President holds opportunities and threats both for the country and for President GEJ himself. On the positive side, the persona with which he won the PDP primaries and the subsequent general election can hardly be counted upon to take the necessary tough decisions that will transform this country. Leadership is rarely a popularity contest so a more decisive President, who is not afraid to give rewards or sanctions, is what the country needs. If the new decisive GEJ is able to bring immediate improvement in the economic circumstances of ordinary Nigerians, the re-invention will be deemed successful. If however nothing changes on the economic front, the new decisiveness will be perceived as emerging traits of dictatorship. Again, there is a risk that in a bid to show that a new tough guy has emerged, the President may fail to realise when his decisions or policy options are truly contrary to popular will. And with so many of his current decisions such as the single term tenure proposal and plans to remove petroleum subsidies being unpopular (at least in the short term), there could be a legitimacy crisis, especially if the implementation of these policies do not lead to an immediate improvement in the material circumstances of ordinary Nigerians. There is a further risk that a re-invented GEJ, seeing that he is able to get away with one tough decision after another, may misread the situation and react in ways that may lead to reversals in our democratic gains. There is equally a possibility that if Sylva Timipre contests and wins the Governorship election in Bayelsa State under another party's banner, the 'fear' of being an 'ordinary' citizen when Timipre will still be Governor, could affect the reported decision of GEJ to leave office in 2015. The re-invented GEJ also means losing the innocence that was part of his political capital before and during the Apri

2011 elections, making it much easier to turn him into a hate figure for counter mobilisation if he decides to contest in 2015.

However this re-invention of GEJ turns out for the country, what is clear is that the President seems to have become more comfortable with the exalted office he occupies. And that too has both its merits and flipsides – for GEJ and for the country.

Daily Trust, 1 Dec 2011

CHAPTER 30

BETWEEN PRESIDENT JONATHAN AND 2015

The threat by President Jonathan to sack any member of his administration campaigning for or holding consultations for the 2015 general elections in the country, has generated remarkable interest. Speaking at the 58th emergency meeting of the National Executive Committee of the Peoples Democratic Party (PDP) held in Abuja on February 20 2012, the President was quoted as saying:

'In a situation where a Governor has not even stayed for a year, the president has not stayed for a year and you start harassing people for 2015, it is another way of saying everything is about election. There must be time to work' (Vanguard [online], February 21, 2012). The scepticism with which the remark was received was a sign of the times. Distrust and suspicion, not just among the constituent units of the federation but also for the government and its representatives, are perhaps are their lowest ebb in our political history. In better times, the president's remarks would have been seen as value- neutral: don't' get distracted and don't distract others and more importantly don't use your official position to bolster your chances of becoming a State Governor or President. That was the kernel of the President's message and ordinarily it ought not to generate controversy. But we are living in such unremarkable times that the remarks, as harmless as they may seem, only succeeded in raising several issues:

One, the remark reminds everyone that 2015 is another election cycle and that some people have already started strategising and positioning themselves for it. Since perception tends to be everything in politics, the President's remark, though directed at officials in his administration, could paradoxically intensify hush-hush politicking as those who suddenly feel left behind may try to cover lost grounds. In other words, the President might have unintentionally blown the whistle for the start of the 2015 politicking and jockeying for positions, especially for the highest political office in the land, the presidency. For most Nigerians, the key election in 2015 is the presidential election, which for some, is simply a contest to decide which geopolitical zone will be in charge of the distribution of lucre.

Two, by publicly warning that officials of his administration campaigning or holding consultations for the 2015 general elections in the country would be sacked, the President may have publicly appropriated and legitimated an additional tool of control. This is because henceforth any official – appointed or elected - seen to be stepping out of line could be fired or 'damaged' irredeemably and impeached ostensibly for flouting the President's directive on 2015. In fact, there are suspicions that the President's remark could be watering the ground for resurrecting his proposal for single term tenure of seven years for the President and Governors. It should be recalled that when the Presidency first mooted the idea of single term tenure shortly after his inauguration, the main rationale was that 'everything seemed to be about elections'. The President's recent warning might have been choreographed to lend credence to the argument that some appointed or elected officials behave as if 'everything is about elections', which will then justify measures to fight that mentality with his single term tenure therapy. If the President resurrects the idea of single term tenure and manages to push it through to become law, not many people will believe that he will not present himself to benefit from it – despite his denial that this was the intention of the proposal.

Three, it is possible that the President's recent remarks were aimed at those in his regime already campaigning for him for a second term – without his say-so. No regime, especially in our type of society, is short of sycophants. But what we can learn from the way Jonathan kept very close to his chest the decision on whether he would run in the April 2010 election or not is that not showing his cards is probably one of his political strengths. I am beginning to believe many of us are grossly underestimating the President's political skills because of his humble and simple public persona. I now openly wonder whether anyone could emerge from the 'machine politics' in some states of the federation – Bayelsa, Anambra, Oyo, Adamawa etc and be truly as politically naïve as some of us paint Jonathan to be. Jonathan was Deputy Governor of Bayelsa and later the Governor of that State.

Four, while the question of whether Jonathan will seek re-election in 2015 or not will remain a matter of conjecture, it will be fair to surmise that he stands in the way of any one or geopolitical zone strategising on how to succeed him. We know that both the North and the South-east have been subtly beating their political drums about 2015 while some elements from the South-south openly talk of their 'right for a second term'. If Jonathan decides to seek his party's nomination, the truth is that he has more than 70 per cent chances of clinching the nomination.

Historically Presidents get the nomination of their parties, and in our type of society with weak institutions and deeply entrenched prebendal politics, a President has the leverage to divide even members of a family. One has to go as far back to the 19th century to find the lone instance of a sitting US president who was denied his party's nomination. This happened in 1852 when Franklin Pierce, who was elected the 14th President of the USA failed to secure the Democratic nomination in 1856. In Nigeria, not only does the President control the structures of his party, he has enormous resources – from patronage to security report and EFCC which he can use to muscle his way to his party's nomination irrespective of his track record.

Five, despite the obvious weaknesses of the PDP, the party's presidential candidate will always have more than 60 per cent chances of winning not just because it has the advantage of incumbency but even more importantly because each of the opposition parties rests on the charisma of its founder or presidential candidate. One of the consequences of this is that opposition parties in the country tend to be organisationally weak outside a few enclaves. And precisely because the opposition parties tend to be the extension of the charisma or ego of its founder or presidential candidate, it has been historically difficult for the opposition parties to come together present a common front during elections. Though the Action Congress of Nigeria has made remarkable progress outside the South-west, it remains doubtful if it has done enough to defeat a PDP candidate on its own.

Six, a key challenge for the geopolitical zones or individuals angling to succeed Jonathan will therefore be how to convince the President not to run in 2015. Though only the most biased supporter of the regime will argue that the President is on top of any of the key challenges facing the country, my personal opinion is that showcasing the President's incompetence is unlikely to be sufficient to make the party deny him nomination. Intimidation and threats are also unlikely to work because we are increasingly realising that despite his humble mien, the President is not incapable of fighting 'dirty'. In fact threats and intimidation may have the opposite effect. Though Jonathan is not by any stretch of the imagination President Mugabe of Zimbabwe, I have often wondered whether Mugabe would still have been in office at 88 years of age if the West had adopted a different type of politics to engage him. It may not just be enough to convince the President not to run, those backing him, including beneficiaries of the current order and sectional interests, will also have to buy into it. Therefore, a different form of politics would be required by those eyeing 2015 to convince the President to step aside.

Seven, one of the concerns of those who wish the president to run in 2015, is that his running and winning may create a new scenario where by any zone that produces the President will have to contrive reasons to hang on to the position for as long as it can. This will make governments not only increasingly provincial but our democracy, given the depth of our fault lines, may no longer be seen as an opportunity to change governments that do not perform. The main challenge for those who feel it is their right to be there in 2015 therefore is to devise creative ways of engaging the President and his critical constituencies, to persuade him to 'step aside'. This is because unless the President agrees not to run, the political space may not be sufficiently opened for any strategising for 2015 to be impactful.

Daily Trust, 15 March 2012

CHAPTER 31

MAURICE IWU'S FAUX PAS

Professor Maurice Iwu, chairman of the Independent National Electoral Commission (INEC), is constantly in the news, often for the wrong reasons. Even before the conduct of the April 2007 general elections, he had attracted so much controversy that doubts were raised about his neutrality as an umpire in the elections.

To be sure, given the peculiarities of the Nigerian political environment, the zero-sum-nature of our politics, and the 'Nigerian factor' of not taking responsibility for failures, it is doubtful whether anyone could chair any election body in Nigeria without being dogged in controversy or accused of being a lackey of the governing political party. To this extent, some of the criticisms of Iwu are unfair or exaggerated. But Iwu, by his style and body language, has not helped matters. Some critics have gone as far as accusing him of suffering from delusions of grandeur.

Professor Iwu's conduct of the April 2007 elections has been well documented. What has been shocking to many Nigerians and international observers was not only that the elections were very shabbily and incompetently conducted, but that INEC has continued to thump its chest for 'a job well done' while regarding any critic of the elections as an enemy with an ulterior motive. This is certainly unhelpful to Iwu's image.

Related to this is that Professor Iwu sometimes conducts himself as a politician rather than an umpire of elections. For instance at the height of the criticisms of his conduct of the elections and strident calls for him to be removed, he organised, or at least welcomed, a solidarity visit from some Igbo youths. This is usually the stuff of politicians, not of appointees of sensitive public bodies such as INEC. Similarly the AIT recently showed footage of him being honoured with a chieftaincy title by his village and surrounded by top government functionaries, including Vice President Dr Jonathan Goodluck and other PDP bigwigs. That most of the dignitaries on the occasion were top members of the PDP could hardly engender confidence in him as a neutral arbiter of the electoral process.

Professor Iwu again seems to have borrowed from the book of our politicians when he turned, or closed his eyes to his Chief Press Secretary, Andy Ezeani, turning himself into an attack dog. For instance when Professor Wole Soyinka criticised the INEC chairman, Andy

Ezeani retorted with uncomplimentary references to his age. Similarly when Ken Nnamani, former president of the Senate, condemned the electoral body, Ezeani again fired back by accusing him of having exerted undue pressure on INEC to postpone the elections so that he would emerge as the nation's interim president. He also reportedly threatened that after the completion of the work of the Election Petition Tribunals, INEC would "prosecute the likes of Chief Nnamani whose electoral offences in the 2007 elections are well documented." Vituperations such as these and a penchant for using intemperate language often makes INEC and its principal look petty, and incapable of taking or responding professionally to criticisms.

Rather than an attack dog what professor Iwu probably needs is someone who is likeable, polite and measured. An attack dog will only reinforce the perception of his own negatives, rather than complement his weaknesses.

INEC's communication strategy also appears flawed. One would think that INEC, following the criticisms that trailed the April 2007 election would start with mapping out the various constituencies that are critical of its work, and then devise appropriate strategies for selling its own side of the story to each constituency. The lack of strategy here is evident in the very disagreeable way INEC responded to criticisms from Professor Wole Soyinka. While even the most ardent supporters of critics like Wole Soyinka, Chinua Achebe and Gani Fawehinmi would very readily accept that these social critics are not always right, and that they do indeed sometimes go overboard in their criticisms, they do not doubt their integrity, honesty and patriotism and would not want to see them insulted or humiliated. In fact acolytes and admirers of these three critics could be said to constitute the core of the 'vocal press' and the online 'ambush journalists', known for their idealism and constantly spoiling for a fight, especially with top government functionaries. Therefore by being rude and trying to humiliate Wole Soyinka, INEC may have succeeded only in giving the 'vocal press' and 'ambush journalists' the fight they naturally crave for. It is remarkable that Nuhu Ribadu, the former chairman of INEC, despite his shortcomings, achieved the unique feat of winning over these three critics to his side, and by so doing also won over the 'vocal press' and the online 'ambush journalists'. Writing, says Camilo José Cela, the Spanish winner of the 1989 Nobel Prize in Literature, is necessarily a denuciation of the times in which the author lives. If you extend this to these three critics, it becomes easier to understand where they are coming from.

One may also wonder which constituency INEC directs its communication to – apart from the Yaradua presidency and the PDP hierarchy - because even when Iwu makes presentations, the undeniable flourishes of brilliance in his papers are often lost in the fact that they are usually crafted as angry repudiations of the points marshalled against him by his critics. His presentations would be more effective if they were aimed at presenting and selling his own side of the story in the political marketplace of a clearly identified constituency.

Recently there was news report that INEC last year gave the National Association of Nigerian Students (NANS) N11,743,000 for the student body's maiden Leadership Training Workshop in Abuja. If INEC's un-stated aim was to win over the students as a constituency of support, then the money is simply misplaced because as a former student leader, I know there are so many political tendencies within the student body and leadership that sustaining any support from students is difficult. This is worsened by the fact that the leadership of student bodies such as NANS tends to drink from the same ideological fountain as Soyinka, Gani, Achebe, the 'vocal press' and the online 'ambush journalists'. Therefore to insult and humiliate Soyinka while apparently wooing NANS doesn't seem to make a strategic sense.

Daily Independent, 21 January 2009

CHAPTER 32

RIBADU: COMEUPPANCE AND LESSONS FROM HISTORY

The current travails of Nuhu Ribadu, the former boss of EFCC, the dreaded anti-graft agency, have received extensive media coverage. Mallam Ribadu was eased out of the EFCC in January this year ostensibly because he needed to attend a career development course at the National Institute of Policy and Strategic Studies (NIPSS) in Kuru, Plateau State. Suspicions that the so-called career development course was a mere ploy to shove him aside from EFCC have since been confirmed by events. Not only has he been demoted from being an Assistant Inspector General of Police to a Deputy Commissioner of Police, he now literally lives in fear of the same agency he once headed.

Beyond Mallam Ribadu's regrettable travails, there are very important lessons from his experiences that should not be lost.

One of the important lessons is that what goes around comes around. Though it may appear sadistic to regale in any one's troubles, such experiences could be useful if they end up teaching us valuable lessons about the need for restraint when we find ourselves in positions of authority. There was no doubt that Ribadu loved his job as the boss of EFCC and discharged his duties with passion and gusto. He was energetic, fearless and apparently determined. But he also went to extremes, unnecessarily courted media attention, and turned the agency into a behemoth that investigated, prosecuted, judged and condemned, not just the political class but also anyone of prominence. In more advanced societies, such agencies work surreptitiously, rarely courting media attention but still quietly very effective. Ribadu's style therefore not only made him powerful enemies but also excited the envy of his colleagues. Though Ribadu appears to have been prematurely canonised by a section of the media and the remnants of the Nigerian left, I still fail to see how abusing or criminalizing elected officials before such people are convicted by a competent court of law furthered the work of the agency. We cannot clamour for the rule of law, a key element of democracy, while embracing Ribadu's methods that clearly undermined the rule of law, however much we may loathe those suspected of corrupt enrichment or other forms of malfeasance.

Another important lesson from the Ribadu saga is that in the discharge of public duties, having good intentions are not enough. The goals pursued, and the means used in pursuing those goals, do matter. Mallam Ribadu hounded candidates for political offices into detention, sometimes on the eve of elections in which they were candidates. In Plateau state for instance, the EFCC was reported to have supervised the illegal impeachment of Joshua Dariye. However the gravity of the allegations against him, due process, a key element of protecting everyone's right to fair trial, ought to have been respected. In more advanced societies, you remain a suspect, and treated as such, until convicted by a competent court of law, even if you were caught with your hands in the cookie jar. Ribadu's supporters have sought to excuse some of the unorthodox ways he went about his business by arguing that he meant well or that desperate times demanded for desperate measures. Unfortunately intentions, however noble they may be, remain at best unborn revolutions. Lawrence Anini, the notorious armed robber who terrorised Benin and its environs during the regime of Babangida, was known for stealing from the banks and spreading part of the loot to poor peasants in the local markets. He too could point to this as evidence of his good intentions.

An equally important lesson from Ribadu' apparent persecution is that it may be utter foolishness to fight your employer frontally, especially if that employer is an African government. It is debatable whether it was wise of Ribadu to have employed, caused to be employed, or closed his eyes to the employment of media attacks on the government when it began to emerge that he was going to be removed from EFCC. If the aim was to twist the arm of his employer and safeguard his job, then it was a disastrous PR job. Rather than highlighting Ribadu's achievements and how he will complement or further the regime's declared interest in fighting corruption, the focus of his strategy appeared to be to rally media support on grounds that he was to be removed in order to protect some powerful interests. This strategy came across, rightly or wrongly, as blackmail, and may paradoxically have helped to seal his fate because it put the government in a position where to back down would have been a humiliation and also seen as a sign of weakness. Ribadu had genuine admirers in high places within and outside the country. A more surreptitious use of those contacts, without appearing to be engaging his employer in a David versus Goliath type of square-off, could perhaps have led to a different outcome.

I believe he made similar mistakes with the hide-and-seek game he played with the EFCC when he was invited for questioning: first he refused to honour the invitation (turning it into a media campaign once again), then later honoured it (revealing he had buckled under pressure); he went to court to obtain an injunction to stop the agency from arresting him (a questionable move), then had to withdraw the case (tacitly admitting another defeat). There may therefore be an additional lesson of learning to discern between bravery and bravado, and hubris and firmness. While it may be difficult to be the chairman of EFCC without stepping on powerful toes, a wise navigation of the aforementioned boundaries would perhaps have enhanced his effectiveness at EFCC without necessarily making enemy of every powerful foot stepped upon. Smart diplomats and administrators are known to have the skills to separate the sin from the sinner, to ask you to go to hell and still be able to politely invite you out for a drink. We all know that whatever legalese may be used to cloak Ribadu's current troubles, some people are obviously taking their pound of flesh.

I do not think it is opportunistic or cowardice to use pragmatic means to secure one's job or negotiate for soft-landing, if one must be shoved aside. It is, on the contrary, wisdom to know when to stoop to conquer, when to throw a punch, when to endure being turned into a punching bag, and when to counter-punch. Yes, your African government employer must be challenged in extreme cases of oppression, but as an individual still under their employment, you fight them sideways, not frontally. This strategy not only prolongs your fighting life but preserves your fighting capability.

Ribadu's current problems also show that while power may be the ultimate aphrodisiac, it is equally ephemeral, transitional and ultimately a vanity. The quickness with which the halo departs from men and women of power in Nigeria once they vacate their authority position could be astounding. In his hey days, the fear of Ribadu was the beginning of wisdom in Nigeria. Today, he appears to be a lonely man in need of friends. An additional lesson from his experience therefore is the tendency of the predator to become the prey, and of the prey to become the predator, in Nigerian politics. Hopefully this lesson will also not be lost on Ribadu's traducers.

Daily Independent, Dec 29, 2008

CHAPTER 33

RIBADU'S QUEST TO BE PRESIDENT

The recent declaration by Nuhu Ribadu, former boss of the Economic and Financial Crimes Commission, that he would run for the presidency of this country in the 2011 elections, may not have come as a surprise to many people. Mallam Ribadu, who became a celebrity public servant by the way he ran the EFCC with pomp and bravado, became even larger than life after he was shoved aside from the job, humiliated, and forced into self-imposed exile. Though some saw the manner he was eased out of the job as a necessary comeuppance for his over-indulgence as boss of the financial crimes buster, there was a significant flow of compassion for his travails, which morphed into a certain mythologisation of his time at the EFCC as the golden era of corruption fighting in Nigeria.

While in self-imposed exile, his fellowship at Oxford University and numerous speaking engagements in the West, was interpreted by many as a tacit endorsement of his own side of the story, if not his era at the EFCC, by these countries. In fact Ribadu's persona, post EFCC, was such that he was not only a much sought-after speaker across the world but also often constantly had to evade the question of whether he planned to run for President.

Several observations could be made regarding his formal declaration of intent to run:

One, Ribadu's candidacy is likely to generate more interest than that of Professor Pat Utomi, who, though liked by the literati and the intelligentsia, appears to be without the sort of political base that Ribadu seems to have. For instance, while Professor Utomi often approaches elections as if they were a matter of who would present the most brilliant paper in a seminar, Ribadu strives to be populist and cleverly exploits language to create a 'we' versus 'them' type of struggle, in which he constantly casts himself as a champion of the underdogs. For instance in an unscripted talk he delivered in Ibadan, on September 13, 2010, as a guest at the 80th birthday remembrance lecture in honour of Bola Ige, the former Federal Attorney-General and Minister of Justice, Ribadu was quoted by The Nation, (online) of Sept 17, 2010 as saying: "I have always been fighting in my life. When I was in the Police Force, I fought armed robbers, I survived. I fought gangsters, I fought 419 fraudsters, big time corrupt people and I have survived. I am still standing as Nuhu Ribadu; I believe I will also survive this."

Two, once he was appointed the pioneer chairman of the EFCC, Ribadu carefully cultivated the support of a faction of the civil society allied to the late Gani Fawehinmi, Wole Soyinka, Femi Falana and prominent Awoists. For instance not only did he publicly declare Gani as his hero, he even smuggled himself back to Nigeria to pay his last respect to the great man after his death – despite reportedly being wanted by the Nigerian police. In return, this constituency, which has a tremendous noise value and the support of the Lagos press and the 'radical' online community, appears to have adopted him as one of its own.

Three, though Ribadu may have a well-deserved reputation for being loquacious - as EFCC chairman he often found people guilty even before proper investigation had commenced on their cases – he is, from all indications, not politically stupid. Not only was he successful in using the Lagos press and its allied civil society to project himself when he was the boss of the EFCC, he also appears to know which popular sentiments to lap on to. For instance he listed his priorities, if elected President as security; effective power supply; free education; sound medical facilities; and collective leadership. He even bragged that with only 5,000 dedicated police officers, he would wipe out crime in the country! For someone who made his name from fighting corruption, one would wonder why fighting corruption was not listed as one of his priorities. The reason may well be that he knows that he too will have questions to answer on corruption because there is virtually no one who has held a public position in the country, including himself, who does not have one allegation of financial malfeasance or the other hanging around his neck.

Four, one of the major challenges facing Ribadu's quest for the presidency will be whether he has the emotional intelligence and level-headedness needed for the top political job in the land. While his tenure as EFCC chairman will continue to evoke extreme emotions, there appears to be a consensus that he brought bravado, emotions, love for a fight and some recklessness to the job – qualities that could be disastrous in a President. There are also concerns of whether he has sufficient organisational and financial resources to effectively mount a presidential campaign – especially against the likes of President Jonathan, Atiku Abubakar and Ibrahim Babangida. This was perhaps what Ribadu alluded to when he said it was going to be a David versus Goliath type of fight.

Five, though on face value Ribadu appears to be running only for the consolation prize of 'also ran', he may end up playing a decisive role in the outcome of the presidential election. If, as suspected, he ends up running on the platform of Action Congress of Nigeria, and most likely chooses someone from the South West as his running mate, he may effectively be positioned as a candidate of that geopolitical zone in the election. In the North, his fortunes may depend on who is fielded by the PDP as its presidential candidate, and how the party resolves the thorny question of zoning. If for instance the PDP implodes or atrophies as a result of the zoning issue, Ribadu may either share the Northern vote or become its main beneficiary. As improbable as it may seem, Ribadu emerging as the President is not impossible if the zoning issue leads to a sort of Mutually Assured Political Destruction among the key PDP candidates – President Jonathan, Atiku Abubakar and Ibrahim Babangida.

Six, a Ribadu presidency will exacerbate, rather than attenuate the zoning controversy, and the North-South divide. Though zoning was a strictly PDP arrangement, the equation of the PDP to the government by many, means that the zoning debate will follow whoever becomes the President, irrespective of the party platform the election was won. In this sense, the zoning controversy could represent one of the biggest challenges in our journey nationhood.

Daily Trust, 21 September 2010

CHAPTER 34

NUHU RIBADU: NIGERIA'S NEXT OBAMA?

It is difficult to meet Mallam Nuhu Ribadu without having some sort of likeness for him. I saw the embattled pioneer chairman of the Economic and Financial Crimes Commission for the first time at a 'state of the nation' symposium organised by the Nigerian Liberty Forum at the Metropolitan University, London, on May 29, 2009. A man whose slender frame and boyish looks often mask his lion heart and iron resolve, Mallam Ribadu easily stole the show at the gathering. He was literally mobbed as he entered the hall, and as he stood to speak, almost everyone, as if by some sort of invisible instigation, stoop up in respect, and remained standing for a long time.

I was never a fan of Nuhu Ribadu's methods as the EFCC chairman. I still hold the EFCC under his watch partly responsible for the joke that was the 2007 elections. I had written about his recent travails as a comeuppance for his misdeeds as chairman of the financial crimes buster. I had strongly disagreed with arguments that he meant well despite his obvious excesses, noting that even the road to hell is paved with good intentions.

Mallam Ribadu spoke on Nigerian unity, making what some people would regard as a populist appeal for Nigerians to overcome their differences and come together to reclaim the Nigerian state from a corrupt and visionless elite. He argued that there was really no substantial difference in the needs and aspirations of ordinary Nigerians, irrespective of their ethnicities and other primordial differences, because "all they ask for are the basic necessities of life." For Ribadu, the Nigerian elites like to harp on the differences among Nigerians, because it is in their interest to do so, to "keep us divided". He called himself a simple Fulani man, whose role model had always been Gani Fawehinmi, a man he said he would name Abuja after, if he had his way. He rhetorically asked, to thunderous applause, whether we are being fair to the likes of Wole Soyinka and Anthony Enahoro, who had given over 50 years of their life in the struggle to make Nigeria better, but are still forced to remain in active service because the problems of the country appear to remain intractable.

I respected Mallam Ribadu for not using the forum to get back to the Nigerian government, his current traducers. He wisely focused on positive messages, admitting that mistakes were made when he was boss of EFCC. There was something about the way he spoke that touched most people in the audience, including those of us who are his ardent critics. It was easy to believe that he spoke from his heart rather than from his head.

As Mallam Ribadu spoke, I noticed that a Nigerian lady sitting next to me was struggling to hold back her tears. "This is a very honest man, a very rare Nigerian", she muttered, more to herself. I tried to engage her in a discussion. I agreed that Nuhu was obviously an honest man, who meant well and had a lot of passion for the job he did as EFCC chairman. I however disagreed that his good intentions were enough excuses for some of his unacceptable methods. Her facial expression changed as if I had uttered a heresy.

"Whether any one likes it or not, he will be our next president", she muttered and moved farther away from me as if to clearly indicate that she did not want to pursue that discussion any further.

Nuhu Ribadu for president? Though not his supporter, I have always believed firmly that in Nigeria's game of musical chairs, his rehabilitation would be only a matter of time, and his traducers would inevitably one day take their own turn of being painted as villains. This is one of the iron laws of our politics: there are no permanent messiahs or permanent villains. Just think of Abacha, the poster boy of Nigerian dictatorship and corruption, and the efforts made not long ago by a section of the country to rehabilitate him.

In the Tube (underground train) on my way home from the symposium, I found myself standing next to three gentlemen who had apparently also attended the event. The discussion was again on Nuhu Ribadu.

"He is very inspirational. He is our Obama", one of the three men, who looked Caucasian to me, declared. I decided to barge into the discussion but resisted the temptation to ask the gentleman if he was indeed Nigerian. I asked whether the genius of Obama was because he was inspirational or because he was post-racial, and a reconciler, with wisdom and good organisational sense.

"Nigeria needs an enlightened leader who can inspire confidence in Nigerians, whom Nigerians will be proud of, and who genuinely wants to transform the country," he declared.

I agreed that Ribadu inspires confidence and will make a genuine effort to transform Nigeria if he becomes president of the country but again expressed concerns about his democratic credentials. I reminded them that when he was boss of the EFCC he virtually kidnapped or forced some House of Assembly members in Plateau state to impeach their

Governor. I also reminded the three gentle men that during the 2007 elections Ribadu appeared to sit in his office and decide people to disqualify from running for office before finding evidence against them.

"I don't think you will vote for him, will you? Your question to the founder of *Sahara Reporters* [the online blog] gave you away", the bulkiest of the three, with obvious Nigerian features asked, with a smile of superior wisdom. I had asked Omoyele Sowore if he ever saw anything good in the Nigerian government. I also accused him of appearing to romanticise the Niger Delta militants, and of failing to distinguish between the cause they espouse (which most Nigerians support) and their methods (which many find abhorrent).

"Look brother", began the third man, "we Nigerians made Obama President of the United States. More than 25 percent of the people who organised and knocked on doors for Obama are Nigerians. Nuhu is not perfect. But do you think any of the people currently being touted as presidential candidates in Nigeria will be better than Nuhu". He had a slight Igbo accent.

I agreed with him that if Nuhu ever becomes Nigeria's president, it would never be business as usual and that he will be prepared to give his life to make a difference. I however once again reiterated my concern about his antecedents, including a tendency to be carried away by emotions.

As we disembarked and went our different ways, what became obvious to me is that Nigerians have not heard the last of Nuhu Ribadu.

Daily Independent, 3 June 2009

CHAPTER 35

OBASANJO 2: ATIKU 6

The recent report that Obasanjo caricatured the emergence of Atiku Abubakar as the consensus candidate of the Northern faction of the PDP brings to mind echoes of the epic battle between the duo during their second term in office. When asked what he thought about Atiku's emergence as the North's consensus candidate for the PDP presidential ticket, Obasanjo, an ultimate political comedian when he chooses to be, was said to have dabbled into a sarcastic laughter and then declared in Pidgin English: 'I dey laugh'. The Atiku Campaign Organisation quickly retorted, also in Pidgin English that 'we too dey laugh oo', after reminding the Ota Farmer of the declining fortunes of the PDP in the South West, which it blamed squarely on Obasanjo's mismanagement of the party in that zone.

Since it is now obvious that the battle of wits between Atiku and Obasanjo has continued unabated since it first blew open in 2003, it may be worth assessing their score lines.

Round one: Some have traced the origin of the deep mistrust between Obasanjo and Atiku to April 2002, when the Owu chief reportedly organised an event and deliberately left out the Vice President from the protocols. It was said that Atiku not only felt humiliated at such a public event but also took it as a confirmation of the rumour that Obasanjo was contemplating to drop him as his running mate in the 2003 presidential election. It was said that from that time Atiku began to plan a counter attack, including preparations to run against his boss in the party's primaries, if need be. Sensing that Atiku had the support of most of the PDP Governors and delegates, Obasanjo, it was said, had to literally 'beg' Atiku for his support. Atiku acquiesced, allegedly on the condition that he would be retained on the ticket. If this version of the origin of the mistrust between the two were correct, then **round one** went to Atiku Abubakar, for successfully preventing Obasanjo from dropping him from the ticket

Round two: Atiku developed ambition for high political office quite early in his political life. At the age of 47, and with only three years experience in politics, Atiku had sought the presidential ticket of the Babangida-created SDP after his mentor, the late Shehu Musa Yaradua and the other presidential candidates in both the SDP and the rival NRC were disqualified because of alleged irregularities in the parties' primaries. In March 1993, Atiku emerged as the SDP presidential candidate from Adamawa State and headed for Jos to vie with 27 others, including 55-year old MKO Abiola, for the party's presidential ticket. The late Musa Yaradua instructed him to step down for Abiola on the understanding that Abiola would make him (Atiku) his running mate. Though Abiola eventually settled for Babagana Kingibe as his running-mate and Atiku was later to contest and win the Governorship election in Adamawa State, it is natural to surmise that Atiku nursed presidential ambitions and had hoped to succeed Obasanjo at the end of the latter's two terms in office.

It was said that Obasanjo felt that one way of retaliating for the perceived humiliation of having to beg Atiku for his political support in 2003 was to stop him from realising his presidential ambitions. He therefore started a process of not only dismantling Atiku's PDM political structure but also of whittling down his political influence in the government. The mistrust between the two reached its crescendo when Obasanjo decided to amend the Constitution to 'elongate' his tenure and Atiku chose to oppose it vociferously. Obasanjo successfully prevented Atiku from succeeding him – just as Atiku succeeded in preventing Obasanjo from elongating his tenure.

Score card: Atiku 1: Obasanjo 1.

Round three: Though Obasanjo succeeded in stopping Atiku from realising his presidential ambition, Atiku won the hearts of many Nigerians not only by the way he carried himself in the face of humiliation by Obasanjo and his acolytes, but also for literally fighting Obasanjo with 'bare hands'. He was said to be among the few with the courage to fight Obasanjo toe-to-toe when the Ota farmer held sway at Aso Rock. Therefore, though Obasanjo succeeded in preventing Atiku from succeeding him, the epic fight between the duo raised Atiku's profile both as a democrat and as a dogged fighter. In this sense, Atiku scores an extra point.

Round four: Both Obasanjo and Atiku vacated office in May 1999. After the Supreme Court affirmed the 'victory' of Umaru Yaradua in the sham that was the 2007 election, Atiku quickly found that his political influence was waning, especially as his new party, the AC (which has now renamed itself ACN) was rapidly being turned into a reincarnation of the Yoruba-dominated AD, with Alhaji Bola Tinubu as the unofficial leader. Efforts to build a credible opposition capable of wresting power from PDP had tumbled. It could be argued that Atiku suddenly found himself with only two options - to return to the PDP, which, despite its weaknesses, remained the only vehicle for him to realise his ambition of becoming President, or to allow himself to drift into political oblivion. He began subtle moves to return to the PDP. On January 19 2009, Obasanjo allegedly lured Atiku to what was supposed to be a top secret 'reconciliation' meeting between the two but tipped the press about it. It turned out that Atiku had not informed his party, the AC, or his loyalists of the planned meeting. The leaked meeting not only undermined Atiku's political image but also succeeded in shifting media focus from the daily negative reports about Obasanjo to speculations of the import of that meeting. Score line: Obasanjo 1 Atiku 0.

Round five: After the infamous meeting of January 19, 2009, Atiku became part of the efforts to create a mega political party that would be capable of defeating the PDP at the polls. When that idea fell through, and he began contemplating a return to PDP, all manner of obstacles were erected on his way – allegedly with the fingerprints of Obasanjo all over it. He was eventually re-admitted into the party after several allegations and counter-allegations. After the re-admission, came the huge hurdle of getting a 'waiver' to enable him contest for the presidency under the PDP. Despite stiff opposition from several quarters, Atiku not only secured a waiver but went ahead to become the consensus candidate of the Adamu Ciroma-led Northern Political Leadership Forum. Before this, many political pundits had concluded that the PDP presidential primary would be a direct contest between Ibrahim Babangida and Goodluck Jonathan.

Score card: Atiku 3: Obasanjo 0.

Among Atiku's supporters, the common salutation these days is 'three down – two to go'. By this they mean that they have surmounted three key obstacles – re-admission into the party, getting a waiver and their Principal becoming the consensus candidate. The 'two to go' are – their candidate becoming the PDP's flag bearer in the 2011 presidential election, and eventually winning the presidency. From all indications, Obasanjo will do his best to stop the victory runs of Atiku, now daubed the ultimate comeback kid.

Daily Trust, 01 December 2010

CHAPTER 36

OBASANJO: BEYOND THE DEMONISATION

It is now common to see Obasanjo's eight year-rule (May 1999 - May 2007) as representing everything that is evil in Nigerian political history. There is usually an erroneous assumption that things were better when Obasanjo came to power in 1999. For some, Obasanjo epitomised a betrayal of hope, what with the enormous revenues earned from oil under his watch, and the paradoxical increase in destitution, unemployment and insecurity of life and property under his regime.

It is possible to identify at least five strands of criticisms: The remnants of the Nigerian left criticise him for his wholesale embrace of market economics - typified in his privatisation programmes (and the redundancies and corruption they spurned) and other policies that were couched in the brand of economics usually espoused by the Bretton Woods institutions. Those who consider themselves urbane or morally-driven pick quarrels with his personal style (including his alleged overflowing libido and countless concubines), his undeniable garrulity ('roforofo' – a la Reuben Abati), his obvious issues with manners, his apparent hypocrisy in a number of issues such as fighting corruption and his grand-father-knows-it-all stance on many issues. There are also those who criticise Obasanjo from ethno perspective. For this class of critics, Obasanjo was out to "undo" or "marginalise" their "people", and each group can reel out many instances of this, or what they would call deliberate acts of denial of "federal presence" in their ethnic enclave under his regime. Obasanjo is equally criticised by the religious right: the Christians criticise him for lacking the balls to stop the introduction of Sharia in some Northern states while some Muslims accuse him of deliberate policies to undermine their religion such as the building of a Chapel at Aso Rock and the removal of the Islamic inscriptions on the Naira notes. There are equally those who criticise him for not living up to the Obasanjo myth – a man who, for a greater part of the last 30 years, was regarded as ascetic, frugal, incorruptible and ultranationalist.

In many ways therefore, there is a room for everyone to find an angle to take a swipe at Obasanjo. Criticisms, sometimes very harsh ones, come with the territory of politics and public service, and are typified in the saying that politics is the "art of the possible". Those who cannot take the heat are usually counselled to stay away from the kitchen.

But I feel that criticisms of Obasanjo are grossly overdone, without due recognition for his achievements. I believe that despite Obasanjo's obvious failures and personal weaknesses, he remains the greatest Nigerian leader to date. He remains the only leader that has recorded irreversible developmental achievements – in banking reforms and in the uptake of mobile phones and internet penetration. Is there any developmental achievement from previous Nigerian regimes that had been sustained? Curiously while the numerous failures of the regime are rightly attributed directly to Obasanjo, his obvious successes are attributed to others - Professor Charles Soludo (banking reforms) and inevitable invisible hand of the globalisation process (internet and mobile phones penetration). There is no doubt that his regime failed in the provision of infrastructure, power, jobs, and in poverty alleviation. If the regime of Umaru Yaradua can record just one irreversible change in any sector (energy, transport, education etc) the nation will be irreversibly moving forward. Development after all is a continuous and incremental process, and part of the Nigerian tragedy is that we have been unable to record irreversible successes in any area (besides the aforementioned two under Obasanjo). Most regimes that are considered successful in many parts of the world often leave their marks in one or two areas. For instance, in the UK, many people consider Tony Blair as a successful Prime Minister despite his unpopular decisions such as the war on Iraq and numerous policy failures such as in the reform of the National Health Service, education and arresting the increasing wave of gun-crimes. He is regarded as successful largely because the economy boomed under his watch. Though many people put the success of the economy down to the then Chancellor Gordon Brown, the credit rightly goes to Tony Blair because he provided the enabling political environment. It will generally be deemed myopic to judge any weather only by its sunny or inclement side. A successful general is not one who never suffered any defeat but one who registered at least one strategic success.

System Dynamics

The harshest critics appear to be those who judge Obasanjo by the man he was, or was perceived to be in his first coming, in 1976-1979. At that time, he stuck to the transition programme of the slain Murtala Mohammed and handed power to an elected civilian government – a rarity in those days. Embedded in that action was a man who could be relied upon, and had a sense of purpose. So with Obasanjo infamous for not keeping his words, and for using and abandoning friends during his second coming, what really happened?

Part of the answer could be found in 'system dynamics' – every system operates in a given way and will often throw up people who will conform to its tenets or try to 'swallow' those who try to change it too quickly. Chinua Achebe in his powerful but less recognised novel, No Longer At Ease gave an insight into this phenomenon in the 'Obi Okonkwo complex'. The novel's main character, Obi Okonkwo, was his own man at a time in Igboland when the voice of the community and the elders was regarded as sacrosanct. First, they sent him to England to study Law so that he would come back to handle their land cases. He defied his people and read English. On his return, when the villagers amassed at the airport to receive him (most of them wearing suits and ties in the brazen sun), they expected to see a man clad in the best suit England could offer. But Obi Okonkwo disappointedly showed up wearing a simple shirt. He was to prove an even greater disappointment at a reception organised in his honour, for while the secretary of the town union reeled out the "English that filled the mouth", Obi Okonkwo, who was expected to thrill them with the type of bombastic English they never heard of before (after all he had just come back from England!), spoke only the "is and was" type of simple English. Above all, Obi Okonkwo went against the ingrained custom of his people and married an 'osu' –a religious outcast. As if these were not enough, he refused to use his senior position in the civil service to help people from his town to get jobs in the service (which was then a common practice among the ethnic unions in the colonial enclaves and new townships) and instead distanced himself from the community. Yet, despite his idealisms, hatred of bribery and corruption and proving beyond doubt that he was his own man, Obi Okonkwo was compelled by the exigencies of survival imperatives and living up to societal expectations to take bribe – and was caught! Some people have used this story to challenge the conclusions in Achebe's later work The Trouble With Nigeria that the problem with Nigeria is leadership, rather than the system.

So what has this got to do with Obasanjo? This means that the Obasanjo of 1976-1978 could not possibly be the Obasanjo of 1999-2007 because the system has changed – the values, ethos, political culture and people's orientation have changed from what they were in 1976-1979 and Obasanjo, as a product of his environment unwittingly had to change to adapt to the demands and expectations of the new system. This is not an excuse for his suspected avarice while in office but an explanation of why it probably happened.

One of the first of these changes Obasanjo felt he had to make to adapt to the new systemic mores and expectations was with respect to his looks and sartorial tastes. Obasanjo had always been known and respected by many for his ascetic and spartanic clothes and life style (remember the photographs of him on his 'Long-John' type of bicycle and usually dressed like a peasant?). Once he was drafted into the Presidency and allegedly given so much money, there appeared to be a systematic "killing" of the old Obasanjo of simple life style. First went the bohemian moustache and the simple shirts and in came numerous designer 'agbadas', glasses and even manner of speaking English. The type of friends he kept also changed and there was a new embrace of men of wealth and the nouveaux riche in tune with the new societal norms of wealth adoration. Some wicked tongues sniped that the deprivation he faced after handing over power the first time, and the humiliation of the near bankruptcy he faced when he was released from Abacha's gulag, made him distance himself from the old Obasanjo and resolved not to be "foolish again" at the second opportunity. The failure of the third term plot, it seemed, brought out the worst in Obasanjo. There are many who believe he completely lost the plot when he embraced the third term plot, as many projects from then on were either to actualise the third term or to punish those who he perceived worked against it.

The Zik complex

Virtually every group has a grouse against Obasanjo. He is uncharacteristically criticised more by his Yoruba brethren than perhaps by any other ethnic group. This is remarkable, coming from an ethnic group that is believed to passionately protect one of its own in Nigeria's competitive ethnic environment. Unlike the late Awolowo, Obasanjo was unable or unwilling to rally the Yorubas behind him. This is due partly to his garrulous style and partly to what I will call the "Zik complex". Zik was obsessed with being seen as a detribalised African/nationalist and enjoyed being called 'Zik of Africa'. He would often openly distance himself from known Igbo positions in the vain hope that such would enhance his Africanist and nationalist credentials. Believed to be de-tribalised, Obasanjo would often descend heavily on known Yoruba positions (eg the massive Yoruba support for Awo presidency in 1979), institutions (AD, Afenifere) and leaders (Awolowo, Obas, Abiola, Abraham Adesanya, Fela etc), often in the hope that it would enhance his nationalist credentials. One of the consequences is that while, like Zik, he may have surreptitiously promoted the interest of his ethnic group in many ways, members of the ethnic group remain suspicious of him and even fail to see his effort in promoting the interest of the ethnic group

This is perhaps one of the reasons some believe that Obasanjo is a hated figure in Yorubaland who cannot win a free and fair election, even in his Owo village. Another reason why every one seems to be against Obasanjo is his style and love of 'fearless' men/women who use 'garrison commander' tactics. The Igbos for instance are among the ethnic groups that complained bitterest against his regime for marginalisation and high-handedness. This is in spite of the fact that, as far as the ethnic arithmetic of 'who gets what', goes, they did rather well under him. For instance, at a point in the regime, the Governor of the Central Bank, Finance Minister and Chief economic Adviser to the president were all Igbos, and one of his closest aides was an Igbo! He also empowered a number of other Igbos (whether the appointments benefited the Igbos as an ethnic group is irrelevant here). Obasanjo as a matter of fact empowered individuals from across the ethnic divide – from plum jobs to contract awards. A more politically savvy person, or one not obsessed with having a certain image, could have turned these into constituencies of support.

Despite the 'Igbo empowerment' for instance, few Igbos (or other ethnic nationalities for that matter), have kind things to say about him, not least because of the mayhem he was suspected to have encouraged in Anambra state. Obasanjo's admiration of men and women with "garrison commander" mentality, helped to undermine whatever empowerment he gave various ethnic groups. Besides the well known excesses of EFCC under Nuhu Ribadu and El Rufai's senseless demolitions in Abuja, there was also the extra legal activity of Professor Dora Akunyili, who, in my opinion, is wrongly seen as heroine in some quarters for fighting drug adulteration using "muscle man" methods. While fighting drug fake drugs must be encouraged (fake drugs is also a big problem in the UK but is fought using intelligence and moles), Mrs Akunyili was applauded for using such a crude and thoughtless method as closing an entire market for months, depriving in the process many honest traders of the chance to earn honest livelihood to care for their families and train their children in schools. Was there any relationship between that primitive method used in fighting a worthy cause and an upsurge in crime in Onitsha? This will be a good matter for research. The traders' 'sin' was that they failed to fish out the fake drug traders (as if it was the traders' job to do so and she had never heard that governments elsewhere use paid moles for the job). Could Prof Akunyili have tried such in any civilised country? Can the police in any civilised society close an entire street for months because drug dealers live there and the residents of the street are unable to hand over the culprits? I feel it is contradictory that people would accuse Obasanjo of disobeying the courts while applauding the likes of Nuhu

Ribadu, El Rufai and Dora Akunyili, who, while they did some good, got carried away by the protection offered by a leader that hugged "tough people". Therefore, the numerous 'celebrity' functionaries created by Obasanjo hurt so many innocent people and are part of the reasons why he is seen as a hated figure across the ethnic divide.

No regime in our political history has empowered women as much as Obasanjo has done, but how many women have stood up to defend him against the barrage of criticisms he faces? Again, I believe this is again down to Obasanjo's style and proclivities, his penchant for empowering and disempowering individuals, the ubiquitous activities of the "celebrity" functionaries and his lack of skills or unwillingness to deliberately cultivate a constituency of support. Obasanjo seems to want to be feared rather than respected. Like Zik, he seemed to fear that deliberately creating a constituency of support would detract from his nationalistic credentials. The consequence is that one way or the other, everyone and every group felt Obasanjo's tough actions and hated him for that.

History will be kind to Obasanjo

Despite Obasanjo's many failings, I believe history will judge him kindly. When the current anti-Obasanjo sentiment settles (and I believe it will settle within the next two years), people will begin to deconstruct him. First, no one will take away the fact that he followed a programme of transition enunciated by Murtala Mohammed and was one of the first military regimes in Africa to willingly give up power. The credit for that belongs to Obasanjo, not Murtala Mohammed, because as the experiences with Gowon and Babangida showed, having a transition programme does not necessarily mean that power will eventually be handed over, or that the goal post will not be changed numerous times. No one therefore can be certain that Murtala Mohamed would have handed over power to civilians had he lived.

Obasanjo also left an enduring legacy in the banking sector reform and in communication (internet and mobile phone penetration). The credit for these successes, which we now take for granted, should be given to him just as the failures of other sectors are rightly attributed to him.

If the Umar Yaradu'a regime does well, the credit must also be partly given to Obasanjo for his wisdom in fishing out Umar Yaradua out from his obscurity and guided him though his apparent initial fear of the responsibilities inherent in the job. On the other hand, if Yaradua's regime remains wobbly or continues with its present indecisions and self-reversals, people will begin to miss a decisive Obasanjo, who is not afraid to back policies he believes in, even unpopular ones. Leadership after is more of a vision contest, not a popularity contest. So head or tail, Obasanjo will win when compared with the Yaradua regime.

While the third term plot would always remain a blithe on his CV, he could, with time, claim that he decided to overlook the massive imperfections in the conduct of the April polls because he was determined to break the jinx of civilian-to-civilian transitions in our politics. If he successfully sells the idea, with time, a description of Obasanjo as the founder of modern Nigeria, which currently elicit sneers and mock laughter, may no longer be seen as a misnomer.

Daily Trust, 23 June 2011

CHAPTER 37

OBASANJO'S 'FATAL EMBRACE' OF BUHARI AND BABANGIDA

Three former Heads of State, Olusegun Obasanjo, Mohamed Buhari and Ibrahim Babangida were reported to have 'sunk their differences' at the public presentation of a book in honour of Governor of Niger State, Dr Mu'azu Babangida Aliyu, at Abuja, August 5, 2010. According to several news reports, Obasanjo, while presenting the book entitled, "Praxis of Political Concepts: Clichés in Nigeria's Fourth Republic" to the public, had to practically drag both Buhari sand Babangida to the podium to help him perform the duty. It was reported that Buhari and Babangida initially resisted but later acquiesced as a result of physical pressure from those sitting around them.

It is an open secret that the three former Heads of State are not the best of friends. Obasanjo, thought to be the main brain behind an anticipated Jonathan Goodluck's presidential candidacy, has a vested interest in the 2011 election in which Babangida has declared his candidacy, and Buhari is likely to do so under his newly registered Congress for Progressive Change. Additionally, Babangida, believed to be one of the arrowheads for an Obasanjo presidency in 1999, is thought to have felt betrayed by some of Obasanjo's actions as President and in supporting a Jonathan candidacy for the 2011 elections.

That Obasanjo, who is the oldest of the three, and also their senior in the military took the initiative for that public show of 'all is well' (rather than Buhari and Babangida approaching him for pleasantries as African custom demands), could be interpreted in different ways. It could, for instance, be seen as showcasing an Obasanjo, who, contrary to the stereotype of a grudge-bearing man, is actually capable of being broadminded and rising above pettiness. Another possible message is in the power relations purveyed by the symbolism of Obasanjo being the one who 'dragged' Babangida and Buhari to the podium. In power relational terms, the one 'dragging' is obviously more powerful than the one being 'dragged'. Is Obasanjo, by that gesture, sending a coded message to both Buhari and Babangida about the game of cat and mouse that the three, (especially Babangida and Obasanjo) are playing on the issues of zoning and 2011 elections?

There could also be a more sinister deconstruction of the 'all is well' gesture based on Obasanjo's history. The Ota farmer has made a career from luring his adversaries into a false sense of security before striking lethally when their guards are lowered. Instances of this are legion. In January 2005 for instance, what was supposed to be a reconciliation lunch between Obasanjo and the then PDP Chairman, Audu Ogbeh, turned out a week later to be the latter's last supper. After Obasanjo fell out with Ogbeh over the latter's letter on a suspected interference by the presidency in the then political imbroglio at Anambra state, several reconciliation meetings were purportedly held between the two. To convince everyone that they had truly reconciled, Obasanjo drove in the same vehicle with Ogbeh to the latter's residence where they reportedly feasted on pounded yam and egusi soup. Ogbeh, fooled by that dummy, went on NTA Network News and announced that any misunderstanding between him and Obasanjo had been settled. Less than a week after this however, the Owu General struck. He invited himself to Audu Ogbeh's home, not to eat pounded yam again, but to demand for his resignation as party chairman.

There was also Obasanjo's celebrated quarrel with the late Chuba Okadigbo in 2001. After a seeming truce had been brokered, Obasanjo was on hand to commission Okadigbo's new residence as the Senate President. They had dinner together and Obasanjo even danced with his host's wife. Few days after that celebrated dance he engineered Okadigbo's impeachment. In a similar move, Obasanjo during an official visit to Anambra state in 2006, showed a lot of 'public love' for Peter Obi. Barely a day or so after the visit, the PDP-dominated state House of Assembly began impeachment proceedings against the Governor reportedly with the active connivance of the Obasanjo presidency. Atiku was to suffer a similar fate after he had successfully battled Obasanjo's attempts to remove him as Vice President and prevent him from contesting for the presidency in the 2007 elections. After the duo left office, and with Atiku possibly trying to rebuild his political base through a planned return to PDP, a number of clandestine contacts were said to have been brokered between the two. Lured by a false sense of security, Atiku accepted to meet Obasanjo for what he thought was a secret meeting – without informing his party members. But the wily Obasanjo tipped the press about the meeting in what was thought to be a move to create disaffection between Atiku and his loyalists. It is debatable whether Atiku has fully recovered from the fallouts of that deft move by Obasanjo.

True, Obasanjo has since left office and that gesture at the book launch may be all that was to it – just a friendly gesture. But with Obasanjo you never know. For many years Obasanjo fooled his opponents by projecting the persona of a dullard to mask his extreme cunning and political astuteness. The dummy was of course helped by his dour, uncharismatic personality. Many of his political opponents who fell for the dummy and underestimated him have lived to tell their stories. As the number of political casualties from underestimating him mounted, another image of Obasanjo as an extremely calculating bugaboo began developing. In the new ascribed persona, any move or gesture by Obasanjo must not be taken at face value, with many people routinely warning the late Yaradua and President Jonathan to avoid Obasanjo. Curiously, embedded in this 'fear' of Obasanjo is also a narrative of his ever relevance, for never has any one in our political history been so closely identified with the soul of our country as Obasanjo.

My take is that a single storyline of being evil will not appropriately capture the Obasanjo essence. Obasano is more an enigma than evil. He appears to be capable of both good and evil in equal measures. Here is a man who is perhaps the most folksy president we have ever had – comfortable in his skin to speak pidgin English or reportedly stop by the road side to buy cobs of roasted corns from roadside hawkers and yet capable of demonstrating unnerving arrogance and temper to both common and uncommon people. Obasanjo likes to flaunt his religiosity but leaves no one in doubt that he never forgives a wrong; he is adept at building up people from relative obscurity to political leadership roles only to set up such people to fail; he helps to build governments but often turns out a vociferous critic of the same government he helped to create; he brooks no one double-crossing him (and few dare try to do so, anyway) but he has no qualms in reneging on agreements he entered with others. Obasanjo was probably the most hardworking of all Nigerian Presidents, but a good chunk of this hard work was often in plotting intrigues that were aimed at bringing down his opponents, not in bettering the country. Obasanjo's genius – or notoriety - however remains in knowing when to lend support, when to criticise and when to deliver a mortal strike. So if I were Buhari and Babangida, I would err on the side of caution and watch my back very closely in the next couple of weeks.

Daily Trust, 18 Aug 2010

CHAPTER 38

OBASANJO'S RESIGNATION AS CHAIRMAN OF PDP'S BOARD OF TRUSTEES

The recent report that Obasanjo has resigned as Chairman of the PDP's Board of Trustees (BOT) took many people unawares. The resignation however also offers an opportunity for reflection on the nature of political power and why our former leaders often opt to remain politically active rather than play the role of statesmen and women as is often the case in the more politically advanced countries.

I see some parallels between crude oil and political power. In the 1970s for instance, at a time oil was bringing unprecedented wealth to the South American country of Venezuela – and other oil producing countries - the country's then oil Minister and OPEC's co-founder Juan Pablo Perez Alfonzo took a rather pessimistic view of the country's overnight, crude oil induced affluence. Alfonso maintained that 'in ten years or twenty years from now...oil will bring us ruin' because 'oil is simply the devil's excrement'. Alfonso's fears about the negative impact of the country's sudden oil affluence was vindicated when oil boom suddenly became oil glut, unsettling regimes that had become so used to the easy money from oil. This is the whole notion of 'resource curse' – the tendency for African countries endowed with natural resources to mismanage them leading to worse development outcomes than before the resource-induced wealth.

As with oil-induced wealth, so with political power – in our type of society. Like oil wealth, political power has the potential of being deployed for public good but quite often former powerswielders get so addicted to power that they often contrive ways of hanging onto it or spend years trying to recapture the power that slipped out of their hands. In the process most are diminished politically as they are perennially political aspirants, party leaders or political godfathers. One of the consequences is a serious dearth of statesmen and women who enjoy acceptance from across the major fault lines and who therefore have the legitimacy to mediate in a time like this, when the country is perhaps facing the worst crisis in its nation-building process. It is in this context that Obasanjo's resignation as the chairman of the PDP's BOT, even if it is belated, must be situated.

Though the real reasons for Obasanjo's unexpectedresignation remains unclear, he was reported as saying that he took the decision "to give some attention to mentoring across the board nationally and internationally in those areas that I have acquired some experience, expertise and in which I have something to share" (Nigerian Tribune, online, April 4, 2012). Obasanjo, 75, also said he wanted to use the period of his gradual disengagement from active party politics to develop his presidential library and mobilise and encourage investment in Africa. Going by his formal reasons for stepping aside, Obasanjo is not retiring from public life. He is merely 'changing gear', re-directing his energy in a new and wholly welcome direction.

Much of Obasanjo's reputation as a statesman hinged on his voluntary handover of power to elected civilians in 1979 at a time when the tendency was for military dictators to either renege on their promises of handing over power to civiliansor civilianise themselves. His reputation was further burnished when, after he stepped down as Head of State on October 1 1979, he set up the Obasanjo Leadership Forum, which among others, intervened in national and international policydiscourses. As the 4th Republic was to be ushered, many of his former colleagues in the military who drafted him into the presidentialrace felt he had the stature and statesmanship to rebuild a country largely fractured by the consequences of the annulment of the June 1993 elections won by Abiola. This was why it surprised many people that Obasanjo appeared to forget a critical reason for his elevation as a statesman when he sought to elongate his regime at the end of his second term in office as a civilian president. It also surprised many that Obasanjo reportedly engineered the amendment of his party's constitution so that only former Presidents could be made Chairman of the PDP's BOT. He has, until his recent resignation, been the chairman of the party's BOT since 2007. Some have openly wondered why a man who has had the fortune to rule this country both as a military Head of State and a civilian president would not let go, and still wanted to be chairman of the PDP's BOT when he has very impressive credentials to be a highly respected statesman?

What is true of Obasanjo is also true of IBB and Buhari. The crucial issue is whether these former Heads of States would have served the country and themselves better if they had chosen to become statesmen rather than being actively involved in the political process and by extension being seen as partisan in the controversial issues of the day?

Perhaps as ordinary citizens we play unintended roles in some of the reasons why these senior citizens refuse to become statesmen. Without patronages to dispense or being seen as close to the centres of power, there may be the fear that we may relegate them to the background and confine them to irrelevance. Perhaps we cheer uncritically when people who bow out 'gracefully' are used o 'shine' by their successors who will tell us how much they stole while in office and other sundry sins they committed. In countries where the institutions for dispensing justice are strong, a former Governor, President or Head of State should rightly be made to account for his or her years in office. In our type of society however, where successors often play to the gallery and the line between vendetta and fighting corruption is blurred, perhaps we need to reflect whether some form of constitutional protection against frivolous and trumped up charges against former political leaders could be more beneficial to the political system in the long run. Perhaps this could help to assure former political leaders that they do not need to hang on stubbornly to power or control a party machinery to feel safe. In fact the fear that their successors or political enemies could come after them could also be one of the reasons why some of these leaders steal us blind while in office. It is possible that some will calculate thatthey will need plenty of money for lawsuits and to meet continue to dispense patronage once they are out of office.

As I applaud Obasanjo for taking the bold step of opening up the political space in his party by stepping aside as the chairman of BOT, I will urge him to go a step further by honestly reconciling with some political elements he seems to have sworn to fight to total annihilation such as his former Vice Atiku Abubakar and others. I am among the admirers of Obasanjo's courage, decisiveness (even if this is sometimes just impulsiveness), hard work, energy, nationalism and folksiness.Unfortunately these virtues in Obasanjo often compete with certain traits his admirers wish he does not have – tendency to be vindictive, utter disregard for agreements or even to indulge in barefaced lies as an elder. I suggest that Obasanjo should start with re-engaging Nigerians and re-inventing himself, especially among people and constituencies that feel he must never be trusted or that he never does anything where there is no personal gain in it for him. People must have implicit trust in him and his agenda for his new role as a statesman to flourish.

As Obasanjo gradually relinquishes control of the PDP's party structure, and with it access to power and distribution of privileges that comes with it, it is in the nature of politics that new elements will want to limit his influence within the power loop, which will in turn make him feel 'marginalised'. Obasanjo is believed not to forgive such slights. He has in fact made a career of being a virulent critic of any government he is not part of which he feels has tried to slight or marginalise him. He is conscious that his voice has powerful echoes around the world and he knows how to choose the time and place to get back on any regime that tries that 'nonsense' with him. He is in this sense often seen as both a voice of courage and a voice of opportunism.

As Obasanjo begins the retreat from partisan politics, Nigerians await with suspense on how he will re-define that term 'statesman'.

Daily Trust, 5 Apr 2012

CHAPTER 39

DIM OJUKWU AND PETER OBI'S RE-ELECTION CAMPAIGN

Former Biafran leader, Dim Chukwuemeka Odumegwu Ojukwu, has reportedly vowed to return Peter Obi to the Government House, Awka, after the February 2010 polls. Speaking at the Basilica of the Most Holy Trinity, Onitsha, Anambra State, at the flag-off of APGA's campaign for Governor Peter Obi, Ojukwu was quoted as saying: "I urge you all who are my friends and sons to come out en masse and vote for my political son, Obi. Let it be the only thing I'm asking you to do for me" (*The Nation* online, 18/12/09). Obi rode on Ojukwu's coattails to power.

Ojukwu's call on the Igbos to vote for Peter Obi as a favour to him, has a number of implications, which goes beyond the question of whether Obi deserves a re-election or not. At issue are the implications, for the Ojukwu myth and legacy, of the Ikemba being drawn into the extremely polarising waters of Anambra state politics, at an age when he should be more of a unifying figure? If the Igbos hearken to his plea, will a victory in only one of the five Igbo states add anything to the persona and myth of the *Ikemba Nnewi*, who is also known as *Eze Ndi Igbo* (King of the Igbos)? On the other hand if Peter Obi loses, will that be taken as a referendum on Ojukwu's claim to Igbo leadership?

There are a number of parallels between Zik's NPP in 1979 and 1983, and Ikemba's APGA in 2003 and 2010:

One, in 1979 when Zik agreed to become the Presidential candidate of NPP, it was perhaps reasoned that since the Yorubas were likely to vote en masse for the UPN, and the North for NPN, there was also a necessity for an 'Igbo party', that would rally the Igbos together, and use their bloc vote as a bargaining chip. If this was really the idea, it succeeded for the NPP swept the then two Igbo states of Anambra and Imo - and also won in the then Plateau state. Zik declared NPP 'the beautiful bride' of Nigerian politics and subsequently went into alliance with the ruling NPN.

It is thought the idea of APGA during the 2003 elections was to mimic what the NPP was for the Igbos in 1979. If this was so, then APGA was unsuccessful as it won only one of the five Igbo states

(Anambra state), though many of the party's supporters believed they were rigged out of some states such as Imo and Enugu states.

Two, while it was perhaps right for Zik to come out in 1979, not many people believe he should have run again in 1983, at the age of 79. There is a feeling that those who rode to power on Zik's back, especially in Anambra state, failed to appropriately reward Zik by consciously expanding the base of his support in Igboland or reconciling him with some of his disenchanted followers in the First Republic, especially members of the Zikist movement. In Anambra state for instance, NPP's support base, especially among the notables, shrank considerably.

It is generally thought that Zik's participation in that election, when the political environment in his home state had become extremely polarised, undermined his perception and aura in Igboland. It is instructive to note that today most of those who rode on Zik's back to power in 1979 appear to have little interest in projects that will preserve his legacy.

Many people are today drawing parallels between the way Zik was 'used' in 1983 and the current efforts by the rump of APGA to get Ojukwu, who is 76 years old, and with a failing health, to get involved in the murky politics of Anambra state. Just like some people accused Jim Nwobodo of failing to use the victory of NPP in Anambra state to build up Zik's image by expanding his support base, there are people who similarly believe that Peter Obi failed to appropriately reward Ojukwu by expanding the base of Ojukwu's APGA to be the party to beat in Igboland. Compare the fate APGA in Anambra state with how Bola Tinubu, the former Governor of Lagos state, has successfully repositioned AC to become a reincarnation of the AD, which was itself a reincarnation of Awo's UPN. There is a legitimate concern that to lure an ageing Ojukwu into the political terrain as Jim Nwobodo did with Zik in 1983, especially when the APGA platform has shrunk considerably, will only lead to a further diminution of the Ikemba.

Three, like Zik, there is something Ojukwu evokes in many Igbos even among those who have not met him, or agree with his political options, which makes it untenable for one party in Igboland to try to appropriate him. This perhaps explains why many of his Igbo critics will often come to his defence at any hint that he will be publicly ridiculed. I can recount my own minor contributions to the Ojukwu legend, which I feel entitle me to a feeling of rage, at what I consider a selfish attempt to 'use' Ikemba, even when it is obvious such that such will end up diminishing him.

I was a freshman at the University of Nigeria, Nsukka, when Yakubu Gowon was pardoned in 1981. Most of us, who were aspiring writers, immediately began 'flooding' the newspapers with articles calling for Ojukwu to be also pardoned. As a student leader (Director of Transport, UNN, 1982-1983; President Nigerian University Students Association, September 1983 until Buhari's coup), we passed numerous resolutions, pestered NPN chieftains with proclamations, and even made threats. Like many people, I was rather disappointed when Ojukwu returned in 1983 and immediately entered politics.

Notwithstanding my disappointment, I successfully convinced Chief Jerome Udoji (of the Udoji Award fame) to tone down his criticisms of the *Ikemba* in his well-received memoirs: *Under Three Masters* (Spectrum, 1995). I had been involved in the research for the memoirs from about 1987, and also read the drafts before publication. Again knowing how bitter Udoji -a man I deeply respected - was with his perceived mistreatment by Ojukwu before and during the civil war, I used the opportunity of working on his selected speeches, (*Which Way Nigeria*, Spectrum, 2000), to persuade him on the need for public reconciliation with Ikemba. I believe I was making a strong headway on this when circumstances, including illness, derailed the plans.

My only substantial encounter with Ikemba was in 1988 – a few months before I left Nigeria for further studies. Ojukwu and Chief Arthur Nwankwo had sent me, alongside two others (Comrade Victor Kalu, a lecturer at the then Awka College of Education, Awka, and Dr Vic who was a Director-General in the short-lived administration of the late Christian Onoh in old Anambra state) to 'represent the Igbos' at the first anniversary of Awolowo's death. Babangida had then just announced one of his many political transitions, and we were mandated to make contacts with eminent Yoruba Awoists such as Ebenezer Babatope – to begin the process of the 'handshake across the Niger.'

Just like I feel that the minor role I played in the preservation of the Ojukwu legend entitles me to a certain rage at what I perceive as an attempt to diminish him for selfish reasons, it is likely the Onitsha trader who regularly picks a fight with anyone he feels has insulted Ojukwu, may feel the same. It is simply not right to give Ikemba the sort of treatment that Zik was given in 1983 by people who pretended to love him but were only interested in riding on his coattails to power.

Daily Independent, 25 December, 2009

CHAPTER 40

PRESIDENT YARADUA: YOU GO THIS WAY, I GO THAT WAY

The recent report that President Yaradua has directed the Revenue Mobilisation, Allocation and Fiscal Commission (RMAFC) to review downwards the remuneration of certain political office holders has continued to generate controversy. In a letter dated February 10, 2009 and addressed to the Chairman of RMAFC, the President inferred that the token measure was aimed at aligning salaries of the affected functionaries to the present economic realities, and by extension, at empathising with the plight of ordinary Nigerians. Critics from the Nigerian Labour Congress have however argued it was more of a pre-emptive move to scuttle labour's demand for a higher minimum wage.

When the emoluments of political office holders are paired with those of other public servants, it becomes obvious that the symbolic gesture from the president is bound to raise a wider debate. According to RMAFC the federal government spends annually the sum of N1.3trillion as emoluments to political functionaries for the three tiers of government. A break down of this mind-goggling sum shows that the nation spends annually N29 million for each minister, N29 million for each of the 109 senators, N22 million for each Member of the House of Representative, N1.4 billion for all the presidential aides, N593 billion for all Local Government Council chairmen/women and N36 billion for Houses of Assembly members in the 36 states.

To put these figures in perspective, a lecturer with a fresh PhD degree employed in a Nigerian University earns a basic salary of about N50,000 or N600,000 per year, meaning that the emoluments of a Minister can employ nearly 50 of such fresh PhDs at current salary levels. Similarly, an average school headmistress in Anambra state earns less than N50,000 per month. In Enugu state some teachers with a Master's degree and over ten years teaching experience earn less than N30,000 per month. If therefore we take the 'average' salary of a fresh graduate employed in the public sector to be roughly N30,000 or N360,000 per year, then a Minister's salary could employ some 806 of such graduates. In this sense, any measure at reducing the income gap between political officer holders and other public servants should be welcome, for as the UK supermarket group Tesco would say in its advert, every little helps.

But the main import of the gesture will be more in the opportunity it provides for discussing related issues, including the size of the government at various levels, and whether the measure goes far enough for whatever objective it is designed to achieve. Here there are legitimate concerns about the non-disclosure of the size of the proposed pay cut, the target level of savings from the measure, and where any savings should be channelled to, and strategies for impact assessment. What perhaps underlined the cynicism that greeted the announcement is that we have seen similar measures before – the forced salary deductions under both the Buhari and Babangida regimes in the name of fighting economic distress and avoiding the IMF/World Bank- recommended austerity measures (which the nation embraced any way) and the much hyped efforts at returning the so-called Abacha loot from Switzerland and the UK. Not many people believe those measures made any positive difference in their life, or knew what happened with the deductions (or the retrieved loot in the case of Abacha). There is very little to suggest that the measure announced by the president would be any different.

There appears also to be a certain belief that a greater threat to the nation's treasury is not so much the salaries of political office holders – despite the abhorrent disparity with the salaries of other public servants- but the 'creative' use of such political offices for personal enrichment. As if to lend credence to this thinking (or perhaps to make mockery of the president's directive) Reuters reported on February 11 - just a day after the presidential directive - that the European Union, which is the largest donor to the Economic Financial Crimes Commission (EFCC), would cut its funding unless the financial crime buster shows clearer results in its fight against graft. This logic appears to suggest that reducing the number of political offices rather than the emoluments of each office would be a more effective way of reducing leakages and avenues for corrupt enrichment.

Over and above that gesture however, is that we can use the opportunity of the announcement to respectfully tell the President that the measure cannot be a substitute for effective leadership. Part of providing this leadership will be resolving the contradictory signals that come from his regime, not tuning up the volume on the sloganeering about Servant Leader or Rule of Law – which Nigerians are becoming weary of. For instance at a time when many Nigerians are honestly concerned about whether the president has what it takes for the job – in terms of stamina, vision, purposefulness and decisiveness - kites are being flown about a possible second term. Such a signal comes across as an insult to

Nigerians, especially when it has been indirectly admitted that the President has so far not delivered.

Again while the regime publicly charges its appointees to deliver results, and had dissolved its first cabinet ostensibly because many of the appointees failed to live up to expectations, the regime's body language seems to be saying something different. For instance unlike Obasanjo who allowed some of his appointees to become 'celebrities' (triggering a sort of competition for 'excellence' and media attention among the appointees), with President Yaradua it would seem that any official who strives to excel or consistently attracts media attention becomes suspected of harbouring illicit ambitions. This appears to limit the willingness of many officials to take the sort of risks necessary to excel. It would also seem that this suspicion and discomfort with excellence partly explains some of the rash dismissal of some appointees and the reported marginalisation of the Vice President Dr Jonathan Goodluck from the scheme of things at Aso Rock.

In essence the persona of the president projected onto the public space tends to clash with the president's body language, making it difficult to decipher his real intentions at any time. His style reminds one of the Zodiac sign of Pisces, in which two 'umbilically' tied fishes choose to constantly swim in opposite directions, meaning that they end up swimming to nowhere.

Nigerianvillagesquare 26 February 2009.

CHAPTER 41

SANUSI: A RADICAL IN A CONSERVATIVE JOB?

S anusi Lamido Sanusi is a very brilliant man. He writes the English language with remarkable authority, and even speaks it better. This could however be both an asset and a liability. Too much love of 'grammar' (*turenci*) could lead to an undue love for the podium and limelight, with attendant risks of gaffes in moments of rhetorical flourishes.

Central Bank Governors are thought to possess so much crucial information about their country's economy that investors and analysts closely monitor their utterances even after they have left office. For instance when Alan Greenspan, who retired as chairman of the US Federal Reserve on January 31, 2006, predicted on February 26, 2007 that the US would enter into recession before or in early 2008, the Dow Jones Industrial Average dropped by 416 points (or 3.3 percent of its value) the following day. At that time, it was the worst one-day loss since September 17, 2001, when it lost 684 points (7.1 percent) after reopening in the wake of the 9/11 terrorist attacks.

It is perhaps because of the 'oracular' nature of being the boss of a country's central bank that emphasis is often placed not just on the professional qualifications of candidates for that office but even more importantly on their character and temperament. Willem "Wim" Frederik Duisenberg, first president of the European Central Bank (1998-2003) was generally considered a failure for not having the appropriate temperament for the job. In a special report on February 8, 2002, aptly captioned, "The Wrong Man for an Impossible Mission", the *Financial Times* (London) summed up the angst against the late Dutch economist and financier: "The biggest criticism of Mr Duisenberg is not over the substance of his decisions, but over his presentation. His willingness to talk off the cuff and his often vivid turn of phrase has frequently raised eyebrows among other policy-makers." About his critics, Duisenberg was quoted as saying: "I am direct - some say I am too direct... It is part of my character. Even if I wanted to change my character, I do not think I could."

You may be forgiven if you think the FT was writing about Sanusi Lamido Sanusi. While I do not necessarily think that Sanusi is the wrong man for the job, I also feel that he has not been as discreet and meticulous as he ought to be in his utterances and actions. I do not however believe the allegations that he harbours any hidden agenda – ethnic or religious. He appears simply too polished to be clannish.

At an event earlier this year in London to talk about the reforms in the banking sector, I asked Sanusi, if, professionally speaking, he saw a tension between where he now found himself, and where in his heart he felt he ought to be. I have read a few of Sanusi's writings on Gamji.com and never ceased to admire his brilliance. I also always felt his 'natural' calling would be as a radical academic.

Sanusi said he did not consider himself a radical but admitted that when he was in merchant banking, he did feel that tension.

Despite his protestations, I am inclined to see him as a 'radical' or 'revolutionist' – in the sense of someone who favours extreme or fundamental changes in the way the society is organised. As with most revolutionists, Sanusi's approaches to complex issues tend to be simplistic, and as the contradictions in his chosen options become obvious, the proffered solutions tend to appear contradictory or hastily taken. Consider the following examples:

In what would appear to be a reckless outburst of emotions, Sanusi was quoted as saying that the sacked bank executives now standing trial at the various courts in the country deserved to die by firing squad for eroding public confidence and raping the institutions that were entrusted to their care through reckless credit and loan administration processes. Sanusi was later to recant, perhaps after he realised the enormity of the statement. He now claimed that Nigerian bankers are honest, hardworking professionals and not the crooks he had made them to appear.

In a similar display of speaking from both sides of the mouth, the CBN announced on October 2, 2009, the removal of Dr Mike Adenuga as a non-executive director of Equatorial Trust Bank. About a month later, the apex bank changed its mind and restored the business mogul to the board of the bank, claiming that it had not established any criminal activity against him. It also said it had granted the request of the shareholders of ETB to be allowed to rectify lapses identified in the bank and to subsequently take it over.

Virtually every major move since Sanusi became the helmsman of the apex bank, including the publication of the list of bank debtors, have been dogged by self-inflicted controversy, with the CBN often admitting errors. Recently Chief Aderemi Oyepeju, chairman of Ibadan Zonal Shareholders Association of Nigeria, was quoted, as saying that Mallam Sanusi had promised that shareholders that could recapitalize the troubled banks would be allowed to do so. This thus raises the question of why

Sanusi did not consider that the first line of action before unduly panicking the financial system? It is instructive that of the ten advisers appointed recently by the CBN for the 'troubled' banks, at least two - KPMG and Akintola Williams Deloite- were the same auditors who apparently saw nothing wrong in the books of the same banks they are now asked to advise and help out of the mire.

Even more worrying is that some policies pursued by CBN verge on dictatorship and could undermine risk-taking, which is at the heart of entrepreneurship. Take this recent directive from the CBN: "Any Director of the 24 banks who fails to redeem loans by November 30 will have his appointment terminated by the CBN, and may face arrest and prosecution" (Times of Nigeria online Sunday, November 21, 2009). It was also reported that the EFCC would investigate to see if prospective borrowers have previous records of non-performing loans. Is the CBN under the guise of reform undermining the autonomy of banks?

In an article for the *Financial Times'* Economists' Forum in March 2008, Alan Greenspan warned that while we "will never be able to anticipate all discontinuities in financial markets...it is important, indeed crucial, that any reforms in, and adjustments to the structure of markets and regulation not inhibit our most reliable and effective safeguards against cumulative economic failure: market flexibility and open competition." While Greenspan has his own critics, Sanusi's CBN should bear this advice in mind so that it does not continue to give its critics the ammunition to strike.

Daily Independent, 26 November 26, 2009

CHAPTER 42

SANUSI'S BANK TSUNAMI: LESSONS FROM OTHER 'REVOLUTIONS'

Since 14 August 2009 when Sanusi Lamido Sanusi, Governor of Central Bank, sacked the chief executives of five banks – Intercontinental, Oceanic, Afribank, Union Bank and FinBank - for allegedly awarding non-performing loans to the tune of N780 billion, supporters of the Governor have tended to describe the move in revolutionary terms. Given the zeal and gusto with which the CBN boss pursues the programme, including a promise to resign if the move turned out to be wrong, it appears he too believes the move is revolutionary. But are 'revolutions' really worth the effort?

Revolution, derived from the Latin word, *revolutio*, meaning "a turn around", implies a fundamental or radical change in power or organizational structures that takes place in a relatively short period of time. The goal of any revolution is often lofty and populist – a desire to quickly change the society or its institutions for the better. However, the tendency for revolutionists to use a very simplistic approach for a highly complex problem usually means that when the dust settles after the revolutionary flourish, so many unintended consequences usually beget the question of whether the entire effort is worth it. Consider the following examples:

The American War of Independence (1775-1783) was spurred by a noble protest against taxation without representation. Though America's victory helped to spread a belief in the principles of republicanism, it also sharply polarised the country and subsequently led to a bitter civil war. Some critics today argue that looking at how America has shaped up since independence in terms of education, freedom of expression and quality of life, it is not substantially different from Canada, Australia and New Zealand, which did not follow such a revolutionary path. The cost of the war was also to bankrupt France, without whose military and financial support, America would not have won the war.

There was also the French Revolution (1789–1799), fought primarily to overthrow absolute monarchy with its feudal privileges for the aristocracy and Catholic clergy. The revolution, fought under the noble ideals of 'freedom, equality and fraternity', quickly became a caricature under Robespierre and his Reign of Terror. Not only did the revolution fail to give France a representative government by the people, or prevent a rapid return to autocratic rule, 'revolutionary' France also fought the most savage of all wars in the 1790s to preserve slavery in Santo Domingo (present-day Haiti and Dominican Republic). So much for freedom, equality and fraternity! In fact, some historians today regard the French Revolution as a terrible waste of time and blood because whatever positives came out of it were equally accomplished by many countries such Britain and America with much less bloodshed.

Again consider the Russian Revolution - a collective term for the series of revolutions in Russia in 1917, which succeeded in destroying Tsarist autocracy and creating the Soviet Union. Today, the Soviet Union has since imploded and Russia is not more democratic or more economically advanced than most other European countries that did not embark on such a revolution. Many historians today question whether there was indeed any benefit from that revolution, which led to the loss of millions of lives and replaced Tsarist autocracy with other dictators – from Lenin and Stalin to Putin.

Consider equally the Iranian revolution that toppled the rule of Mohammed Reza Shah some 30 years ago. The revolution ushered a period of unprecedented hostility to the West and helped to radicalise the Middle East. Almost overnight, the West's most steadfast ally in the Muslim world became a violent and volatile enemy, where mass crowds raised their fists to chant "death to America". Within months of the revolution however, the euphoria had evaporated as rival factions began a brutal battle for the control of the country, which ended with a repressive state that imprisoned and executed thousands of political prisoners – including many of the revolutionaries. Today some Iranians, including those who participated in the revolution, openly wonder whether it was worth it and what the country really achieved from it.

In Nigeria, benefits from what could be called our own 'revolutions' are also questionable. Consider these two instances:

In 1966, Major Chukwuma Nzeogwu's Supreme Council of the Revolution of the Nigerian Armed Forces, which said it wanted to "establish a strong, united and prosperous nation, free from corruption and internal strife", ended up unleashing forces that culminated in a civil war. Today, more than forty years after Nzeogwu's 'revolution', Nigerians look with nostalgia to the society the young Majors riled against.

There was also the Buhari regime and its signature War Against Indiscipline. Buhari's declaration that "this generation, and in deed future generation of Nigerians have no other country but this. We must remain here to salvage it together", is widely regarded as the most patriotic sentiment ever uttered by any Nigerian leader. However, in the name of overhauling the society for the better, Buhari's thin moustache quickly became a veneer symbol of dictatorship. He repressed the press, sacked civil servants with impunity, disregarded the federal character principle in appointments and engaged virtually everyone and every social group as an enemy. By the time he was toppled in 1985, he had become such an odious figure that Nigerians yearned for liberation from him.

From the above, it would seem that the system dynamics in most countries favour evolutionary social progress rather than a revolutionary one. While the philosophy of most revolutions has an emotional appeal, in reality, only few revolutions are successful or worth the effort. With regards to Sanusi's 'revolution' in the banking sector, there are a number of observations:

One, as criticisms of the way Sanusi handled the situation continue to grow, crucially overlooked is that he has scored a major victory in taking control of framing the discourse. These days it has become axiomatic to talk of 'the crisis in the banking sector', 'sanitising the banking sector', or 'the rot in the banking sector' when discussing Sanusi's recent interventions. This implies an acceptance, without debate, of Sanusi's position that that there is a crisis in the banking sector, when prior to August 14, not many people felt so.

Two, while critics of Sanusi accuse him of harbouring a Northern agenda, there is also a possibility that the CBN Governor could be a victim of ethnic and sectional prejudice – a certain belief that intelligence has ethnic/regional character, and that people from certain sections of the country are lower in the intelligence hierarchy. Some openly question whether Sanusi has sufficient theoretical groundings in economics and finance for the position he occupies.

Three, there are some who suspect Sanusi of being a closet Islamist, and for who every move by him must be closely scrutinised. This set of critics for instance wonder why, after resigning from Merchant Bankers (now Intercontinental Bank Plc), where he rose, after about seven years, to become Area Manager, Kano Area Office, he took the unusual step of going to Sudan for a bachelor's degree in Arabic and Islamic Studies. Sanusi remained in Sudan (a country that is often associated with radical Islam and where Osama bin Laden once lived) between 1991 and 1997. He returned to join UBA as a Principal Manager 2 in the Credit Risk Management division. His critics continue to suspect the essence of that study, which had apparently nothing to do with his career.

Four, Sanusi has not helped the suspicions around him by the peculiar manner he carried out the banking tsunami. That an article by the Vanguard in March 2009 accurately predicted the manner in which the five banks were taken over appears to further strengthen the suspicion about his agenda. The matter is not helped by his apparent determination, in concert with a suddenly rejuvenated EFCC, to prevent the accused from giving their own sides of the story.

Five, if criticisms of Sanusi accentuate the legitimacy crisis around the Yaradua regime, the president is likely to withdraw support for him, especially if there are revelations that Sanusi, while boss of First Bank, had been guilty of the same offence for which he sacked the bank executives. Already one newspaper has alleged that while at First Bank, Sanusi gave a N1.57 billion loan to a newspaper publisher introduced to him by Mallam Nassir el-Rufai, the former boss of the Federal Capital Territory.

Six, going by our history, it is most likely that the Sanusi 'revolution', if continued, will certainly be reversed after the Yaradua regime – the same way the bank consolidation is being surreptitiously challenged now and previous controversial policies such as Ironsi's Decree No 34 and the sale of some choice property and state-owned enterprises under Obasanjo were reversed after regime change.

Seven, if the Sanusi revolution is not pursued to its logical conclusion, it would leave anarchy in its wake while widening the north-south divide. On the other hand, if it succeeds, it would be difficult for the average Nigerian to have a feel of this success - unlike the bank consolidation, which led to such visible innovations as the introduction of ATMs and online banking. This means in essence that it is not going to be easy for Mallam Sanusi Lamido, especially if he continues with his predecessor's style of hugging the limelight and seeing himself as a celebrity.

Daily Trust, 6 June , 2012

CHAPTER 43

KANU'S HONORARY DEGREE FROM
UNIVERSITY OF JOS

I received with joy the news report that the University of Jos would honour footballer Kanu Nwankwo with a Master of Arts degree honoris causa (Latin phrase, meaning 'for the sake of the honour') during its 25th convocation ceremony on May 12 2012.

I must confess that I have not really been a great follower of Kanu Nwankwo's football career, especially after he left Arsenal in the summer of 2004. Though I have never met the lanky footballer, there is an aura of humility and purposefulness around his person that I have always found very appealing. Even before his football began to decline after 2004, I had come to see him as someone much bigger than the round leather game that literally thrust him onto the national stage. His Kanu Nwankwo Heart Foundation, which he set up in 2000, was for me a statement on how to achieve immortality. More about the Foundation later.

Born in Owerri, Imo State, on August 1 1976, Kanu's journey to stardom started at the Nigerian league club Federation Works, from where he later moved to the then Iwuanyanwu Nationale. Following a distinguished performance at the 1993 U-17 World Championship in Japan where he emerged as the most valuable player of the tournament, he was signed by the Dutch team Ajax. In 1996 he was bought by the Italian team Inter-Milan (Internazionale). In the summer of the same year, he captained the Nigerian team that won gold in the 1996 Olympics in Atlanta where he was also voted the best player of the tournament. Kanu, a two- time winner of African Footballer of the Year award, was once rated among the top 20 footballers in the world. By far Nigeria's most decorated footballer, he has won the prestigious European cup competition now known as the European Champions League with Ajax of Amsterdam and also won the premiership and FA cups with Arsenal, among other awards.

After a triumphal return from the 1996 Olympics, routine medical examination at Inter, Kanu's club at that time, revealed that the lanky footballer had a serious heart defect. He underwent a successful surgery in November 1996 to replace an aortic valve and did not return to his club until April 1997.

Though Kanu had a successful surgery to correct his heart defect and his football career appeared to blossom even better after his return than before the surgery, he never forgot the shock of a sudden discovery that things could have gone awry. Therefore in the year 2000, when he was only 24 years old, he started the Kanu Nwankwo Heart Foundation to hel p"underprivileged African children and young adults, living with heart ailments in Nigeria and other African countries respectively to obtain the cardiac surgical operations needed". The first two beneficiaries from the Foundation were Master Oluwatofunmi Okude and little Miss Enitan Adesola who were operated on at the Crown Hospital London in 2000. Since its establishment, several hundred children have benefited from the Foundation, which has a success rate of about 98 percent.

With his Foundation, Kanu, who holds the Nigerian honours of MON, OON, and is also a UNICEF ambassador, joined a growing list of athletes who are genuinely using the name and money they made from sports to make a difference outside the field. Among known athletes who have established foundations to make a difference outside their core competence of sports include:

Adonal Foyle, a former player for the NBA's Orlando Magic, who together with his parents, Joan and Jay Mandle, both of whom are Colgate University professors and life-long organisers, founded 'Democracy Matters' to empower college students to strengthen democracy through grassroots organising. The foundation says that its chapters across the US work to "remove the corrosive and corrupting influence of big private money in the political process. Our vision is a democracy that includes and is accountable to all voters – not just big campaign contributors".

Dikembe Mutombo, an NBA player from the Democratic Republic of Congo, founded the Dikembe Mutombo Foundation to improve the lives of people living in his native, DRC. In 2007, the Foundation opened the Biamba Marie Mutombo Hospital and Research Centre to provide modern healthcare and employment opportunities for the area's underserved population. Those listed as supporters of DMF include Bill Clinton, Kofi Anann, and Jimmy Carter.

Warrick Dunn started 'Home for Holidays' in 1997 as the flagship programme of Warrick Dunn Charities. 'Home for Holidays' was set up during Warrick's rookie season in the National Football League (NFL) with the Tampa Bay Buccaneers to help single parents purchase homes for their families. A native of Baton Rouge, Louisiana, USA, Warrick grew up as the oldest of six children and experienced the privations that often inhere in a single-parent family. His mother, Betty Smothers, was a police officer who often worked security shifts to provide for her family. Her big ambition was to one day realise the American Dream of home ownership. Tragically, Warrick's mother was killed in an armed robbery attack during an off-duty shift, leaving him, as an18-year-old, to care for his five siblings.

There are several celebrity athletes, including Africans, who are utilising their fame and money for good causes and I believe they should be encouraged – as Unijos has just done with Kanu. It is remarkable that UniJos decided to honour a young sports personality who is not even from its geo-political zone, and who is unlikely to have donated handsomely for the honour. Kanu does not seem to fit into the breed of Nigerians favoured by most universities to receive such honours - big time politicians, wealthy traditional rulers, billionaire business people and retired army Generals.

Does Kanu, who does not have a bachelor's degree, deserve an honorary Master's degree in Arts? Or should he have been awarded the better known honorary doctorate? These are the prerogatives of a University. Suffice it to add that contrary to the belief in some quarters, you do not necessarily need to have earned a degree to be awarded an honorary degree, including an honorary doctorate. Retired heavyweight boxer Mike Tyson for instance was awarded an Honorary Doctorate in Humane Letters by Central State University in Ohio, USA, in 1989 even though his only formal education was graduating from reform school to boxing. Honorary degrees could even be conferred on non-persons – depending on what the awarding institution wants to achieve by that move. For instance in 1996 Southampton College at Long Island University, USA, (now a campus of SUNY Stony Brook) awarded an Honorary Doctorate of Amphibious Letters to the Muppet, Kermit the Frog – one of the puppeteers in Jim Henson's famous Muppet creations. Though Southampton College claimed the award was in recognition of the Muppet's efforts in the area of environmentalism, some people suspected it was deliberately aimed at attracting media attention.

An institution could also award or deny an honorary degree to someone to make a point. For instance in 1985, as a deliberate snub, the University of Oxford, United Kingdom, voted to refuse the then British Prime Minister Margaret Thatcher an honorary degree in protest against her cuts in funding for higher education. The award had previously been given to all Prime Ministers who had been educated at Oxford.

What does University of Jos hope to achieve by the award of an honorary degree to Nwankwo Kanu? The Vice Chancellor of the University Professor Hayward Mafuyai was quoted by the *Vanguard* of May 9 2012 as saying that the award was to "honour a youth who has striven to be exemplary as a footballer and became even more exemplary with the heart foundation which had offered treatment to many who would not have been able to afford the treatment". The VC was quoted as further saying that "we have not done enough to honour our own young men and women". In honouring Nwankwo, Unijos also makes an eloquent statement about itself – that despite a general belief that things have fallen apart in every nook and crevice of our national life, there are still individuals and institutions that remain sources of hope and redemption. In the current conjuncture in the country where many decisions and actions are often filtered through the lenses of the dominant fault lines in the society or pecuniary advantages to be gained, UniJos shows there are still institutions that can rise above the fray and be forward thinking. As I celebrate Unijos, it is also important to give the thumbs up for Lagos State, which, since the time of Tinubu (like him or hate him), has tried to involve non-indigenes of the State in running the State. In Lagos State, some non-indigenes are Commissioners or head important agencies in the government. Compare this with say Abia State where some people who have been working for years in the State's civil service were reportedly sacked because they are not indigenes of the State. In essence, when some are trying to tap the excellence inherent in a 'melting pot of cultures' others are glorifying primitive village irredentism that can hardly lead to any progress.

Daily Trust, 10 May 2012

CHAPTER 44

ZUCKERBERG, FACEBOOK AND THE Y-GENERATION

There is something about Mark Zuckerberg, co-founder - or more appropriately the main founder of Facebook - the eponymous social networking website- which I find very fascinating. Zuckerberg is both an affirmation and a negation of the debate in some Western countries on whether college (university) education really matters. An embodiment of the generation Y, a portraiture of Zuckerberg immediately beams a searchlight on the Nigerian youths and the impediments that militate against the emergence of such prodigies in our dear country.

Born on May 14 1984, Mark Elliot Zuckerberg was brought up in Dobbs Ferry, New York, USA, and raised Jewish. His father was a dentist who ran his practice from home while his mother was a psychiatrist. At Ardley High School, Zuckerberg excelled in the classics before transferring to Phillips Exeter Academy where he also won prizes in mathematics, astronomy and physics. In college, he was known for reciting lines from epic poems such as The Iliad. In addition to English he could read and write French, Hebrew, Latin and ancient Greek.

Zuckerberg began using computers and writing software as a child. In the 1990s, his father, noticing that he had a passion for computers, taught him Atari Basic Programming and later hired a developer to tutor him privately. So much was his passion for computers that while still in High school, he took a graduate course in programming at Mercy College near his home. One of the early programmes he built was software he called 'ZuckNet' which allowed the computers in their home to communicate with the ones in the part of their home that served as his father's dental practice. ZuckNet was considered a primitive version of AOL's Instant Messaging Service, which came out the following year. While still in High school, he also built a music player called Synapse Media Player, which used artificial intelligence to learn the user's listening habits. AOL tried to buy Synapse and recruit Zuckerberg but he declined the offers and chose to enrol at Harvard University in September 2002. By the time he began classes at Harvard – in psychology and computer science - he had already achieved a reputation as a programming prodigy. While a freshman he created a programme known Facemash, - just to have fun with his fellow students. The site had books called 'Face Books', which included the names and pictures of everyone who lived in the student dorms. Here Zuckerberg would place two pictures or pictures of two males and two females and urged visitors to the site to choose who was "hotter". Though several students complained that their photos were used without permission, the site proved so popular that students began requesting that the university should develop an internal website that would include similar photos and contact details. It was said that when Zuckerberg learnt of the demand by some students, he decided that if the university would not accede to the students' request, he would build a site that would be even better than what the university could offer. Zuckerberg launched Facebook from his Harvard dormitory room on February 4, 2004. Though it started off as just a "Harvard thing", Zuckerberg later decided, with the help of his roommate Dustin Moskovitz, to spread it to other schools, starting with other Ivy League Universities - Stanford, Dartmouth, Columbia, New York University, Cornell, Pennsylvania, Brown and Yale. Zuckerberg later moved to Palo Alto, California - headquarters to a number of Silicon Valley high-technology companies - with Moskovitz and some friends. There they leased a small house that served as an office. Over the summer, Zuckerberg met Peter Thiel, the German-born American entrepreneur and co-founder of the online payment system Paypal who invested in the company.

Despite the controversies that dogged Facebook's recent IPO, there are several important lessons from the story of Zuckerberg. One, Zuckerberg typifies those known in the West as the 'Generation Y' (also variously called the Millennial Generation, Millennials, Generation Next, the Net Generation or the Echo Boomers). Though there is no unanimity about when Generation Y starts and ends, most definitions of the concept include at least those born between 1981 and 1989. Members of Generation Y are believed to be incredibly sophisticated and technology-wise, having been born and grown up in the era of Cable TV channels, satellite, the Internet and e-zines. The generation is also more racially diverse and more tolerant of diversities. Though they believe in success and education, it is not exactly in the same way the preceding Generation X did. Though Generation X is often said to be the best educated generation, it is equally said to exude unacceptably high levels of scepticisms with 'what is in it for me' attitudes. What can we say of the Nigerian youths who fall within the age-bracket of the Y Generation? My personal opinion is that while many can use mobile phones better than their elders, they also seem to suffer the sort of existential crisis their elders at home and peers abroad are largely immune from. With most of them being unemployed or under-employed amid generalised insecurity and identity issues in the country, most Nigerians in the age bracket of the Generation Y are still at the level of struggling to 'liberate their stomachs', and therefore are unable to manifest the traits that produce the likes of Mark Zuckerberg. Two, Zuckerberg, who dropped out of Harvard without earning a degree, has through his Facebook impacted on the world more than most people with a chain of degrees. By joining the seemingly endless list of people who have 'changed the world' without a college (university) degree, Zuckerberg immediately re-opens the debate about the value of college (university) education. The list of people who 'changed' the world without formal qualifications include: Bill Gates of Microsoft (who dropped out of Harvard); Amadeo Peter Giannini, founder of Bank of America (dropped out of high school); Andrew Carnegie, famous industrialist and philanthropist and one of the first mega-billionaires in the US (dropped out of primary school); George Eastman, founder of Kodak (dropped out of high school); Henry Ford, founder of Ford Motors (did not attend college), John D Rockefeller, billionaire founder of Standard Oil (dropped out of high school just two months to graduation), Michael Dell, founder of Dell Computers (dropped out of College) Ray Kroc, founder of McDonald's (dropped out of high school), Walt Disney, founder of the Walt Disney (dropped out of high school), Richard Branson, founder of Virgin Atlantic and more (dropped out of high school), Steve Wozniak, co-founder of Apple (did not complete college) and Simon Cowell, TV producer and music judge of American Idol, the X Factor and Britain's Got Talent (dropped of out of High school).

The point of the above is not to encourage people to drop out of school but a statement that we all have different talents and not everyone may be cut out for university education. This will help temper the current situation in Nigeria where people believe that they need degrees – even though they could more meaningfully have used the time in trying to discover or polishing their God-given talents. If Zuckerberg had been a Nigerian, he would most likely have been derided for dropping out of school, banks and potential investors will stick it to his face that he couldn't even complete a University education and his parents would have done 'whatever it takes' to make sure he gets a degree or even a master's degree, preferably in prestige disciplines like law and medicine, even if his talents and aptitude lie somewhere else. I have come across many postgraduate students I honestly believe have no business 'wasting' their time in something that they are obviously not cut out for. Yet, such students believe they will 'somehow' pass. To find out one's true talent is often a tough undertaking.

Daily Trust, 31 May 2012

CHAPTER 45

MO IBRAHIM: CELEBRATING OUR OWN

Writers are often accused of being good at finding what has gone wrong but rarely of what is going right. I believe this is an extreme view, though I concede that because the writer or analyst is often comparing society as it ought to be with the society as it is, there is often a tendency to focus on the imperfections of the existing order, which the writer/analyst believes, if fixed, will close the gap between the real and the idealised worlds. This is perhaps what Camilo Cela, the 1989 Spanish laureate in literature meant when he said that writing is necessarily a denunciation of the times in which the author lives.

Today I will like to do what does not seem to come naturally to a writer/analyst: celebrate an African whom I believe is not as much sung as he ought to be. I am talking about Mohamed 'Mo' Ibrahim, the Sudanese-British telecommunications billionaire whose foundation started the Mo Ibrahim Governance Index in 2007. The foundation also funds the Mo Ibrahim Achievement in African Leadership prize in which the winner gets $5million over 10 years and subsequently $200,000 annually for life. The winner of the African Leadership Prize also has the possibility of getting a further $200,000 per year for 10 years towards public interest activities and good causes. The Ibrahim Achievement prize is the largest annually awarded prize in the world, dwarfing by far the better known Nobel Prize. Both the Governance Index and the African Leadership award are clearly aimed not just at promoting good governance in Africa but also at making African leaders resist the temptation of dipping their hands in the public till or sitting tight in office beyond the constitutionally allowed term limits. The Governance index provides 'objective' criteria for measuring the performance or non-performance of African governments - along the lines of the UNDP's Human Development Index. The Ibrahim Index compiles 86 indicators, which it groups into 14 sub-categories and four overarching categories to measure the effective delivery of public goods and services to Africans.

Though cynicism, as should be expected, greeted the launch of both the Governance Index and the African Leadership Award, it is obvious that both are increasingly, even if grudgingly, winning international respectability. In the recently released Governance Index 2011 for 2010, Mauritius, Cape Verde and Botswana came tops, with an overall score of

82.46, 78.98 and 76.12 respectively. Ghana was ranked 7th with an overall score of 65.99 while Nigeria was ranked 41 with an overall score of 41.2. Of more significance is that Ghana performed far better than Nigeria in each of the four main criteria – Safety and Rule of Law, Participation and Human Rights, Sustainable Economic Opportunity and Human Development. The methodologies used in arriving at these rankings, though not without their shortcomings, are generally seen as credible. Many activists in Africa increasingly rely on the Ibrahim Governance index to clamour for an improvement in the quality of governance and the process of leadership recruitment in their countries. In Nigeria for instance, many activists are calling for a variant of the Ibrahim Governance Index for assessing the performance or non-performance of the state governors. The argument is that at the moment most of the proclaimed achievements of the State Governors can only be found on bill boards, advertorials and sponsored write-ups.

It is gratifying that four years after the African Leadership Award and Governance Index initiatives, there is still no sign that fatigue is setting in on the 61-year-old Mo Ibrahim. In April 2011 for instance his foundation added into the mix the Ibrahim Leadership Programme - in partnership with the African Development Bank, the United Nations Economic Commission for Africa and the World Trade Organisation. Under the arrangement, the AfDB, UNECA, and WTO will each host an Ibrahim Fellow in their executive offices. The expectation is that Ibrahim Fellows will go on to play a major role in the governance and development of the African continent. Though this approach to leadership recruitment could be criticized for being narrowly focused on acquiring economic skills, no one doubts the patriotic thoughts behind the initiative.

It is not often that initiatives from Africa or Africans reach the sort of respectability that Mo Ibrahim's have. True, there are many distinguished Africans both in the continent and in the Diaspora. Few however have come up with initiatives that are effectively competing with rival international brands. Despite their increasing respectability however, there is a feeling that their acceptance, especially by Africans, would have been more, if they were driven by some quasi government organisations in London, New York or any of the Western governments. Colonial mentality unfortunately still thrives among us, including among our governments.

It is remarkable that the companies founded by Mo Ibrahim in the UK also transcended both the colour and ethnic lines and competed effectively with similar brands on a global level – despite the fact that he was already a young adult when he arrived in the UK. After working for several telecommunications firms in the UK, including British Telecom, Mo Ibrahim founded the consultancy and software company MSI in 1989, which he sold 11 years later to the Marconi Company. Before it was sold, the company had 800 employees and had in 1998 spun off MSI-Cellular Investments, later renamed Celtel, as a mobile phone operator in Africa. In 2005, Mo Ibrahim sold Celtel for $3.4 billion. He is listed on Forbes' 2011 Billionaire List as the 692nd richest man in the world with a personal worth of some $1.8 billion.

Born in 1946 in Sudan of Nubian heritage, Mo Ibrahim earned a bachelor's degree in Electrical Engineering from the University of Alexandria, Egypt and a master's degree in Electronics and Electrical Engineering from the University of Bradford, UK. He also has a doctorate degree in Mobile Communications from the University of Birmingham. With his academic qualifications, Mo Ibrahim becomes a negation of the myth that acquisition of a chain of degrees is incompatible with being successful as an entrepreneur. In the pantheon of successful entrepreneurs it is easier to point at Bill Gates, Richard Branson and Steve Jobs – men who either did not complete their university degrees or never even went to university at all than the likes of Mo Ibrahim who, in addition to being successful entrepreneurs, also have doctorate degrees.

African Union misses an opportunity to offer Global Leadership

First it was the anti-cut protests in London, also known as the March for Alternative. The demonstration, which held in Central London on 26 March 2011 had quickly spread throughout the UK and ran out of control. It was in the main a protest march against planned public spending cuts by the Conservative-Liberal Democrat coalition government that was formed in May 2010. In the heat of the protests, a furious Prime Minister David Cameron reportedly said that any young person old enough to engage in acts of vandalism should also be old enough to go to jail. He was also quoted as saying that he would not be willing to listen to any sociological explanations of the riots.

The current Occupy Wall Street protests in the US against economic inequality and corporate greed essentially meant the globalisation of discontent, essentially youth anger, in the affluent countries of the West.

I was rather disappointed that the African Union and many leaders in Africa did not recognise both the London riots and Occupy Wall Street protests as an opportunity to offer global leadership. Would it have cost the African Union anything to offer to mediate in these conflicts – even if for symbolic reasons? Would it have cost them anything to suggest that the affected countries should resist any temptation to kill an ant with a sledge hammer but should instead strive to understand the underlying bases of these discontents and carry out any needed reforms? Will the Western world have kept mute if these riots were taking place in Africa? By not speaking out, African leaders give the wrong impression that they lack the self-confidence to play leadership roles at the world stage or that critical advice, including suggestions for needed reforms, can only flow from the West to Africa and not also the other way round.

Daily Trust, 20 October 2011

CHAPTER 46

AGAINST ALL ODDS: CELEBRATING AKI'S WEDDING

The 'white wedding' between Chinedu Ikedieze, (a.k.a Aki), and his heartthrob Nneoma Nwajah on December 9, 2011 was front page news for a number of newspapers, including the Sun and the Vanguard. True, some newspapers made it front page news for the wrong reason: to show the comic contrast in height between the pint-sized ace Nollywood actor and his much taller wife, who is a graduate of Enugu State University of Science and Technology. From the wedding photograph, Aki, a graduate of Mass communication from the Institute of Management and Technology, Enugu, who suffers from dwarfism, was barely up to his wife's waist. If providing a laugh was the main reason why the wedding became front page news by any newspaper, then such a paper, honestly, ought to hide its face in shame.

I have never met Aki, nor am I particularly a fan of Nollywood 'movies'. But there is something about Chinedu Ikedieze and his screen twin Osita Iheme (a.k.a. Pawpaw) that greatly appeals to me: their ability to overcome the challenge of dwarfism and all it entails. At barely three feet or so tall, it is easy to imagine the sort of discriminations, if not dehumanisations, Aki and Pawpaw must have suffered in life before getting to where they are today. There is often a knee-jerk tendency among many of us to 'lock out' those who 'do not look like us'. That Aki 'who does not look like us' was able to study and graduate from a tertiary institution can only be a tribute to a can-do spirit that consciously rejects that which others have tried to make of him. Many faced with similar challenges as him and Pawpaw faced while growing up, could decide to take the easy option and hide from the curious stares, if not mockery, that inevitably followed them wherever they went. This would have meant accepting that which others have tried to make of you – namely that you cannot possibly be good enough because you do not 'look like them'. This is the whole notion of self-fulfilling prophecy. Had Aki and Pawpaw accepted such a societal notion of people suffering from the medical condition of dwarfism, they would today probably have ended up as beggars, court jesters or at best sidekicks in a few Nollywood 'films'. Aki's marriage to Nneoma, a University graduate 'who is normal like us', could therefore be seen as a consummation of his resilient quest to prove to a prejudiced world that his physical challenges do not make him any less capable or different from us. In any case, some of us also have our own medical conditions to deal with – hypertension, diabetes, asthma or whatever.

Aki and Nneoma's wedding, which was variously described by the PM News of December 12 2011 as a 'celebration of true and undying love' and 'one of the best celebrity weddings of the out-going year' was attended by the crème-de-la-crème in the society including Richard Mofe-Damijo, Segun Arinze, Monalisa Chinda, Uche Jombo, Rita Dominic Kate Henshaw and Ifeanyi Uba who was the Chairman of the occasion. The wedding celebrates not just a triumph over the sort of adversity we have no control over but also reminds us of numerous others who have similarly overcome what would seem to be insurmountable natural hurdles to leave lasting legacies to mankind. The list is indeed very long, as most books on motivation will readily confirm. Consider the following examples:

Vincent van Gogh (1853 - 1890), an epileptic, was one of the most famous painters of all time. In fact his epilepsy once drove him into running after his friends with an open razor but ended up cutting off his own ear lobe.

Alfred Bernhard Nobel (October 21, 1833-December 10, 1896) was a Swedish chemist, engineer, innovator, armaments manufacturer and the inventor of dynamite. By the time he died he held more than 350 patents and controlled factories and laboratories in 20 countries. But from infancy Nobel suffered from severe migraine and convulsions. In 1895 he laid the foundations of what is today called the Nobel Prize when he wrote his last will leaving much of his wealth for its establishment. Since 1901 the Nobel Prize has been used to honour men and women for outstanding achievements in physics, chemistry, medicine, literature, and for work in peace.

Charles Proteus Steinmetz (April 9, 1865- October 26, 1923) was a distinguished German-American mathematician and electrical engineer. Though like Aki and Pawpaw he suffered from dwarfism, this did not stop him from fostering the development of alternating current that made possible the expansion of the electric power industry in the United States. He also made ground-breaking discoveries in the understanding of hysteresis, which enables engineers to design better electric motors for use in industry. Steinmetz was President of the American Institute of Electrical Engineers (AIEE) from 1901 to 1902 as well as the first vice-president of the International Association of Municipal Electricians (IAME)—which later became the International Municipal Signal

Association (IMSA)—from 1913 until his death. He wrote 13 books and 60 articles.

There are several blind people who have risen above their adversity to excel. The list includes:

Louis Braille (January 4, 1809-January 6, 1852), who accidentally stabbed himself in the eye and became blind from the injury. He later invented and designed the Braille writing which enables blind people to read from a series of organised stumps.

Stevie Wonder (May 13, 1950), an American singer, songwriter, record producer and multi-instrumentalist. His hits include 'Ebony and Ivory' that aided the civil rights cause in a non-violent way.

Marla Runyan (January 4, 1969), an American runner who is legally blind. Runyan is a three-time national champion in the women's 5000 meter run in the USA. She was also the first legally blind athlete to compete in the Olympics Games, where she placed eighth in the 1,500-meters race in the 2000 Sydney Olympics, making it the highest finish by an American woman in that event.

Franklin Delano Roosevelt (January 30, 1882 -April 12, 1945), one of the most popular American presidents in history, had several disabilities including vision impairment.

One of the important lessons from the above is that the human spirit has the capacity to rise above challenges – whether from nature or the environment such as unemployment- if there is sufficient determination, persistence, hard work, focus, diligence and of course prayers and God's grace. Aki's path to becoming a superstar in Nollywood from his days as an undergraduate was not strewn with gold. As he explained: 'Most often, when I was on campus, I usually buried my head in the library and also read ahead of my mates, knowing that there may be times that I would not have the time to come for my lectures. Despite all these sacrifices on my part, there were still many times that I will go out for auditions and come back empty handed. But despite the above, I did not give up, I persisted, I insisted on being part of Nollywood, I insisted on living above the frustrations. So I kept going from one audition to the other.'

Related to this is the importance of tolerance. Being able to accept people 'who do not look like us' is virtue. Aki and Pawpaw, just as the examples above, worked hard to get to where they are today. However without people being willing to give them a chance, they would not have been able to prove themselves. This is why I am particularly impressed by the broad-mindedness of Aki's father in-law, Lawrence Nwajah. When asked how he felt when he discovered that Aki was to be his son in law, Mr Nwajah, a retired civil servant, was quoted by the Vanguard of December 11 2011 as saying: 'I only said to her, "You have come of age, and I cannot choose a husband for you. Since you have found the man you want to marry, go ahead and marry the person. You will have my blessing."

Another important lesson from Aki's wedding is that we all need to love and be loved – no matter how different we look. After some two years of courtship, it is likely that both Aki and his wife now see the humanity and weaknesses in each other rather than just the comic differences in their heights. I believe this is what will happen to us as Nigerians if we are able to keep aside our prejudices and stereotypes and relate to one another as members of the same human family rather than as purveyors of particular religious or ethnic

Dialy Trust, 15 December 2011

CHAPTER 47

THE CIROMA GROUP'S BIG MISTAKE

In my column last week, I raised a pertinent question of whether we are in the throes of a new political alliance – that between the South-west and the political North, also known as the 'core North'. I observed that the political protests over the removal of subsidies were more successful in the South-west and the political North than elsewhere. I also noted that the 'civil society' groups pushing for the continuation of the protests after the federal government had reduced the per- litre price of fuel from N141 to N97 appeared to come mostly from these two zones. Another pointer to this putative alliance is that prominent columnists from the South-west are now alluding to a presumed alliance between the South-east and the South-south against the rest of the country. For instance Olusegun Adeniyi, one of my favourite columnists, in a surprising intemperate lampoon of the 'Ijaw handlers' of President Jonathan wrote in his column of January 19 2012: "And following the protests of last week, they [Jonathan's 'Ijaw handlers'] are now trying to recreate a president whose support base is restricted to the South-south and the South-east of the country, and yet they don't see anything wrong with that". The ill-advised drafting of the army to Lagos following threats by some groups to continue street protests after the NLC and the TUC had called off the strikes and protests seems to be another 'evidence' to some that the Jonathan administration is moving against the Yoruba. I shall return to this later.

With the political North widely suspected of having issues with President Jonathan, will the presumed grievances of the South-west against the Jonathan administration lead to an alliance of the two political blocs as 2015 approaches? An old aphorism tells us that the enemy of my enemy should strategically be my friend. The putative re-alignment in the traditional forms of political alliance in the country is really interesting. For instance the South-east and the South- south (essentially the ethnic minorities in the former Eastern region) have had uneasy relations with each other from the time of the spat between Zik and Eyo Ita following the fallouts of the 1951 elections in the Western Region through the Civil War and the abandoned property issue that followed. While the two geopolitical zones distrust each other, they are the traditional political allies of the political North. For the South-west, apart from the period of the civil war when Awolowo was released from prison by Gowon and made Vice President of the Federal Executive Council, attempts at political alliances between the political north and the South-west have often been problematic. For instance though Lt General Diya, (South-west) was the second in command to general Abacha (North), Diya was disgraced out of office and accused of plotting a coup. Again the putative alliance between the two blocs during the Obasanjo regime (1999-2003) ended in the epic hauling of brickbats between Obasanjo and his deputy Atiku. Even the alliance between the two blocs during the civil war seemed to have run into difficulties by 1979 with Chief Obafemi Awolowo choosing Philip Umeadi, an Igbo as his running mate. Shagari also chose an Igbo, Ekwueme, as his running mate.

What are the possible implications of these putative changes in the traditional pattern of political alliances for 2015?

My position is that the way the narrative of any political battle is framed could be more important in influencing its outcome than overt mobilisation on the basis of region, ethnicity and religion. While tapping into primordial sentiments could succeed in state or regional elections, it could be counterproductive in the competition for the presidency which usually requires support from other ethnic and geopolitical zones. This is where I feel the Adamu Ciroma-led Northern political group made a strategic error. And it is a mistake that those currently sticking their ethnic/regional identities on the face of others should learn one or two lessons from.

When President Goodluck Jonathan decided to contest the April 2011 presidential elections, some Northern politicians rightly felt he was reneging on the zoning and power rotation agreements the PDP had reached at an enlarged caucus meeting of the party in 2002, in which as Deputy Governor of Bayelsa, Jonathan was the 35th signatory. But they got it all wrong when they framed their campaign in regional and ethnic terms – Northern Political Leadership Forum and Northern consensus candidate. By using an irredentist narrative, it unwittingly narrowed the base of involvement and aroused the worst fears of non-Northerners, making it easier for the supporters of President Jonathan to counter by mobilising primordial sentiments in the South and also exploiting the internal contradictions in the North itself.

I strongly feel that the Ciroma group could have achieved more if it had framed its political narrative differently, say, as a struggle to force political leaders to show honour, integrity and respect for agreement as a basis for building trust.

When a faction of the Yoruba elite led the struggle for the revalidation of Abiola's mandate, it was framed as a struggle for democracy, not to avenge an ethnic insult. Similarly when the former Vice President Alhaji

Atiku Abubakar and others led the struggle to stop Obasanjo's tenure elongation bid, it was framed as a struggle to respect our Constitution and protect our nascent democracy and not a campaign for the North to take its turn in 2003. By framing these struggles in altruistic terms, the base of participation was broadened and international sympathisers were attracted. Few international organisations will want to be identified with ethnic or religious issues in another country

I feel that by framing its campaign for trust and integrity in regional terms, the Ciroma Group unwittingly did a disservice to the candidates that participated in the consensus arrangement by diminishing them in the eyes of many non-Northerners. A small window of opportunity for that to be corrected was not properly utilised. This was at the National Stakeholder in December 2010. Most political pundits expected Atiku to use the opportunity to re-define his candidacy and throw off the regional toga that was one of the unintended consequences of his involvement in the consensus candidacy arrangement. For a candidate who had invested time and money in developing a policy document on the critical issues in our political economy, there was an expectation that he would use the opportunity of the forum to make major policy pronouncements that would convince Nigerians he was truly more prepared for the job than his rivals. This unfortunately failed to happen. Rather his speech was brief. His quotation of Franz Fanon "those who make peaceful change impossible, make violent change inevitable" (John F Kenney also had a variant of the quote), became an ammunition in the armoury of his political opponents because the quote was not properly hung on any context.

The point from the above is that the way we frame the cause we espouse in our type of society is crucial for the base of support it will enjoy and consequently for its outcome. In this sense, I will respectfully disagree with those who believe that militarised ethnic/regional militias could be used in the quest for presidential power. It is true that NADECO made the country ungovernable under Abacha and helped to pave the way for Obasanjo to emerge as a civilian president in 1999. However I strongly feel that without the broad participation of other Nigerians in that struggle – something that would not have happened if it was framed as a Yoruba struggle – it would not have succeeded. In the same vein, while the militarisation of the Niger Delta struggle helped to draw the attention of the government and the international community to the area, I doubt that the struggle would have enjoyed the sympathy it does if it was framed simply as a matter of 'resource control' rather than environmental degradation from oil exploration. Precisely for the same reason, OPC, MASSOB and Boko Haram will be counter-productive if they get involved in the campaigns by any region for presidential power because of their irredentist orientation. It is for a similar reason that historically politicians with cult following in one ethnic group or region rarely do well outside their enclave.

Back to Olusegun Adeniyi. While I agree with him that many supporters of President Jonathan from Ijaw and the South-south are making Jonathan look extremely very provincial - like Yaradua before him - I am disappointed he fell into the same mistake the Ciroma group made and the Ijaw people he accused are making, namely to frame his own discourse in irredentist terms. What Mr Adeniyi may have succeeded in doing with his rather unfortunate piece is to diminish himself as a respected journalist and arouse the suspicions of others against his ethnic group.

Daily Trust 2 February 2012

SECTION TWO

CHALLENGES OF NATION BUILDING

CHAPTER 48

BETWEEN MAJORITY TYRANNY, DEMOCRATIC SPACE AND PDP'S ZONING

Alexis Tocqueville, the French political thinker and historian, developed the phrase 'tyranny of the majority' in his treatise on possible threats to representative democracy in America, including the tendency for democracy to degenerate into 'soft despotism' and 'tyranny of the majority'. Since Tocqueville, representative or liberal democracy has come a long way, with different political states developing policies to prevent their system from being corrupted into a 'tyranny of the majority'. The notion of human rights, which is necessarily anti-majoritarian in principle, and which is vigorously protected and defended in many mature democracies, is one such safeguard. In other political states, where the basis of statehood remains contested or where the state is made up of an agglomeration of different ethnic nationalities, the notion of 'concurrent majority'- in which great decisions are not arrived at through numerical majorities but often require agreement or acceptance by the major interests in the society – is quite popular. In such political states, contrivances like 'government of national unity', the need to reflect the 'federal character' of a country in appointments and 'zoning' are often popular political vocabularies.

A liberal democracy is an embodiment of a gamut of civic rights and individual liberties geared towards preventing it from degenerating into a tyranny of the majority. The extent to which these liberties are guaranteed and the degree to which they are protected differ from one democracy to another, and could be regarded as the democratic space available in each state. Obviously the democratic space is elastic, and can contract or expand based on new laws, policies, conventions and the activities of relevant social groups.

This raises the question of the interface between the fear of majority tyranny in Nigeria, the need to defend the country's democratic space and the PDP's zoning arrangement. Several observations could be made.

One, zoning could both extend and contract the democratic space depending on the way it is applied. In a zone where the elites are Cohesive, Conscious and Conspiratorial, there is a real possibility that such elites could hijack the process that throws up candidates from that zone. In such an instance candidates 'produced' by that zone will become an imposition on the rest of the country since popular candidates who may not be in the good books of those elites will not be allowed to emerge in the first place. In this sense the freedom to choose elected representatives becomes circumvented, leading to a corruption of the democracy and a contraction of the democratic space.

There is however a sense in which zoning could actually help in expanding the democratic space by removing the threat of majority tyranny. For instance one of the common complaints, especially by people from the Southern part of the country, is the domination of the North in the country's politics. This charge is not totally unfounded. Statistically, the Yorubas have held the executive presidency of the country for 12 years (between Obasanjo in his military and civilians incarnations and Shonekan as head of Interim Government); the political North for 37 years, the South South for approximately 18 months (under Jonathan until May 2011) and the Igbos for six months (under Ironsi). Although this domination is essentially through military coups and counter coups, it was feared that given the role of ethnicity and religion in Nigerian politics, the North, with its population and number of States, might continue its domination in a democratic dispensation. This was perhaps one of the immediate reasons why the defunct NPN came up with the idea of 'zoning' in the Second Republic. Of course there were also those who believed that zoning could facilitate the country's journey to real nationhood by assuring every group that they have a realistic chance of producing key political officers of the country. The policy of zoning was subsequently borrowed by the PDP.

Two, the decision by Goodluck Jonathan to contest for the presidency in 2011 despite being a signatory and beneficiary of the zoning arrangement, simultaneously benefits and undermines our democracy. It benefits our democracy in the sense that arguments for, and against his running, has contributed immensely to the vibrancy of our marketplace of political ideas – a key bedrock of any democracy. Few issues have dominated political discourse in our history more than the controversy surrounding the decision of GEJ to run for president. True, there have been threats and counter threats from both the pro-and anti-zoning forces but there has not been any substantial recourse to violence by the two contending groups. In other words, the decision by GEJ to contest has generated robust discussions and arguments which have benefited our democracy by enriching the vibrancy of our marketplace of political ideas. On the other hand, if GEJ contests and wins, it could undermine our democracy because zoning, a key safeguard against majority tyranny in our type of society, will have been discarded. This will then be a reversal of the gains from our experiments in democratic governance since the Second Republic and will throw us back to the era of

WAZOBIA, when the country's politics rested on a tripod – Hausa/Fulani (or North), Igbo and Yoruba. In other words, if zoning is removed, and our democracy becomes an unfettered electoral competition in which one person has one vote, and the winner is determined by simple majority, the prospect of majority tyranny becomes real.

Three, there is a sense in which zoning could be salutary to development. It is true that having a President of one's own ethnic stock will not, on its own, bring development to such an ethnic group. However it is generally recognised that having one of your own at the top can generate a 'hurrah effect' and a certain 'can do' attitude among members of the ethnic group, which could be salutary to development. It is largely on the basis of this that African Americans and indeed Africans in general supported Obama's candidacy during the last presidential election in the USA. Has any one noticed for instance that some Ijaws now walk with a certain swagger? It is certainly a good development and some are bound to convert the self confidence into economic risk taking.

Four, just as zoning could lead to rule by incompetent people, it could also improve the quality of governance if it leads to the various zones competing to produce candidates that will excel, and in the process do the geo-political zone proud. We are already seeing this among Governors as they now compete to make a mark and leave lasting legacies. In this sense, zoning could be improved if each zone is given the power to recall a representative of the zone seen not to be performing satisfactorily.

In summary, zoning could both undermine and advance our democracy –depending on how it is applied. Perhaps it is time to advance the debate on zoning by focusing on how it could be applied such that its negatives are blunted while the positives are accentuated.

Daily Trust 27 October 2010

CHAPTER 49

ZONING: THE FIRE NEXT TIME

From all indications the issues raised by the PDP's zoning and power rotation arrangements during the party's acrimonious presidential primaries are far from resolved. At that time the anti-zoning lobby advanced several arguments why zoning and power rotation arrangements were either not good for the country or should not be a hindrance to Jonathan contesting. The zoning proponents too had their own arguments. In the end Jonathan contested and won. In theory that would have resolved the zoning controversy. But going by the fallouts from the media reports of the proposed zoning formula of the principal offices of the National Assembly, it seems that the issue will for a long time continue to generate controversies especially whenever a new government is to be instituted.

PDP members of the House of Representatives have reportedly sworn not to abide by the party's recommended zoning formula. In the South East, (which has the second largest concentration of anti-zoning elements going by the results of the just concluded presidential elections), the umbrella Igbo socio-political organisation, Ohaneze as well as prominent traditional rulers and former political office holders have cried 'foul'. In some other places, a number of previously anti-zoning elements have turned into proponents of zoning and power rotation. So why do many Nigerians seem to flip-flop on the zoning issue? There are several salient issues here. It will appear that many people instinctively recognise the benefits of zoning but at the same time do not want a rigid application of the principle - perhaps in order not to ossify the political process. This approach-avoidance attitude, including by some PDP stalwarts, has created regrettable fuzziness around the issue, especially on conditions under which it should be strictly applied and when it should be discarded. Former President Olusegun Obasanjo, (and current Chairman of the party's Board of Trustees) has for instance taken at least four stances on the issue - first he denied that zoning existed in the party's constitution and then shifted into an obscurantist 'when you are there you are there and when you are not there, you are not there'. He had also, at different times, argued that zoning was suspended to enable Jonathan run for the presidency and equally contradictorily held that the party's zoning arrangement was still very much alive. But Obasanjo was not alone in flip-flopping over the matter. In Imo Sate for instance, there is reportedly a zoning arrangement among the three senatorial zones in the area when it comes to producing the State Governor. Under this arrangement, the Okigwe senatorial district (where Governor Ikedi Ohakim comes from) was expected to produce the Governor until 2015. However in the just concluded Governorship election in the state, it would seem that the electorate favoured a dispensation for Rochas Okorocha who actually comes from Orlu Senatorial district – where Ohakim's predecessor in office Achike Udenwa hails from. Again if reports in the media were anything to go by, most serving and newly elected members of the Senate want David Mark to retain the Senate Presidency. A strict application of the PDP's zoning and power rotation arrangements would have meant the office would be zoned to the South because under the Obasanjo presidency, (from the South West), the post was also zoned to the South (South East) while under the Yaradua presidency (North West) it was zoned to the North (North Central). This presupposes a tradition of zoning the Senate presidency to the North if the president is from there or the South if the president is from the South. These instances show that both the zoning proponents and the anti-zoning elements during the acrimonious contest for the PDP presidential primary have sufficient grounds to claim vindication. Which, of course, only compounds the problem.

Not resolving the issue of the conditions under which the zoning and power rotation would be strictly applied and when they could be dispensed creates uncertainty such that any reconfiguration becomes vulnerable to suspicion, manipulation or being unduly politicised- some of the reasons why the zoning arrangement was put in place in the first instance. My personal opinion is that despite the obvious imperfections of zoning and power rotation arrangements, in a multi-ethnic country like ours, where the constituent units deeply distrust one another, the certainty that a zone would occupy a certain position at a defined political moment could help to muffle cries of marginalisation, and by so doing, remove a major clog in the nation-building process. In essence what seems to be lacking is not so much whether there are circumstances in which zoning could be dispensed but how to compensate for the certainty that zoning and power rotation arrangements offer. True, that someone from one's ethnic group/geopolitical zone occupies a certain office does not necessarily guarantee progress for such a zone/ ethnic group. Unfortunately we have across the country a group of 'ethnic watchers' who have the capacity to press the right emotional button to throw a regime into a legitimacy crisis – if they are given the ammunition to strike. We saw this during the Buhari regime when this group successfully politicised what I believe was an honest mistake (or naivety) in the constitution of the Supreme Military Council and in Buhari appointing a fellow Northerner and Muslim Tunde Idiagbon as his second in command. Suddenly a regime that was very popularly received became viewed with suspicion such that virtually every action it took was unfairly analysed through ethnic/religious prisms. Up till this day Buhari has not fully shaken off that unfair labelling.

Another danger in not resolving the issue of zoning and when it should be rigidly applied or discarded is the danger of reviving the 'cluster politics' of the First and Second Republics where each major ethnic group formed a party it dominated with the hope of using the control of its enclave as a bargaining chip. The recent sweeping victory of the ACN in the South West in fact raises the possibility of a 'me-tooist' scenario. My personal opinion is that 'cluster politics' is a step backward in our nation-building process.

Related to the above is the emerging tendency for groups that exert an 'overwhelming claim' to a certain entitlement to be pacified with juicy political offices. This trend appears to have started with the annulment of the June 12 election won by the late Moshood Abiola. Though I strongly condemn the annulment, the fact is that primaries and elections had been serially annulled by Babangida and nothing happened. Coups and counter coups had also taken place without heavens breaking loose. With the June 12 annulment however, a faction of the Yoruba elite which was Cohesive, Conscious and Conspiratorial staked an 'overwhelming claim' for that entitlement by making the country 'ungovernable'. They were subsequently pacified with an Obasanjo presidency (the way they resisted Babangida and Abacha however also helped to pave the way for the current democratic dispensation – besides making military coups unattractive to the 'khaki boys'). It could equally be argued that the militarisation of the Niger Delta struggle for equity led to a strong desire to pacify them, which in turn paved the way for the emergence of Goodluck Jonathan first as Vice President and later as President. Some cynics have also argued that the post election violence in some parts of the North, as condemnable as it is, is the area's copycat staking of an 'overwhelming claim' for a certain entitlement. The danger therefore is that without delineating a clear and predictable system of giving constituent units of the Nigerian federation assurances that they are real stakeholders in the Nigeria project, there could be tactical nurturing of militants and purveyors of violence to help groups stake such 'overwhelming claims' to an entitlement.

CHAPTER 50

THE NOTION AND POLITICS OF 'CONSENSUS CANDIDACY'

Since Atiku Abubakar was declared the 'consensus' candidate of the Northern presidential aspirants in the PDP, there has been a lot of aggressive exchange of ideas over the notion of 'consensus candidacy'. While some have condemned the exercise, which was carried out under the auspices of the Adamu Ciroma-led Northern Political Leadership Forum, as either undemocratic or an unwelcome ethnicisation of our politics, others believe the consensus arrangement is legitimate and laudable.

The Vice President Namadi Sambo reportedly claimed recently that the process that threw up Atiku Abubakar as NPLF's consensus candidate was 'illegal'. He reportedly insisted that "there is no consensus candidate," in the PDP or the North, and if any exists for the North, it should be him. Several issues are raised by the claims and counter claims over Atiku's 'consensus' candidacy.

One, in the controversy over whether Atiku Abubakar is the consensus candidate of the North or not, very little effort is made to define the notion of 'consensus candidate'. 'Consensus' simply means an opinion or position reached by a group as a whole. Following from this, a 'consensus candidate' is one selected or elected to represent a grouping, tendency or ideological belief. A resort to a 'consensus' candidacy is often predicated on a premise that if several candidates representing the same tendency or principle compete against another candidate who represents a different interest, the chances of electoral victory are diminished. Organisations that are not formally political can also come together to present a common or consensus front on issues. It can in fact be argued that the whole essence of such ethno-regional groupings as the Ohaneze, Afenifere and Arewa Consultative Forum is to articulate and present consensus positions on issues that affect them.

Two, because a political party is an agglomeration of various interests, it is quite normal for groupings and tendencies within a party to reach an agreement among themselves to present a common front on issues. In the defunct NCNC for instance, the Zikist movement represented an ideological tendency that was often at variance with the political inclinations of the party's leadership. Again in the Babangida-created SDP, Atiku Abubakar emerged as the 'consensus' candidate of the Musa Yaradua-led PF grouping, which later persuaded Atiku to step down for Abiola who then became the 'consensus candidate' of the PF and other groupings in the contest for SDP's presidential ticket against Babagana Kingibe, which Abiola won with a very slim margin. In the 2003 presidential election, the AD decided not to field a candidate and chose instead to adopt Olusegun Obasanjo as its 'consensus candidate'.

Three, it is possible for a grouping that represents a tendency within a political party to make generalisations about its consensus positions. For instance, when the Zikist movement decided on 'positive action', it was possible for it to claim that it was representing Nigerians dissatisfied with the relatively gradualist approach of the NCNC leadership on the question of independence for the country because its position certainly resonated well with the sentiments of some Nigerians across the country's ethnic, religious and political fault lines. Similarly, it is possible for Atiku's supporters to claim that the basis on which the consensus arrangement was negotiated was the PDP's zoning and that the principles this embodies for them such as respect for the party's rules, honour, integrity and protection of minority interests transcend the issue of North versus South, which on a face value, zoning seems to purvey.

Based on this, they can argue that Atiku is the consensus candidate of all Nigerians who stand for those principles. Jonathan has also been chosen as the 'consensus candidate' of a number of groupings – South West PDP, South East Governors and South East Houses of Assembly etc. It is possible to articulate the reasons for the adoption of Jonathan by these groupings and then frame the forthcoming PDP primaries as a direct contest between the principles represented by both zoning and anti-zoning arguments. In this sense, both Jonathan and Atiku could be said to be national 'consensus candidates', over a given set of conflicting principles.

Four, it is puerile to argue that consensus candidacy is undemocratic. It is not. In all political climes, it is not unusual for one or more candidates to step down for a person they feel will have better electoral chances. In terms of democratic value, there is no difference between one or more candidates stepping down for a candidate – as Dr Odili and others were 'forced' by Obasanjo to do for Umaru Yaradua in 2007 - and the Northern political Forum facilitating the process of three candidates stepping down for Atiku. A consensus arrangement also played out in 1999 when prominent Yoruba leaders facilitated the emergence of Olu Falae as their preferred presidential candidate against the late Bola Ige under the platform of the AD. Similarly in 2006, Edwin Clarke and others formed what they called the South South Political Leaders Forum to present a 'consensus candidate' from the South South in 2007. It is believed that pressures from the Edwin Clarke-led Forum partly influenced the choice of Goodluck Jonathan, who is from the South South, as the running mate of the late Umaru Yaradua in the 2007 presidential election. Just as it is wrong to regard a consensus arrangement as undemocratic, it is a misuse of language to regard it as 'illegal'. If it is illegal, what law of the land does it contravene?

Five, if the other three candidates in the NPLF's consensus arrangement – Ibrahim Babangida, Gusau and Saraki – decide later to pursue their presidential ambitions under different political parties, that will not mean that the consensus deal has flopped because the essence of the arrangement was to pull together their resources to defeat Jonathan in the PDP primaries. The consensus arrangement will only be said to have flopped if at least one of the three candidates decides to re-enter the race as a PDP candidate or works against the interest of Atiku in the PDP primaries. If Atiku does not defeat Jonathan in the primaries and one or all of the three other candidates re-enter the race, it will not be a defeat of the consensus arrangement but a continuation of the candidates' struggle to defend the principles which the party's zoning arrangement represent to them. In this respect, newspaper headlines that the consensus arrangement is on the verge of collapsing based on speculations that the other candidates in the consensus deal could re-enter the race on the platform of other parties, is misplaced

Daily Trust, 9 December 2010

CHAPTER 51

A TWO-PARTY SYSTEM: PANACEA OR COMPOUNDING THE PROBLEM?

The recent call by Abubakar Atiku, the country's former vice president, for a two party system has animated the discussion on the appropriate number of political parties for the country. Many are understandably unhappy with the current state of affairs, in which some 50 political parties are registered. One of the arguments is that with so many political parties, the political space is turned into a sort of Tower of Babel, undermining one of the key functions of political parties - the articulation and aggregation of interests in such a way that choices are simplified for the electorate.

There are also concerns that most of the currently registered parties are just paper tigers, which are incapable of performing the true functions of political parties, and were registered just for the purpose of ego massage and collecting the grants from INEC. It is equally argued that with so many parties, the candidate who gets the most votes will be the one with the broadest constituency, not the one who represents the will of all or most of the voters.

Proponents of a two party system also usually refer to the 1993 elections, contested by two political parties – SDP and NRC, as 'the freest and fairest' in the country's political history.

There are a number of issues with the arguments for a two-party system. One, is a tendency to mistake a two-party system with a two-party **dominant** system. In a two- party system, two parties are imposed by fiat such as Babangida's 'a little to the left' and 'a little to the right' parties. In a two-party dominant system however, other parties are allowed to contest elections if they meet the criteria, but the system is such that only two parties at any time have real chances of forming the government at the centre. A good example of this is Britain where you have the Labour and Conservatives (Tories) as the only viable parties capable of forming the government at the centre but other parties such as the Liberal Party, the British National Party and the Justice Party also contest and field candidates for offices. It is possible for a-two party dominant system to suddenly become a one-party dominant or three-party dominant system depending on the constellation of events and the alignment of political forces. In the UK for instance the Conservative Party was dominant between 1979 and 1997 while the Labour Party was dominant from 1997 until recently. Nigeria is currently a one-party dominant system.

Two, proponents of a two-party system usually refer to the 1993 elections, contested only by NRC and SDP, as the 'freest and fairest' elections ever held in Nigeria without telling us anything about cause and effects. Was the election the 'freest and fairest' because the contest was only between two parties or because it was conducted under the military and the politicians were either so cowered or so eager to wrest power from the military that they decided to be on their best behaviour?

Third, it will also seem that those who refer to the 1993 elections as a model underestimate the latent problems with the Moshood Abiola/Baba Gana Kingibe ticket, if the mandate had been actualised. Theirs would have been the second Muslim/Muslim ticket to rule the country in our political history.

While it is possible that Nigerians wouldn't have cared about a Muslim-Muslim ticket, especially if the regime performed well in office, the first experience of a Muslim/Muslim ticket in the country - that of Buhari and Idiagbon - was not a savoury one. Buhari's experience would suggest that the 'professional ethnic/religious watchers' in the country would have used it to undermine the legitimacy of the regime. For instance, despite the popularity of the coup that brought Buhari to power, the legitimacy of the regime however quickly plummeted after it emerged the Number One and Number Two citizens were from the same religion, and the same North. The regime's every action was subsequently analysed using that filter. There are clear indications that Buhari has continued to pay for that political miscalculation because he remains deeply distrusted by many non-Muslims. The late chief Obafemi Awolowo made a similar mistake when he chose Philip Umeadi, an Igbo, and fellow Christian, as his running mate in 1979. That costly political *faux pas* did an incalculable harm to Chief Awolowo's image, especially in the North and among Muslims. A Muslim-Muslim or Christian-Christian ticket is unlikely to win in a multi-party system in Nigeria. It is in fact tempting to speculate on what would have happened if UPN and NPN were the only political parties in 1979, and what would have happened to the country if the Awolowo/Umeadi ticket had emerged triumphant.

Fourth, a two-party system is also likely to sharpen the North-South divide, and is easier to manipulate to achieve tenure elongation. For instance, while it is increasingly accepted that the North and South should alternate in producing the country's president, it is hypothetically possible to rig this 'arrangement' under a two party system. Take this scenario as an example. The South takes its 'turn' of eight years, using Party A as the ruling party. Towards the end of its 'turn', it deliberately weakens Party A and encourages decampments to Party B, which is likely to have fielded a Northerner as a Presidential candidate in the last two elections. Meanwhile Party B will come under pressure not to field another Presidential candidate from the North for a third consecutive election. The South then fields a Presidential candidate for Party B and claims an entitlement of another eight years. This type of scenario is unlikely if you have more than two parties.

Fifth, a two party system will also freeze out the possibility of cause and fringe groups having the opportunity to ventilate themselves, and subject their ideas to the competition of the political marketplace. Without this possibility, such ideas could be driven underground, making them more romantic and attractive to some.

There is no doubt that a-two party dominant system will simplify choice for the electorate without ossifying the political system. Such a system however normally evolves from a muti-party base, and not imposed by fiat. There are in fact indications that the country is already moving in that direction. What is perhaps needed is for INEC to develop more stringent conditions for the registration of political parties and benchmarks, assessed periodically, which parties must meet to continue to enjoy its recognition.

Daily Trust 8 June 2012

CHAPTER 52

DON'T CRY FOR ME, NIGERIA

It must have been around 1984 that Wole Soyinka declared his generation, 'the wasted generation'. The 1986 Nobel Laureate in literature had accused anyone who was 40 years old or over, of belonging to a generation that wasted the opportunities to take the country to greater heights. I was then a 22 year-old young man, and my generation and the one following us were perhaps expected to correct the errors of the 'wasted generation'.

A quarter of a century after, members of Soyinka's 'wasted generation' are paradoxically today held up as the only true heroes and heroines the country ever produced. Similarly, the society that the Nigerian wordsmith riled against at that time is today benchmarked as the country's golden era. Meanwhile, Soyinka, at 75, is still very much in the trenches.

In 1984, at about the time that Wole Soyinka unveiled the 'wasted generation' thesis; celebrated novelist Chinua Achebe published the well-received slim book, *The Trouble With Nigeria*. For Achebe, who is generally regarded as the father of modern African novel, the trouble with Nigeria was squarely a failure of leadership.

I was a final year student of political science at the University of Nigeria, Nsukka, when *The Trouble With Nigeria* was first published. The book sharply divided our class. At issue was whether the trouble with Nigeria was really that of leadership or whether it was systemic. The orientation of the class was overwhelmingly Marxist, so the system argument got a good hearing. Some argued that even Achebe himself had bought into the system argument through the Obi Okonkwo character, in *No Longer At Ease* (1960), Achebe's sequel to *Things Fall Apart (*1958).

In the novel, the portraiture of Obi Okonkwo was that of a very independent-minded - man at a time when individuals were subordinated to their communities in Igboland, and the elders were revered. Though he was sent to England by his community to study law so he would handle their land cases on his return, Obi Okonkwo chose to read English. On his return, he again disappointed the entire community by arriving at his reception venue in simple T-shirt when every one had expected him, a returnee from England, to dress in the best suit money could buy. As if to add insult to injury, while the secretary of the town union thrilled the audience with the "English that filled the mouth", Obi Okonkwo only spoke the 'is' and 'was' type of English. Additionally, Obi Okonkwo decided to marry an 'osu' (a social outcast), which was an abomination among his people. He also refused to use his position as a senior civil servant, to 'fix' jobs in the civil service for people from his village – as was the norm in those days. Obi Okonkwo simply did not want to have anything to do with the prevailing nepotism and corruption. Yet, despite being morally upright and independent minded, Obi Okonkwo, was eventually forced by pressures and survival imperatives to take bribe – and was caught, meaning that in *No Longer At Ease,* the trouble with Nigeria was systemic, not leadership.

Though many in my class in those days believed that the trouble with Nigeria was systemic rather than leadership, we also agreed there was a conundrum: if the Obi Okonkwo complex showed how system dynamics could corrupt a good man, what would then be required to change the system? It is like the argument of whether the chicken or the egg came first.

A quarter of a century after our argument about *The Trouble With Nigeria,* the 'systemic problems' we talked about had degenerated into 'system collapse', and talks of Nigeria being either a failed or failing state. As for leadership, while Achebe implied 25 years ago that the trouble with Nigeria was that of poor leadership, today, with President Yaradua hospitalised for an indeterminate duration in Saudi Arabia without reportedly formally handing over power to Vice President Goodluck Jonathan, many feel the country has no leadership at all, not to talk of whether it was a poor one or not.

Understandably, pessimism seems to have taken over in the country - with the negatives seemingly growing in their grotesqueness – armed robbery, kidnapping, joblessness, corruption, ethnic and religious chauvinism etc. The problems in the country, as real as they are, however mask some grounds for optimism:

One, despite the current challenges, the possibility of the country breaking up seems more remote now than ever. The federating units, despite the occasional grandstanding, appear to have accepted their marriage of convenience with one another. There is a feeling that most Nigerians would in fact feel diminished were the country to break up.

Two, despite our problems with elections, it is highly unlikely that the military can successfully intervene in Nigerian politics again. Freedom of expression is for instance today enjoyed on a scale never before seen in the country. It is easy to forget that as recent as 1984, we had a decree (Decree No 4), which prohibited criticisms of public officials – whether such criticisms were right or wrong - if such would embarrass the government of the day. Similarly while the crisis generated by the 1983 elections provided the ammunition for the military to strike, in 2007, despite the shoddiness of the elections, no one dared suggest that the military should take over.

Three, in the current global recession, we are actually doing better than some countries in the West. For instance, despite talks of Sanusi's revolution in the banking sector, no Nigerian bank has collapsed – thanks in large part to the bank consolidation exercise. In the US, 133 banks or an average of 11 banks collapsed every month this year. In the UK, the official cost of bank bailout by the government is £850bn. Similarly while only a few years ago, you would need to spend hours in our banks to even withdraw you money, these days you have ATMs, credit cards, online banking and even international transfers that are successfully effected within 48 hours.

Four, while the country undoubtedly faces numerous challenges, it is likely that some of our frustrations may actually be the result of rising expectations or improvement in reporting systems. For instance though statistics show the incidence of corruption is increasing, I remain unconvinced that the current crop of politicians are more corrupt than the 1960s' politicians we like to regard as heroes – if we consider the stupendous wealth and property most of them accumulated during their time. Similarly, while we are right to complain about epileptic power supply, we seem to forget that there were many parts of the country without even electric poles by the 1980s. And even at UNN in the 1980s, it was not uncommon for us study with lanterns.

Daily Trust, June 6 2012

CHAPTER 53

A NATION IN COMA: BEYOND CONSTITUTIONAL PROVISIONS

Nigeria is once again at one of those junctures where tripping over the precipice cannot be ruled out. At issue is the President's serious illness, and increasing calls by some Nigerians for him to hand over the reins of government to Vice-President Goodluck Jonathan. Militants from the Vice-President's Niger Delta area have threatened to secede from the country if Jonathan is pressured to resign, as is being rumoured, so that another Northerner would succeed Yaradua, if he is unable to continue in office. The Oodua Peoples Congress (OPC) recently joined the fray, warning that any attempt to force Jonathan to resign could push "the country down the precipice on which it currently and dangerously balances" (The Sun News Online, December 6, 2009).

Supporters of Jonathan anchor their position on section 146(1) of the 1979 Constitution which says: "The Vice-President shall hold the office of President if the office of President becomes vacant by reason of death or resignation, impeachment, permanent incapacity or the removal of the President from office for any other reason in accordance with section 143 or 144 of this constitution." The ire of this group is further fired by reports that Yaradua has never formally handed over power to Goodluck during the numerous times he has been away for health check-ups, including in 2008 when he spent 17 days in Germany. They contrast this with George W Bush handing over power to Vice-President Dick Cheney on August 29, 2002, just because he had to undergo a routine health screening (colonoscopy) with important side effects.

Those said to be leading the move for Jonathan to resign to pave way for another Northerner to complete Yaradua's term in case of his demise or inability to continue in office, appear to base their own arguments on the fact that under the PDP's zoning arrangement, the South had taken its 'agreed turn' of eight years, so to prevent the North from completing its own 'turn', would be unfair and unjust

There are a number of important observations on this issue.

One, no one wishes the President death (or even incapacitation), as only God can give or take life. However death is an inevitability to all of us, and just as some people who are healthy make certain contingency plans against their own death (such as writing a will), when a President gets ill, it will not be out of place to have a national discussion of what happens in a worst case scenario. Scenario mapping and future strategic plans are important tools for ensuring that a company, organisation or society is not overwhelmed by unexpected developments. As the cliché goes, if you do not plan, you plan to fail. It is therefore wrong to accuse those discussing the issue of Yaradua's possible demise or resignation of being enemies of the nation.

Two, an essential spirit of the Nigerian constitution is anchored on rules that will help the various federating nationalities to co-exist amicably. The letters of the law do not always effectively capture its spirit, hence you have conventions, traditions, and other supplementary arrangements such as the PDP's zoning formula to help build the necessary trust, sense of justice and fair play among the federating units as envisaged by the constitution makers. In other words, while Grover Cleveland, the 22nd and 24th President of USA might have been right that no "man has ever been hanged for breaking the spirit of a law", it is equally true that advantages secured through a recourse to legalese tend in the long run to be a pyrrhic victory. Though the letters of the law trump its spirit in formal relationships, most people will prefer to deal with people, who, in selfless pursuit of justice and fairplay, are flexible enough to keep the spirit of the law, even if its letters, are not fully observed.

Three, despite its numerous shortcomings, the PDP – at least at the national level - has been able to respect its zoning principle. For instance, under the Obasanjo regime, the Senate churned out five presidents. However because that office was zoned to the Igbos, only Igbos ran each time a vacancy occurred. Thus we had Evans Enwerem (1999), Chuba Okadigbo (1999-2000), Pius Anyim (2000-2003), Adolphus Wabara (2003-2005) and Ken Nnamani (2005-2007). Under Obasanjo the post of Speaker of the House of Representatives was zoned to the North-West and produced Salisu Buhari ([Kano state], 1999-2000), Ghali Umar Na'Abba ([Kano state], 2000-2003), and Aminu Bello Masari (Kano state, 2003-2007). The Yaradua regime has continued to respect the zoning principle of the party. The post of Speaker of the House of Representatives is for instance zoned to the Yorubas. Thus when Patricia Olubunmi Foluke Etteh, from Osun state, was forced to resign, only Yorubas vied to succeed her, ensuring that she was succeeded by Oladimeji Sabur Bankole from Ogun state. In none of these instances was there any talk of the deputy stepping up to the substantive position. This means that if we apply the principles of justice, fair play and tradition (zoning in this case), we should not be too dismissive of some people who argue that they too shall be allowed to complete their 'turn'.

Four, while in the perception of some people from the north, the South has had its 'turn', it is not clear-cut that the Niger Delta, which is conscious of providing the bulk of the country's wealth, sees itself as part of the political South. It is believed that they prefer to be treated as a special case. There is a fear that they may feel a certain conspiracy to deny one of their own a constitutionally enshrined right of acceding to the presidency just because they are not among the dominant ethnic groups. This could in turn heighten their sense of injustice, alienation and exclusion, with its implications for militancy in the region.

Five, the current quagmire raises a number of pertinent questions: If Goodluck Jonathan is made the president to serve out Yaradua's turn; will it not be unconstitutional to prevent him from seeking a second term in office? If the letters of the constitution are enforced and he goes for a second term in office, will that not be regarded as treachery by the North, which has so far respected the zoning arrangements in the PDP? If on the other hand Jonathan is made to resign so that a Northerner will complete Yaradua's turn, will we not be setting a dangerous precedent that explicit constitutional provisions could be disregarded at our whims? What will be the implications of any solution adopted for the PDP's zoning arrangement and the current nation-building efforts? However this issue is resolved, it will be worth taking a long term perspective that will engender mutual trust.

Daily Independent, December 10, 2009

CHAPTER 54

BRAND NIGERIA: DO WE REALLY NEED A RE-BRANDING?

Nation branding has become a popular phrase ever since Simon Anholt coined the phrase in 1996. In a seminal article, 'Nation-Brands of the Twenty-First Century' (1998), Anholt noted that most of the really successful international brands have come from countries that are successful brands in their own rights such that a substantial transfer of brand imagery and brand equity seems to occur naturally between the two. This suggests that a brand is often a complex mixture of attributes, one of which is the brand's provenance. In fact, the relationship between a brand and its provenance could be so strong that it may be difficult to assess whether the perception of a brand is because of the product or its place of origin.

The above presupposes that a country's brand is best appreciated if it is woven as a narrative around its famous products, services or attributes – samba in Brazil, reggae in Jamaica, resilient technological products from Japan and Germany, enthralling wild life in Kenya, wonderful nature in Uganda, and mysticism in Tibet.

There are some crucial questions in the current drive to 'rebrand' Nigeria: What is Brand Nigeria? Which products or attributes of the country are woven around the brand? What do we hope to achieve by re-branding? How do we measure the success of a country brand?

Nigerians have, at least since the oil boom of the 1970s, branded their country as the 'Giant of Africa', a slogan that despite its lack of humility rightly reflects our relative huge population and leadership in many areas in the continent - from the struggle against Apartheid South Africa to peace keeping initiatives and sports. In July 2004, the Obasanjo regime decided to change this subsisting brand when it launched the 'Nigeria Image Project', which later metamorphosed into the Heart of Africa Project. The new brand was notorious not just over accusations of plagiarism and theft of other countries' intellectual property but even more importantly for the lack of any association between its implied narrative and any of the country's known attributes. When the Minister of Information, Professor Dora Akunyili, announced the jettisoning of the brand, part of her reasons was that "we need to re-brand Nigeria, so that we as Nigerians will appreciate ourselves and our country, which will put us in a position to present ourselves positively to the outside world."

There are a number of issues with the new drive to 're-brand' the country. First, a country 're-brands' to improve its ability to attract tourism, inward investments and export sales, not so that the citizens will better appreciate themselves. If the aim of the exercise is for citizens to better appreciate themselves, then what is required is not rebranding but some form of mass psychotherapy or the use of historiography to imbue national and racial pride along the lines of the Black History Month.

Second, the minister said nothing about the interwoven association between a brand and its provenance, implying some ignorance of a key fundamental in the success of any brand. For instance though India, China and Jamaica could have more conmen than Nigeria, the fact that these countries are perceived to work while Nigeria is not means that the criminals from those countries cannot be used to define them while those from Nigeria will. This suggests that for as long as Nigeria remains a fraudulent failing state, campaigns to correct the purported negative image of the country abroad could be misconstrued as a whitewash, further feeding into the perception that Nigerians are deceptive people. It is pretty much like Black people believing that the celebration of Black History Month will radically change the stereotyping and perception of the Blackman in the West. Of course the criminal activities of some Africans are unlikely to affect the perception of blacks and Africans in areas they are historically seen as doing well –music, sports, dancing. But perceptions in these areas were built up over the years, not through media whitewash.

Third, when a country's image suffers – as that of Britain did at the turn of the century when it was known as the 'sick man of Europe', and America did under Jimmy Carter, what they often do is to get their acts together and then create new narratives around their success areas, not create a new brand symbol. People and companies from such countries concomitantly benefit from the improved perception of the country.

Fourth, there are contradictions that suggest that the new effort to 'rebrand' the country was hastily put together. For instance one of the reasons given for abandoning the Heart of Africa Project was that it "was launched in overseas, thereby disconnecting the ordinary Nigerian from the project, which makes it look elitist." This argument is rather unconvincing, for one can in fact argue that launching the project overseas rather than at home would have a better impact since the key aim was to correct the apparent misperception of the country abroad and not to induce behaviour changes at home. Besides, since when has a project being home grown an indication that it would succeed?

Fifth, the Minister also claimed that the Heart of Africa project failed to achieve its objectives without telling us how she carried out the impact assessment or how her own will be different. Nothing was also said about budget, time frame and impact assessment.

The above is not a defence of the Heart of Africa Project, which had a whopping budget of N600 million (enough to offer full time employment for some 1.4 million graduates for one year). The argument is simply that the country does not need another white elephant project - a poorly articulated one at that - at a time of global recession and unacceptable levels of unemployment at home. We already have a good brand name, Giant of Africa, and our brand symbol/logo remains our flag.

You cannot be prouder as a Nigerian to visit the Odeon cinema chain in Surrey Quays, south east London, and discover that a Nollywood film is on the menu, with many non-Nigerians, including Caucasians, queuing up for tickets. Or to know that the $450 million industry is the third biggest in the world, after America's Hollywood and India's Bollywood. This is a far more effective image-making effort for the country than the government can possibly do.

Daily Independent, March 12 2009

CHAPTER 55

BEYOND A SOVEREIGN NATIONAL CONFERENCE

There was something strange about the inaugural lecture delivered on behalf of President Goodluck Jonathan on Thursday May 26 2011 by Professor Ladipo Adamolekun. Entitled, "A Transformation Agenda for Accelerating National Development," an assertion from that speech that most of those lobbying for positions are selfish was widely reported, and seemed to strike the right chord with many Nigerians. For many people, that our office seekers are mostly selfish would seem self-evident, given that such offices are more often than not seen as an opportunity for accumulation rather than for service.

One of the intriguing but less reported aspects of the lecture however is the apparent juxtaposition of Professor Adamolekun's voices/opinions with those of the President. Traditionally, when a lecture or speech is given on behalf of an official, say the President, the views or comments expressed by the person delivering the lecture/speech, are expected to reflect the views of the official on behalf of whom the speech or lecture is given. And this is where I had difficulty fathoming whether a controversial opinion expressed by the learned Professor indeed reflected the views of Mr President.

It was reported by the *Tribune* of Friday May 27 2011 that Professor Adamolekun called on "President Jonathan to yield to calls by eminent Nigerians, including Professor Wole Soyinka, to convoke, within the shortest possible time, a Sovereign National Conference, where issues affecting the nation could be discussed." Though this appeared to be the personal opinion of the Professor, the fact that it was proffered when he was officially representing the President raises some crucial questions: Has the President turned into an advocate of a Sovereign National Conference (SNC)? Since a person delivering a lecture on behalf of the President is assumed to be a confidant of sorts, what was exactly the import of that public proposal? And is SNC really a credible vehicle for resolving some of the contentious issues which had dominated national discourse under different names at different times – the national question, enthronement of true federalism, resource control, zoning etc?

It is important to underline that calls for a sovereign national conference have always had both political and economic undertones. Politically the calls reflect an implicit recognition that virtually all the constituent units of the federation feel dissatisfied with the Nigerian arrangement and believe that they are either short-changed or will fair better under a different structure. In fact, every unit of the federation has a scar to convince the others that it is indeed being 'marginalised'. In this sense, the SNC is a euphemism for a clarion call for the constituents of the federation to come together to renegotiate the basis of their 'marriage of convenience', including what would be the appropriate number of states for the federation, and the way each unit should be made to feel that it is a real stakeholder in the Nigeria project. Yes, among the proponents of the SNC are those who believe that everyone will be better off with a peaceful divorce.

The calls for a SNC are equally economic-driven. Over and above the concerns of the ethno-regional forces are issues about the appropriate revenue-sharing formula not only among the states but also between the centre and the states. Despite the fact that our constitution is almost exclusively consumption-oriented – spelling out who gets what, when, and how (but largely silent on how the national cake should be baked or expanded) the issue of sharing the 'national cake', including power at the centre, remains one of the most divisive issues in our political history.

My personal opinion is that the issues that the SNC seeks to resolve are crucial and vital – and must be confronted honestly and decisively if we genuinely hope to fashion out a nation out of the mosaic of nationalities that make up the Nigerian state. What is however unclear is whether the SNC is the best vehicle for resolving those vital issues. There are indeed several sources of concern: apart from the elected representatives, who should be invited to such a Conference? What should be their claim for being the authentic spokespeople of the constituencies they purport to represent? Wouldn't SNC exacerbate the very problems they are meant to resolve as many of the conferees are likely to see the platform as an opportunity for grandstanding? Throw onto these the ethnic profiling and name calling that usually follow such conversations in the media and one wonders whether SNC might not be the last straw that could push the country, ever on the precipice, onto the abyss. Even more worrying for the President is the Republic of Benin scenario being played out.

It should be recalled that when President Matthew Kerekou was forced to convene the National Conference of Active Forces on February 19 1990 (the events that led to this were triggered by student protest in January 1989), the 488 conferees soon declared themselves sovereign, suspended the republic's constitution, dissolved the national assembly and created the post of prime minister. This likely scenario is one of the reasons why it seemed rather odd that someone representing the President would use the occasion to propose a vehicle that could unravel the presidency.

My personal opinion is that rather than a SNC, which could well become a platform for grandstanding and trading blames, the various political parties could be encouraged to articulate their positions on some of the issues the SNC proposes to resolve and then use such as part of their bases for canvassing for support. This could then become a basis for distinguishing one party from the other. This is why I believe that the PDP's zoning arrangement – as imperfect as it is and as pedestrian as the party has been in governing the country in many respects - is a major effort in this direction. I believe that the party should have the courage of its conviction to debate and refine that policy. Parties that say they are opposed to zoning and similar interim arrangements in the nation-building process could come with competing options. And since it seems that votes are beginning to count in this country, the ultimate decision on which direction the country should go will then be left directly for the citizens to decide rather than self-serving conferees under a SNC.

There is often an erroneous assumption that once the problems of inter-ethnic and inter-regional relations are resolved, the 'national question' will also have been resolved. My personal opinion is that the contentious issues that play out at the national level also find expressions at the regional and state levels. In some states or geopolitical zones for instance the contradictions among the various sub-national, sub-ethnic and special interests are more virulent than you find at the national level. This is why I believe that at both the national and state levels, we should have bicameral legislatures, with one chamber emphasising the equality of states or local governments (at the state level) and the other chamber, with about 50 percent of the members appointed, aggregating the various special interests and contending forces. The two chambers should serve as checks and balances to ensure that vital and special interests are taken into considerations in making laws that affect the country or the state. But will a bicameral legislature not further bloat the cost of governance? I have elsewhere called for the collapse of the current 36 state structure into about 18, three from each geopolitical zone. My personal opinion is that the Constitutional requirement that each state shall produce three Senators and a certain number of members of the House of Representatives based on population is actually responsible for bloating the size of the national assemblies. Reducing the number of states in the federation will therefore automatically reduce the number of Senators and Members of the House of Representatives. I also feel that apart from the principal officers of the legislatures, legislative work should be part-time, with legislators paid only a sitting allowance.

Daily Trust, 2 June 2011

CHAPTER 56

POLITICAL PROTESTS, PROTEST POLICING AND OTHER MATTERS

The tragedy which attended the nationwide strike against the 'ambush' removal of subsidies on premium petroleum products raises fundamental questions about the relationship between political protests and protest policing in a democracy. According to the organised labour, at least eight people were killed by the police on the first day of the strike on Monday January 9. The strike had grounded some states and cities to a halt.

The right for organised protest in a democracy, while not absolute anywhere in the world, is generally seen as a manifestation of three important fundamental human rights - the right of assembly, the right to freedom of association and the right to freedom of speech. In fact the International Covenant on Civil and Political Rights – a multilateral treaty adopted by the United Nations General Assembly on December 16 1966 and which came into force on March 23 1976 - commits its parties to respect the political and civil rights of individuals, including the three aforementioned rights. Although Articles 20 and 21 allow states to restrict these freedoms 'in the interests of national security or public safety, public order, the protection of public health or morals or the protection of the rights and freedoms of others', in mature democracies such prohibitions are rarely applied unless they can pass the 'clear and imminent danger' test. This means that the burden is on the state to prove that without such a prohibition, there will be a 'clear and imminent danger' to the society. It is also often believed that suppressing popular discontents will drive them underground, making them politically more dangerous. In this sense the attempt by the government to use the courts to stop the protest against the removal of subsidies could be seen as a form of censorship and therefore a threat to our democracy.

Political protests tend to be a coalition of various interests. This means that in the current protest while the rallying issue is the removal of subsidies on premium petroleum products, it should also be expected that the protest would naturally attract other interests - from opposition political elements who will gladly use any opportunity to push for regime change to those who merely want the regime to grant the public minor concessions. For this, the goal of a political protest can quickly change depending on which faction in the protest coalition gains ascendancy, the duration of the protests and how the regime handles it.

This is where the issue of protest policing comes in. Methods used by the police in quelling a riot could be counterproductive in managing political protests in a democracy and could in fact play into the hands of the political opposition faction of the protest rally. For instance police brutality against those protesting against the removal of subsidies will very readily attract the attention and sympathy of human rights activists, which could broaden the base of the protest or even change its goal. The Daily Trust of January 10 2012 reported that organised labour has lodged a formal complaint at the International Criminal Court against President Jonathan and Inspector General of Police Hafiz Ringim for the murder of the protesters. The government, in what is clearly damage control announced that the DPO who killed a protester in Lagos would face murder charges. The Lagos State Commissioner of police Mr. Yakubu Alkali was quoted by ThisDay of January 10 2012 as saying: "I did not send him or others to kill innocent Nigerians and since he has flagrantly disobeyed, he has to face the law" This should be a lesson to other overzealous police officers but also raises questions about how well trained the police are for protest policing.

Other matters

There are several other issues that the current protests against the removal of fuel subsidies have raised:

One, in my column of December 1 2011, I drew attention to the re-invention of Jonathan as a man of conviction – from his pre-April 2011 persona of a 'weak' gentleman who did not mind changing his mind several times on an issue. I noted that one of the dangers of the new persona is that as he gets away with one tough decision after another, he may be carried away into thinking he can get away with virtually any decision, irrespective of the feeling of the public on the issue. It is true that leadership is not a popularity contest and that effective leadership does not necessarily mean following the diktat of public opinion. In a democracy however, a leader does not stick it to the face of the general public that it is going against the popular will. This is part of the anger of the protesters against the government, which pretended it was 'consulting' stakeholders, only to spring a surprise on them even while the 'consultation' was still going on. Smart political leaders contrive ways to make their decisions seem to be the popular will. It is the difference between a democracy and a dictatorship.

Two, if popular protests lead to President Jonathan reversing himself on the removal of the subsidies, then his new persona as someone who can take tough decisions and stand by them would have taken a heavy pummelling. Such a reversal will also portray the President as someone who does not think through his decisions before taking them. On the other hand, if he clings stubbornly to the image of a resolute president while the protests persist and are sustained over a number of days, the regime could become embroiled in such a legitimacy crisis that no option could be ruled out. I believe the key challenge for the President's handlers at this point is how to contrive a good 'soft landing' that will not exacerbate the crisis of trust that seems to have engulfed his regime.

Three, while the Boko Haram challenge has been one of the issues that make people question President Jonathan's competence as the chief security officer of the country, paradoxically the sect is also his bulwark against the protests bringing down his government in popular anger. This is because each time Boko Haram – or group acting in its name – claims responsibility for any gory attack that injures or kills innocent people, sensitive ethnic, regional and religious nerves are touched. In such a situation, a knife is thrust in the pan-Nigeria consciousness needed to sustainably oppose policies that are seen to be inimical to the public interest.

Four, when the fuel subsidy dust has settled, there is likely to be a re-evaluation of some 'radicals' and 'activists' who made their names from opposing 'unpopular' government policies only to now commit 'class suicide' by allying with the government against the people on the issue of fuel subsidy removal – usually disguising their somersault under a grandiloquent rhetoric. Those to be 'demoted' to the rank of 'ex-radicals' will most likely include the CBN Governor Sanusi Lamido Sanusi and Governor Adams Oshiomhole of Edo State. Depending on how the issue is resolved the government may also sacrifice some of the regime's most powerful advocates of removing fuel subsidy as a way of rebuilding trust with the public.

Five, the more the government tries to justify the de-subsidisation move, the more unconvincing it sounds. One of the ridiculous mantras is that the government wants to move from a regime of subsidising consumption to that of subsidising production. Forgotten is that the distinction between subsidising consumption and subsidising production is very blurred. For instance if a company decides to subsidise meals for its employees by paying say 50 percent of the cost of each meal directly to the caterer, the subsidy will enable more staff to buy the food (consumption) but will also help the catering company to maintain an artificially high level of sales (production). A similar effect will be achieved if the company decides to directly pay 50 percent of the cost of the caterer's purchase of raw foods to enable it sell its meals at lower price. There is therefore something that does not add up in the mantra about subsidy removal being aimed at ending the subsidisation of consumption.

It is also interesting that these days the purported money to be saved from the de-subsidisation is being presented as the magic elixir for all our development challenges. The savings, we are told, will not only provide rail transport, roads, and healthcare facilities and build refineries but will also solve the problem of high mortality rate for pregnant women. Yes, it may even help men and women looking for life partners to get one! The sad thing is that these rationalisations have a familiar ring to the el Dorado we were promised during the campaign for debt cancellations or debt forgiveness for many African countries. Am I the only one who has not noticed what difference that debt cancellation or payoff has made?

Daily Trust 12 January 2012

CHAPTER 57

REVOLUTION AND NIGERIA'S 'ECONOMY OF AFFECTION'

In a very influential work, *Beyond Ujamaa in Tanzania: Underdevelopment and the Uncaptured Peasantry* (1980), Swedish-American political scientist Goran Hyden argued that African small cultivators prioritise their informal support networks such as familial and ethnic obligations over the pursuit of profit. For Hyden, African peasants are trapped in subsistence production because the 'economy of affection', which is their comfort zone, will not allow them to engage in economically rational pursuits. The latter, according to him, means that the peasants remain largely 'uncaptured' by state and capital. Those who believe that the type of revolution that is currently sweeping through the Middle East and the Maghreb regions cannot happen in Nigerian have relied on a variant of the 'economy of affection' argument – namely that the country's ethnic, religious and other primordial fault lines are so deep that Nigerians are unlikely to rise above their sentimental attachments to these cleavages for a concerted revolutionary action. But is this argument correct? Several observations could be made:

One, those who argue that a Middle East type of revolution is impossible in Nigeria appear to underestimate the power of contagion or domino effect. When, after the Second World War, Macmillan's 'wind of change' triggered a wave of anti-colonial movements in Africa; did this wind not also sweep through Nigeria despite the existence and politicisation of the current fault lines? When Gorbachev's perestroika and glasnost triggered a chain of events that culminated in the fall of the Berlin wall and unleashed a wave of democratisation forces across Eastern Europe and Africa, did ethnic, religious and other cleavages prevent this from snowballing into the National Conference in Benin Republic (February 19-28, 1990), which forced President Kérékou to turn over effective power to a transitional government? And did our primordial cleavages prevent the democracy wind from blowing through Nigeria and other African countries?

Two, it can in fact be argued that two 'revolutions' have already succeeded in Nigeria. The first was when General Ibrahim Babangida annulled the June 12 1993 elections won by Moshood Abiola. The annulment aroused popular anger, which snowballed into an organised resistance that eventually led to Babangida 'stepping aside'. An interim government headed by Ernest Shonekan could not dowse the resistance. Even when General Abacha took over in a military coup, the resistance, which was well co-ordinated, continued. After the death of Abacha the political transition programme that followed was designed in such a way as to pacify the leadership of the resistance, which had succeeded in making the country ungovernable.

Another instance of a successful demonstration of people's power was when the late Umaru Musa Yaradua became terminally ill and a 'cabal' held the nation hostage. People's power, typified by the activities of internet bloggers and protests by civil society groups helped to pile pressure on the legislature to embrace the doctrine of necessity, which in turn paved the way for the then Vice President Goodluck Jonathan to become the Acting President.

Three, it may be necessary to interrogate why the above two instances of relatively mild revolutions succeeded – despite our deep rooted ethnic and religious cleavages. My personal opinion is that the success of the 'revolution' against the annulment of the June 12 1993 election was principally because it was led by a faction of the Yoruba elite, which was Conscious, Cohesive and Conspiratorial but which carefully ensured that a cross –section of Nigerians were co-opted into the resistance. The 'revolution' was largely waged under the banner of the struggle for democracy even though it was a largely Yoruba-led struggle against perceived injustice. In the revolution against the 'cabal' Jonathan's humble public persona and the victimhood storyline were used to galvanise sympathy for him, especially among people from the South and the South South who were subtly made to believe that the 'cabal' equated to the 'core North'. At the same time, there were careful attempts to prevent the 'silent revolution' from being hijacked by ethnic champions by making prominent Northerners such as Bala Mohammed as the arrowheads of the pro-Jonathan group. My belief is that if these two mild 'revolutions' could succeed, there is no reason why a more radical revolution cannot succeed here. It will seem that for a revolution to succeed in Nigeria, its leaders must be politically astute enough to anticipate the moves of the ethnic/religious arithmeticians and take measures to pre-empt their moves. Again, if, as generally believed, frustration is a general trigger for a revolution, then the generalised frustration among ordinary Nigerians will suggest that unless something is done to change the direction the country is going; a radical revolution cannot be ruled out, especially when the avenues for ventilating pent-up frustrations are increasingly being foreclosed.

Four, an important reminder from the Middle East revolutions is that the strategic interests of the West drive their relations with countries. An ally who is about to be consumed by people's anger will be very readily sacrificed, and indeed branded a 'dictator' so as to appear to be on the side of the people, and more crucially play a key role in choosing the new set of leaders after the revolutionary flourishes. From Gobarchev through Mubarak the philosophy appears to remain unchanged.

Five, though radical revolution may be useful in overthrowing regimes when peaceful options are denied, it remains debatable whether a revolution is really worth the trouble - apart from its cathartic function of being used to ventilate pent-up frustrations. Consider for instance the American War of Independence (1775-1783), which was spurred by a noble protest against taxation without representation. Though America's victory helped to spread a belief in the principles of republicanism, it also sharply polarised the country and subsequently led to a bitter civil war. Some critics today argue that looking at how America has shaped up since independence in terms of education, freedom of expression and quality of life, it is not substantially different from Canada, Australia and New Zealand, which did not follow such a revolutionary path. There was also the French Revolution (1789–1799), which was fought primarily to overthrow absolute monarchy with its feudal privileges for the aristocracy and Catholic clergy. The revolution, fought under the noble ideals of 'freedom, equality and fraternity', quickly became a caricature under Robespierre and his Reign of Terror. Not only did the revolution fail to give France a representative government by the people, or prevent a rapid return to autocratic rule, 'revolutionary' France also fought the most savage of all wars in the 1790s to preserve slavery in Santo Domingo (present-day Haiti and Dominican Republic). Consider equally the Iranian revolution that toppled the rule of Mohammed Reza Shah more than 30 years ago. The revolution ushered a period of unprecedented hostility to the West and helped to radicalise the Middle East. Almost overnight, the West's most steadfast ally in the Muslim world became a violent and volatile enemy.

It is in fact precisely because of the uncertainty of the order that will be created after the revolutionary flourishes that many people continue to urge governments not to make peaceful change impossible.

CHAPTER 58

LESSONS FROM NIGERIA'S 'PAW-PAW REVOLUTION'

T he recent street protests and labour strike over the removal of fuel subsidies, which literally shut down the country for one week, is the closest to a revolution the country has had in modern times - if we define a revolution as a change in the configuration of power relations between the political establishment and the people in favour of the latter. For the one week it effectively lasted, it was a triumph of people's power, with the leadership of organised labour and its allied civil society groups successfully mobilising and framing the 'struggle' as a simple matter of people versus state and capital. There are several lessons from the one week revolution that nearly changed the country:

One, is that it has partly answered the lingering question of whether a 'proper revolution', *a la* Arab Spring, is possible here. I have always taken the position that those arguing that such is not possible in the country underestimate the power of globalisation and the domino effects of events in other parts of the world. For instance when, after the Second World War, Harold Macmillan's 'wind of change' triggered a chain of anti-colonial movements in Africa, was Nigeria spared despite the existence and politicisation of our current fault lines? When Gorbachev's *perestroika* and *glasnost* in the former USSR triggered a chain of events that culminated in the fall of the Berlin wall and the unleashing of a wave of re-democratisation forces from Eastern Europe to Africa, was Nigeria spared despite the persistence of our traditional fault lines? Is it not instructive that many of the protesters even appropriated the vocabulary of the protest groups in the West, hence we had various 'Occupy Nigeria' rallies from London to Toronto and from New York to Hamburg competing to lend their support to the protesters at home?

For the time the 'revolution' lasted, the protesters – from Ibadan to Akure and from Kaduna to Kano - submerged their primordial identities to the larger contradiction of a collective struggle against perceived state callousness, if not wickedness. It was a telling sign that under the right leadership and conditions, a Nigeria-nation will be a viable project.

Two, part of the answer of whether a proper revolution is possible here is also an examination of the efforts to counter the protests, using a combination of state coercion and mobilisation of primordial identities. Such should always be expected in our type of society and was perhaps what those who expected the revolt to fizzle out within a day or two counted on. There were various efforts to portray the protesters as people trying to bring down the government of Jonathan 'because he is from the South South'. How did the leaders of the protest movements counter the expected state response and counter-mobilisation? What were their strategies for sustaining the people's anger – a key ingredient in sustaining the protest? Utilising the power of the new social media, supporters of the protest constantly released information that fed people's anger against the state and its functionaries: hyped reports of President Jonathan's N1 billion budget for feeding, Ngozi Iweala's alleged purchase of N1.2bn mansion in Maitama, Abuja, Justice Minister Adoke Mohammed's several bulging bank accounts. After about a week of shutting down the country, many people began to yearn for life to return to 'normal', especially given the government's symbolic climb down when it reduced the price of fuel from N141 per litre to N97 per litre. It is true that the protesters did not achieve their declared aim of forcing the government to reduce the price to N65 per litre. What was proven was that Nigerians could close ranks to sustain a protest against unpopular policies. Our primordial identities and other contradictions may not disappear but they can be submerged to a higher cause. This is an important lesson the leaders of this country must take to heart. The protesters and a faction of the protest movement interested in regime change must have also absorbed that lesson.

Three, the street protests were muted in the South East, Bayelsa state and other South South states. During that period President Jonathan wore Igbo caps in a number of his public appearances. These have raised questions of whether the protests portend a shift in the traditional pattern of political alliances in the country? Traditionally the South East and the South South are bastions of support for the political North in the South. In fact until recently the political North seems to take such support for granted. With the street protests more successful in the South West and the North, not a few people are asking whether a putative alliance between the South West and the political North is in the offing?

There are perhaps several reasons why the protests are muted in the South East:

Because of their diasporic nature, most of the non-Northern victims of the Boko Haram attacks in the North were Igbos, giving an impression that the Igbos were specially targeted. One blogger who defended the muted nature of the street protests in the South East asked rhetorically: 'when they were killing the Igbos in the North why didn't they come out for a mass protest?' Another possible explanation is that there is a preponderance of traders in the South East and street protests on issues that do not specifically target traders, is unlikely. Additionally the political leadership of the South East tends to have this theory that the goat should follow the man with the palm fronds. Thus during the Yaradua regime when a group of self-serving cabal held the country hostage, the Governors of the area – just like most of the State Governors - supported the cabal against Jonathan; today they are with Jonathan against the protesters – just like many other State Governors. The Governors of the area actively discouraged the street protests.

Four, the political North and the South East are becoming increasingly alike in the way they frame the narratives of their quest to produce the president of the country in 2015 – if the position is vacant: while the Igbos cry marginalisation and remind anyone who cares to listen that it is the only major ethnic group in the country not to have produced the President of the country (apart from the brief Ironsi regime,(January –July 1966), some from the North appear to rely on the politics of 'entitlement'. The latter derives from two sources: The first is a belief that the South West dominates the corporate life of the country, the Igbos the commercial life and therefore the North needs political power to ensure they are not totally dominated. The second is a belief that going by the PDP's zoning and power rotation agreement, the North ought to have been allowed to serve out Yaradua's entitlement of two terms of four years each.

A crucial question is how the removal of the subsidies and the subsequent street protests will affect how political discourses are framed by the various contending politicians and political zones. I had argued elsewhere that with the removal of the subsidies, the Jonathan administration has taken a high risk manoeuvre that will make it either a phenomenal success or a monumental failure. Either way, it is likely to make zoning, politics of entitlement and cries of marginalisation anachronistic as strategies for capturing the ultimate political prize. Politicians and geopolitical zones who desire to capture the presidency will be be forced to go back to the drawing boards and develop new narratives and storylines.

What appears to be clear is that whoever succeeds Jonathan in 2015 – if his position becomes vacant – will be determined by the balance of political forces and the political choices the various geopolitical zones make to win the trust of the other zones. Since democracy is never about choosing the most competent but the most acceptable, candidates that are most likely to allay inter-ethnic suspicions, will always be preferred to candidates marketed solely on the basis of their competence or incorruptibility. Also historically candidates with cult following in their geopolitical zones do not do well in other political zones. In fact part of the reasons for Obasanjo's national acceptance in 1999 and in fact a major reason for his claim to being a nationalist remains his difficulties with his Yoruba political base.

Daily Trust 19 January 2012

CHAPTER 59

NIGERIA @51: HAS THIS HOUSE REALLY FALLEN?

When Karl Maier published his book *This House Has Fallen: Midnight in Nigeria* (2000), I was probably among the first people given an advance copy of the book a few months before it was formally published. I was at that time the Books Review Editor of the London-based monthly magazine, *Africa Today*. Maier, a former correspondent for the London daily, *Independent,* called a few times to ask my opinion of the book, before I got to review it. I was unequivocal that some aspects appeared contrived and unbelievable and subsequently did what could be regarded as a 'negative review' of it. To his credit, this did not stop him from inviting me to a party he held for his girl friend, which turned out to be just another opportunity for a healthy disagreement on several aspects of the book.

Maier's book appeared to me at that time to be more popular for its prophetic and catchy, if depressing title, than for any rigorous analysis of the Nigerian condition. Accepted, he interviewed several shakers and movers of the society. I felt however that like most reportages and travel writings, in several instances he elevated the institutional manifestations of a phenomenon to its defining characteristics, thereby missing the point. I also accused him of peppering his reportages to enthral his publishers and the British reading public.

Barely a year after relocating to the country, I am beginning to feel I was perhaps unfairly touchy about Maier's book. I left the country as a young adult and was away for only twenty years. Maier was only a correspondent and his referents were the worlds he grew up in and knows well – USA and UK. Perhaps my reaction to the book in the UK was typical of the way most people would react if a non-family member told them that their mother's 'soup' tasted awful. In hindsight, Maier's book was perhaps the way outsiders would interpret our country: one chunk of chaos that was destined to implode at some point. These days people are bandying around Karl Maier's book as despondency holds the nation captive.

In October 2003, some three years after Maier's doomsday book was published, a survey of more than 65 countries published by the UK's *New Scientist* magazine suggested that the happiest people in the world live in Nigeria. Nigeria had not imploded; rather it inhabited the happiest people on earth, according to the survey. We flaunted the results of this survey – directly where we could and by innuendo where etiquette would frown at such. We were unconcerned about the 'scientificness' of the survey and very few of us took issues with the *New Scientist* that had published that survey.

Karl Maier and the *New Scientist's* 2003 survey on happiness in many ways mirror the contradictory relationship many Nigerians have with the Nigeria project. While faith in the Nigeria project seems to have declined when Gaddaffi suggested that Nigeria should be balkanised along its most obvious fault lines, most Nigerians, even those that have represented centrifugal tendencies, jumped on him. This for me suggests that despite the consensus that most of the constituent units of the country are unhappy at the contrived marriage, we seem to have become so used to one another that, like most dysfunctional marriages, we bicker and threaten divorce all the time and at the same time paralysed by fear of what would be our fates if the divorce option is pursued conclusively.

For me, it appears obvious that Nigerians need a forum where the basis of the marriage should be renegotiated. And a continued resistance to this, when things are obviously not going in the right direction in the country, stiffens the challenge to the current arrangement. I am not for a 'Sovereign' National Conference, which, knowing the Nigerian temperament, will easily be turned into a forum where a vocal minority will tyrannize the rest and engage in all sorts of unhelpful shenanigans and grandstanding. We may need something along the lines of a Constituent Assembly where all critical stakeholders are represented, and no subject is declared off limits. In fact declaring any subject off limit, such as any discussion of the break-up of Nigeria, drives such an idea underground, glamorising it in the process. In such a forum to renegotiate the Nigeria project, every idea must be allowed to compete freely in the political marketplace of ideas.

My gut feeling is that most Nigerians will feel diminished if the country were to be dismembered. It appears that most Nigerians simply want a greater devolution of power from the centre to the federating units such that local peculiarities will be preserved and allowed to blossom within the Nigeria project. Curiously, while popular sentiments is for 'true federalism' quite a number of the actions of the federal government, including the proposed constitutional amendments, will invariably push the country towards greater centralisation. The proposed constitutional amendments even included the creation of more states – at a time most of the existing ones are economically unviable and popular sentiments are towards collapsing existing ones to a more manageable number to save the cost of governance. Such a forum to renegotiate Nigeria must also take a critical look at the current system of revenue allocation just as it has to consider the possibility of state/zonal police.

I believe that beneath the façade of 'happiness' exuded by many Nigerians is the stark reality that for an overwhelming majority of the populace, life is truly nasty, brutish and short. At 51, it is true that the house has not fallen; it is however equally true that it has continued to leak badly and is becoming progressively inhabitable, with wobbly structures. At 51, we can no longer continue to skirt around issues when there is a pervasive existentialist crisis and a rapid withdrawal from the Nigeria project into primordial identities where people are trying to seek meaning for life. At 51, many increasingly see the Nigeria project as a hindrance to their self actualisation and therefore see the country as a legitimate target.

The crisis in our nation building project was brought to the fore by the selfish way a group of self-serving members of the late Yaradua's kitchen cabinet - otherwise known as the cabal - took the nation for a ride during the last days of the late President. The opportunity for a new beginning offered by the collective anger against the 'cabal' was sadly lost by the decision by Goodluck Jonathan to contest the April election. For some Nigerians therefore, Jonathan became just another hope betrayed. Regaining the trust of Nigerians should consequently be the number one priority of the president. I however honestly can't see how his idea of a-single term tenure of seven years for the President and Governors, which he continues to push despite contrary popular sentiments, can aid the rebuilding of trust.

War of the militias?

The *Tribune* of September 30 2011 reported that the Egbesu Mightier Fraternity has threatened to fight MEND to a standstill over the latter's threat to plant and detonate explosives within the vicinity of the Eagle Square on October 1 2011. In an email to the paper through its "European representative Mr Peter Timi" who claimed he was "mandated by the leader of the group, Mr Jomo Gbomo", to issue the statement, MEND said one of the reasons for planning the attack was "to express the displeasure of the group at the continued prosecution of the leaders of MEND, Henry and Charles Okah."

It should be recalled that MEND once threatened to bomb Kaduna just as Boko Haram had threatened to bomb Bayelsa State. Similarly both MASSOB and OPC had warned Boko Haram of possible retaliation if it bombed their respective enclaves. Can the threats and counter threats lead to peace through balance of fear? Or would it escalate to arms race, a full blown war among these outfits, which could become politicised with the possibility of a civil war, and the implosion of the country?

Daily Trust 6 Oct 2011

CHAPTER 60

PERVASIVE KIDNAPPING IN NIGERIA: SYMPTOM OF A FAILING STATE?

Kidnapping, the taking away of a person against the person's will, usually for ransom or in furtherance of another crime, is becoming everyone's nightmare in our dear country. Daily, we read nightmarish stories of people being abducted as they go about their daily business. A criminal act, which first attracted national attention on 26 February 2006 when Niger Delta militants kidnapped foreign oil workers to press home their demand, kidnapping has since become ubiquitous and commercialised. It has spread from the Niger Delta to virtually all nooks and crannies of the country, with some states of course being hotspots. Similarly victims have changed from being predominantly foreign oil workers to Nigerians, including parents, grand parents, and toddlers and about anyone who has a relative that could be blackmailed into coughing out a ransom. Those behind the recent wave of the despicable act have also changed from being exclusively Niger Delta militants to dodgy elements from different walks of life - armed robbers, unemployed, professional 419ers, and at least one Catholic priest

There is no doubt that Nigeria is today one of the major kidnapping capitals of the world. This has obvious implications for investments, the country's development trajectory and even the quality of governance.

The common tendency is to blame the pervasive wave of kidnapping outside the Niger Delta exclusively on the unacceptable rate of unemployment in the country, an inefficient and corrupt police force that is ill-equipped to fight crime, and collusion between kidnappers and politicians. These factors however appear to be mere symptoms of a larger malaise, namely that pervasive kidnapping, is one of the major symptoms of both 'failed' and 'failing' states. Most of the countries where kidnapping have been pervasive have been either failed or failing states – Baghdad after the 2003 invasion of Iraq, Columbia from the 1970s until about 2001, and Mexico between 2003 and 2007.

A 'failed state' is often used to designate a state, which has become incapable of fulfilling the basic functions of a sovereign government. These functions include physical control of its territory, provision of security of life and property for its citizens, the monopoly of the use of legitimate physical force and ability to provide reasonable public services or to interact with other states as a full member of the international community. A "failing state" on the other hand denotes a state in transition to a failed state. Here while the state remains nominally a sovereign and fulfils a modicum of the functions of a sovereign government, the central government has become so weak and ineffective that it has little practical control over much of its territory, leading to an upsurge in pervasive insecurity such as kidnapping, organised assassinations and robberies. A failing state is also characterised by a weakened ability to provide basic public services and widespread corruption as people think of themselves first, following the failure of the state to perform its traditional functions. Most of the countries in the developing world involved in civil wars or protracted internal conflicts could qualify as 'failing states'.

Following from the above, while Nigeria is not yet a 'failed state', it could arguably qualify as a 'failing state'. This in essence means that while addressing the problems of unemployment and inefficient and corrupt police force could be good palliative measures in combating kidnapping, any lasting solution to the menace will inevitably have to address the key question of the nature of the Nigerian state, including why it has transited from a weak state to a 'failing state' and rapidly gravitating towards being a failed state. I would recommend the following:

One, there is a need to restructure the Nigerian state to enthrone true federalism, including true fiscal federalism. Classically, federalism is regarded as a system of government in which the centre and the federating units are each, within a sphere, co-ordinate and equal. A true federalism cannot work in Nigeria under the present condition where the federating units are atomised into 36 unviable states, (with the possible exception of two or three states), which are dependent on the centre for their survival. Instituting true federalism will require merging the present unwieldy number of states into about six to make them manageable and cost efficient. The federating units should be allowed to run their own police force and to take measures they deem fit, within the law, to protect the citizens within their territory. Each federating unit ought to have a database of people living in its territory, including what such people do.

Two, the cost and efficiency gains from the consolidation of the present 39 state-structure could be channelled towards improved provision of public services and better quality of governance. A computerised national identity card scheme has become an imperative.

Three, states should invest in smart security, especially preventative security, which could involve phone tapping, extensive use of moles, and possible use of private armies and private military companies in protracted conflict areas. In this sense, the recent call by Governor Peter Obi of Anambra state that he would hold traditional rulers in the state in whose domain kidnapping takes place culpable, appears misplaced. Traditional rulers, especially in the Southeastern states, only have ornamental value and should therefore not be expected to be the chief security officers of their kingdoms. They are not paid security agents of the state, and should therefore not be expected to play the role of moles, which was never part of the duties of traditional rulers. There is however merit in the proposal that kidnapping should attract capital punishment.

Four, in the social contract theory that created the notion of sovereign (monarch or constituted national authority), a key argument is that prior to the creation of the sovereign, there was what the English political philosopher, Thomas Hobbes, called the 'state of nature'. This 'state of nature', he argued, was characterised by the 'war of all against all'. People agreed to the creation of this sovereign, and willingly gave up their right to self-help because they were very eager to escape the conditions in this 'state of nature' where life was 'short, nasty and brutish'. This is the underlying philosophy of the social contract between the government and the governed. It could therefore be argued that pervasive insecurity is a key manifestation of the breach of this social contract by the government. This raises an interesting question of whether citizens should continue to be bound by this social contract when one of the parties – the state- is increasingly failing to keep its own side of the bargain? A state becomes a failed state when citizens and groups conclude that they too should no longer be bound by the terms of the social contract. In this scenario, the Hobbesian state of nature reigns. Is Nigeria moving in this direction?

Daily Independent 18 June 2009

CHAPTER 61

EFCC'S CALL FOR SPECIAL COURT FOR FINANCIAL CRIMES

Almost from the time she became the boss of the financial crimes buster EFCC, Mrs Farida Waziri has been persistent in her calls for a special court to prosecute corruption cases. For instance speaking at a G-6 security summit organised by the FCT administration to expedite trial of criminal cases in Abuja on February 16 2011, Mrs Waziri reportedly explained that her demand for a special court is not borne out of lack of interest in the regular courts but to ensure "that corruption cases are not stalled endlessly in the regular courts in a way that may create the impression that the nation is not committed to the anti-graft war." She was further quoted as saying: "We have all identified corruption as our major problem and as such we all have to identify ways of tackling the problem. We have seen how the accused persons manipulate our procedural laws and criminal justice system to frustrate and prolong their trials and that is why we have come forth with the special court option as a way out."

I have serious issues with Mrs Waziri's repeated clamour for special corruption courts. The impression given is that if we can have a special court for corruption cases, the trial of suspects will be accelerated, leading concomitantly to higher convictions, which will then serve as deterrence to people who are contemplating engaging in corrupt practices. I think the premise on which this assumption is based is rather weak. If the rate of conviction could be sufficient deterrence to corruption, then we shouldn't be talking of corruption today because under the Buhari regime, most of the overthrown politicians were tried expeditiously and summarily convicted, with some bagging as many as 250 years. Abacha's Failed Banks Tribunals also pursued and dealt 'ruthlessly' with those implicated in shady deals that led to the collapse of banks. The quickness of the trials and the extremely high level of conviction however did not stem the growth in corrupt practices in the country just as the relative efficiency of the courts in the UK and the US in convicting and jailing drug barons has not stopped the trade in illicit drugs in those countries. Ideally the courts should be only one of the several tools for combating a social ailment as pervasive as corruption in Nigeria.

The impression one often gets is that Mrs Waziri has been struggling to get out of the shadow of Nuhu Ribadu, the pioneer Chairman of the

EFCC. It is a sort of 'Ribadu-envy' - a condition Governor Peter Obi of Anambra State also suffers from whenever his predecessor in office, Dr Chris Ngige, is mentioned. Though Nuhu Ribadu's method was unorthodox and certainly contributed in abridging our democratic space under Obasanjo, he was seen as a hero by some people, including some international organisations, who admired his 'courage' in harassing the high and the mighty. Ribadu often accused, tried and convicted his suspects in the media even before he had gathered sufficient evidence to charge them to court.

Mrs Waziri, who does not seem to have Ribadu's cantankerousness and 'courage', sometimes gives the impression that she has been underappreciated in her work because of these 'deficits'. She has tried, especially under Yaradua, to define herself as someone who believes in the rule of law, and who therefore should not be judged by the drama and methods used by her predecessor. The problem in defining herself in such a mould however is that she feels she needs a high level of conviction of the high and mighty by the courts to be seen as effective in her job. Ribadu did not need a high level of convictions by the courts to be seen as effective by some people because he had already secured such convictions through media trials before any case was sent to court. As Mrs Waziri confronts the fact that she has neither been convicting enough suspects in the media and courts of public opinion nor in the law courts, one senses a sort of desperation which issues either in strident calls for special courts for corruption cases or occasionally in trying to embrace the 'Ribadu method'. One of the fallouts from this is that a uniquely Mrs Waziri's approach to fighting corruption has not emerged even though her tenure is fast coming to an end.

I abhor the 'Ribadu method' just as I do not believe that emphasis on the number of people tried and convicted of corruption is necessarily an indication of one's effectiveness in the fight against corruption. How for instance does improving the rate of conviction of high-ranking politicians affect the police extortion of N20 at checkpoints, or examination malpractices by secondary school students or of the endemic corruption among the rank and file in the civil service? I am not against the demand for improved prosecution and conviction of those suspected of dipping their hands in the public till. The concern however is that it appears that many people are mistaking the tool for fighting corruption with a strategy for combating the menace.

There is an additional worrying danger in having special courts for corruption cases. With the line between the fight against corruption and political vendetta often blurred, and with our judges not being exactly insulated from the malaise, a special court for corruption will be a dangerous tool in the hands of contraptions such as the EFCC. Under a character like Nuhu Ribadu, the media prosecution, judgment and conviction of people the EFCC chooses to go after will be given a legal backing by such a special court. And under a chair person like Mrs Waziri who seem to believe that her perceived non-performance should be blamed on the courts, such a special court could also be deployed to quickly churn out conviction of suspects.

There is no evidence that special courts, even where the judges are relatively non-corrupt, will positively affect the war against corruption. In India where you have special courts, it has often led to a proliferation of the demand for more special courts – special courts for rape, special courts for spousal abuse cases, special courts for armed robbers etc. A proliferation of special courts will obviously undermine our regular courts.

Again assuming that Mrs Waziri is right that the fight against corruption is undermined by corruption cases being stalled in regular courts, wouldn't a better solution be to call for a reform of the judiciary such that the causes of such stalling are removed? Without reforming the regular courts to remove the sections of our law that unnecessarily cause the delay in the dispensation of justice, how will a special court for corruption cases for instance stop lawyers from applying for interlocutory injunctions or stay of execution of court judgments? And assuming the special courts are manned by non-corrupt judges, how will they help Mrs Waziri in cases where prosecutorial capacity is limited or evidence gathering is weak? The truth is that the slow machinery of justice in this country affects everyone, not just the fight against financial crime.

I believe that contraptions like the EFCC and the ICPC are unlikely to succeed in the war against corruption for as long as they continue to see the social ill as an issue of moral lapse rather than a manifestation of a more fundamental systemic crisis. This, coupled with the fact that those prosecuting the fight and those judging those being prosecuted are not believed to be free from the malaise, makes the 'war' unwinnable.

I believe that Nigerians will be more accommodating of the EFCC if it could show that the money it has recovered from corrupt people have been well utilised. For instance Mrs Waziri claimed that since coming into office in 2008, the EFCC has instituted about 70 cases and recovered more than $11 billion. This is a huge sum of money and Nigerians will like to know how it was spent. I would love to see the EFCC clamour to be given powers to deploy money saved from corruption to some projects such as creating employment or providing electricity in identified areas.

By monitoring the use of resources in such projects and ensuring their success, the EFCC will practically demonstrate what could be accomplished if corruption is reduced to the barest minimum.

Daily Trust, 27 Oct 2011

CHAPTER 62

CORRUPTION: TIME FOR GENERAL AMNESTY?

The fight against corruption – the abuse of public office by officials – predates Nigeria's independence and has always been embroiled in politics. Corruption was thought to be so pervasive in the First Republic that anger against the malaise partly triggered the first military coup of January 1966. Every subsequent regime in the country has made fighting the cankerworm a key policy.

The intertwining of the fight against corruption with political witch-hunting is rooted in the country's political history. For instance one of the earliest attempts to use charges of corruption to smear political opponents was in 1946 after the NCNC raised £13,000 from its well publicised tour of the provinces (April 1946 to December 1946) to send a delegation of seven people to London to protest against the Richard's Constitution, and its 'four obnoxious ordinances'. The delegation, which was led by Dr Nnamdi Azikiwe and included Mrs Funmilayo Ransome Kuti and Mallam Buka Dipcharima, left for London in June 1947 and returned two months later. Though it was welcomed by an enthusiastic crowd of over 100,000, the initial euphoria was quickly overshadowed by insinuations of corruption. The Governor-General of the time, Sir Arthur Richards, had never hidden his displeasure at Zik's brand of radical nationalism. In July 1945 for instance the colonial regime banned Zik's two Lagos dailies, West African Pilot and Daily Comet, for 'misrepresenting facts relating to the 1945 labour strike' – a move that eventually led to Zik writing his 'Last Testament' and claiming plots to assassinate him. But to what extent were insinuations of corruption and wasteful spending part of the government's efforts to tarnish Zik and the NCNC? It is instructive that the government-owned Daily Times, in its editorial of August 15, 1947, led the charge: "We would like to remind the delegation that what has been achieved could have been obtained in Nigeria by airmail at the very modest cost of one shilling, whereas the delegation has been ever so expensive. If therefore this is the sort of unthinking and wasteful leadership being thrust on us, we will have none of it". The rival Nigerian Youth Movement gladly made political capital out of this.

The blurring of the boundary between the fight against corruption and political vendetta has become a feature of every civilian dispensation in the country. For instance though both the Foster-Sutton Tribunal and the Coker Commission found Zik and Awolowo respectively guilty of corruption, everyone knew that politics intruded in their findings. In the same vein, could Bode George, a strong Obasanjo ally, have been convicted of corruption under the regime of Obasanjo? If the cabal around Yaradua had emerged victorious in their battle of wits with supporters of Goodluck Jonathan, would Vincent Ogbulafor have been made to face corruption charges over allegations that he had purportedly already been cleared of a decade ago? Could the federal government have withdrawn the charges against Nuhu Ribadu, including allegations that he sold confiscated properties to fictitious companies, if Yaradua had remained the President? Would the EFCC have been mandated to bring Ibori dead or alive if Yaradua had remained the President? What role did vendetta play in Obasanjo's celebrated pursuit of the 'Abacha loot'?

There are additional reasons for recommending a general amnesty programme:

One, the current system of fighting corruption is very distractive. Virtually everyone who has ever occupied a public position has one corruption allegation against him or her and even those convicted by competent courts of law believe they are victims of political persecution. You could be convicted today and your conviction quashed with the change of a regime. On the other hand, being cleared of corruption charge today does not mean that you may not be re-tried of the same offence tomorrow.

Two, despite the setting up of high profile contraptions like the EFCC and turning some of their key personnel into celebrities, there is no evidence that the fight against the malaise is being won. It is a mistake to equate the humiliation of some politicians with progress in the fight against corruption. A true measure of effectiveness is the extent to which any measure helps to reduce corruption or serve as deterrence to others. Telling us how much was recovered from corrupt individuals is also not a sign of progress especially when the alleged recovered loot has not made any difference in the material circumstances of the people or can even be properly accounted for.

Three, countries all over the world have used amnesty programmes to deal with problems that appear intractable. In 2004 for instance, George W Bush enacted tax amnesty programme, which allowed US corporations to bring home, tax-free, the billions of dollars they stashed away in tax havens. The US also routinely offers amnesty to illegal immigrants who met certain conditions. Similarly, the Italian government in October 2009 launched a tax-amnesty plan, the third in the past eight years, which allowed Italians to repatriate funds deposited in tax havens. In 2006, the government of Colombia granted amnesty to some 21,000 paramilitaries linked to drug cartels. In South Africa, the Truth and Reconciliation

Commission offered amnesty to people who confessed and apologised for crimes committed under apartheid. Just before he became gravely ill and subsequently died, Yaradua also offered amnesty to militants of the Niger Delta in exchange for their laying down their guns. These instances suggest that there is a history of granting amnesty to people who have broken the law, including people who have committed murders, in exchange for everlasting peace or to ensure a new beginning. The proposed amnesty shall be one-off, and shall extend to drug barons and those accused of advanced fee fraud because their crimes are no worse than the crime of those who have benefited from amnesty here or in other countries. The amnesty shall of course be predicated by certain conditions. Four, an amnesty programme will encourage the repatriation of much needed funds hidden in different parts of the world to help accelerate the economy. People repatriating money shall not be questioned on the source of their money but shall forfeit a certain percentage to the state, which shall be managed as trust fund solely for employment generation and combating the problem electricity. Five, to ensure a complete separation between vendetta and a future fight against corruption, a special corruption tribunal shall be set up to speedily and transparently try corruption cases. Those found to have maliciously accused others of corruption shall be made to pay both reparative and punitive damages to deter others from wilfully damaging others' reputations. Six, a future fight against corruption shall recognise it as a systemic problem rather than an issue of moral laxity, which appears to underlie the philosophy of the current strategy used in the fight against the malaise. For instance a future strategy must pose the question of the extent to which aspects of our culture such as gift giving, glorification of materialism and unbridled display of affluence facilitate corruption. It should also recognise that it is just not a problem that is exclusive to the political class but something that is pervasive. For instance, is the policeman who asks for N100 bribe better than the politician who steals N10bn? Is the social critic who corners the funds donated by some foreign agencies better than the politician he constantly riles against? Is the lecturer who demands money or sexual favours to pass an undeserving student any better than a corrupt politician?

Nigeria needs to re-think the fight against corruption, and a general amnesty programme could offer the needed break with the unproductive, selective justice and vendetta-driven strategies of the past.

Daily Indpendent, 12 March 2009

CHAPTER 63

BETWEEN FREEDOM OF INFORMATION AND WITCH-HUNT

The recent call by Nobel laureate Professor Wole Soyinka for President Goodluck Jonathan to test the workability of the recently passed Freedom of Information (FoI) Act generated deserved headlines. Speaking at the Newspaper Proprietors' Association of Nigeria (NPAN) Town Hall Meeting on the FoI Act at the MUSON Centre,Lagos, Soyinka reportedly said: "It is not enough for the government to conceal issues of public interest. There is need to put FoI Act to test. One human being was concealed for months and came back to the country and was concealed in the night with the lights put off." (ThisDay, July 22 2011). A little disclosure here may not be out of place: I am one of the admirers of Wole Soyinka's creative genius. I also admire his outspokenness. Spanish writer Camilo José Cela, who won the 1989 Nobel Prize in literature, once said that a writer should be a denunciation of the times in which he or she lives. Soyinka personifies that dictum. Quite often Soyinka's voice is one of courage, of speaking truth to power, even if his prognoses for identified problems rarely rise above romantic idealisms or mere stringing of flowering phrases whose values start and end with enriching one's repertoire of quotable quotes. Professor Wole Soyinka was right when he implied that the activities of some members of the late Umaru Yaradua's kitchen cabinet– those that came to be labelled as the 'cabal' in Yaradua's last days - were deplorable. I will however respectfully disagree with him that the Freedom of Information Act should be used to find how they smuggled a dying Yaradua from Saudi Arabia to the country, at an inhuman time of the night, with lights switched off, and without the knowledge of the then Acting President Goodluck Jonathan. My personal opinion is that to embark on such 'inquiry' will not only be a needless distraction but could also be a misuse of the FoI Act, if not an outright witch-hunt. Given the current crisis in our nation-building project, it will amount to doing the right thing at the wrong time. As we all know, doing the right thing at the wrong time is the wrong thing to do.

True, the public has a right to know what really happened during those dark days. This is the whole notion of 'public interest', a key requirement not only in leaning on the FoI Act to request for information from public bodies but also a veritable defence by media houses against invasion of privacy or defamation proceedings. But what is 'public interest' (also known as 'common well-being', the 'common good' or the 'general welfare') is not always clear-cut, especially given the increasing diversity of most societies, not just in class terms, but also in racial, sociological, cultural and regional terms. I do not believe that what is in the interest of the majority constitutes 'public interest', especially when it is remembered that the whole notion of human rights is based on protecting the individual from the tyranny of the majority. Democracies also recognise the need to protect the minorities from the tyranny of the majority. So it is not clear-cut that the interests which the 'cabal' purported to represent do not deserve protection or form 'public interest' to a section of the population. Additionally, 'public interest' is usually balanced with other values – privacy, reputation and national security concerns. In our type of societies, there are certain types of information, which the public has a right to know, but which, if brought into the public domain at the wrong time, could exacerbate the crisis of the nation state. Therefore public interest – whatever its purveyor takes it to mean - must also be balanced against the imperative of inter-ethnic/regional harmony. Because President Jonathan, as the Vice President, was on the receiving end of the activities of the 'cabal', any attempt to use the FOI Act to bring into the public domain the activities of the 'cabal' in the dying days of Yaradua could expose him to charges of witch-hunt or being actuated by express malice.

There is also the issue of common sense. With the last PDP's acrimonious presidential primaries and the events they spewed as well as the politicisation of the Boko Haram menace, it may be safe to argue that we are facing the worst crisis in our nation-building project since the end of the Civil war in 1970. In a situation like this, my personal opinion is that emphasis should be on healing the wounds and pacifying various aggrieved factions of the elites – and not doing the right thing at the wrong time. There is a time for everything under the sun. A good deed done at the wrong time will become a bad act. Flowers sown where they are not wanted will become weeds. Acts that could be construed as triumphalism rarely takes any politician or section of it very far in our political history. What will the knowledge of how the 'cabal' smuggled a dying Yaradua into the country serve us at this time? I actually believe that Jonathan has so far handled the issue of Yaradua and the cabal with wisdom. The 'cabal', as reprehensible as what its members did were, were not the first faction of the Nigerian elite to defend an ethnic/regional interest in a way that manifestly undermines the nation's constitution or makes mockery of our collective intelligence. This is obviously not a case for impunity, but just to put it in perspective.

Reminiscences on the 'good ol' days'

Reading an article by Wole Olaoye 'Falling quality of leaders' (*Daily Trust*, June 27, 2011), I cannot but remember the words of the American journalist and columnist Franklin Pierce Adams when he said: 'Nothing is more responsible for the good old days than a bad memory'. In the said article, Wole bemoaned the quality of the present crop of leaders and declared: "The only time we ever had leaders of Triple-A grading was in the FirstRepublic; the survivors of the era (Zik, Awo, Aminu Kano) still kept their halo and were rewarded electorally by the people.... There are no thinkers any more. You can't even find one golden voice". Really?

I always feel amused by certain uncritical romanticisation of our FirstRepublicpoliticians. For instance, if, as Wole postulated, there are no thinkers any more among today's leadership, what do you say of the likes of Ngozi Iweala, Chukwuma Soludo, and Professor Ibrahim Gambari? I think the capabilities of the politicians of the FirstRepublicare often exaggerated because they were around when the level of literacy was very low and so it was easy to venerate them as sort of oracles (the Zik *ekwugo* phenomenon – Zik has said therefore it must be right). If theFirstRepublic politicians were as astute as we often ascribe to them, how come that ethnicity, thuggery, violence and strife were endemic in their dispensation? My personal opinion is that if the present crop of leaders appear less capable, it is most likely because our times have moved from the era of uncritical veneration of leaders to judging them by global standards of excellence. In the same vein, I am not sure that our current politicians, as corrupt as many of them are – are worse than many of the politicians of the first Republic. When I look at the material acquisitions of some of the first Republicpoliticians it is difficult to believe they accumulated such wealth from their legitimate earnings. Again when you consider the modest resources available to them at that time, and how much many of them are suspected to have stolen from that public pool, it is not clear to me that the present crop of leaders, relative to the resources available to them, are stealing more. Additionally, it is unclear the role played by improvements in reporting methods for corruption in the current era (emergence of the internet, weblogs, more educated people and recently the passage of the Freedom of Information Act) in perceptions that the current crop of leaders are stupendously corrupt. This is of course not an excuse for the current crop of leaders that pilfer public resources.

CHAPTER 64

THE HYPOCRITE IN ALL OF US

We are probably all guilty of this. We constantly project beliefs, opinions, values, feelings, qualities and standards that are at variance with what we practice. Admittedly, what we practice is not necessarily what we will want to practice, making hypocrisy more than inconsistency between what is advocated and what is done. The English author and moralist Samuel Johnson in fact tells us that nothing "is more unjust, however common, than to charge with hypocrisy him that expresses zeal for those virtues which he neglects to practice; since he may be sincerely convinced of the advantages of conquering his passions, without having yet obtained the victory, as a man may be confident of the advantages of a voyage, or a journey, without having courage or industry to undertake it, and may honestly recommend to others, those attempts which he neglects himself."

It is often said that man is completely sincere only when he is alone, away from the prying eyes of anyone. As the American poet and essayist, Ralph Waldo Emerson, adumbrated: "Every man alone is sincere. At the entrance of a second person, hypocrisy begins."

If there is a bit of the hypocrite in all of us, then our hypocrisy is often at its highest when discussing public officials, especially politicians, in the context of money and sex. Consider this story:

The *New York Times* of December 26, 2009, carried a story of Narain Dutt Tiwari, an 86-year Governor of a southern Indian state who was forced to resign after a television news channel broadcast a tape showing him having a tryst with three women. Though Tiwari's office had denounced the tape as a fabrication, opposition and women's rights groups held protests in Hyderabad, Andhra Pradesh's capital, demanding for his resignation. Tiwari later resigned, citing health reasons.

Admittedly the alleged sex escapade, which apparently took place in the privacy of Tiwari's bedroom, will be morally revolting to some, but does that amount to a crime? Apart from the comedy of imagining an old man of 86 being naughty, does the alleged dalliance in any way affect his ability to perform his official duties? Was the Governor's right to privacy breached? Will the protesters be willing to honestly share with the public their activities when they are completely alone or in the privacy of their homes?

While our hypocrisy as ordinary citizens can often go undetected and unpunished, sometimes public officials who take a high moral ground to enhance their image and career are not always so lucky. Consider these cases:

On 10 March 2008, New York Governor Eliot Spitzer admitted that he was a customer of a prostitution ring which charged as much as $3,100 to $5,500 an hour. What irked most people was not so much the act of patronising prostitutes as the hypocrisy of it all because Spitzer was known for his moral high grounds. For instance as Attorney General of the state in 2003, he had brought a suit against a company suspected of planning sex tourism trips to Asia. He was then quoted as saying that the "company purports to be a traditional travel agency, but through its actions promotes prostitution and the abuse of young women." He resigned on March 12, 2008.

Wayne Hayes , an Ohio Democrat, was regarded as one of the biggest bullies in the US Congress in the 1970s, intimidating lawmakers and staff alike as chairman of the House Administration Committee. He had a carefully cultivated image of a moralist and a puritan. Then Elizabeth Ray, a woman he hired to be a secretary and receptionist, confessed to *The Washington Post* that her real 'job' was to provide sexual favours to the congressman. "I can't type, I can't file, I can't even answer the phone," she said. The scandal forced Mr. Hayes out of Congress. Similarly, it was found that Newt Gingrich, who, as Speaker of the House of Representatives, led the effort to impeach Bill Clinton for lying about sexual dalliances with former White House intern Monica Lewinsky, was himself having an affair with a House aide.

In the UK, John Major, the British Prime Minister and Leader of the Conservative Party (1990-1997) had in 1993 launched a Back- to- Basics campaign in an attempt to re-launch his government. The effort backfired when the media began scrutinizing the campaign's moral aspects and consequently exposed "sleaze" within the Conservative Party and, most damagingly, within the Cabinet itself. A number of ministers were then revealed to have committed sexual indiscretions, and Major was forced by media pressure to dismiss them. It later emerged that prior to his promotion to the cabinet, John Major himself had a long-standing extramarital affair with a fellow MP, Edwina Currie.

In countries like France and Nigeria, where infidelity by politicians and others is usually regarded as a 'non-issue', it is easier to grandstand on corruption or incompetence of public officials. Take Olusegun Obasanjo for instance. For years he had a carefully cultivated image of an 'incorruptible' man, and during his regime as civilian President (1999-2007), he had accused sundry politicians of corruption and even used the EFCC to hunt them. Today not few people question the source of his suspected stupendous wealth, especially as it was revealed that he was almost a bankrupt when he was drafted to run for President in 1999.

What are the lessons from the above?

One, most of us should consider ourselves lucky that as private individuals, the media really have no interest in beaming their searchlights on us. Were they to do so, it will be easy to find a dissonance between the values we profess (sometimes very honestly) and the way we live our lives. This should help us to temper our criticisms of public officials, by consciously balancing an official's good deeds with his/her shortcomings. As Edward Wallis Hoch, the seventeenth Governor of Kansas, USA, would counsel us:

> "There is so much good in the worst of us, And so much bad in the best of us, that it hardly behooves any of us to talk about the rest of us."

Two, while as citizens and writers we have an obligation to hold public officials to account, there is a related question of how we should do this responsibly without appearing like the biblical hypocrite, who revels in pointing out the speck in another's eyes while neglecting the log in his own eyes. No sensible person judges the weather only by its inclement or sunny side. Today, there are 'social critics' who believe that once you have been in public office, then you must have 'stolen us blind', and must consequently be ostracised because nothing good will ever come from you. I know for instance of one 'social critic', who 'vamoosed' with money given to him by a friend, whom he convinced to sell his plot of land in Lagos to raise money for a certain "assured business deal". Some two years after the money was handed over to the 'social critic', the "assured business deal" has still not materialised and the money still not returned. Yet, in his articles, he has no qualms taking absolute moral positions, permitting no room for mistakes or human imperfections, as he lampoons, in the most flowery phrases, those who have 'stolen us dry'.

Nigeriavillagesquare, 1 February 2010

CHAPTER 65

THE BURDEN OF BEING VICE PRESIDENT

I t is not easy being a deputy to anyone, in particular being the Vice President of a country. On the face of it, it is a prestigious position because nominally you are the Number Two in the power hierarchy. However, substantially you are only as powerful as the President wants you to be. In essence, to be a 'good' Vice President is to be good at playing a second fiddle, which may not be as easy as it sounds. Though it is seen as a joint ticket in a Presidential system of government (albeit the bottom part of it), once elected; it is a mortal political sin for a Vice President to see his position as such. The American entertainer Will Rogers summed up the job description of a 'good' Vice President: "The man with the best job in the country is the Vice President. All he has to do is get up every morning and say, 'How is the President?'" For Hubert H. Humphrey, the 38th US Vice President under President Lyndon B Johnson (1965-1969): "Anyone who thinks that the Vice President can take a position independent of the President of his administration simply has no knowledge of politics or government. You are his choice in a political marriage, and he expects your absolute loyalty".

In countries like USA where the level of literacy is high, and constitutionalism has a long history; friction between the President and the Vice President is well managed, often away from the public glare. A President who demeans the Office of the Vice President by completely sidelining the occupant risks a political backlash as much as a Vice President who is seen as disloyal or too ambitious. In sharply divided and low-trust societies however, the story is often different. Consider these stories:

In Malaysia, Mahathir bin Mohamad, the country's fourth and longest-serving Prime Minister (1981–2003), had a running battle with Anwar Ibrahim, a Malay of Indian extraction, when the latter was the Deputy Prime Minister and Minister of Finance (1993-1998). Though Anwar had risen as a protégé of Mahathir, matters came to a head when he began asserting himself, forgetting, so to say, that he was simply meant to be a spare tyre. For instance during the Asian Financial Crisis in 1997, in his capacity as finance minister, Anwar publicly favoured options that were antithetical to Mahathir's, such as supporting the International Monetary Fund's plan for the country's recovery, which included instituting an austerity package that slashed government spending by 18 percent and deferring major investment projects. Mahathir's supporters subsequently began suspecting Anwar of nursing an inordinate ambition to replace the Prime Minister, inspired by the downfall of Indonesia's President, Suharto, who was forced to resign in 1998 following the hardship caused by the Asian financial crisis. In 1998, the Malaysian government brought charges of sexual misconduct and abuse of power against Anwar, who was later fired from the Cabinet amid other allegations of being a homosexual and a serial sodomite.

In South Africa, President Thabo Mbeki had a running feud with Jacob Zuma when the latter was Deputy President (1999-2005). It was said that Mbeki had little regard for Zuma, the rough-hewn but popular farm boy who spent ten years in jail on Robben Island prison. Zuma, an uneducated, self-confessed polygamist, who at 67 recently married his third wife, claimed that when he became Deputy President in 1999, Mbeki stripped the role of any real power. Within a year of coming to power, Zuma, discovered he was under investigation over corruption allegations linked to the purchase of frigates for the South African navy. Zuma, who was also accused of raping an AIDS activist, was convinced that Mbeki was behind the allegations. Eager to save his political career, Zuma went on television and pledged loyalty to Mbeki but it was apparently insufficient to mollify Mbeki who later fired Zuma from the government. Zuma decided to fight back, with support from his Zulu ethnic group, trade unionists and left-leaning groups. In 2007, Mbeki lost to Zuma in a contest to be the Chairman of the ANC. In 2008, High Court Judge Chris Nicholson ruled that Thabo Mbeki had used 'presidential powers' to interfere in the legal action against Jacob Zuma. Radicals within the ANC forced Mbeki to resign as President of South Africa - in one of the rare cases of victory for a Vice President in any contest with the substantive President. In May 2009, Zuma was elected President of South Africa.

In Nigeria, there was the epic feud between Obasanjo and the then Vice President Abubakar Atiku, which dominated much of the regime's second term in office (2003-2007). While the open quarrel effectively prevented Atiku from succeeding Obasanjo, it however turned out to be a pyrrhic victory for the Ota farmer as his carefully cultivated public image of an incorruptible statesman was severely battered by counter allegations of corruption and innuendos about sex escapades from the Atiku camp. Supporters of Obasanjo locate the root of the discord to their principal's doubts about Atiku's loyalty to him, while Atiku's camp believed their principal was being persecuted for opposing Obasanjo's third term plot.

In the three instances cited above, we have Vice Presidents who clearly nursed ambitions of succeeding their bosses, which in turn could have led to suspicions (real or imagined) of disloyalty. In the case of Goodluck Jonathan, he appeared to be an apotheosis of the good Vice-Preside: almost without an ego, self-effacing, comfortable with playing a second fiddle, not bombastic and shuns the limelight. So if Jonathan is in theory the ideal Vice President, why is he apparently not trusted by the kitchen cabinet of an ailing President who has been away from duty for more than a month and a half?

We can all speculate on this or attribute it as part of the transaction costs in low-trust societies - the fear, real or contrived, of being double-crossed in any gentleman's agreement. In essence, while Yaradua's prolonged illness and lack of formal transfer of power to the Vice President may have brought us on the throes of a constitutional crisis, the situation more importantly calls attention to the special burden of being a Vice President (and also Deputy Governor) in our type of societies. How many Deputy Governors in Nigeria have become substantive Governors? Can a Vice President in Nigeria ever become the President? In the situation we found ourselves today, can the Vice President appropriate more functions to himself under the doctrine of necessity? If he does, will that make him a closet power hawk? If he chooses to be extremely cautious - seeing banana peels everywhere, so to say - will that reinforce suspicions of some critics that he is perhaps too weak and not up to the job of being President?

For the Vice President, it is a dicey situation, which calls for understanding. As Donald Rumsfield, the US Secretary of Defense (2001-2006) under President George W Bush would counsel: "Being Vice President is difficult. Don't make it tougher".

Daily Independent 2 February 2010

CHAPTER 66

OUR DEMOCRACY PROJECT: THE JOURNEY SO FAR

The Governorship elections of April 26 (April 28 in Bauchi and Kaduna) drew a curtain on the current election season. And with these, it may be worth assessing the democracy project, which the nation embarked on May 29 1999 when the Fourth Republic was inaugurated under Olusegun Obasanjo's presidency. How have we fared so far?

If politicians are like diapers that require periodic change, then an examination of our conduct of elections and the issues such elections throw up will provide an insight into how far we are faring in our democracy journey. Several issues were thrown up by the just concluded election cycle:

One, Jega had two things coming into the elections – one worked in his favour, the other against him. His predecessor in office, Professor Maurice Iwu, had organised a sham in 2007 which any breathing goat would have no difficulty dismissing as non-election. The baseline for comparing Professor Jega's efforts was therefore extremely favourable. But Jega also came with an over rated credibility tag, which raised expectations beyond realistic limits. Fortunately for him, the high expectations nose-dived on April 2 when he announced the abortion of the National Assembly elections that were already under way. Paradoxically the false start of April 2 and the extremely low bar of public expectation, which it engendered (in addition to the 'no bar' of expectation set by the 2007 elections), helped to exaggerate the perception of success of the National Assembly elections. The euphoria that followed muffled all contrary voices as killjoys or sore losers.

Two, based on the above, the presidential election of April 16 and the Governorship elections that followed are better baselines for assessing Jega and the new INEC. Though the violence that trailed the outcome of the Presidential elections in some Northern States cast a dark shadow on the exercise, my personal opinion is that Jonathan won hands down, despite legitimate complaints by the opposition parties, essentially Buhari's CPC. While there may have been rigging, I had in two previous articles on General Buhari taken the position that his charisma and credibility might not be enough for him to win the election. CPC's organisational weaknesses for instance showed in the elections and were not helped by the deleterious effects of the in-fighting among the CPC's gladiators in the North. It also appears that Buhari remains distrusted by some Northern power brokers who probably felt that Jonathan's non-threatening personality would be easier to live with than the assumed unpredictability that would come with a Buhari presidency.

Three, the popular explanation for the outbreak of the violence in some Northern states after the presidential poll is that people took to the streets because they felt the outcome did not reflect their wishes. This, in my opinion, is at best only a partial explanation. While it is true that some people probably equated the support for General Buhari in their locality and among their peer groups to his support across the entire North or the country, my personal opinion is that people resorted to violence for unconscious reasons that were beyond Buhari's performance in the elections. Eminent Nigerian political scientist Professor Isawa Elaigwu has for instance argued that the North- South interaction has been held together by a sort of balance of fear. The South, he argues, fears political domination from the lopsided nature of the federation in which the North accounts for some 79% of the land mass and 53.5% of its population – according to the 1963 census. Elaigwu argues that the North equally fears the South's 'tyranny of skills', (arising from its head start in Western education), which it allegedly uses to dominate the economy and the bureaucracy. In essence in this balance of fear, the North holds the political lever while the South holds the economy/bureaucracy lever, with each suspecting the other of trying to use its lever to neutralise the other's advantage. In this sense, the violence that followed the presidential election in the North may be less a show of support for Buhari than an unconscious outpouring of the fear of total Southern domination. To allay the fears of some people in the North about a Southern presidency therefore, Jonathan needs to convince them that the old levers used in maintaining the balance of fear have become anachronistic (the skills gap between the North and South has for instance closed up considerably) and that he will be a fair President to all.

Four, the elections threw up conflicting signals about the direction of our democracy. On the positives: The number of incumbent governors that were defeated in the elections – in Oyo, Nasarawa, Zamfara and possibly Imo States – showed that the ballot box is becoming a more potent vehicle of regime change. The influence of political godfathers also seemed to have become less significant in electoral outcomes. For instance candidates backed by Obasanjo, Governor Gbenga Daniel, Olusola Saraki, Edwin Clarke and Dr Chimaroke Nnamani all lost woefully. The elections equally showed that the political space is opening up in many parts of the country. In Anambra, Benue and several other states of the federation, the ACN, generally seen as a 'Yoruba party' gave a good account of itself. In the South West however, the ACN swept the polls, meaning that with the exception of Ondo State (which is controlled by the Labour Party), the entire Yorubaland is now under the control of ACN. It remains however debatable whether the victory of the ACN in the South West is a triumph of Yoruba irredentism or triumph of progressive politics.

Five, the elections also revealed that while the perception of INEC as a neutral umpire has improved, several gaps need to be plugged to improve the integrity of the process. For instance the number of votes that were voided remained unacceptably high, calling for a massive voter education campaign. Also there remain issues with the voters' register, which calls for the routinisation of the registration and clean-up exercises. Our politicians also showed that they are always ahead of efforts to cage them, meaning that INEC has to step up its game to be at least one step ahead of the politicians when it comes to ballot snatching/stuffing, rigging, underage voting and falsifying the results at the collation centres. In summary while it is still not *Uhuru* for our democracy, we are making steady, even if slow, progress.

Governor Peter Obi's revenge

As chairman of the South East Governors' Forum, Governor Peter Obi was very visible in the negotiations between the South East ASUU and the governments of the South East States over the implementation of a new salary structure for academics. The university lecturers had gone on strike insisting on the implementation of the new salary structure. After some six months of strike, the governments of the area largely acquiesced to the lecturers' demand. In Anambra State however Governor Peter Obi seemed to have taken his revenge on the largely indigent students of the State-owned Anambra State University by hiking the school fees from about N35,000 per annum to more than N100,000 per annum. While it is understandable that school fees have to be increased, I struggle to find decent words to describe the level of increase.

Governor Peter Obi also needs to level up with Local Government Chairmanship aspirants under APGA who were made to pay 1 million Naira each for the expression of interest forms as far back as July/August 2010. The indication then was that the elections would hold in December 2010. Though the elections have been postponed indefinitely, there has not been a word about refunding the aspirants their money. And given APGA's relatively poor performance in the just concluded National and

State Assembly elections, not many people believe that Local Government elections will be held any time soon. Has Governor Peter Obi lost his halo?

Daily Trust 5 May 2011

CHAPTER 67

HOW TO BECOME A BEAUTIFUL POLITICAL BRIDE IN LOW TRUST SOCIETIES

In a very remarkable book, *Trust: The Social Virtues and the Creation of Prosperity* (1995), the American political scientist Professor Francis Fukuyama, divided societies into high trust and low trust categories. In high trust societies members readily trust their compatriots and assume that they will 'follow the rules' – whether formalised in a contract or not. While in high trust societies a person is trusted until the person proves otherwise, in low trust societies, members deeply distrust one another, and you have to go the extra mile to win and sustain people's trust.

Though Fukuyama's categories are at best ideal types, it is obvious that in low trust societies such as ours, individuals and groups that possess that rare quality of keeping to their promises will become 'beautiful brides'. In this sense, going out of one's way to win people's trust becomes a smart, long-term investment. Once one is unable to resist the temptation to repudiate an agreement for short-term gains, one makes a dishonourable contribution towards consolidating the mistrust in the society. As Friedrich Nietzsche, the German philosopher would put it in such a situation: "I'm not upset that you lied to me, I'm upset that from now on I can't believe you."

Much has been written about the domination of the country's politics by the North but without concomitant attention paid to how this is facilitated by their perception as people who keep their words. Even outside politics, it is not uncommon to hear people from the South say that 'if an Alhaji from the North gives you his word, he is likely to keep it.' Contrast this perception for instance with the politics of extreme distrust among many politicians from ethnic groups in the South and it becomes easier to understand why the North has remained the 'beautiful bride' of Nigerian politics. It is time we began to pose the question of why many nationalities from the South seem incapable of working together.

There are several implications of the above for the current discussion about whether President Goodluck Jonathan should contest the 2011 presidential elections:

One, both the supporters and critics of the PDP's zoning arrangement often deploy the politics of language to disguise their real motives in their stances. For instance it is suspected that some critics of the PDP zoning arrangement are trying to blackmail others into repudiating an arrangement their zone has benefited from simply because they have 'taken their turn' and now shudder at the prospect of having to wait for a long time to take another shot at the presidency. Similarly many of the proponents of zoning mask their hurt feelings for being 'outsmarted' or taken for a 'mugu'. The cumulative impact of this is the deepening of the distrust that already permeates the society. As distrust is deepened, the nation building process becomes even more complicated.

Two, critics who say that the PDP zoning arrangement is unconstitutional tend to forget the difference between the spirit (intent) of a Constitution and its letters. The 1979 Nigerian Constitution recognises the need to reflect the federal character in political appointments as a way of allaying fears of marginalisation by any constituent part. The decision by a political party to zone or rotate power among different geographical blocs is therefore in consonance with the spirit of the Constitution on ensuring a sense of belonging to all the federating units. It could in fact be argued that zoning, which was first explicitly practised by the defunct NPN, has proved more potent in allaying the fears of ethnic minorities than state creation (the fears provided the basis for agitations for state creation in the First Republic) because while each state creation exercise created new minorities and therefore triggered demands for new states, zoning successfully ended WAZOBIA politics (the dominance of the country's politics by the three major ethnic groups – Hausa, Igbos and Yorubas). Besides, what we call zoning is not significantly different from the increasing recognition in the USA that political appointments should reflect the 'changing demographics' of the country. Similarly, in the UK, there are discussions that 'positive discrimination' aimed at boosting the chances of people who are likely to be disadvantaged in an unfettered competition for jobs such as women and ethnic minorities should be taken a step further into the political process.

Three, critics of zoning have questioned whether it really matters who governs a country, provided the right sets of people are doing so. This line of reasoning underestimates the force of nationalism and the psychological impact of a feeling of belonging in nation building. If it really does not matter who rules, why did an overwhelming majority of African Americans and Africans turn out to support Barrack Obama during the last Presidential election in the US? What was the point of the whole anti-colonial struggles, and the Nigerianisation and Northernisation policies they spurned? Why do we all feel a sense of elation when our national football side does us proud? Those advocating the abrogation of the PDP's zoning that has worked relatively well for the party are in essence calling for a return to the era of WAZOBIA politics.

Four, those who know Jonathan well say he is truly a gentle and unassuming man. If he decides to run in 2011, he will be putting his honour on the line and giving the cabal around Yaradua, who held the country to the jugular for months, an opportunity to re-invent themselves. They can easily rationalise their actions by claiming to have discovered that Jonathan was a closet power hawk and therefore had to do what they thought was necessary to protect the 'national interest'. If Jonathan shuns the temptation to run in 2011, it will boost not only his personal standing as a man of honour but arguably that of the entire Niger Delta. If he decides to run, all the actions he has taken so far, including the forced resignation of Ogbulafor and a resurgent EFCC being sent after known Yaradua supporters, will be seen as witch-hunting geared at neutralising those who will stand between him and his ambition.

Five, Jonathan will become much more respected as a statesman if he chooses not to run than if he runs and wins. Nigeria is such a complex country that most of the leaders come out of office diminished in stature. With just one year to go, making it clear he will not run in 2011 will spare his regime intense scrutiny and distraction while guaranteeing him the status of a global statesman once out of office. Much of Obasanjo's stature as an international statesman in fact stemmed from his singular act of voluntarily handing over power to elected civilians in 1979.

Six, if Jonathan decides to contest and the cream of the Northern politicians flocks into another political party, many of the ethnic nationalities will have to weigh who they will trust more 'to carry them along': Jonathan who has already betrayed a trust or the North, who, rightly or wrongly, are believed to be good in keeping their words? If our political history is anything to go by, especially on the issue of trust, the North will once again be the beautiful bride, even among groups that 'despise' them 'for behaving as if ruling the country is their birthright'. More worrying will be the fate that awaits Jonathan if he contests and loses. With witch-hunting as part of our inglorious political culture, we will likely be treated to revelations of the litany of sins he committed while in office, quite a number of them of course contrived.

Hollerafrica.com, May 19 2010

CHAPTER 68

FORGIVENESS AND THE CULTURE OF CYNICISM

When Hannah Arendt, the late influential German political theorist, coined the phrase the 'banality of evil', you might think she was being prophetic about 21st century Nigeria. The staple of uncomfortable news from our dear country could sometimes border on the horrendous. This apparent ubiquity of evil has helped to spawn a culture of cynicism, even for deeds that are ordinarily extolled as virtuous.

Take for instance, 'forgiveness'. A virtue highly extolled by the major religions and even by medical science, once it is embraced by public figures, the citizens become very cynical, even suspicious, and perhaps rightly so.

On January 19, 2009, Alhaji Abubakar Atiku, the former vice president, reportedly met his former boss and nemesis, Chief Olusegun Obasanjo. Obasanjo's perceived persecution of Atiku while in office included unconstitutionally sacking him as the VP, virtually preventing him from running for the office of president of Nigeria in the 2007 elections, marginalizing and humiliating him at the Federal Executive Council meetings, and framing corruption charges against him. Atiku's associates explained that the former VP's visit was a demonstration of his forgiving spirit. Many Nigerians shook their heads in disbelief.

In early June 2009, it was reported that former military president General Ibrahim Babangida, had 'forgiven' Professor Saliba Mukoro, one of the eggheads of the April 22, 1990 bloody coup that attempted to topple him. The 'reconciliation', which was reportedly brokered by Governor Olagunsonye Oyinlola of Osun State, marked the first time Babangida and Mukoro would see each other in 19 years. Both Governor Oyinlola and Saliba Mukoro were Babangida's students. Once the news broke out, Nigerians quickly remembered that Babangida's nickname is 'Maradona' and began wondering what he was up to. If it is Babangida, goes the consensus, then any foot he puts forward is likely to be 'Maradonic', a decoy.

The above two instances of high-profile acts of 'forgiveness' and 'reconciliation' raise a number of questions, especially among the growing community of cynics.

One, bearing a grudge means retaining the memory of an offence against you, which, in extreme cases, could lead to the wronged party seeking revenge. This may in turn lead to both the aggrieved and the perceived aggressor living in fear. Could it be that the balance of fear created by the enmity between powerful public figures, and the need to feel safer, is a major reason why feuding public figures often want to make up after a period of bearing grudges?

Two, while true forgiveness is a noble act, usually carried out only by the very strong and confident, and to be encouraged, is there a condition where enmity between powerful officials will be deemed beneficial to the public interest? If we accept the theory that one of the reasons the elites get away with much impunity is because they are cohesive, conscious and conspiratorial, can we consider a division in their ranks as progressive? In particular, could such a division be deemed beneficial to the national treasury, especially if it encourages the adversaries and their associates in government to be conscious of powerful forces monitoring their moves?

Three, what are the implications of the reconciliation between feuding powerful public figures for their associates and foot soldiers? It was for instance reported that Atiku's protracted quarrels with Obasanjo led to many of the former VP's associates being victimised by the Ota farmer and his associates. In the attempted rapprochement between the two, were all the associates and foot soldiers part of the reconciliation moves or were they just dispensed with as if their opinions didn't matter and as if the quarrel between the two titans were not principally a proxy war fought by their associates and foot soldiers? Similarly, how many of Mukoro's associates and family members were adversely affected by his involvement in the coup? How many were taken into confidence in the 'reconciliation' with Babangida? Did the 'reconciliation' create any scheme for rehabilitating people who were probably victimised by Babangida for being relatives or family members of the coup plotters? Does any such act of 'forgiveness' by a powerful public figure necessarily create fall guys who may be more adversely affected by the 'reconciliation' between the former adversaries than the status quo?

Four, given the pervasive belief that powerful public figures and business people see 'forgiveness' more as a business tool than a moral and medical injunction, are we justified in being cynical of any attempt by quarrelling public figures to reconcile? If yes, are we turning into sadists, not just cynics, by a certain wish that political adversaries never reconcile – even when we know that a grudge is like a baggage and that there will surely come a time when the burden becomes too heavy for the carrier? If we are turning into cynics and even sadists, are the politicians helping matters? Consider this story: Fani-Kayode, who allegedly led the public humiliation of Alhaji Atiku at the Federal Executive Council meetings, was reported to have also reconciled with the former VP (This

Day, June 6 2009). Fani-Kayode said the quarrel between Obasanjo and Atiku was unfortunate but that he was like a soldier who necessarily had to take orders from 'my General'. It is instructive to note that Fani-Kayode has signified an interest in running for the governorship of Osun state while Atiku remains interested in the presidency. Are we justified in being cynical about this purported reconciliation?

Five, does forgiveness, as practised by our public officials, nullify or undermine justice? Take the case of Babangida's reported forgiveness of Mukoro. Could their kissing and making up deny Nigerians an opportunity of knowing what truly happened in the 1990 coup and in other coups? Have the moves to 'reconcile' Atiku and Obasanjo affected the investigation of the numerous allegations they levelled against each other in the wake of their troubles?

Six, if talks of reconciliation between powerful public figures echo the dictum that in politics there are no permanent friends or enemies, but only permanent interests, what happens to the need for human communities to take a hard look at the truth of the past and courageously acknowledge the evils in it in order to avoid repeating the mistakes of the past?

Perhaps we have become a nation of cynics, where nothing is believed, not even a well-intentioned 'good morning' felicitation at 9.AM by a newscaster. May be being cynical has become an escapism, a way we try to cope with the increasing chaos in our land.

Daily Independent, July 9, 2009

CHAPTER 69

HEROES, DEMOCRACY, AND THE 'PHD' SYNDROME

A nation that does not honour its heroes is not worth dying for –so goes the cliché. This appears to be an obvious truth – or so it seems. Identifying the public hero (or heroine) could however be problematic in a society sharply divided along ethnic, religious, social, political and class fault lines. In such a society, there are rarely living individuals or institutions that enjoy universal legitimacy such that one's hero is often another's villain. No one for instance doubts that a terrorist for Americans could be a freedom fighter for the Al Qaeda - just as a militant adored as a hero by his ethnic group in Nigeria could be regarded as a felon by other ethnic nationalities in the country. Additionally, if we accept that free speech is the bedrock of democracy and that it is applicable not only to information or ideas that are favourably received or regarded as inoffensive but also for "those that offend, shock or disturb the state or any other sector of the population", some important questions are raised: are sharp scrutiny of individuals regarded as heroes by some people contributions to the 'market place of ideas' (which, enrich democracy) or a manifestation of the 'pull him down' syndrome that tends to sharpen the discords in the society? What is the boundary between genuine disagreement with a 'hero's way' and the real 'PhD' syndrome that is often actuated by envy, malice or hidden agenda?

While every nation eventually creates icons that appear, with the passage of time, to be generally accepted by the citizens, even the most iconic public figures faced stiff opposition in their journey to 'immortalisation'. Consider the following examples:

Mohammed Ali (born Cassius Clay) is today a hero to virtually everyone, including people who are against professional boxing. But this was not always so. In his heydays, Ali was regarded as cocky and boastful, and hence nicknamed 'Louisville Lip'. Despite his unquestionable boxing ability, he was seen as a polarising figure, especially after he converted to Islam. It was even suspected that some of his spectacular victories in the ring were fixed. For instance when he knocked out Sonny Liston in the first round in their rematch for the World Heavyweight boxing title in May 1965, journalists quickly began talks of the 'phantom punch', claiming that the Nation of Islam (then known as the Black Muslims) intimidated Sonny Liston into submission. Even in his home town of Louisville, Kentucky, Ali was not especially liked – despite winning the Light Heavy weight gold medal in the 1960

Summer Olympics and being a three-time World Heavy Weight boxing champion. For instance in 1978, three years before Ali's permanent retirement, attempts to rename Walnut Street to Muhammad Ali Boulevard in his hometown was sharply resisted but eventually passed by the Board of Aldermen by a very narrow majority of 6–5. Earlier that year, a committee of the Jefferson County Public Schools considered renaming Central High School in his honour, but the motion failed to pass. At any rate, in time, Muhammad Ali Boulevard—and Ali himself—came to be well accepted in his hometown such that on September 13, 1999, Ali was named "Kentucky Athlete of the Century" by the Kentucky Athletic Hall of Fame. He was also in the same year crowned "Sportsman of the Century" by *Sports Illustrated* and "Sports Personality of the Century" by the BBC.

Consider again Abraham Lincoln, the 16th President of the United States, who successfully led his country through its greatest internal crisis, the American Civil War. Though Lincoln has consistently been ranked by scholars as one of the greatest of all U.S. Presidents, he was not universally accepted as such during his presidency, even within his Republican Party. For instance while opponents of the war criticized Lincoln for refusing to compromise on the slavery issue, the Radical Republicans, an abolitionist faction of the Republican Party, constantly lampooned him for moving too slowly in abolishing slavery. He was also contemporaneously described and ridiculed as suffering from "melancholy" or clinical depression throughout his legal and political life.

Nearer home, the commonly accepted Nigerian public heroes – Dr Nnamdi Azikiwe, Chief Obafemi Awolowo, Sir Tafawa Balewa and the Sarduana of Sokoto, were in their days viewed with suspicions by most people who were not from their region. Even within their region, they faced stiff opposition and challenges and were not universally adored as they are these days. Thus while Zik had polarising quarrels with Professor Eyo Ita in the East, Awolowo had a long-running divisive feud with Ladoke Akintola in the West while the Sarduana of Sokoto and Tafawa Balewa had stiff challenges – on ideological and ethnic grounds - from both Aminu Kano and J S Tarka respectively.

What are the lessons from the above?

One, if the notion of human rights is necessarily anti-majoritarian in principle (i.e. the protection of the right of individuals to dissent from majority opinions), then dissenting from the majority's anointed hero does not necessarily amount to one exhibiting the 'PhD' syndrome but an exercise of the right to dissent. Dissent, which is crucial in any spirit of enquiry and is often richly rewarded in academics and innovations, is a major contribution to the 'market place of ideas', which is itself the lifeline of democracy. In this sense, those who are quick to accuse others of 'PhD' could be guilty of undermining democracy by stifling speech. In the same vein, threat of libel action has long been recognised as having a 'chilling effect' on free speech and explains why it is almost impossible for public officials to win libel actions in many jurisdictions such as the USA and the European Union.

Two, heroes are not people without faults, or people whose contributions were never contested in their time. Because democracy is necessarily rowdy and noisy – just like in any typical Nigerian marketplace- every 'temporary' public hero subjected to the 'endless' haggling of this marketplace of ideas eventually becomes a bore, with question marks hanging over the person's signature achievement.

Three, it will seem that icons are eventually created (even if through agreement by exhaustion) based on the relevance of their specific actions or policies rather than on a balance sheet assessment of their successes and failures. Who for instance will today question that Awolowo's free education in the western region was visionary or that Lincoln's stance on the abolition of slavery was truly progressive? If, as they say, history will vindicate the just, how will history judge Obasanjo, Soludo, Sanusi, Nuhu Ribadu and other candidates for Nigeria's public heroes and heroines? Only time will tell.

Daily Independent, Nov 12 2009

CHAPTER 70

RE-THINKING OUR UNIVERSITY EDUCATION SYSTEM

The recent decision by the federal government to establish six more 'specialised' federal universities in each of the six geopolitical zones in the country, has made headlines. According to Kenneth Gbagi, minister of state for education, who made the announcement, full academic activities will commence in the new universities in September next year. It was reported that the federal government would make available the sum of ten billion Naira for the start of the new universities.

Julius Okojie, the executive secretary of the National Universities' Commission and chairman of the committee that worked on the modalities for establishing the new institutions, said the new universities would expand access to university education in the country, pointing out that out of over 1.3 million candidates that sit for university entrance examinations every year, only about 300,000 are eventually admitted. Nigeria currently has 27 federal-owned universities, 35 state government-owned universities and 41 private universities. The proposed new universities, said Okojie, would be sited within states that do no already have federal universities.

The proposal for the new universities raises fundamental issues about our university education system:

One, it will seem that not much meticulous planning went into the conception and actualization of the new universities. From the report by *Next* newspaper of 17 November 2010, it would seem that it took less than a week between the time a committee was set up and mandated to "work out modalities for establishing the new universities" and the time the committee submitted its recommendations, raising questions about how thorough it was in its assignment, or whether it was merely set up to rubber stamp a decision that had already been taken *apriori*. We were also told the new universities would take off in September next year and that they would be built from scratch. This means in essence that it will have taken less than one year to conceive, construct, equip and recruit competent staff to run these universities. There is certainly a smell of undue haste in all these - which is of course not helped by the rather suspicious decision to site two of the new universities in the home states of the President and the Education minister respectively.

Two, though one of the formal rationales for the establishment of the new universities – the need to expand access to students - makes sense, it is not at all clear that establishing new universities is the best way of doing this. Wouldn't the same objective be achieved if some of the existing universities were funded to expand their student intake? And if there must be additional universities, why must they be built from scratch when it will be cheaper for some polytechnics or colleges of education to be upgraded to degree awarding institutions and given a face-lift? More importantly, at a time when the quality of our university education is at its lowest ebb, what will be the interface between expanding access and further lowering the quality of students admitted into our universities? It would appear that by taking what seems to be a hasty decision to set up these universities, and with a take-off budget of only ten billion Naira, the government may have unwittingly exposed itself as part of the problems of our university education system.

Three, the problems of our university education system are multifarious, of which access is only one of them. The declining quality of university education correlates with the sharp fall in the quality of the secondary education system that feeds into it. In this sense, the poor quality of our university education cannot be fixed independent of the quality of our secondary education system. Obviously the declining quality of our university education is worsened by incessant strikes, poorly motivated lecturers and corruption and sexual harassment within the academia. We cannot solve the problems of our university education system simply by an unbridled expansion of access. Competition for access to available spaces at universities is in fact one of the ways of ensuring that the quality of university education remains high. Democratising access such that any one who wants admission gets it as Mr Gbagi implied (as opposed to anyone who deserves admission) negates the role of relatively high entrance barrier in guaranteeing quality. The challenge of course has always been how to provide access to as many students as deserve it without diluting the need to maintain high entrance barriers so that only those who can, and truly deserve it, get admitted

Four, a fundamental aspect of the need to re-think our university education system is the urgency of interrogating the notion of our universities as 'Ivory Towers'. There is a need for a re-conceptualization of our universities away from 'Ivory Towers' to our universities as conscious agents of development. In the notion of universities as 'Ivory Towers', there is often a tendency for knowledge to be pursued, created, or distributed just for its own sake rather than for such knowledge to be attuned to the immediate needs and developmental aspirations of the society. In our type of society, with its monumental development challenges, the notion of universities as 'Ivory Towers', is a luxury we cannot afford. Our universities need to go beyond their traditional roles and become 'developmental universities'. In a 'developmental university' for instance, teaching and research are organised in such a way as to consciously meet the developmental needs of the country. A 'developmental university' uses its enrolment procedures and its shared intellectual and cultural environments to consciously promote the goal of nation building, economic development and graduate employment.

Five, another area of our university education that cries out for urgent reform is the unnecessarily long number of years spent in pursuing some degree and diploma programmes. Why should it for instance take six years to produce a law graduate and five years to produce an engineering graduate in Nigeria when it takes only three years or less to produce similar graduates in most other countries? What is the sub-text here? That Nigerians are slow learners? Unfortunately in an increasingly competitive international labour market where age is often a big issue, Nigerian graduates are being unnecessarily disadvantaged. There is also an urgent need for the introduction of conversion programmes as we have in many countries. In the UK for instance, a non-graduate in law who wants to become a lawyer can opt to do a one year conversion programme in law and will be deemed to have satisfied the academic stage of legal training if he successfully completes such a programme. In Nigeria such a graduate will be required to spend another four to five years.

In conclusion, the idea of establishing six more federal universities seems hastily conceived, and oozes of political agenda. In this sense, what will ordinarily have been a good idea risks compounding the problems of university education system.

Daily Trust, 24 Nov 2010

CHAPTER 71

BOKO HARAM: SYMPTOM OF CRISIS IN OUR NATION-BUILDING PROJECT (1)

Virtually everything about Boko Haram is contested – including the reasons for its radicalisation after some seven years of being a peaceful group, whether all the atrocities said to be perpetrated by the sect were indeed carried out by it and who its sponsors are. What is not contested is that the sect's methods have become increasingly sophisticated and audacious.

One of the contested domains is whether the sect has links with foreign terrorist groups such as Al Qaeda. The government thinks it does. In fact in June 2009 the Nigerian State Security Service claimed that members of Boko Haram were being trained in Afghanistan and Algeria by members of al-Qaeda. President Jonathan re-echoed that much a day after the bombing of the UN building in Abuja on August 26 2011 when he declared that "Boko Haram is a local group linked up with terrorist activities". But not everyone buys this. Former US ambassador to Nigeria John Campbell and Ioannis Mantizikos, a Greek expert on radical Islamic movements, are among those who argue there is no evidence of any such linkage.

It can be argued that the government has a vested interest in presenting Boko Haram as having such a linkage. One, it will make it easier to attract international sympathy and technical assistance from European countries and USA which are normally paranoid about any group rumoured to be linked to Al Qaeda . Two, linking Boko Haram to Al-Qaeda will blunt criticisms against the government's inability to contain the group– after all, if the USA and the European countries, with all their resources and capabilities have not been able to effectively contain Al Qaeda, why will anyone see it as a sign of weakness that the government has not been able to defeat an organisation it sponsors? Three, by linking Boko Haram to Al Qaeda the government may hope to use innuendos and name-dropping of US involvement to frighten the sect and help to pressure it to the negotiating table.

Paradoxically linking Boko Haram to Al Qaeda will also enhance the chances of such alliance happening – if the sect does not already have such a linkage – because it could help it to attract the sympathy of other international terrorist groups. Another paradox in the portraiture of Boko Haram as an organisation with an external linkage is that if the USA and other European countries get openly involved in fighting the sect, it could mobilise anti- USA forces globally and even domestically behind the sect. It could also fire off a wave of nationalism that may end up winning the sect more members and sympathisers even from Nigerians stoutly opposed to the sect's activities.

Explaining the Boko Haram phenomenon

Though there are several conspiracy theories about Boko Haram, it is possible to group some of the more 'reasonable' explanations of the sect around some theoretical constructs and then interrogate the validity of such 'theories' in understanding both why the sect came into being and the audacity of its activities.

Boko Haram as a Symptom of a Failed or Failing State

There are some who believe that Boko Haram is the clearest indication that Nigeria has become a failed or failing state. Those who argue within this framework often rely on the notion that a state should have the monopoly of legitimate violence in its territory. The argument is that Nigeria is a failed or failing state because it has lost that monopoly – not only to Boko Haram but also to kidnappers and armed robbers.

This argument however is not very convincing because there are countries such as Brazil which are regarded as 'successful' but where some of the cities and sub-states are effectively under the control of militarised gangs, drug barons and god-fathers. Besides, the notion of 'failed' of 'failing' state is often subjectively and politically deployed. In fact Noam Chomsky's famous book, *Failed States: The Abuse of Power and the Assault on Democrac*y (2006) argued that even the US was becoming a 'failed state'.

The closest to an extant taxonomy for measuring a 'failed state' is the Failed State Index published since 2005 by Fund for Peace, an independent Washington DC-based non-profit research and educational institution. The Index, which is published in conjunction with the journal *Foreign Policy*, uses the following to determine the extent to which a state has failed or is failing: (1) Loss of control of its territory or of the monopoly on the legitimate use of physical force. (2) Erosion of legitimate authority to make collective decisions. (3) Inability to provide public services and (4) Inability to interact with other states as a full member of the international community.

Nigeria first entered the league of the worst 20 cases in the Failed State Index in 2007 - before Boko Haram became radicalised. At that time it was ranked 17. In 2008, 2009, 2010 and 2011 it was ranked 19, 15, 14 and 14 respectively. This means that despite the audacity of its actions, Boko Haram only contributed 'marginally' to the worsening of Nigeria's ranking in the Index. In fact if official figures were to be believed, Nigeria with a per capita income of $2,700 and a GDP growth of seven percent cannot be called a failed or failing state – despite current security challenges.

Human needs theory

Human Needs theorists would argue that one of the primary causes of protracted violence is people's drive to meet their unmet needs. The argument here is that the relative poverty in the North, especially in the North-east, the Boko Haram's main base, disposes people to violence. While there is some merit in this position, I will argue that this cannot comprehensively explain the audacity of the sect's actions or why similar groups have not emerged in other impoverished parts of the country.

The Frustration-Aggression Hypothesis

The argument here is that frustration causes aggression but when the source of the frustration cannot be challenged, the aggression gets displaced onto an innocent target. There are a number of explanations of the Boko Haram phenomenon that would seem to fit into this theory. For instance the CBN Governor Sanusi Lamido Sanusi was quoted by ThisDay of January 28 2012 as blaming the rise of Boko Haram partly on economic inequality among states and regions caused by the principle of derivation, which gives 13 percent of oil revenue to the oil producing states. According to Sanusi, who had clarified that he was quoted out of context, "There is clearly a direct link between the very uneven nature of distribution of resources and the rising level of violence."

A variant of this explanation is that the huge sums allocated in training former Niger Delta militants overseas under the Amnesty Programme of the late Umaru Yaradua may have had the unintended effect of triggering envy and frustration or sending a message that violence pays. My position is that while these may be partly true, they cannot comprehensively explain why the Boko Haram type of violence is not generalised in the North or why several states in the South which do not benefit from the 13% derivation or the amnesty programme have also not taken to militancy.

Another argument within the frustration-aggression framework is that after the reintroduction of Sharia law in the 12 Northern states, there was a widespread disillusionment at the way it was implemented, and members of the sect simply tapped into that frustration. As Jean Herskovits, an American expert on Nigerian politics was quoted as saying about it: "You punish somebody for stealing a goat or less - but a governor steals billions of *naira*, and gets off scot-free".

Another explanation within this thesis is that in Nigeria's peculiar mode of sharing privileges, the Igbo controls the commercial economy, the Yoruba the corporate economy and the North political power. It is thought that the loss of political power to the south in 1999 was perceived by some in the North as a loss of the region's lever in ensuring that it is not dominated by the South. This perception is thought to have fed into the bitter debate on the PDP's zoning and power rotation arrangements and Jonathan's decision to contest the April 2011 presidential elections to create generalised frustrations in the North, which Boko Haram simply tapped into. Again why this may be partly true, I will argue that it cannot explain why similar groups have not emerged in other parts of the North.

Next week, I will try to show that Boko Haram is one of the several symptoms of the severe crisis in our nation-building project.

Daily Trust, 9 Feb 2012

CHAPTER 72

BOKO HARAM: SYMPTOM OF THE CRISIS IN OUR NATION-BUILDING PROJECT (2)

In the first instalment in this three-part series, I tried to organise the various explanations of the Boko Haram phenomenon around three theoretical constructs – the failed or failing state argument, the human needs theory and the frustration-aggression hypothesis. I argued that each of these explanatory schemas, while embodying elements of truth, cannot comprehensively explain the Boko Haram phenomenon since the conditions that purportedly led to the emergence and radicalisation of the sect also exists in other parts of the country without giving birth to similarly radicalised groups.

In this instalment I shall try to show that Boko Haram is a manifestation of the severe crisis in our nation-building project.

The notion of 'nation' is highly contentious. There is however fairly a consensus that it has to do with the process of deliberately and consciously constructing or structuring a national identity using the power of the state. It is basically an attempt to use state power to unify the people of competing identities within a state to create what Benedict Anderson, a professor emeritus of International Studies at Cornel University, USA, called 'imagined communities.' For Anderson, a nation is a community socially constructed and imagined by the people who perceive themselves as part of the group. For him, a nation "is imagined because the members of even the smallest nation will never know most of their fellow members, meet them, or even hear of them, yet in the minds of each lives the image of their communion".

What is evident from the above is that a nation-building project, just like the building of a house, involves a mental picture of how the completed structure will look like such that the assignments given to all involved in the project work towards the actualisation of that goal. It is true that Nigeria is 'a mere geographical expression' in the sense that it is inhabited by previously independent ethnic nationalities that were more or less nation-states in their own rights before they were forced into the Nigerian arrangement. But Nigeria is hardly alone in this. In fact, historically nations have successfully been made of previously independent and even antagonistic nationalities forcibly brought together into one country by circumstances. Good examples include Germany, Tanzania and even Ghana. It can in fact be argued that most of the successful nations in the world today were at a point in their evolution made up of ethno-linguistic nationalities that antagonistically competed for scarce social values. They became successful nations through a deliberate use of state power to engender trust and feeling of oneness.

Given how different the peoples that were brought together into the Nigerian arrangement were at the time the Nigerian state was fashioned, I think it will be uncharitable to say that no progress has been made in the nation-building project. There have overtime evolved some shared values including the use of Pidgin English as a sort of lingua franca and pride in the national football team. But it will appear that trust, so critical in welding together the different peoples and nationalities to form Anderson's 'imagined community', was never really appreciated as a foundational element in Nigeria's nation-building project. Rather the actions and inactions of the political leaders over time have tended to promote distrust, which has percolated to even ethnically and linguistically homogenous groups. Today this distrust has become so endemic that not only is the Nigerian state distrusted by all, virtually all the constituent peoples and units of the Nigerian state aggressively distrust one another and openly express such distrust in stereotypes and innuendos that not only further the distrust but also promote hatred. True, unity and creating a real nation may not have been the real intentions of the British imperialists that fashioned the Nigerian state. But to blame them for the lack of progress in making a nation-nation out of the nationalities that make up the country, will, in my opinion, amount to a mere feel-good grandstanding. These people left more than 50 years ago. As someone once said, though some people may have helped to push us down, the ultimate responsibility to get up is our own.

Nigeria without Nigerians?

Following from the above, my position is that a more comprehensive explanation of the Boko Haram phenomenon is the crisis in our nation-building project which feeds into the crisis of underdevelopment to create an existentialist crisis for many Nigerians. For many people, a way of resolving the consequent sense of alienation is to retreat from the Nigeria project and construct meanings in chosen primordial identities - often with the Nigerian state as the enemy. The same process is replicated at the sub-Nigerian state levels – the state and local governments - seen as part of the Nigerian state authority structure. There is therefore everywhere in the country a pervasive sense of what the German - American political theorist Hannah Arendt called the 'banality of evil'. Her explanation of this thesis is that the great evils in history are not executed by fanatics or sociopaths but rather by ordinary people who accepted the premises of their actions and therefore participated in them on the grounds that those heinous actions were normal. This is the so-called notion of 'normalising the unthinkable' or the routinization of evil. And this truly reflects Nigeria's federal character – violent armed robberies across the entire country, kidnapping especially in the South-east and turf war by militarised cults and gangs in Bayelsa State.

Therefore the Nigerian state, contrary to the media hype, is regarded as the enemy, not just by Boko Haram, but by several Nigerians and groups, each attacking it with as much ferocity as Boko Haram's bombs, using whatever means they have at their disposal: politicians entrusted to protect our common patrimony steal the country blind, law enforcement officers see or hear no evil at a slight inducement, government workers drag their feet and refuse to give their best while revelling in moonlighting, organised labour, including university lecturers in public institutions go on indefinite strikes on a whim while journalists accept 'brown envelopes' to turn truth on its head or become uncritical champions of a selected, anti-Nigerian state identity. What all these groups have in common with Boko Haram is that they believe that the premise on which they act is justifiable and that the Nigerian state is unfair to them, if not an outright enemy. What all these tell me therefore is that a big de-Nigerianisation process is going on and that unless the trend is urgently reversed we risk having Nigeria without Nigerians. For instance that many communities in which members of the Boko Haram live know them but are not giving them away to the authorities could mean they are afraid they could be targeted by the sect. But it could also mean that the de-Nigerianisation process is perhaps more pervasive than we think.

In Nigeria, there is a heavy burden of institutionalised sectional memories of hurt, injustice, distrust and even a disguised longing for vengeance. Every unit of the federation has its own story to tell and has several examples to prove its case of 'marginalisation'. This means therefore that any strategy to confront the security challenge in the country – and Boko Haram has become the metaphor for our security challenge- is bound to evoke these ugly memories in some sections of the population. No individual or political authority enjoys universal legitimacy across the main fault lines. Nigeria is therefore a country in desperate need of creating Nigerians. When the Boko Haram attacks lead to Southerners fleeing from the North and Northerners in the South fleeing for fear of reprisal attacks from the South, the de-Nigerianisation process is furthered.

I will conclude this next week by interrogating some of the desiderata for the crisis in our nation building project, especially the idea of sovereign national conference.

Daily Trust, 16 Feb 2012

CHAPTER 73

BOKO HARAM: SYMPTOM OF THE CRISIS IN OUR NATION-BUILDING PROJECT (3)

In the last instalment I opined that several groups and individuals are withdrawing from the Nigeria project into primordial identities where they seek to construct meanings for the existentialist crisis engendered by a confluence of the severe quagmire in the country's nation building process w and the crisis of underdevelopment. I noted that Boko Haram and others withdrawing from the Nigerian state feel justified in regarding the state as their enemy and attacking it ferociously with whatever means they have at their disposal.

In this third and concluding part I will argue that trust – more than economic development- will be required to restart the stalled nation-building process. And talking of trust, it is tempting to speculate on what would have happened if President Jonathan had by-passed the chance to run in the April 2011 elections. Would that have engendered more trust between the North and South or would that have been taken as a sign of weakness? There are no clear cut answers to this even among political scientists. Those who subscribe to the realist school of power believe that Jonathan did the right thing and that once an opportunity to grab power is lost, it could be lost forever. On the other hand those who believe in normative political science will, focusing morality, argue that the President as a signatory to his party's zoning and power rotation arrangements that zoned the office of the president to the North after eight years of a Southern presidency ought to have disqualified himself from running despite the fact that as a sitting President he was constitutionally entitled to run.

It is germane to note that over the years several institutions and processes have been created to facilitate the task of nation-building – the introduction of the NYSC in 1973, enthronement of the need to reflect federal character in appointments in public offices, establishment of the Federal Character Commission etc. The critical question here is why are all these structures and other extant rules apparently ineffective in stemming the rapid de-Nigerianisation process and cries of marginalisation by virtually all the constituent units of the Nigerian arrangement?

Sovereign National Conference

The idea of a Sovereign National Conference in Nigeria gained traction during the regime of Babangida. With the frequent changes in the regime's transition rules, there began a silent murmur across the country that Babangida did not really want to relinquish power. When the presidential election believed to have been won by MKO Abiola in June 1993 was annulled, for some, it indicated not only that Babangida did not want to relinquish power but also that the North was unwilling to let go of the highest political office in the land. This narrative gained currency despite the fact that the victims of previous annulments by Babangida - Maj. Gen. Shehu Umaru Yar'Adua in the Social Democratic Party and Alhaji Umaru Shinkafi and Malam Adamu Ciroma in the National Republican Convention were all Northerners. When a faction of the Yoruba elite in NADECO agitating for the revalidation of Abiola's mandate upped the calls for a sovereign national conference under Abacha, SNC quickly became seen as a euphemism for the constituent parts of the federation to come together to peacefully negotiate terms of the dissolution of the union. My opinion is that this is a time-warped view of SNC.

The truth is that the various factions of the Nigerian elite clamouring for a SNC have different agendas in mind. True, there is a faction for whom SNC simply means meeting to discuss a peaceful dissolution of the Nigerian arrangement. There are however other factions who use it as a bargaining chip or for whom it means anything from 'resource control' to finding enduring solutions to some of the intractable issues in the polity such as the appropriate number of states and local governments in the country or the issue of state police. That SNC, as pushed by various factions of the elites, has no one agenda could be seen in the fact that the idea refused to die down even during the tenures of Southern Presidents – Obasanjo and now Goodluck Jonathan. In fact what all the advocates of a 'Sovereign' National Conference have in common is a deep distrust of the government, hence they want whatever decisions taken at such a National Conference to be implemented unmediated by the government. It is for this reason that the National Assembly, as part of the state structure, is also distrusted by all the advocates of SNC.

Dialogue is good. I am all for a SNC if some of the practical issues are addressed such as the constitution of its membership, leadership and safeguards to ensure that it is not hijacked by a vocal minority who will readily label themselves as 'progressives'. Few people will deny that the intractable problems of nation-building facing the country require new thinking. The problem with the country is not creating institutions or laws but getting people to trust their originators enough to obey them. The history of government interference in apparently 'independent' institutions and constant inaction on reports of the different probes and committees it regularly sets up is does not in fact encourage anyone to trust the government.

I am against the break-up of Nigeria because every country, no matter how successful, has its own fault lines. However I am equally against any notion that the 'unity' of the country is not negotiable. One, to talk of the 'unity of the country' amid the worst crisis in the country's nation-building project is a contradiction in terms, which in fact glamorises the call for the dismemberment of the country. If there is that 'unity' why is the process of de-Nigerianisation moving at the fastest pace in our political history? Two, it is illogical to call a couple in a dysfunctional marriage to a peace meeting with a proviso that divorce is off the agenda. This is because the fear of divorce may actually be what has been keeping the marriage together – as dysfunctional as it may be. It is therefore perfectly possible that those who want the SNC to be a forum for a peaceful dissolution of the country could change their mind when they realise they could be granted their wish and the full implications of such an option dawn on them.

While I do not have a fully developed idea of how the practical issues around representation in the proposed SNC should be overcome, I also do not believe that popularity, as defined by the ability to win elections, should be the sole requirement for choosing members of the SNC. I will therefore favour a sort of a National Conference, which will be made up of both elected members and those selected to represent special interests or those who have been vocal over the years on the issue. It is true that some of the 'usual suspects' who have been agitating for SNC over the years cannot win elections. However given their tremendous noise value, excluding such people from such a Conference will cast a big legitimacy question mark over the whole exercise.

While the idea of SNC is still being debated, the government must, in the interim, think out of the box and find out why the state and its agencies are deeply distrusted by Nigerians. There is a feeling that while inter-personal relations across the fault lines seem to have improved over the years, inter-group relations appear to have worsened. My personal opinion is that while mutual self-interest has been the driver of most successful inter-personal relations across the fault lines, the government has continued to rely on appeal to abstract patriotism to engender harmonious inter-group relations. I strongly believe that more could be achieved if the government appeals to the self interest of the constituent units of the federation. For instance, the government can, deliberately encourage say the groundnuts produced in particular areas of the North to be used in say the manufacture of peanut butter in another part of the country. Such a project, if viable, is likely to lead to a greater harmony of interests between the elites of the areas that produce groundnuts and those that produce peanut butter.

Another area that needs urgent government attention is the use of intemperate language and ethnic/religious profiling. In the USA and many parts of Europe for instance, racial slurs are criminalised and politicians dig their political graves if they make off-the- cuff remarks that are seen as racists. Not so in Nigeria where even the very educated and enlightened regale in ethnic and religious profiling. And the government does nothing about it.

How do we get our people to trust the government and one another? I have no answer to this. What I do know is that trust has to be earned.

Daily Trust, 23 Feb 2012

CHAPTER 74

THE AFTERMATH OF THE CHRISTMAS BOMBINGS

The bomb attacks on Christmas Day have understandably led to palpable anger in the land. The attacks - one at St. Theresa's Catholic Church, Madallah, on the outskirts of the Federal capital Territory, another in a church in Jos, Plateau State and a third one at the state headquarters of the State Security Service at Damaturu, Yobe State - appeared co-ordinated and led to several deaths, with scores of people injured. The anger and collective revulsion that followed the attack suggests that the heinous crime has the possibility of uniting a sharply divided populace against the forces of evil and criminality. However they are also capable of further polarising an already divided populace if it is mismanaged or allowed to be exploited by opportunistic elements.

We call for maturity in the handling of the common challenge posed by the Boko Haram threat. While it is understandable that bombing places of worship should be regarded as crossing the line by Boko Haram, we urge for restraint in the use of intemperate language to express our feelings as this could only worsen what is already a bad situation. In this sense we strongly condemn the statement credited to Pastor Ayo Oritsejafor, pastor of the Words of Life Ministry and President of the Christian Association of Nigeria of CAN, who implied that Boko Haram specifically targets Christians and declared that Christians would henceforth defend themselves. Contrary to Oritsejafor's insinuations, the truth is that Boko Haram seems to target everyone – Muslims and Christians alike. For instance Boko Haram opened its dastardly activities in 2011 on Friday January 28 with the assassination of a prominent Muslim, Alhaji Modu Gobi, who was the ANPP's Governorship candidate for Borno State. He was killed alongside his brother, four police officers and a 12-year-old boy. Boko Haram also killed the Gomari Islamic cleric, Ahmed Ibrahim Abdullahi on March 13 at his mosque. On August 12 2011, another prominent Muslim cleric Liman Bana was shot dead while returning from the main mosque at Ngala. Again as the year drew to a close, an Islamic cleric's family were reported killed in a gun attack in Maiduguri on Dec 30. These few examples show that Boko Haram, which has been denounced by prominent Northern Muslims including Buhari, Atiku and the Sultan of Sokoto, do not discriminate between Christians and Muslims in their gory activities. It is therefore clearly a fallacy and opportunistic to suggest that Boko Haram only targets Christians.

While we condemn Oritsjeafor's unguarded vituperations, we similarly condemn the attempt by the Secretary General of the Jama'atu Nasril Islam (JNI), Dr. Khalid Abubakar Aliyur to join issues with the CAN President. We do not agree as suggested by Dr. Khalid Abubakar Aliyu that Oritsejeafor's purported statement amounted to a contempt on the Sultan of Sokoto and on other Muslim clerics that have condemned the attacks. Two wrongs cannot make a right and it is unhelpful to politicize Oritsjeafor's unfortunate incitement of Christians to violence. We similarly condemn other groups that have tried to opportunistically cash in on the situation such as the Egbesu Mightier Fraternity, which claimed responsibility for bombing a mosque in Sapele, Delta state in a purported retaliation of the supposed targeting of Christians by Boko Haram.

We urge the government to do more to convince the public that it is really in charge of the security situation in the country. We welcome the declaration of state of emergency in some parts of the country where the Boko Haram threat has been more endemic, including the temporary closure of contiguous borders in the affected states. But this must be seen as only a palliative measure. There is a need for a thorough re-organisation of our security services. We are sick and tired of service chiefs who keep assuring us that they are on top of the security situation while the country gradually slides into anarchy and lawlessness. We must put sentiments aside and shove aside those manning our security apparatuses who are really not living up to the task.

While we believe that the criminal members of Boko Haram who perpetrate mayhem must be hunted down and punished, we also urge the government not to completely foreclose avenues for dialogue. We believe that by engaging the more moderate members or factions of the sect, the hardliners will be isolated, making it easier to neutralize them.

Daily Trust 3 January 2012

CHAPTER 75

SHOULD SUSPECTS BE PARADED?

The above question is generating increasing furore among our intellectuals, and 'beer parlour' political activists. Parading of suspects takes various forms: the police calling a press conference and triumphantly showing nabbed suspects of crime, or a top public functionary leaking to press allegations of crime, usually corruption, against another top official or former top official, often with an innuendo that the evidence against the suspect is incontrovertible. It is thought that Ribadu's EFCC took the practice of parading suspects in the media to a dizzying height with his practice of accusing, trying and convicting suspects before remembering to add (as an afterthought perhaps) that 'investigations are continuing' in the case.

The practice of parading suspects is not unique to Nigeria. In the US for instance, while it is common for arrested suspects to be concealed from public view while in police custody to protect their privacy and reputation, it is sometimes unavoidable to expose them to the public while being tansported through public places. This is known as 'perp walk' (the 'perp' is short for 'perpetrator') and could be used as an opportunity by the police to parade the suspects by tipping the media and the public of the planned 'walk'. For instance, Lee Harvey Oswald, the presumed assassin of US President John F Kennedy, was paraded in front of TV cameras several times as he was moved from place to place in Dallas Police Headquarters, and was even allowed occasionally to speak to the media. He was shot dead in one of such "perp walks" by Jack Ruby while being led to a vehicle for transfer to the county jail. In the same vein, Oklahoma City bomber Timothy McVeigh was paraded before television cameras nearly three hours before he was officially arrested for the bombing. 'Perp walks' are also done to politicians or business people accused of white-collar crimes.

In the UK, 'name and shame' - a practice aimed at discouraging anti-social or criminal activity by publishing the names of those involved- is not very different from parading suspects. The UK uses the 'name and shame' policy variously, including against shoplifters, abortionists, graffiti artists and customers of prostitutes. In fact, The Rat Book, the UK's biggest 'name and shame' website, which was launched in late 2009, contained, as of January 2010, the details of over 14,000 criminal charges and convictions on sundry issues, including paedophilia, rape, murder, violent crime, abuse and terrorism.

A major difference between the parading of suspects in USA and UK, and Nigeria, is that the investigative process is so robust in these countries that often the police and authorities would make an arrest only when they feel they have sufficient evidence for a successful prosecution. In Nigeria on the other hand, we seem to act often on the spur of the moment.

There are legitimate concerns about the practice of parading suspects, not least because the presumption of innocence until convicted by a competent court of law, is seen as a fundamental human right. Additionally, the right to one's reputation is universally seen as part of human dignity. Recently the Commandant General of the Nigerian Peace Corps Ambassador Dickson Akor called for legislation restraining the police from parading suspects after the police invaded his office and later called a press conference accusing him of training and arming youths. A Federal Capital Territory (FCT) High Court dismissed the charges brought against him and six others. Similarly in March 2010, Justice Akinjide Ajakaiye of the Federal High Court in Lagos reportedly warned the CBN Governor Lamido Sanusi to stop parading suspects in the media.

In Nigeria, supporters and opponents of parading suspects have their arguments:

One, supporters argue that the humiliation of being publicly paraded could be a good deterrence against crime and unacceptable anti-social behaviour. They also posit that parading suspects helps to reassure the public that the system works and that criminals will eventually be smoked out. As the criminologist Robert McCrie would put it: "When we see that someone has been apprehended, looking forlorn and beshackled, it indicates that the system is working, and that the defendant will get his just deserts." Opponents however fear that the police or public authorities in a desperate bid to show off their crime fighting skills, or to hug publicity or legitimise their policies, may act too quickly before the facts are fully available. A good example here is the Central Bank under Lamido Sanusi publishing the list of debtors to banks, only to later admit, when challenged, that its initial list contained typographical errors.

Two, opponents of parading suspects argue that it prejudices the trial of the suspects by putting the judges under tremendous public and media pressure. They point out that the public, and the vocal media, will often demonise and forever caricature a judge who rules against popular sentiments irrespective of the weight of evidence before the judge in the case. Supporters of the practice however counter that since Nigeria does not run a jury system, the judges, as trained professionals, cannot possibly be swayed by the emotionalism of media and public trial.

Opponents of parading suspects sneer at this point, noting that even the integrity of many judges are routinely called into question.

Three, supporters of parading suspects argue that in our type of system, where justice could be bought or unnecessarily delayed, parading suspects offers instant 'justice' in the court of public opinion – when the case is still fresh and before the suspects have the time to pull the strings. Opponents however counter that given the time it takes to prosecute a case, and the pervasive belief that justice could be bought and sold, even if a suspect is eventually acquitted, many will still believe the person has simply paid off the judges, meaning that the suspect's reputation will remain forever damaged in the court of public opinion. They also note that many who witnessed the initial parade may not be aware of the eventual exoneration of the suspects.

Based on the above arguments and from the practice in other parts of the world, I will argue that parading of suspects does have a place in our society, but needs to be reformed to prevent abuse. I will recommend the following: First, there is a need for an exhaustive taxonomy of the types of crimes and anti-social behaviour that warrants the parading of suspects. Second, there should be a guideline of 'tests' to be met before the suspects are paraded. Part of these tests should be evidence that the suspects were given fair hearing and that a certain number of officials involved in the interrogation of the suspects must agree on such a parade. A component of such 'tests' could be an assessment that without such parading, the accused may elope or cause further danger to the society before they are charged to court. The UK and the US for instance have 'responsible journalism' tests often used by judges in defamation proceedings against the media. Third, crimes in which vendetta or hidden agenda is possible, especially against politicians and public officials, could require more stringent tests before the suspects are paraded. Given the propensity to use allegations of corruption to smear opponents in our culture, this will help to prevent witch-hunting or using others to achieve cheap popularity. Fourth, suspects paraded, and later found not guilty, should equally be paraded when acquitted, and the accusing police or public authority made to publicly apologise to them and pay symbolic compensation for damaged reputation. This will not only help to restore damaged reputation but also put the reputation of the parading authority on the line.

Daily Trust 6 June 2012

CHAPTER 76

AGENDA FOR JCCR: MERGER OF THE STATES

The task of the Joint Committee on Constitution Review is not an enviable one. Reviewing the country's constitution is usually a thorny issue, often compounded by the lack of unanimity on areas that deserve to be reviewed, and in which direction any review should be made. In Nigeria's political history, the only successful attempt by a civilian regime to amend the country's constitution was in 1960, when the independence constitution was amended to produce the 1963 Republican constitution. At that time, the major area of amendment was agreed at a national conference of political leaders a few months before it was given legislative backing. Perhaps the exercise succeeded because the politicians were conscious that the Big Brother eyes of imperial Britain were watching them, and that behaving badly could have unacceptable consequences.

There were no such Big Brother eyes when the Obasanjo regime started a process of the review of the 1979 Constitution on 19th October 1999, with the establishment of the Presidential Committee on the Review of the 1999 Constitution. Though the Committee submitted its report in February 2001, the contentious nature of the exercise and strident calls by some that what Nigeria needed was a sovereign national conference and not a constitution amendment, frightened the wits out of the normally rancorous Obasanjo. Similarly a Bill produced from the proceedings of a committee set up by the National Assembly in May 2000 to review the Constitution did not go beyond second reading before the tenure of the assembly lapsed in May 2003. Any demand for constitution amendment in the country normally triggers emotions and tendencies that remind all of us that the fundamentals of our statehood remain contested. Some are already arguing that the standoff between the Senate and the House of Representatives is an indication that the current exercise could go the way of previous efforts.

Despite the sensitive nerves the exercise triggers, there are fundamental flaws in the constitution that undermine the country's state-building project and national development efforts, which should be urgently addressed. One of these is state creation and the politics it spurns. Originally conceived as part of the strategies of allaying ethnic minority fears of domination by bigger ethnic groups, and of bringing 'development' nearer to the people, the exercise has now run out of control, and has become a major impediment to economic growth and a contributor to the anarchical nature of our politics.

The current 36-state system for instance clearly undermines the principle behind the adoption of federalism in the country, namely, that each of the federating units, should, within its sphere of competence, be co-ordinate and equal. With the possible exception of Lagos and the Old Kano state, virtually all the states in the country are dependent on allocations from the federal government for their economic survival. Many struggle to even pay the salaries of their public servants, not to talk of embarking on any meaningful development project – a situation that is likely to get worse with dwindling revenue from oil.

Related to the above is that the current 36 states have become agents of underdevelopment. For those wondering why there is so much poverty in the land when the country is a major oil producer, consider the economic impact of having 36 state governments spurning a commensurate number of 'His Excellencies', commissioners, hangers-on, thugs, state Houses of Assembly, state public services and other paraphernalia. Add to these a certain percentage of the revenues from the Federation Account embezzled at various levels in each of the 36 states in the country and it becomes easier to see why development has eluded the country. It is instructive that India, whose population is about eight times that of Nigeria, has only 28 states.

I propose a merger of the current 36 states into six regions coterminous with the six generally accepted geopolitical zones in the country. Under this proposal, the current 36 states should be restructured into local governments but should not be recognised as units that share from the Federation Account. Each of the federating states should have the power to create sub-units and devise its own revenue allocation formula among such units. Town unions, which historically have been agents of self-help development in many parts of the country, ought to be recognised as units for sharing revenues at the state level.

Consolidating the 36 states into a manageable number will concomitantly reduce the size of government at the federal level, leading to efficiency and cost savings. Section 14 of the 1979 Constitution for instance makes the states the basic units used in determining whether the government is 'reflecting the federal character' in its appointments, composition of the federal public service and dispensation of privileges. This leads to a bloated federal government, as it has to ensure balanced representation of the 36 states in its appointments.

Reducing the number of states is also likely to impact more favourably on our politics. Section 126 (2-6) of the 1979 Constitution for instance demands that to be elected president a candidate must have no less than 25 percent of the votes cast at the election in each of at least two-thirds of all the states in the federation. This provision gives the number of states in each geopolitical zone a special political salience. Rival geopolitical or ethnic groups such as *North v South* or *Yorubas v Igbos* have therefore been overheating the polity with their politics of state creation to ensure either that they maintain their current power balance or get more states in its zone to redress a perceived imbalance. Of course elites who feel that new states will make them big fishes in small ponds do not help in this regard. Reducing the number of states is therefore likely to reduce the jockeying and bickering for political influence by the various geopolitical zones, which the politics of state creation generates.

Certainly any effort to consolidate the existing states will meet with massive resistance from vested interests, including from Governors and Members of the Federal and State Legislatures whose positions could suddenly become redundant. But it is a position that is likely to serve the country better. The crucial question however is whether we have the nerves to confront this issue head-on?

Hollerafrica.com February 19 2009

SECTION THREE

THE ECONOMY

CHAPTER 77

THE CALL FOR NIGERIA TO BORROW MORE

The recent report that Minister of Finance, Dr. Mansur Muhktar and the Director General of the Budget Office, Dr. Bright Okongu, have made a case for the country to borrow more to enable it achieve some of its economic targets, is bound confuse many Nigerians. Dr Abraham Nwankw, Director General of the Debt Management Office, who was also at the presentation of a breakdown of the recently passed 2009 budget on March 24, at which the duo were said to have made the call, reportedly, argued that the country was under-borrowing. According to Dr Nwankwothe nation's external debt currently stands at less than $3.7 billion, "which is a residue of the Paris and London Clubs debts". He also stressed that the loans were secured to fund education and some other development projects.

It should be recalled that in April 2006 Nigeria announced gleefully that it had paid the last of its multibillion-dollar debt to the London and Paris Club of creditor nations, with President Obasanjo boasting that "Nigeria will not owe anybody in the Paris Club one kobo". The country had reached a deal with the Club in October 2005, which allowed it to pay off about $30 billion in accumulated debt for about $12 billion, an overall discount of some 60 percent. As expected, many Western nations and institutions lauded the country for its 'bold' move when it paid a final instalment of $4.5 billion in April 2006. In fact a few months before the final instalment was paid, two reputed credit rating agencies rated the country's credit as BB-, which is below investment grade but, which at that time put the country on a par with developing nations like Turkey, Ukraine and Brazil.

Though not everyone was enthused about the debt repayment at that time for various reasons, the Obasanjo regime regarded it as one of its most remarkable achievements. In fact at about the time the last instalment was paid, the regime quickly announced a huge development project to provide jobs for Niger Delta youths and build a $1.6 billion highway in the region, giving the impression that the money allegedly saved from servicing the debts would be used to fund development projects like that. Only recently, Dr Ngozi Okonjo-Iweala, managing director of the World Bank, who was the Finance Minister at the time, continued the chest thumping: "It took a great deal of work – blood, sweat and tears to do it. If you had hired consultants to do this work they would have charged the country a great deal of money. Yet those of us who worked on it did it as part of our normal assignment looking at the benefit it would bring the country...I hope Nigerians never forget the freedom that lifting the debt burden has brought us. We must never incur such high levels of debt again" (ThisDay, March 29, 2009).

Given the politics of debt cancellation at the time, the huge amount the country paid to exit the London and Paris Club, and the glee and hoopla that laced the debt cancellation and buyback, the recent kite flying about a possible return to the Club for a new round of borrowing spree raises some uncomfortable questions.

One, why pay almost 20 billion dollars to exit the Club only to return to it for another borrowing just three years after? While it is understandable that given the current economic climate the budget deficit would have to be financed by some form of borrowing, the argument that part of the needed loan would come from apparently the London and Paris Club is worrying. The argument that Nigeria is 'under-borrowing' is similarly a source of concern since it was one of the arguments used to rationalise the borrowing spree of the 1980s. Second, there was a suggestion at the time Nigeria exited the London and Paris Club that the conditions that led to the country accumulating some $35 billion in debt had been addressed, and would apparently not re-occur. In fact, part of the conditions of the deal was that Nigeria agreed to enact economic reforms approved by the International Monetary Fund, which also had to confirm the country's compliance to those economic 'reforms', before the last transfer could be made. If the country is now back on the road to accumulating another round of debt just because the same condition of declining oil revenue that triggered the accumulation of huge debts in the 1980s has re-occurred, is there a legitimate ground to ask who is fooling who? As if to suggest that the country has once again come full circle, the credit rating agency Standard & Poor on 27 March lowered the country's ratings outlook to "negative" from "stable", citing falling oil revenues. It should be recalled that the Obasanjo regime made too much out of the BB- rating of 2006. Were the cynics after all right that the improved rating of 2006 was to massage the ego of the country's leaders for naively transferring so much wealth to the rich nations of the world?

Obviously while there is nothing wrong in a government borrowing to finance its budget deficits, however, for a country that transferred a huge sum out of her treasury just to be freed from an unbearable debt burden three years ago, many Nigerians would feel the government has not levelled up with them. Even the assurance by Dr Nwankwo that the government is "committed to ensuring that Nigeria's borrowing is sustainable" and that it would be "prudent when borrowing", is not likely to assuage the concerns of the citizens. Nor are they likely to be convinced that the new loans would be channelled into projects that would benefit them. In fact, three years after the country substantially paid down its debt, many Nigerians are still waiting to receive the dividends from the debt cancellation as promised by both the government and campaigners. What happened to the argument that the huge debt overhang and amount used to service it undermined investments in development projects such as education, infrastructure and employment generation? Is there any difference in the material circumstances of Nigerians before the debts were substantially cancelled and now? If the government succeeds with its plans to go on another borrowing spree from the 'international financial markets' will debt overhang once again be blamed for the country's poverty five years from now?

Daily Independent 4 February 2009

CHAPTER 78

SOVEREIGN WEALTH FUND (SWF): WHAT THEY ARE NOT TELLING YOU

The recent call by the Nigerian Governors' Forum (NGF) for the suspension of the implementation of the Sovereign Wealth Fund (SWF) has mostly generated angry responses from Nigerians, who are miffed that the Governors do not seem to think of tomorrow. It should be recalled that the SWF was set up ostensibly to conserve a portion of the money due to the Federation Account from oil revenue in excess of the benchmarks used in budget appropriation by the National Assembly. Before the establishment of the SWF, which was signed into Law by the President on May 27 2011, with $1 billion seed capital, such 'excess' revenues from oil went into the Excess Crude Account created by the Obasanjo regime as 'savings for the rainy day'. It is expected that the SWF will be funded monthly with surpluses from the budgetary revenue from oil.

The Governors have hinged their new found opposition to the SWF on its constitutionality because section 162 of the 1999 Constitution, which establishes the Federation Account, requires that such 'excess funds' should be put into the Federation Account and shared. The Governors also argue that given that their roles are increasing, especially with the newly introduced minimum wage, they need all the money they can get in order to perform their duties.

I align myself with the Governors in opposing the SWF. My position is that because of the perception problems most of the Governors have – most are rightly or wrongly perceived as no more than 'thieves' - the public seems unforgiving, and may in fact consider it a moral duty not to separate the message from the messenger once the Governors are involved, and the issue is more money for their states. I believe the whole notion of SWF raises several issues:

One, there is a tendency to discuss the SWF as a sort of fixed savings account, without any risks involved. My understanding of SWFs however is that these are pools of government money invested aggressively for profit. And if this is so, it immediately raises questions about the expertise of those who will manage the SWF, the willingness of the owners of the funds to accept that investments could go awry, and whether the owners of the fund accept the ethical basis of the investments made. While some SWFs have grabbed headlines by their audacious investments such asDubai's SWF's acquisition of big stakes in several Asian companies, including Sony, others have made pretty bad investments. Values of SWFs could also go up or down by changes in the economic climate. For instance in a working paper by the Council on Foreign Relations (CFR) published in January 2009 and entitled 'GCC Sovereign Funds: Reversal of Fortune', its authors Brad W. Setser and Rachel Ziemba estimated that the SWFs and foreign-currency funds of the Gulf Cooperation Council (GCC) lost about 27 percent of their assets, or $350 billion, in 2008 because of the collapse of oil prices in the latter half of the year.

Two, the governors have been lampooned by many commentators for leaning on the side of law to reject the SWF. While many commentators agree that the SWF violates section 162 of the 1999 Constitution, the consensus seems to be that the Governors should look beyond constitutionalism and focus on the spirit behind the establishment of the SWF. I do not buy this. To give the federal government this type of licence on the basis of a so-called good intention is dangerous because even the road to hell was paved with good intentions. This is especially so when the Governors have argued that the federal government has continued to deny them revenues centrally collected from companies paying stamp duties as well as taxes on the income of members of the armed forces and police which are supposed to be fully remitted to the states of residence on the basis of derivation as provided by Section 163 (b) of the 1999 Constitution. I think it is dangerous to give any government the licence to apply the law when it chooses.

Three, just like most States, the Federal Government has no history of prudence in its management of resources. For instance while the Excess Crude Account contained more than $20 billion when late President Umaru Yar'Adua came to power in 2007, by the end of last year it held less than $1 billion. Our foreign reserves were raided and depleted at a time of rising oil prices. On top of all these, the level of our indebtedness has been growing by leaps and bounds. With these backgrounds, why should we expect the federal government to manage the SWF prudently? Similarly, given our notoriety for policy reversals and somersaults, what is the guarantee that the next government will not jettison the idea of SWF, cash the investments and find spurious reasons why the federal government needs the money more than the other tiers of government?

Four, the SWF will widen the financial leverage the centre has over the states, further undermining the calls for true federalism in the country. The current revenue allocation formula, based on a March 2004 circular from the then Minister of Finance, Ngozi Okonjo-Iweala, is 52.68 per cent; 26.72 percent and 20 percent for the federal, states and local governments respectively. With 36 states and the federal capital territory sharing only 26.72 percent (when their responsibilities are increasing), the financial leverage enjoyed by the federal government becomes obscenely enormous. Under the current fiscal system, all but two or three states are dependent on allocations from the Federation Account to meet even the cost of their wage bill. With the federal government increasingly unable or unwilling to discharge its core responsibilities of guaranteeing security of life and property and providing basic infrastructure, I feel there is no rationally defensible reason for entrusting more resources under its care. On the contrary, with the pervasive insecurity in the land, the idea of State Police has become more imperative than ever - and the states will need money for that.

Five, Nigeria's SWF has three components that are potential sources of discord - the Nigerian Infrastructure Fund (to support infrastructural development); the Future Generations Fund, (savings for future generations of Nigerians) and the Stabilisation Fund, (to be used by government to ensure macro-economic stability in the country). Given the bitter politics that usually cloud revenue allocation inNigeria, what formula will be used by the federal government in distributing the funds from both the infrastructure fund and future generation funds? Why will monies that should go to the states be used for macroeconomic stabilisation when this is clearly the function of the central government?

Six, suggestions that any delay in the implementation of SWF will be negatively perceived by the 'international community' and might even lead to credit downgrade, is balderdash and cheap blackmail. We have never been short of projects, development plans and contraptions that are hyped to the high heavens but which rarely deliver on their promises. If abandoning the SWF leads to a ratings downgrade, certainly some Nigerians may be emboldened to ask the rating agencies to declare their interest on the Fund.

Seven, I believe the Governors' opposition to the SWF raises a fundamental question of the appropriate fiscal relationship between the three tiers of government? Are the three tier structures still relevant to our needs? Do we really want federalism for this country? This last question is pertinent because in a true federal arrangement, the federal government will have no reason to nanny the federating units by compelling them to give up a share of revenues that should accrue to them so that it will invest such on their behalf. I also honestly don't believe that reducing the cost of governance in the country is possible under the present 36 state system. My position is that we need to collapse these states into no more than 12 or 18. I also believe the states and the federal government should each have 40% of federally generated revenue. I believe the whole idea of local government as a tier of government that should partake in revenue sharing should be re-visited. Each state should be allowed to decide whether its local governments or town unions will be the most appropriate units for sharing the state's share of revenues.

Daily Trust, 8 September 2011

CHAPTER 79

WHY THE GOVERNMENT MAY BE WRONG ON THE NEW 'MINIMUM' WAGE

The recent 63.7 percent increase in the national minimum wage, from N11,000 to N17,000 (or is it N18,000?) has generally been seen as good news for workers – despite the increase coming short of the N52,000 originally demanded by the Nigerian Labour Congress. The pay rise, effective from August 2010, and graduated across the levels, will make the highest paid civil servant on the highest grade level (i.e. level 17, step 9) earn N453, 444, 67 per month, or N5, 444,336 per year. While this is certainly a victory for the relevant labour leaders – labour leaders tend to measure the success of their tenure by the number and quantum of concessions they are able to extract from employers – it is not clear that Nigerian workers will benefit as much as the nominal salary increases suggest. The new 'minimum' wage in fact raises a number of issues:

One, is that the entire exercise appears to be clouded in ambiguities. It is for instance unclear whether what was effected was an increase in 'minimum wage' as widely reported in the press or a relativity adjustment as argued by Comrade Philips Agbonkonkon, General Secretary of Amalgamated Union of Public Corporations, Civil Service, Technical and Recreational Services Employees (AUPCTRE) who said the new deal was meant to bridge a wide gap in pay differentials among staff of various sectors of the civil service. He said the pay rise "is different from the increase in wage that the Nigerian Labour Congress (NLC), Trade Union Congress (TUC) and Nigerian Employers' Consultative Association (NECA) are working on" (Nigerian Compass of July 12, 2010).

The new minimum wage is also silent on how this affects members of the NYSC, whose current allowances are below this minimum threshold – just as there are conflicting reports on whether it was increased to N17, 000 or N18, 000. It was equally not made binding on the private sector employers – as is often the practice with minimum wage legislations. Similarly, there is a lack of clarity on what really spurred the President to push for the new wage hike: while the President's Facebook claims he took the steps following his survey of the prices of basic goods, which made him realise the difficulties Nigerians are going through, other reports say it was a fulfilment of the promise he made to Nigerian workers on May 1, 2010, when, as Acting President, he persuaded them to suspend a five-day working strike over pay increase.

Two, there are sufficient grounds to be suspicious of a wage increase on the eve of an election year, especially when the President's body language appears to indicate that he will contest the election next year. Critics could interpret this as an attempt to bribe the workers. Additionally, cynics may be looking out for the possibility of the increases being sweeteners to the labour leaders preparatory to the introduction of harsher economic measures, especially as the government has been flying a kite about the need for further increases in the prices of petroleum products. Could the new minimum wage be a pre-emptive strike in which the so-called de-subsidisation of petroleum products will be accelerated after next year's elections?

Three, it is debatable whether the decision to increase wages during a strangulating recession that is accompanied by unacceptably high levels of unemployment, is a wise economic move. At a time when most governments in the world are offering economic stimulus packages to help save workers' jobs and get the unemployed back to work, not much was said about how the measure will affect job security or job creation. In the US for instance, a study by the Ball State University's Centre for Business and Economic Research (CBER) suggests that the increase in the minimum wage between 2007 and 2009 ((1.6% in 2007, 12% in 2008 and 10.7% in 2009) from $5.15 in early 2007 to $7.25 in the summer of 2009, led to the elimination of some 550,000 jobs in the country. It was also thought to have contributed significantly to unemployment rate for the 16-24 year olds (the age bracket that often earns minimum wage) reaching a record 19.6 percent in April 2010, double the US national average – the worst since the 1980s, and possibly since the Great Depression. Summer jobs – a useful way for students to earn cash and job experience - virtually disappeared.

In the UK, the recent increase in the minimum wage was a conscious effort to strike a balance between helping low paid workers and their families and ensuring that the pay rise does not affect their job security or general employment prospects. Thus from October 1, 2010, the national minimum wage (adult rate) will rise from its current level of £5.80 per hour to £5.93 per hour, an increase of just 2.2 percent. The national minimum wage "youth development rate" (for workers aged 18 to 20) will concomitantly rise from £4.83 per hour to £4.92 (an increase of just 1.8 percent).

In Nigeria there are legitimate concerns that the 63% increase in the minimum wage (at one go) could give wrong signals to the market, leading to inflationary pressures that would undermine the expected benefits of the exercise. Wouldn't it have been better if a substantial part of the new wage hike was offered as fringe benefits such as support to help low paid workers with school fees, retraining or medical bills?

Four, it may be tempting to speculate on the profile of Nigerian workers likely to benefit most by the new minimum wage and pose the question of how the increase is likely to affect their job security. It is no news that most state governments struggle to meet their current wage bills, and some owe arrears of salaries. These states are now told they must implement the new minimum wage – without any hint of what will happen if those governments decide to embark on retrenchments to be able to afford the new pay. More importantly is that the announcement of the new 'minimum' wage ought to have been made simultaneously with a federally funded programme for job creation at both the federal and state levels – to forestall the announcement leading to a knee jerk freeze on hiring by employers. The government also ought to have clearly indicated where it expected funding for the new increase to come from.

Five, the possible undertones that informed the minimum wage increase calls to mind our orientation towards 'sharing' as opposed to the 'baking' of the national cake - to increase its size. Not much has been heard about creative ways of increasing productivity, reducing the cost of governance and improving economic efficiency at a time key institutions like NNPC were said to have gone broke (though denied, but as they say, 'no smoke without fire'). While any move to better the lot of Nigerian workers must be applauded, we should at the same time not lose sight of the real factors that have confined them as the wretched of the earth and the rest of us as the laughing stock of the world.

No one will dispute that our workers deserve decent wages that will guarantee social self-reproduction without recourse to moonlighting, bribery and corruption or primitive accumulation. I remain however unconvinced that increases in nominal wages under the current, consumption-oriented structure of the federation and poor infrastructure will be able to guarantee them just that.

CHAPTER 80

THE NORTH, REVENUE ALLOCATION AND THE GAMES THEY PLAY

The call by Governor Babangida Aliyu of Niger State for a review of the current system of revenue allocation, which he argued 'disadvantages the North', has, expectedly generated angry reactions from the South, especially from South-south politicians. Governor Aliyu, who is also the chairman of the Northern Governors' Forum, reportedly took umbrage at the 13 per cent derivation principle, in particular the fact that revenues from offshore explorations are treated as being derived from the Niger Delta, when in his opinion, they shouldn't.

Governor Aliyu's remarks raise a number of fundamental issues:

One, among the nation's political elites, geopolitics is like a game of chess or draught. You make a move; your opponent anticipates your game plan and makes a counter move to block you from realising your objective. In this game of wits, decoy, grandstanding and exaggerated anger are key elements. For instance in the days of agitation for 'sharia' by the North, many of the politicians from the South rallied behind the South-south in its counter agitation for 'resource control' (never mind that most of them will be as disadvantaged as the North if resource control were to be implemented). In the current political climate when the South is 'moving' its game of 'Sovereign National Conference', it is not altogether impossible that Governor Aliyu's 'umbrage' at the 13 per cent derivation principle is meant to be a counter move to the South's SNC. In this sense I truly sympathise with Nigerians who work themselves up when the different ethnic and regional factions of the elites play this game. The truth is that when these politicians meet in their hideouts with their mistresses over the best foods and drinks, they review with hilarity the 'moves' they made as they played this game. Honestly most of our politicians are self-interested creatures- despite their grandstanding and pretensions of being champions of the best interests of their regions.

Two, assuming that the call by Governor Aliyu was not just part of the games the different ethnic and regional factions of the political class play, how correct was he that the 13 per cent derivation principle disadvantages the North? The truth is that derivation - a percentage of the revenues, which states retain from taxes on oil and other natural resources produced in their state – is only one of about five main criteria used in sharing revenue from the Federation Account and the North has the advantage in the other principles. In fact historically, the bulk of the allocation (about 70 per cent) has been on the basis of 'equality ofstates' and 'population', and the North enjoys advantage in these two criteria because it has more States and more population. Also the North has strategic advantages in the key units that share the revenues: it has more States and far more local governments than other geopolitical zones. And if you take into consideration the current system of sharing the revenue among the three tiers of the government: Federal government (52.68%); States (26.72%) and Local Governments (20.60%), you will realise the quantum of money the region as a whole gets. In essence while Governor Aliyu was right that individual States from the North get less from the Federation Account than the Niger Delta States because of the 13 per cent derivation principle he was wrong to extrapolate from that to arguethat the entire North is disadvantaged by that systembecause most of the States from the South do not benefit from this. Governor Aliyu's position was therefore a classic case of committing a 'fallacy of composition' - the mistake of assuming that what is true of an individual or unit is true for the group as a whole.

Three, derivation has always been a 'principle' for sharing the national revenue from 1958 when the Raisman Commission recommended that it should be 50per cent. It has never been under 10 per cent under any regime. Even under Abacha, it was 13 per cent and has remained 13 per cent since 2001. So what is the big deal about the current 13 per cent derivation? True, it has remained controversial whether the derivation principle should apply to revenues from off shore exploration but so have virtually all the principles used or suggested to be used for revenue sharing from the Federation Account. For instance States from the South- east and the South- west which tend to have more people in schools than other parts of the country have always favoured the use of 'primary school enrolment' as a key principle in sharing revenues because as they argue, having a large number of people in schools require increased revenues – not just for paying teachers' salaries but also for building and equipping schools.Similarly, the North, with population and land mass advantages,hashistorically always favoured these two 'principles' in the sharing of revenue from the Federation Account. Thus while the North accuses the South-south of 'resource tyranny', it is in turn accused by the South of 'population tyranny'.

Four, it is a myth to believe that the States that get more money from the Federation Account perform better than those which do not. For instance, not long ago, Senator Olubunmi Adetunmbi, in a motion entitled 'Looming danger of bankruptcy in states: the need for fiscal evaluation', declared that most of the 36 states in the federation are in dire financial straits. Based on figures from the Nigerian Governors' Forum, Senator Adetunmbi declared that only four States - Abia, Akwa Ibom, Anambra and Jigawa - were in good financial health. The remarkable thing here is that Akwa Ibom is the only oil rich State that was certified to be financially healthy. In fact Rivers and Bayelsa States which receive huge revenues from the Federation Account were classified along with Oyo, Bauchi, Nasarawaand Gombe as being unhealthy. The conclusion from this therefore is that there is no correlation between the amount of money available to a State and its financial health or what the government is able to achieve if it manages its resources prudently.

Five, there is a need to revisit the myth that the Northern states underperform their Southern counterparts or that they are 'disadvantaged'. For instance in the list published by Senator Adetunmbi on the financial health of the States, a Northern state - Jigawa was among the four States regarded as being in good financial health. In the same list, of the 15 States classified as being in 'critical condition' - Ekiti, Plateau, Benue, Edo, Borno, Adamawa, Cross Rivers, Enugu, Taraba, Ogun, Kogi, Yobe, Ebonyi, Ondo and Kaduna – the North accounted for eight States while the South accounted for seven (a parity between the two regions if one realises the North has more States). In the same vein, the notion that the North will be worse off in the event of a break-up of the country is a myth. True, currently most of the States in the Federationdepend on the monthly allocation from the Federation Account to meet even their wage bill. But we will never know how the various units of the federation will fare without the monthly allocation from the Federation Account because, as they say, necessity is the mother of invention and no one can predict what each State can achieve if pushed to the wall. If we use Internally Generated Revenue (IGR) as a percentage of total revenue as a guide on how the States could fare without the monthly allocations from the Federation Account, then only Lagos and Sokoto States will survive. According to Mrs Ifueko Omoigui-Okaru, the chairperson of the Federal Inland Revenue Service (FIRS), Lagos had the highest IGR in 2008/2009 of 60 per cent followed bySokoto State which had an IGR of 46 per cent. Apart from Lagos and Sokoto, other 'good' performing States had IGR of 20 per cent or a little above this. And of these, two Northern States - Borno and Gombe made the list along with others like Rivers, Osun, Oyo, Ogun and Abia States. Based on these, the alleged underperformance of the North or that it will be the worse off in the event of a break-up of the country is a myth.

Six, while I believe that some of the 'real' grouses over the principles used in sharing the revenues from the Federation Account could have some merit, I am also mindful they could be used to mask non-performance and corruption by the State Governors and Local Government chairpersons. What is perhaps more important at this point is developing a mechanism to ensure that the capital projects in the Federal Government's share from the Federation Account are fairly distributed across the country. This could be one way of muffling the perennial cries by all sections of the country of being 'marginalised'.

Daily Trust 8 May 2012

CHAPTER 81

LYING WITH STATISTICS – NIGERIA AS THE 'THIRD FASTEST GROWING ECONOMY'

n a very influential book, *How to Lie with Statistics* (1954), the American writer, Darrell Huff, discusses the funny business of lying Iwith figures, telling us how intentional or unintentional errors could lead to inaccurate conclusions. The book, which was meant to be an introduction to statistics for the general reader, quickly became one of the most widely read statistics books in history- despite the fact that the author was not a statistician. I suspect that the popularity of the book had largely to do with the fact that using graphs and figures to prove one's point could make one look really clever, and knowing that you are using such uncanny methods to bamboozle the gullible, probably will give an extra illicit sensation.

This brings me to the latest report that the International Monetary Fund (IMF) has ranked Nigeria the 'third fastest growing economy in the world after China and India'. IMF claimed that the country's economy grew "from 6.9 per cent in 2009 to 7.4 per cent this year". Minister of Finance, Dr Olusegun Aganga, was reported as saying that the rating by IMF at a time when the economies of the developed world were contracting was a good development and attributed the supposed growth to new policies initiated by the Federal Government.

There are several observations about this supposedly new status as 'the third fastest growing economy in the world'.

One, most statistical projections are based on certain assumptions – once the assumptions are changed, the conclusions also change. For instance the IMF has based its ranking on the assumption of a GDP growth rate of 7.4 per cent as supplied by the Nigerian government. Not many people will agree with this growth rate. For instance the website, www.theodora.com, based on figures from the CIA World Fact Book and other sources, estimated that the (GDP) real growth rate for the country was 6.4 per cent in 2007, 5.3 percent in 2008 and 3.8 per cent in 2009. In a country notorious for its poor statistical records and for brandishing figures on a whim (notice how different Nigerians and even researchers brandish different figures regarding our population), most statistical figures given are suspect – and often rightly so. And when these figures come from a government source, on the eve of an election year, when the government is roundly criticised for its handling of the economy, they become even more suspect.

Two, assuming that the growth rate of 7.4 percent given to the IMF by the Central Bank of Nigeria is correct – and that is a big assumption - it actually says very little about the management of the economy. Economic growth – the quantity of goods and services produced in a country- in our oil-dependent economy is often driven by an increase in oil exports and high global prices. It should be emphasised that economic growth is not the same thing as economic development, which is a sustainable boost in the standard of living of the people of a country, including an increase in their per capita income. It may therefore be disingenuous to make a political capital out of this supposed economic growth by suggesting that things are getting better.

Three, since the supposed 7.4 per cent growth rate will imply, in our type-of economy, an improvement in revenues from oil, the government is actually put on the spot to explain to Nigerians what has happened to the extra earnings especially against the backdrop of recent reports on the depletion of the $7bn excess crude account, the country's rising debt profile and the whopping 15 per cent drop in the country's foreign reserve in just one year. Figures issued by the Central Bank of Nigeria on October 7, 2010, showed that the country's foreign reserves fell to $34.57bn as at October 5, 2010, compared with $40.75bn at the same time a year ago.

One of the crucial questions that beggar answer is: how has the supposed growth in the economy impacted on job creation, the education sector, pervasive feeling of insecurity and the poverty line? Growth figures are meaningless to ordinary Nigerians if they cannot feel some changes in the quality of their life. And please do not tell them that the benefits will percolate to them in the 'long run' because as the British economist John Maynard Keynes would put it, in the long run we are all dead.

Four, there is a strong suspicion that the current rash of 'positive' news on the economy are contrived to blunt the regime's perceived vulnerability on the economy. It should be recalled that the news of Nigeria's ranking as the 'third fastest growing economy in the world' came at about the same time that Sanusi Lamido Sanusi, Governor of Central Bank, was also named the African Banker of the Year by the global business magazine, *Emerging Markets*, and the rating agency Standard & Poor (S&P) assigned Rivers State a 'B' international rating, "owing to its strong cash holdings, low debt and a healthy operating balance". Forgotten is that many of the bank chiefs that Sanusi criminalised had also received similar international awards. In fact, Sanusi's predecessor in office, Professor Chukwuma Soludo, now blamed by the government for being partly responsible for the economic woes of the country after he wrote an article expressing concerns over the direction of the economy, was also named African Banker of the Year during his tenure. We should also not forget that the rating agencies, Standard & Poor and Fitch, had once told us (after Sanusi's bank 'reforms' unearthed some rots in the system) that the glowing ratings they gave our banks and economy were simply based on figures supplied to them.

Five, while it will be unfair to attribute all the problems in the economy to the current government, there are real concerns that the government should address, and politicians should eschew playing politics with. Eminent Nigerians including Dr Ngozi Iweala and Professor Pat Utomi have for instance expressed grave concerns over the country's increasing debt profile at a time of rising oil receipts. Recently another request by the presidency to borrow additional 4.4 billion dollars was sent to the National Assembly. It should be recalled that in November 2005, the country won Paris Club approval for a debt-relief deal that eliminated $18 billion of debt in exchange for $12 billion in payments - a total package worth $30 billion of Nigeria's total $37 billion external debt. Many people will recall the international campaign for debt relief and debt cancellation of the late 1990s and early 2000s. It will therefore be uncharitable to regard any criticism of the handling of the economy as being anti-Jonathan. And if contriving a ranking by the IMF as the 'third fastest growing economy' is one of the strategies to blunt these criticisms, then it is a disservice to the country.

Daily Trust 20 October 2010

CHAPTER 82

THE POLITICS OF DE-SUBSIDISATION

The plan by the federal government to remove fuel subsidies, effective from January 2012, is the latest in the seemingly endless stream of controversial policies that has been flowing from, and unwittingly increasingly defining the Jonathan regime. According to the supporters of de-subsidisation, subsidising the prices of finished petroleum products costs the government some N500 billion annually. Removal of the subsidies will purportedly help the regime to save some "N1.2tn, part of which can be deployed into providing safety nets for poor segments of the society to ameliorate the effects of the subsidy removal", according to a letter to the National Assembly by the President conveying his administration's Medium Term Expenditure Framework (MTEF) and a N4.8tn budget for the 2012 fiscal year. Estimates vary on how de-subsidisation will affect the price of petroleum products. After de-subsidisation, the price of a litre of petrol, which currently sells at N65, is estimated to sell at between N120 and N150.

Several issues are raised by the current round of de-subsidisation politics.

One, Dr Ngozi Iweala, the Finance Minister and Co-ordinating Minister of the Economy, has by virtue of her elevation as the *de facto* Prime Minister in charge of the economy and her pedigree in the World Bank become the new face of the de-subsidisation lobby. This has provided a convenient cover for some politicians to distance themselves from the de-subsidisation lobby without appearing to be opposing the President. For instance in a report on October 10, 2011 aptly entitled: 'Fuel subsidy: National Assembly, Okonjo-Iweala on collision course,' the Punch reported that "members of the National Assembly, especially Senators, were not satisfied with the MTEF and Okonjo-Iweala's alleged insistence that it would only take the removal of fuel subsidy for the framework to be successful." The paper further reported that "even before the letter was submitted, the lawmakers were not happy with the minister's utterances which the legislators believed meant that her positions on economic policies should be final."

It may be sheer happenstance but the truth is that Dr Okonjo-Iweala's return as Finance Minister and *de facto* Prime Minister also coincided with a period of more strident push by the government for both the removal of fuel subsidy and the devaluation of the Naira. Dr Okonjo Iweala, as most people know, has worked most of her adult life in the

World Bank, where she rose to become one of its Managing Directors. The World Bank and its sister institution the International Monetary Fund are notorious for their brand of economics for the developing world, which almost always hinges on the removal of subsidies and the devaluation or flotation of the exchange rate regime. In the 1980s and early 1990s, such policies, encapsulated in the structural adjustment programmes (SAPs), which were forced on African countries by these two institutions, contributed in ruining African economies and reversing the developmental gains recorded since independence. Remarkably many people who were against Dr Okonjo Iweala's appointment as Finance Minister hinged their opposition on fears that her economic prognoses may be a simple rehash, by reflex, of the discredited economic desiderata of the two Bretton Woods institutions.

Two, the proposal to remove fuel subsidies did not originate with the Jonathan administration. It dates back to the Babangida regime and has since become more or less a tool of blackmail by every subsequent regime. The 'game' is often played this way: the regime in power proposes to remove fuel subsidies, all of it in one go, making a mountain of how much it costs the government, and how the money saved from such removal would be used to transform the country into an el Dorado on earth. Organised labour and civil society come out fighting against the proposed removal. The government hardens its stance and organised labour and civil society also harden theirs. Some political, religious and traditional rulers are recruited to play the good cops by pleading for dialogue between the two contending sides. A dialogue subsequently ensues, which results in subsidy being removed by say 30 percent, enabling labour and civil society leaders to claim some victory and the regime to achieve its original aim. This pattern has now become too predictable.

Three, when the government talks about how much it spends in subsidising petroleum products, it conveniently forgets that subsidies, in one form or the other, are facts of life in several countries across the world. TheUnited Statesfor instance currently pays around $20 billion per year to farmers in direct subsidies as "farm income stabilisation". These subsidies had their origins in the US Farm bills, which date back to the economic turmoil of the Great Depression of the 1920s. Since then a tradition of government support to farmers has been maintained. It is in fact estimated that for every dollarU.S.farmers earn, 62 cents come from some form of government subsidy. The estimated total subsidies to US farmers in 2009 from all levels of government were $180.8 billion.

Subsidy regime is also very strong inEurope. For instance the Common Agricultural Policy (CAP), a system of European Union subsidies, represented 48 percent of the EU's budget of €49.8 billion in 2006. In 2010, the EU spent €57 billion on agricultural development, of which €39 billion was spent on direct subsidies.China has several export subsidies. So the whole talk about how much subsidies cost the government is, in my own opinion, simply bunkum. It is like moaning about how much you spend to keep your children healthy and happy.

Four, by emphasising on the quantum of money to be saved from de-subsidisation, the government wrongly implies that lack of money is the cause of the current problems facing the country. But if lack of money is really the problem, what impact has the money we purportedly saved from exiting the sovereign debts owed to theLondonand Paris Clubs made on the material circumstances of the average Nigerian? Has any ordinary Nigerian really felt the impact of the billions of Naira allegedly recovered from politicians by the EFCC and ICPC? Our fundamental problem, in my opinion, is the lack of the vision thing, and being repeatedly saddled with leaders who are either not prepared for the job or are incapable of thinking outside the established dogmas and wrong policies that have failed in the past. As part of the social contract in every country, the citizens must have something to show for giving up their right to self help and giving loyalty to a central authority. Without anything substantial from the government to justify itself in the eyes of the people, many citizens will willy-nilly begin to withdraw from the state and transfer their loyalty to any primordial identity where they feel they can best negotiate the meaning of their existence.

Five, it may be necessary to interrogate the claims by the de-subsidisation lobby that petrol is too cheap in the country. The truth is that at N65 per litre, it is actually not, especially given the per capita income. In the UAE and Saudi Arabia for instance, where per capita income is several times higher than what you have in Nigeria, a litre of petrol sells for around 1AED (N45) and SRO 0.45 (N18) respectively. In these countries, the citizens additionally enjoy their God-given natural wealth in several other ways. As one of the largest oil producing and exporting countries in the world, in which way does citizen Okeke, Musa or Banjo feel the impact of the wealth that crude oil brings to the country?

Six, it is tempting to speculate on how the regime will cope with the legitimacy crisis that is gradually engulfing the administration from all corners as one controversial policy feeds into the other amid pervasive insecurity and rising poverty. There appears to be an increasing loss of faith in the ability of the regime to guarantee the security of life and property; there is an unprecedented crisis in our nation building project, organised labour is up in arms over the non-implementation of the Minimum Wage; the Academic Staff Union of Universities have already gone on one week warning strike over the regime's apparent refusal to honour an agreement it reached with it and the level of unemployment is unprecedented in our history. Amid all these, the regime is pushing for a single- term tenure of seven years contrary to popular sentiments and at a time it is very deeply distrusted. It will be interesting to see how the regime will manage this escalating crisis of legitimacy.

Daily Trust 13 October 2011

CHAPTER 83

DEMOCRATISING THE LANGUAGE OF ECONOMIC DISCOURSE

There is a real danger that the title of this piece alone may scare away many potential readers – just for having the word 'economic' in it and the quantitative method it conjures in the mind of average readers. Nigerian government and its economists tend to capitalise on this to obfuscate or cabalise discourses on how our economy is really faring. For instance when President Jonathan's handling of the economy was put on the spot in the run-up to the PDP's acrimonious presidential primaries in December 2010, the then Finance Minister, Mr Segun Aganga, ill-advisedly declared that the economy was too technical for some people to understand.

Which is why I believe that the first step in having honest discussions about our economy is to democratise the language of discourse. If an averagely intelligent secondary student can read The Economist of London and understand an essay on even the most technical economic issue, there is no reason why we should allow a cabal to appropriate more intelligence to themselves than they really are simply because they bandy around jargons and hide under obfuscation. In the UK, the Plain English Campaign, an independent lobby established in 1979, has been leading a successful campaign must be written in clear, concise and accessible English. The Campaign has been strongly against what it regards as 'gobbledygook, jargon and misleading public information', including the use of obfuscation and inaccessible language in public communication. Many agencies these days boldly proclaim on their public information materials that the language used in the writing meets the standard of the Plain English Campaign. In Nigeria, speaking in arcane, inaccessible and obfuscatory language is perceived wrongly as a sign of intelligence – as we saw when many government officials tried to sell their argument for removing subsidies on premium petroleum products.

There are several aspects of our economy that require the democratisation of the language of discourse to ensure greater citizen participation. Take for instance the recent ranking of the country as the third fastest growing economy in the world by the Islamic Development Bank. The IDB said Nigeria's economy grew by 7.68 per cent behind Mongolia's (14.9 per cent) and China's (8.4 per cent). It should be recalled that in the run-up to the PDP's presidential primaries in

December 2010, the IMF also ranked Nigeria as the third fastest growing economy in the world behind India's and China's.

While the high ranking of Nigeria's economy in the world brings joy to those who believe in the figures, especially the government, it equally elicits anger from those who feel that the figures are simply massaged or that the government is taking the citizens for fools or has been overdosing on Darrell Huff's influential book, How to Lie with Statistics (1954). In essence, such a lofty ranking could have the unintended consequence of increasing the distrust of government.

There are several things to note about this recent thumb-up of the economy:

One, it could be a coincidence but the first time our economy was ranked the third fastest growing economy was in late 2010, in the run-up to the PDP presidential primaries when President Jonathan was perceived to be especially vulnerable on the economy. At that time there were a rash of other supposedly positive news on the economy: Sanusi Lamido Sanusi, Governor of Central Bank, was named the African Banker of the Year by the global business magazine, Emerging Markets, and the rating agency Standard & Poor (S&P) assigned Rivers State a 'B' international rating, "owing to its strong cash holdings, low debt and a healthy operating balance".

Now the recent ranking by IDB comes as the politicking for 2015 is transiting from hush-hush to open beer parlour talks amid media speculations on whether Jonathan will run or not. As citizens, we need to question whether these agencies that garland us with honours are merely doing their jobs as impartially as they can or whether their figures could be construed as interferences in our domestic politics, in so far as they seem deployed as instruments for blunting criticisms over the general belief that the government has not managed the economy well.

Two, economic growth - – the quantity of goods and services produced in a country - is usually distinguished from economic development, which is more of a sustainable boost in the standard of living of the people of a country, including an increase in their per capita income. While it is possible to have economic growth which does not immediately issue in economic development, it is often believed that an economic growth rate which is higher than the population growth rate or a growth rate as high as Nigeria is purported to have recorded since the Obasanjo civilian regime cannot fail to impact positively on the human development indicators. For instance since 1992 when China's economic growth rate averaged over ten per cent, over 400 million Chinese have been lifted out of poverty. It is in fact predicted that by 2015 only 0.3 per cent of the Chinese people will be living on less than $1.25 dollars per day. In the same vein, India's rapid economic growth since 2000 is expected to lift some 367 million Indians out of poverty. Now compare this with the situation in Nigeria. We are told that during Obasanjo's second coming, the country's growth rate averaged six per cent until 2009 when it crossed the seven per cent mark. Paradoxically while a similar growth rate elsewhere led to significant improvements in most of the human and social indicators, in Nigeria the reverse seems to be the case. For instance figures released by Nigeria's Bureau of Statistics on February 13 2012 showed that despite - or because of our economy's purportedly high growth rate, the number of people living below the poverty line – defined as those who live on less than a dollar a day - rose to 61.2 per cent in 2010 from 51.6 per cent in 2004. In real terms, the report noted that no less than 112.5 million Nigerians are by this definition squalid poor or those Franz Fanon, the Martinique-born French psychiatrist, philosopher and revolutionary, would call the 'wretched of the earth'.

Again while high economic growth rates elsewhere often lead to higher inflow of foreign direct investment, in our own purported high growth rate, the reverse seems to be the case. For instance the United Nations Conference on Trade and Development, UNCTAD in a report released in Geneva on January 17, 2011 revealed that foreign direct investment (FDI) into Nigeria dropped by as much as 62 per cent in 2010, from $6 billion in 2009 to $2.3 billion in 2010, the worst in many years, and even worse than during the global crisis. Foreign direct investments are important to any nation because they are often sources of job creation. With rising indebtedness and a sharp deterioration in most of the human development indicators, there is simply something that does not add up with the figures of high growth rate that are being bandied around. Nigerians want an honest discussion of this apparent paradox in an accessible language because we have for long been intimidated by the unnecessary recourse to technicalese: when we ask for simple uninterrupted power supply, we get lectures on megawatts, when we ask for affordable fuel; we get lectures on premium petroleum products, de-subsidization and impending economic collapse.

Three, there is a feeling that the high growth rate being bandied around to show that the government is managing the economy well may have boomeranged. Now rather than show that the government is managing the economic well, it is portraying managers of the economy and those trying to reap political capital from such figures as being 'out of touch' with what Nigerians will call 'the realities on the ground'. For instance the Minister of State for Finance Yerima Ngama was quoted as saying that the recent ranking of the Nigerian economy by IDB showed 'growing investor confidence in Nigeria'. He also claimed that the standard of living "has improved in Nigeria as a result of this growth, as at December, 2011, our income per capita grew from 1200 Dollars to 1400 U.S. DOLLARS and this actually moved us from low income countries to Middle Lower income countries per World Bank classification." I am sure I won't be alone in wondering whether the Minister lives in Nigeria or in Planet Jupiter.

Four, while it will be unfair to attribute all the problems in the economy to the current government, it must also be recognised that there are genuine concerns about the direction of the economy and how it is being managed or mismanaged. The government needs to level up with the citizens. It needs to get them involved in earnest discussion about what it is doing to alleviate the suffering of the generality of Nigerians. And it needs to do so in accessible, honest, non-obfuscatory language that will be inclusive.

Daily Trust 19 April 2012

CHAPTER 84

THE DAY MADEMOISELLE LAGARDE CAME TO TOWN

There are still speculations about the import of the recent visit to Nigeria by Ms Christine Lagarde, the French managing director of the International Monetary Fund (IMF) since July 5 2011. It was the second visit to the country by the six-foot tall Lagarde, who had held various ministerial positions in France prior to her appointment as the IMF boss. The visit on December 19-20 2011, was Ms Lagarde's first since she was appointed to head the IMF. She reportedly met separately with President Goodluck Jonathan, Senate President David Mark, Speaker of the House of Representatives Aminu Waziri Tambuwal and of course Finance Minister and Co-ordinating Minister of the Economy Ngozi Iweala.

Officially Ms Lagarde was in the country partly to discuss how the potential fallouts from the European debt crisis could possibly affect the country. In a press release by the IMF on December 12 2011 announcing the visit to Nigeria and neighbouring Niger, Ms Lagarde was quoted as saying: "African economies have made significant progress over the last few years. However, the world economy is in a critical phase, and in these difficult times, we have to make sure we all work together to tackle the challenges facing all IMF member countries, in Africa and around the globe." Implicit in this is that Ms Lagarde was here partly to assess whether the economic programme of the country is heading in the 'right direction'. And her opinion was that it was – or so it was reported to be. "I was extremely impressed with ... the energy and pace at which he [President Jonathan] wants to transform the economy, create jobs, focus on agriculture ...." she was quoted as saying by the Vanguard of December 19, 2011. However, when all 'diplomatese' are peeled off from the 'endorsement', it becomes debatable what she really said of Jonathan's economic programme: She was merely 'extremely impressed' with the 'energy and pace' that the President 'wants to transform the economy....' Not that an unabashed endorsement of President Jonathan's economic policies would have blunted the local challenges to his economic options. On the contrary!

Ms Lagarde and Okonjo Iweala, who was thought to have facilitated her visit, share many things in common: While Ms Lagarde was the first woman to become the Minister of Economic Affairs of a G8 country, Ngozi was the first woman ever to be Minister of Finance or Foreign

Affairs in Nigeria; both Ngozi and Ms Lagarde are associated with the Bretton Woods institutions, they were both born in the mid 1950s – Lagarde on January 1 1956 and Ngozi on June 13 1954; their fathers were academics - Lagarde's father Robert Lallouette, was a Professor of English while Ngozi's father, Chukwuka Okonjo was a professor of economics. Ngozi was appointed to her current position in July 2011 while Ms Lagarde assumed her position as boss of the IMF on July 5 2011. Given therefore the many things both women share in common, it could well be that the 'real reason' for Ms Lagarde's visit was to show solidarity with a fellow high flyer, and by extension the regime she works for. Whatever the real reason for the visit, it raises several issues:

One, supporters of the Jonathan administration has sought to reap political capital out of the visit by making much about the purported pass mark given to the Jonathan administration's economic policies. The truth is that expression of support by the IMF, with its rather sad history of engagement with Africa, could hurt more than it can help at the domestic level. In fact, Alan Greenspan, the former Chairman of the equivalent of a Central Bank in the US - the Federal Reserve Board (1987 -2006) - once reportedly attributed his success in managing the US economy to doing the opposite of the economic advice from the Fund. If the IMF is notorious for giving bad advice, especially to the developing countries, it means that an outright endorsement of President Jonathan's economic policies by Ms Lagarde could well be the clearest flashpoint that we are heading in the wrong economic direction.

Two, there has been a tendency to use the opportunity of Ms Lagarde's visit to 're-invent' the IMF as an institution that has changed from its sad past. The Compass of December 22 2011 quoted Ngozi Iweala as saying: 'The Fund now allows nations to build their own capacities while it provides support; the Fund expects nations to seek its assistance. If any seeks, it will find. If it does not, the Fund keeps its hand to itself.' With all due respect to Dr Okonjo Iweala, this was not the gravamen of the misgivings against the IMF. In fact, even in the 1980s, the Fund and its sister institution the World Bank never accepted that they forced their economic options on African countries. And in many ways they didn't since they allowed countries to come up with 'acceptable' reform packages. But the problem was that most African countries then had little option but to embrace IMF's standard package because to reschedule one's debts with either the London or Paris Clubs or even obtain letters of credit, required that a country's economic programmes must have been approved by the two Bretton Woods institutions. This led to talks of 'explosion of conditionalities' and 'cross conditionalities' because several agencies, including donors, also began to tie their assistance to a country's economic programme being endorsed by IMF/World Bank. And the only reform measures the Bretton Woods institutions approved were the ones that embraced the key instruments they favoured. It is in this sense that African countries argued that the SAPs were forced on them by the two Bretton Woods institutions.

A key measure of whether IMF has changed on not however is not necessarily on whether countries are still forced to embrace its favoured economic reform measures or not but whether it has changed in its favoured brand of economics. The key planks of the IMF/World Bank-supported SAPs in the 1980s centre on downward exchange rate adjustment, removal of subsidies, liberalisation of trade, privatisation, de-regulation and massively reducing public expenditures (all of which were labelled 'rolling back the state'). These remain the key policy prescriptions of the IMF. In fact as the damages done by the failure of SAPs became very obvious by the 1990s, the mantra changed from 'rolling back the state' to 'bringing back the state' as it was realised that in countries like Africa, where the private sector remains small, the state has still a key role to play in economic development. In other words, the failure of the IMF/World Bank-supported SAPs was a failure of the economic doctrine of neo-liberalism - a contemporary form of 'liberal' economic thoughts championed by the likes of the British economist Adam Smith. The key idea in liberalism is to 'roll back the state' and transfer control of the economy from public to the private sector. 'Bringing back the state' doctrine that became popular in the 1990s was therefore a repudiation of neo-liberal economics and is usually associated with the economic ideas of John Maynard Keynes, a 20th-century English economist, who had argued that private sector decisions sometimes lead to inefficient macroeconomic outcomes and therefore advocated active policy responses by the public sector and the government. Interestingly when Ms Lagarde was asked her economic philosophy in a Vogue magazine interview of August 22 2011, she replied that she was 'with Adam Smith' - meaning, in 'economics-speak' that she was neo-liberal, an adherent of the failed brand of economics aggressively pushed by the IMF and the World Bank in Africa in the 1980s. How can anyone therefore argue that the IMF has changed when its boss has openly declared she is an adherent of its failed brand of economics?

Three, an important symbolism of Ms Lagarde's visit is that it came at a time of intense debate about the government's proposal to remove subsidies on petroleum products. Ms Lagarde's visit and reported endorsement of President Jonathan's economic programme is by extension an endorsement of the government's stance on removing subsidies – one of the key instruments in a standard IMF/World Bank supported economic reform programme. This can only bring powerful sad memories of the SAP of the 1980s, which will most likely harden the stance of the opposition forces against de-subsidisation. Obviously if the government succeeds in removing the subsidies, it is likely to lead to a general increase in the cost of living and subsequent agitation by labour for a new wage structure to ameliorate hardship. If this happens, the government is sure to roll out 'poverty alleviation programmes' and talk of 'giving adjustment a human face' - as happened in the 1980s and 1990s. In this sense, President Jonathan's 'transformation agenda' will once more amount to moving forward to the past.

Daily Trust 29 December 2011

CHAPTER 85

PLAYING MARADONA WITH STATISTICS

In his highly regarded book, *Lying With Statistics* (1954) the American writer, Darrell Huff, discusses the funny business of lying with figures, telling us how intentional or unintentional errors could lead to inaccurate conclusions. Though Huff was not a statistician, his book, which he had meant to be a witty introduction to statistics for the general reader, quickly became one of the most widely read statistics books in history.

When in late June 2011 several newspapers and weblogs reported that a research note from Morgan Stanley has suggested that Nigeria's economy could overtake South Africa's economy (currently about four times the size of Nigeria's) by 2025, I remembered Darrell Huff's book. According to the reports, two of Morgan Stanley's Johannesburg-based economists, Andrea Masia and Michael Kafe, wrote in a report that was released on June 29 2011 that "Nigeria could match SA's gross domestic product (GDP) of $400bn before the end of the decade and overtake SA by 2025". The report further claimed that the "Nigerian economy is on a growth charge", buoyed by "retail trade, deepening financial markets, and current account surplus".

There are several issues with this report:

One, I do not consider myself a killjoy. As a proud Nigerian I would love this projection to come to pass. I can imagine the number of Nigerians that have already acquired an extra swagger because of that report. I do not intend to spoil their fun. But we have to be realistic. Every projection of this nature is based on certain assumptions (the 'all things being equal' clause). Once the assumptions are changed, the conclusions also change. The basic assumption in the Morgan Stanley's analysis is that Nigeria's GDP would grow by 8.4 percent this year and 8.5 per cent next year whileSouth Africa's would grow by 3.6 per cent this year and 3.9 per cent next year. Because in real life 'all things are rarely equal', these assumptions could easily, and in fact are likely to be wrong. For instance any major event such as earthquake, terrorist attack, sharp economic meltdown or the discovery of alternative sources of fuel in China or USA (the two main importers of the country's crude) would fundamentally alter this assumption as it would sharply reduceNigeria's revenue from oil. In the same vein a prolonged resurgence of insecurity in the Niger Delta or a sudden collapse in oil prices in the international oil markets will also mean that the growth assumption for the country will have to be sharply revised downwards because revenues would dip sharply. Add to this the monocultural nature of our economy which is characterised by policy reversals and instability amid one of the worst crises of nation-building in our history, and you will find how difficult it is to sustain this growth rate – assuming it is ever achieved in the first place. There is also a ridiculous assumption thatSouth Africawill be incapable of accelerating the growth of its economy or that by surpassing the size ofSouth Africa's economyNigeriawill automatically surpass the country in economic development or move ahead ofSouth Africain the Human Development Index. One of the things about lying with figures is that because you are speaking with the 'specificities of a statistician', it makes you appear cleverer than you really are before your uninitiated audience.

Two, while I recognise that Morgan Stanley may not have deliberately set out to bamboozle and lie with figures, I am honestly suspicious of the motives of some of the international bodies who are, with one eye, targeting a business opportunity and how to warm itself to a regime, while with the other eye they seem to prod their affiliates to garland or castigate a regime as the case may be. In fact, among investment banks, the potential conflict between their research departments (which can put favourable or unfavourable rating on a stock or country) and their investment, brokerage or advisory arms, have long been recognised. And do not forget they often get their projections wrong – which is why some like Merrill Lynch have been successfully sued by their clients for misleading advice.

And what about those institutions that organise or sponsor awards for our critical office holders? Have we forgotten the numerous awards given to the managers of the banks that the CBN Governor Sanusi Lamido later accused their managing directors of monumental frauds? How do we reconcile the fact that Soludo and his successor in office Sanusi Lamido Sanusi were both named African Central Banker of the Year – despite representing different banking philosophies?

Three, I suspect that some of these organisations, including institutions like the IMF and World Bank, have a way of surreptitiously getting involved, or being dragged, into our domestic politics. For instance in October 2010, at the heat of the PDP's acrimonious presidential primaries in which President Jonathan was perceived as being vulnerable on the management of the economy, the IMF came out with a report ranking Nigeria as the 'third fastest growing economy in the world after China and India' as it claimed that the economy grew from 6.9 percent in 2009 to 7.4 percent that year. The IMF cleverly made it sound as if economic growth is the same thing as economic development, implying that contrary to the position of Jonathan's critics on the handling of the economy, things were actually getting better. I find similar suspicious positions in Morgan Stanley's recent research note. For instance the researchers wrote: "External debt levels are among the lowest in emerging markets." Although this was merely a comparative statement, it was couched in such a way that it could also be taken to mean thatNigeriais under-borrowed - at a time many are justifiably worried at the level of debts being accumulated by the regime.

Local firms also do get involved in projections that appear too good to be true, raising also questions about their motives. For instance FN Capital Ltd, a wholly owned subsidiary of First Bank Plc, recently projected that the country's foreign reserves - which fell by some 14% to $32.3 billion as of June 24 compared with a year earlier despite the fact that Bonny Light crude added 38 percent over the same period - would rise to 24 percent because of the creation of Sovereign Wealth Fund. Depletion of foreign reserves was one of the vulnerable points of President Jonathan during the last presidential election.

I am of course not implying that all positive analyses or projections of our economy are wrong or done with ulterior motives. The point is that some are simply too good to be true. Take for instance Morgan Stanley's declaration in the aforementioned research note that the Nigerian economy is "on a growth charge". Many Nigerians would wish this were so. But if this were really true, in which sectors of the economy are the effects of such 'growth charges' being felt at the moment- employment generation, the manufacturing sector, nation-building or what? IfNigeria's economy is truly on a 'growth charge', the benefits must be trickling down to some people - apart from political office holders.

Why Col Kangiwa Umar declined a ministerial appointment

Following reports that Col(retired) Kangiwa Umar, the radical former military Governor of Kaduna State (August 1985 to June 1988) turned down an offer for a ministerial appointment; I sent him a text message disagreeing strongly with his decision. I argued that rejecting the appointment was wrong because social critics like him needed to prove that they can not only talk the talk but also walk the walk.

In his reply Col Umar argued that by declining the offer he merely wanted to make the point - especially at a time many public figures appear to be in a sort of rat race for political offices - that one does not necessarily need to have a political appointment to be able to contribute to national development. He further wrote: "Government critics are doing both talking and walking. If we were to make ourselves readily available for service under every government, we will be accused of opportunism." I believe opinions will be sharply divided on Col Umar's position on this. What do you think?

Daily Trust 17 July 2011

SECTION FOUR
UNITS OF THE FEDERATION

CHAPTER 86

THE SOUTH EAST AS A 'PROBLEM' AREA

The recent call by the South East wing of the Manufacturers' Association of Nigeria on President Goodluck Jonathan to declare a state of emergency in the five states in the zone and replace their Governors with military sole administrators generated deserved headlines. The manufacturers were of the opinion that the South East Governors have proved incapable of "guaranteeing security of lives and property" in the area after one of their members, Dr Chike Obidigo, was kidnapped at Okigwe, Imo State, while travelling to catch a flight at Owerri. The manufacturers also accused the Governors of failing to address the problem of rising unemployment and of being indifferent to the strike by the Academic Staff Union of Universities, which has shut down the state-owned universities in the area for some six months.

A number of issues are raised by the recent kidnap saga in the zone, and MAN's proposed solutions.

One, the pervasive sense of insecurity in the area is a double whammy. While creating jobs can partly be used to fight the kidnapping menace, individuals who have created jobs in the area by investing there or have the resources to make such investments are paradoxically the chief targets of the kidnappers. MAN is only partly right when it blamed the problem of insecurity in the area on the quality of governance. In reality the problems in the South East go beyond governance and insecurity such that it is often difficult to separate the causes from the effects of these problems.

Two, MAN's desideratum – sole military administrators for the South East - could complicate issues not only for the area but for the entire country. For instance, if military sole administrators are brought in and they succeed in bringing the problem of kidnapping and armed robbery under control, will that not trigger agitations for military sole administrators for the rest of the country, and even a military takeover of power at the federal level? Will Igbo politicians not exploit such a measure as evidence that the Igbos are 'hated'? Does the military sole administrator option not embody a subtle narrative that the Igbos are incapable of governing themselves? And if so, will such an option not be used by politicians from other parts of the country as evidence that the Igbos are not yet 'ripe' to produce a president of their ethnic extraction for the country?

Three, kidnapping and the pervasive sense of insecurity which it engenders, while a serious issue, is only one of several serious problems in the South East, which often feed into one another. For instance the Igbos rightly complain that the five states in the South East (compared to the six in the South West) disadvantage them because the number of states in each geopolitical zone has implications for the number of representatives they will have in the national legislatures, the federal government and what the zone is able to attract from the Federation Account. However, given the relatively small revenue base of the states in the zone, additional states in the area could be anti development since whatever revenue that is received from the Federation Account will hardly be enough to fund the setting up of bureaucracies for the new states and paying salaries and emoluments of civil servants and political office holders not to talk of financing development projects.

Another example in this regard is the issue of state- owned universities. Given the high number of qualified students who sit and do well in JAMB examinations from the South East, the zone deserves, more than many others, to have state-owned universities. Paradoxically, setting up such universities and maintaining them make serious demands on the already lean resources of the states in the area. It is within this context that the current stand-off between the state Governors and the South East ASUU should be seen, rather than just accusing the Governors of indifference.

Four, there is a sort of identity issue which interfaces with many of the problems in the area. A good example here is the current debate on zoning and the offer of a VP slot to the area in 2011 and the presidency in 2015 by the pro-zoning candidates of the PDP. At face value, it is an enticing offer, especially given the Igbos' constant complaints of marginalisation and perpetual project of producing a president of the ethnic group's extraction for the country. However the choice may not be that easy for many Igbos for a number of reasons: the Igbos believe that *'agbatobi onye bu nwanne ya'* (one's neighbour should be regarded as one's own sibling'), meaning that as they are neighbours with the South South, some see Jonathan as their 'sibling'. There is also the issue of affinity with the Ibos of the South South. In fact, the current President of *Ohaneze* Ralph Uwechue is an Ibo from the South South. It is possible that the alleged endorsement of Goodluck Jonathan by the *Ohaneze* reflects the growing chasm between the Igbos of the South East, and their 'cousins', the Ibos of the South South. There is equally an identity issue linked to the diasporic nature of the Igbos.

Being highly mobile people, and entrepreneurs at heart, some Igbos will often say that they are more interested in a person who will provide them a 'level playing field' than the ethnic identity of a candidate while the more business or opportunistic minded will simply argue that 'a goat follows the person with the palm fronds'. In essence while the Igbos are very proud of their Igboness, they have other affinities and identities that they sometimes prioritise over their ethnic identity. Therefore if the Igbos appear to sing discordant tunes on the zoning issue, it can be located on the tension between a very enticing offer from the pro-zoning Northern PDP candidates and the competing identities and affinities that they bear.

Five, while the Igbos' extreme individualism and 'can do' attitude have helped to produce many high achievers in all fields of life, the same attributes tend to undermine a sense of collective action embodied in the existence of a set of elites who are Cohesiveness, Conscious and Conspiratorial and who command universal respect and legitimacy among the in-group. This is perhaps why people often say that while the Igbos are good entrepreneurs and individual achievers they often make 'bad' politicians and do badly in inter- group bargaining.

Daily Trust 16 December 2010

CHAPTER 87

REFLECTIONS ON STATE CREATION

Please permit me start to start this piece with a confession: I have been an ardent opponent of state creation. My reasons have been the conventional explanations deployed by opponents of the exercise, namely that it escalates the cost of governance by increasing the number of political appointees and bureaucracies.

Another key argument of the naysayers is that the atomisation of states increases their dependency on the federal government, which in turn deepens the current mockery of federalism as a concept for sharing power, responsibilities and privileges between the centre and the constituent units of a country. Our federalism, like most things Nigerian, is a far cry from what that nomenclature means elsewhere. Ours is, at best, unitarism or centralism in federal clothing.

I am now re-thinking my opposition to state creation. While I haven't become a convert in the sense of being an advocate of the creation of more states, I have now considerably watered down my opposition. If I were a politician, I would say that my position on the issue is 'still evolving' in 'the light of new evidence'.

I now realise that in my previous contributions on the issue I had not given sufficient weight to the fact that State creation has facilitated the emergence of new urban centres without which the old ones – Lagos, Ibadan, Enugu, Kano, Kaduna etc – would probably have been overwhelmed by now as people naturally move from the rural areas to urban areas in search of greener pastures. I also now realise that I had not sufficiently recognised that the new urban centres spurred the emergence of new elites, including entrepreneurs, who flock into the new enclaves in search of commercial opportunities such as contracts. These new elements often form the hub of the private sector and the middle class that play critical roles in any economy.

Does my re-thinking my position on State creation mean a support for endless State creation so there will be more urban centres? No. But I will come back to this later.

I feel that opponents of State creation have overstated the issue of the non-viability of the current states because they wrongly imply that each exercise increases the non-viability of both the new states and the states from where they were carved out. For this argument to be valid, certain key questions need to be answered: at what point in the State creation exercise did states (not the regions) cease to be viable? Are there services a State was providing which it suddenly feels unable to provide because it has been balkanised into two or more States?

There were several States in the old 19 state-structure which struggled with paying salaries of workers and could therefore be regarded as 'non-viable'. In the old Anambra State for instance, 'teachers to smile' was a common newspaper headline whenever the State Governor made a pledge to pay part of the backlog of salaries usually owed to teachers and other civil servants. Is there any evidence that states that have been balkanised into two or more states are less viable than States that were never balkanised?

A key challenge is to find out why State creation is so steeped in acrimonious politics that only the military has been able to create States in the country. My opinion is that it is possible to address the reasons why the exercise is so contentious while recognising that it could also be a potent instrument for stemming rural-urban migration or recognising the uniqueness of certain culture areas.

What are the key arguments against state creation? And how can we blunt the negative impacts of the politics and exercise of State creation?

One argument is that it bloats the size of the federal government because of the Constitutional requirement on the 'reflection of federal character'. For instance in ministerial appointments, there is a constitutional requirement that at least one Minister must come from each State, meaning that if we have 50 states then the minimum number of ministers will be 50. Similarly each State is entitled to produce three senators and a given number of Members of the House of Representatives. In the same vein, given the constitutional requirement that to be elected President of the country, a candidate must obtain 25 percent of the votes cast in at least two-thirds of the States of the federation, there is often a perception that the more States a zone has, the better its chances of fulfilling that constitutional requirement.

Another key argument against State creation is that because States (and the local governments) are constitutionally recognised units that share the country's revenues with the federal government, the politics of State creation often feeds into, and is in turn fed, by the politics of regionalism and North-South divide. In essence because the number of States (and local governments) in each zone has implications for the quantum of federal resources flowing into that region, state creation will remain inherently contentious in our type of society.

My feeling is that we can blunt most of the negative effects of having more states by simply removing them (and the local governments) as the units for sharing revenues and political privileges and substituting them with the current six geopolitical zones. I will further recommend a sharing formula of 40 percent for the federal government, 50 percent for the six geopolitical zones and 10 percent as ecological and natural disaster fund (for fighting erosion, desert encroachment, oil spill etc). The government of each of the six geo-political zones will be constitutionally empowered to determine whether it wants to have a bicameral legislature or not, the number of States and local governments it wants to have and which units within its boundary (States, Local Governments and Town Unions) will be used in sharing its own revenues and on which formula. I also favour granting such geopolitical zones the power to have their own police which will be subordinated to the federal police.

There are, in my opinion, several advantages of using the six geopolitical zones as units for allocating political privileges and sharing money from the Federation Account: First, it will automatically reduce the size of government at the centre. Second, since the zones are sufficiently large, it will moderate the pull of the centrifugal forces by moving substantially the site of the contest from the centre to the geopolitical zones, which are likely to have challenging internal contradictions. Third, making the geopolitical zones the only units that share resources and privileges with the federal government will be a very close approximation of what some people call 'true federalism'. Fourth, perpetual cries of marginalisation by virtually all the units of the federation, which have undermined the country's nation-building project, will become muffled. I do not think there should be any fear that any geopolitical zone may one day break away from the federation because the internal contradictions in each zone will be a sufficient bulwark against such.

I believe the greatest challenge we have in the country today is not poverty and underdevelopment but politics, stupid. Our nation-building project is in deep crisis. Trust, a key ingredient in that building project, has long evaporated. Nigeria has become a country without Nigerians as there appears to be a stampede to withdraw from the Nigeria project into primordial identities. In such a situation individuals and groups consider the Nigerian State as an enemy and therefore a legitimate target: those entrusted to look after the common patrimony steal it blind; workers drag their feet and refuse to give their best; law enforcement officers look the other way at a little inducement, organised labour, including members of the Academic Staff Union of Universities go on indefinite strike on a whim while students riot, embrace cultism or destroy the property of their institutions on a slight provocation.

My personal opinion is that at the centre of the crisis in our nation-building project is the distribution of political and economic privileges. By making the geopolitical zones the units for sharing these privileges, the site of the struggles will in many ways be moved to these zones while the anarchical struggle for who will control the centre will also be moderated. It will, in my opinion, be one of the surest ways of resolving the serious crisis in our nation-building project.

I also believe strongly that a creative application of the principles of zoning and power rotation arrangements both at the centre and the units will be useful in giving the constituent units that psychological sense of belonging. Nigeria is facing a lot of very serious challenges but I honestly do not believe the country is a lost case.

Daily Trust 24 May 2012

CHAPTER 88

THAT PEACE MAY REIGN IN JOS AGAIN

I attended a strategy review conference on 'Peace in Jos: Arresting the Cycle of Violence' – a project hosted by the Institute of Governance and Social Research (IGSR), Jos, and sponsored by the UK Department for International Development (DFID). IGSR is led by eminent Nigerian political scientist, Professor (emeritus) J Isawa Elaigwu.

Some 200 participants, including former State Governors and Pauline Tallen, the popular former Deputy Governor of Plateau State and Labour Governorship candidate in the April 2011 gubernatorial election in the state, attended the event, which took place from October 23-26, 2011. The conference also attracted several retired top ranking army and police chiefs, former ambassadors, including the erstwhile Nigerian ambassador to the United States, Professor George Obiozor, and a horde of top- flight academics.

Basically the conference wanted the participants to review its approach to a DFID-funded project it carried out in 2010 and 2011 on bringing peace to the once tranquil city. The project had several components, including Youth Peace Camps, (where it has so far trained over 2,500 youths in conflict management), Skills Acquisition (where over 290 youths have been trained in various vocations), Capacity-building for Security Agencies (where some 500 security agents have been sensitised on how to manage the ever recurring conflicts in the city), Football for Peace (where some 3,000 youths from four local governments have been engaged in football tournaments to promote peace) and Mediation (where it organises peace rallies and trains peace ambassadors for the city).

There are a number of lessons for me from the review conference:

One, Alhaji Ahmed Makarfi, the former Governor of Kaduna State, was the star of the conference as speaker after speaker eulogised his approach to the 1998 violence in Kaduna State, which is often credited with bringing enduring peace to the State. After Makarfi, who is now a Senator, has shared his experiences in Kaduna, Professor Nuhu Yaqub, former Vice Chancellor of the University of Abuja, was moved to remark: 'Makarfi shows that you do not need to be a giant to solve Nigeria's problems'. The frail-looking Makarfi seems an unlikely candidate for the sort of courage required in resolving a volcanic eruption of violence as happened in Kaduna in 1998. Many of the conferees made repeated references to Makarfi's approach to the Kaduna crisis as a possible template for managing similar conflicts in the country.

Two, many of the 'timbers and calibres' (apologies to the late K.O. Mbadiwe) who attended the conference talked of how they had to abandon other engagements because they received a 'marching order' from Professor Elaigwu, whose IGSR hosted the event. Professor Elaigwu is neither a politician with patronages to dispense nor a Dangote. The deference with which he is regarded shows that despite the crisis of values engulfing the country, people of integrity will not go unrewarded, even if it is in intangible ways.

Three, one of the greatest accomplishments of the review conference, in my opinion, is bringing together people from different sides in the conflict. Many of the conferees were moved when the SSA to the Plateau State Governor on Youths, who chaired the closing session, asked a strident critic of the State government's approach to the Jos crisis to meet him after the session for an 'honest discussion'. The participants were apparently impressed that the SSA to the State governor was conciliatory, not defensive – in line with the spirit of the conference.

Four, another important lesson from the conference for me is a re-affirmation that from our small cubicles in the world, there is always a way we can make a little positive difference to a most daunting situation. True, our modest efforts may not dramatically change the world over night, but were we not taught in primary school that it is drop by drop that an ocean is made?

Baba Suwe and the politics of defecation

The arrest and detention of Alhaji King Babatunde Ayinla Nurudeen Olasunkanmi Omidina, aka Baba Suwe, on October 12 2011, has continued to generate headlines. The National Drug Law Enforcement Agency (NDLEA) arrested Baba Suwe, who was on his way to Paris, after its scanner at the Ikeja airport allegedly showed that the popular Yoruba actor had ingested a large quantity of a substance suspected to be narcotics. Though Baba Suwe is said to have defecated several times since his arrest, he has reportedly not excreted any hard drugs. NDLEA said it remained convinced that Baba Suwe would eventually do so. An Ikeja High Court has ordered that Baba Suwe must be released on November 4 2011 if no drug is found in his body.

The Baba Suwe saga is a clear demonstration of how an issue that would, in other climes, be simple and straightforward, could become extremely complicated, even intractable, when it interfaces with what is often called the 'Nigerian factor'. Both Baba Suwe and the NDLEA have questions to answer: For Baba Suwe, how come the scanning machine, whose reliability appeared to have been established beyond doubt over the years, found traces of substances suspected to be hard drugs in his stomach? Is it true that another scanner at the Lagos State University Teaching Hospital confirmed that substances suspected to be hard drugs were actually lodged in the actor's stomach? Is it true, as claimed by NDLEA and confirmed by the Vanguard of October 26 2011, that the anti-narcotics agency's offer for the comedian to be released to his family and lawyers for an independent scanning was not taken up? And for the NDLEA, is there really no other way in this modern age to prove that a substance suspected to be hard drugs was lodged in the actor's stomach than to wait for him for over two weeks to excrete it out? How would a similar case have been resolved in say the United Kingdom or the USA?

The tales surrounding the arrest and detention of Baba Suwe confirm what we already know about Nigerians – that we may lack everything but never a fertile imagination. Nigerians, no matter their vocations and stations in life, seem to have ready explanations for any issue – be it nuclear physics, landing in the moon or why Okada riders do not want to wear helmets. Problem is that some of these opinions, usually presented as facts obtained from authoritative sources, when repeated often enough through the grapevines and occasionally in the broadsheets, begin to sound like truth, or at best make the search for the truth more arduous. In the Baba Suwe saga there are those who swear that the actor had since defecated out the hard drugs but had bribed his way out of trouble. Others swear that he had used a powerful juju to hide the drug in his system. Yet others allege that he was a victim of a frame-up gone awry, and that the NDLEA is bidding an opportune moment to plant hard drugs it will claim was excreted by the actor. An additional twist was added to the competing tales when an online weblog (saharareporters.com) reported that Dr. Subhash Vijayvargiya, the consultant radiologist at the Lagos State University Teaching Hospital who carried out the CT-scan for NDLEA, is an ex-convict in India who was "sentenced to three years in prison and fined 5,000 Rupees in 2007 after Indian authorities found out his centre had no records of any kind regarding existence and maintenance records of ultrasound machine."

One of the consequences of these tales is that no matter how the saga ends, many people will remain sceptical. ThisDay's editorial of October

24 2011 captured the cynicism that will certainly accompany whichever way the saga ends: "If at the end of this show of shame, NDLEA comes forward with some substances allegedly excreted by Baba Suwe, we will recommend a second opinion. Indeed a DNA test should be conducted to confirm that whatever the NDLEA brings forth actually came from inside Baba Suwe as it is most likely that some unscrupulous, overzealous Agency officials in a face-saving move could 'manufacture' evidence to prove their case."

Another issue that the Baba Suwe saga revealed is that while in most parts of the world, the State increases its legitimacy any time it punishes members of the elite or high profile individuals like Baba Suwe, the same rule may not apply in Nigeria. In fact, in a polarised, multi-ethnic and low trust society like ours, while everyone agrees that the State should be firm, any attempt by the State to be as firm as theoretically demanded by the citizens paradoxically increases the suspicion with which it is viewed by some people. This means in essence that some of the incompetence we see in public officials may be deliberate 'self-censorship' as doing their jobs as they ought to may have unpalatable consequences for them.

Daily Trust, 3 Nov 2011

CHAPTER 89

IGBOLAND: WHEN DID THINGS REALLY BEGIN TO FALL APART?

That the level of insecurity in Igboland has reached unacceptable level is no longer news. In virtually all parts of South East, daily reports of kidnapping, armed robberies and ritual murders have morphed from the gory to the macabre. The *Daily Independent* (online) of July 1, 2010 reported that commercial and industrial activities in the entire South East zone risk unravelling if the situation is not halted soon. The paper for instance reported that in Anambra state, a "total of 62 wealthy businessmen have fled Nnewi industrial town, while half of the businessmen in Igbo land have relocated to other parts of the country for fear of falling victim to kidnappers and armed robbers."

True, Igboland is not the only area of the country with security problems. The distinguishing feature however is its absurd level, which recently prompted President Jonathan to order joint military operations to flush out the hoodlums in the area. Okey Ndibe, an activist columnist and novelist, who himself is an Igbo, used the metaphor of war to describe the near state of nature that the area is fast degenerating into. In a brilliantly written piece, "The War in Igboland", (NVS, June 22, 2010), Ndibe appears to suggest that the cause of this 'war' in Igboland is "crisis of values" typified in people's apparent deification of wealth. He blames the 'oti nkpu' (praise singer) musicians like the late Oliver De Coque and Osita Osadebe for contributing to this "crisis of values" with their songs that seemingly glorified charlatans who came into wealth by questionable means as "owners" of their community.

While I agree with many aspects of Okey's arguments, I am however not too sure that 'oti nkpu' musicians should be blamed for the alleged crisis because praise singing is often an important leitmotif of the folk music genre in many parts of Nigeria. Every type of music – just like in literature or any work of art – tends to have a defining characteristic: racial soldering in reggae, social rebellion in rap, love in blues, spiritual awakening in gospel and political rascality in Fela's afrobeat. Most people enjoy music for what it invokes in them, not necessarily because of its message: the rhythm, the voice and the creative mix of voice and sound. Similarly many people read a novel more because of an author's narrative skills than for his/her message. I feel blaming 'oti nkpu' musicians for the assumed "crisis of values" in Igboland will be akin to blaming Western thriller novels, war films, wrestling and boxing for violence and crimes in these societies.

I share the frustration in Okey's voice in the aforementioned important article. I am however not sure I agree with his suggestion that the alleged "crisis of values" is a recent phenomenon in Igboland. It could in fact be argued that "crisis of values" was a primary concern of the Igbos at the turn of the century. We can see this in Chinua Achebe's most famous work, *Things Fall Apart*, first published in 1958. The novel is not only a great work of fiction but also one of the most important narratives on Igbo sociology. Here Achebe tells us how the introduction of Christianity and subsequently colonialism led to the adoption of new values by the Igbo town (or village) of Umuofia, and how the new values "put a knife" in those things that held the community together. The novel's main character, Okonkwo, on returning from a seven-year exile, found to his chagrin, that the Umuofia he left behind had fallen apart because of the new values: people no longer acted like one and respected personalities and institutions had lost their prestige and relevance. In what is perhaps an echo of the "crisis of values" identified by Okey, in which wealthy Igbo ruffians are now 'crowned' as "owners" of their community, Okonkwo returned to find that people previously regarded as social outcasts and scoundrels (who were of course the first to embrace the new ways of the White man and his religion) had become the new elites. Okonkwo did his best to re-awaken the old values in his people but it was a futile and solo effort that was doomed to fail. This could be called the first "crisis of values" in Igboland.

In many ways the first "crisis of values" was successfully resolved by the onset of full colonialism and the creation of the colonial urban centres. Though there was no consciousness of being Igbo before colonialism, and many Igbo villages were in fact oblivious of the existence of one another, in the colonial enclaves the consciousness of being Igbo was developed as they competed with other ethnic groups for scarce values like jobs and scholarships. The first "crisis of values" was therefore successfully resolved through efforts to develop a pan-Igbo identity (buoyed by the prestige of prominent Igbos like Zik, Nwafor Orizu and K.O. Mabdiwe as well as institutions like Igbo State Union) and aggressive encouragement of Igbos to embrace the new values of the White man. The project of pan-Igbo nationalism was given a further fillip during the events that preceded the civil war, which culminated in the proclamation of the Republic of Biafra. It will seem however that since the end of the civil war, the Igbos have been engulfed in an identity crisis that has remained unresolved.

Okey is right that Chinua Achebe is not given the sort of recognition accorded to many moneybags in Igboland by the folk musicians. But this has probably nothing to do with "crisis of values" but more because Achebe as a novelist has a specialist skill set, which only people familiar with such skills will appreciate. Among the educated, Achebe remains one of the symbols of Igbo pride. In virtually every society, it is often easier for the masses (especially when most are hungry) to know and lionise men of wealth than it is for them to recognise people who have distinguished themselves in specialist fields like medicine, IT, sports or creative writing. 'Oti nkpu' musicians want to reach the masses, and the more successfully they can do this, the more they will get more moneybags to pay them to make songs in their praise – pretty much the way newspapers need high circulation numbers to win the heart of advertisers. I agree with Okey that there is less scrutiny these days on how people come about their wealth. But this is not peculiar to Igboland. I will therefore argue that what Okey identified as the "crisis of values" in Igboland is more a crisis of the Nigerian state writ large because as often happens, any practice borrowed by the Igbos – whether home video making, kidnapping or 419 – is guaranteed to be taken to dizzying heights. I do not think the Igbos necessarily love money more than other ethnic groups in the country.

My take is that the fundamental crisis in Igboland today is the crisis of the elites – not that of values. In the 'Iron Law of Oligarchy', the German sociologist Robert Mitchels tells us that all forms of organisations or societies are eventually effectively controlled by an oligarchy – a small group of elites distinguished by either royalty, wealth, family ties, military control, or religious hegemony. This oligarchic group - whether called cabals, mafias or kitchen cabinet – are usually Cohesive, Conscious and Conspiratorial. It could be argued that any society without a set of elites with these three important Cs is unlikely to be able to present a common front or effectively defend the group's interest. I will argue that since the end of the civil war, the crisis in Igboland is the inability to produce enlightened elites with the aforementioned three Cs.

Despite the current challenges however there are many grounds for optimism that the Igbos will successfully re-invent themselves as they did after the first "crisis of values" following the Christian and colonial intrusions.

CHAPTER 90

THE (ABORTED) MEETING OF THE IGBO POLITICAL FORUM

The recent blocking of a planned meeting of the Igbo Political Forum (IPF), which was to take place at the Banquet Hall of Hotel Concorde, Owerri, on Monday September 27, 2010, has generated headlines, editorials and condemnations by various groups. According to the story, the organisers had paid N100, 000 to use the hall two weeks before the scheduled event. However, just a few days to the date, riot police men 'invaded' the hotel, claiming they had 'orders from above' not to allow the event to take place. The organisers tried to move the event to a nearby All Seasons hotel only to be rebuffed by the hotel's managers, who allegedly also claimed they were acting on 'orders from above'.

Several issues are raised by the debacle that surrounded the planned confab.

One, the blocking of the meeting turned out to be a public relations coup for IPF as it enabled it to attract far more media attention than would have been the case had the conference been allowed to hold as planned. The notion that some respected Igbo leaders like former Vice President Dr Alex Ekwueme, former Governor of old Anambra State Chief Jim Nwobodo, former Senate President Ken Nnamani and former CBN Governor Professor Chukwuma Soludo - among others - were prevented from holding a political meeting in their homeland and had to resort to having such a confab in an open field, amid an inclement weather, played into a certain persecution narrative and disrespect for Igbo leaders. Since the IPF is thought to support PDP's zoning arrangement, implying that it is opposed to the candidacy of Goodluck Ebele Jonathan (GEJ), the situation was happily exploited by Jonathan's political opponents, with innuendos suggesting that the lockout could not have taken place without the active connivance of both the federal government which controls the police and the Imo State government, which owns Hotel Concorde.

Two, suggestions, even if by innuendo, of the federal government's complicity in the lockout, undermines the 'moving train' storyline on which much of GEJ's campaign has so far been premised. This storyline, accentuated by the mammoth crowd that came to the Eagle Square at Abuja to witness the president's declaration of his intent to contest the 2011 presidential election, suggests that GEJ winning the PDP primary and even the general election is a fait accompli. There are a several stories and events – some probably contrived- to feed into that narrative. These include reports that the PDP in the South West pledged the support of the entire geopolitical zone for GEJ; news that the South East Governors and Speakers of their respective Houses of Assemblies unanimously endorsed the candidacy of GEJ, news reports that Dr Alex Ekwueme, former Vice President, has accepted to work for GEJ's campaign and ThisDay's 'trends analyses' which suggest that President Jonathan would win an overwhelming majority of the delegates in the PDP primary.

Critics have argued that if the 'moving train' storyline is true, then there would not have been any need for such a panicky measure as stopping a group of people in a democracy from exercising their right to free assembly. The critics also point out other incidents that cast a big question mark on the 'moving train' story line such as the fact that Dr Alex Ekwueme, who was recently reported to have accepted to work for GEJ's campaign actually turned out to be the chairman of the IPF's conference at Owerri. In the IPF's communiqué, which was read in an open field, Ekwueme insisted that the Igbos would not compromise on their right to take a shot at the presidency in 2015.

Three, GEJ's political opponents have tried to use innuendos to link him to the lockout with the aim of raising questions about his democratic credentials. Though it is perfectly possible that the Presidency had absolutely nothing to do with the lockout, the suggestion that GEJ could have been involved puts a big dent on the image he projects onto the public space. There is no doubt that the President is genuinely popular with some people, most of whom respect him as an unassuming gentle man. During the late President Yaradua's terminal illness, when a 'cabal' within the presidency tried to prevent GEJ, who was then the Vice President, from being named the Acting President, his public persona helped to galvanise support and compassion for him. In this respect, any action that will undermine the President's public persona of an affable, tolerant and easy-going gentleman will undermine his support among many Nigerians. In recent times however, there have been quite a couple of such stories that may end up hurting the President's image. For instance, Chief Raymond Dokpesi, chairman of Babangida's campaign organisation, claimed the presidency was after him for agreeing to work with the Minna General. Similarly, some critics have accused GEJ of using a suddenly resurgent EFCC to go after state Governors who refuse to support his candidacy. Again, few days before the lockout of Igbo leaders at the Hotel Concorde, Owerri, the Secretary-General of the Igbo

Political Forum, Chief Chyna Iwuanyanwu, was reportedly whisked away by security operatives at the Sam Mbakwe Airport, Owerri and allegedly detained at the State Security Service, (SSS) offices for five hours before being allowed to go. Stories like these – some of these obviously exaggerated by the President's opponents – do no political good to his image.

Four, the contentious meeting of the IPF also raises questions about Igbo political leadership. Is there really any particular set of people who can claim to speak on behalf of the extremely republican Igbos? At least one faction of the Igbo elites led by First Republic Minister of Aviation Mbazuluike Amechi had already endorsed the candidacy of GEJ. The South East Governors, who have a tendency of supporting whoever is in power at the centre under the thesis that the "goat follows the person with the palm fronds", have, as expected, already declared their support for Jonathan (they also voted that Jonathan should not be made Acting President even though it was obvious the late Yaradua had become terminally ill). The IPF and some other Igbo groupings have expressed preference for other political options. So which of these groups could be said to be representing the interest of the Igbos? There is a feeling that before the lockout, those genuinely supporting and opposing Goodluck Jonathan in Igboland appeared to be evenly divided. The crucial question now is the likely impact of the lockout and the emotions it stirred, not to talk of their exploitation by politicians, on possible support for GEJ in Igboland.

Daily Trust 7 October 2012

CHAPTER 91

NIGERIAN GOVERNORS AND THE MOU WITH HARVARD UNIVERSITY: A CONTRARY VIEW

For critics, the recent report of a Memorandum of Understanding (MOU) between the Programme on Intrastate Conflict and Conflict Resolution (PICCR) of the John F Kennedy School of Government at Harvard University, United States, and the Nigerian Governors Forum (NGF), was in bad taste. The suspicion is that Nigerian Governors, hiding under NGF, merely wanted to find another avenue for primitive accumulation, and an opportunity to acquire an ego-massaging honorific, perhaps a P.tH (passed through Harvard) in much the same way that the top military brass who passed through Staff College were entitled for life to the exclusive use of the suffix, 'psc' after their names.

Bayo Okauru, NGF Director General, was reported as saying that the purpose of the four-day trip to the USA by representatives of NGF during which the MOU was signed with PICCR, was to "to seek partnership with credible institutions in the United States to assist in building the capacity of the NGF Secretariat and exploring avenues for benchmarking global best practices especially in the operation of democracy in a federal system like Nigeria." Okauru also said the trip was equally aimed at opening up a working relationship with their US counterparts, the National Governors Association (NGA).

While the pernicious behaviour of some Governors give legitimate grounds for suspecting any initiative from them, the near consensus that the deal is scandalous appears rather hasty. The controversial deal however raises a number issues, not only about the level of trust we have on our elected officials but also on our own temperament as ordinary citizens and critics, including possible implications of our intemperate utterances for the future willingness of foreign institutions to partner with public agencies from our country.

One, the formal reasons given for signing the MOU with PICCR should ideally be an opportunity for a sober discussion of the pros and cons of the deal. I believe that some of the critical concerns here ought to be: what benefits should accrue to the states that participate in the programme? What criteria should be used for impact assessment of the programme? How much will this cost? Have quotations been obtained from other credible alternative providers? Where will the training be delivered – in Nigeria or in the USA? How will a possible collaboration between NGF and NGA be used to strengthen the quality of governance in Nigeria and reduce corruption? Is there a way PICCR could include performance benchmarks by Governors as minimum qualifications for participating in the programme?

While the negative attention the trip and the MOU attracted is understandable, it is also in many ways unfortunate. In these days and age, few people will deny the value of continuous capacity building and networking in our extremely fast- changing world. In fact, even conservative institutions such as the police and the army make promotion to certain ranks dependent on an officer attending and passing some capacity-building courses. Similarly many public and private firms have long recognised the value of capacity building through in-service training, both at home and abroad. Academics who fail to constantly refresh their capacity for handling abstract ideas by following changing trends in their disciplines such as through regular participation in seminars and workshops are known to quickly degenerate into what celebrated political scientist Professor Ali Mazrui called 'ex intellectuals'. Seen from this perspective therefore, a wholesale condemnation of the MOU with PICCR becomes akin to throwing away the baby with the bathwater. The impression is wrongly conveyed that we are a nation that does not understand the value of continuous capacity building or networking.

Two, is the question of whether it was morally wrong of PICCR to have entered the MOU with the NGF. I do not believe so. I also do not think it was necessarily wrong of the governors to have chosen Harvard University, especially if the prestige that is associated with the name of the institution could convince most of the governors to buy into the idea. In fact, the name of the institution could cut both ways – it could convince most of the governors to come on board the programme while Harvard, conscious of its worldwide reputation, is unlikely to lower standard to accommodate the ego of the governors. The institution could in fact be influenced to introduce 'entry qualifications', a sort of performance benchmarks that could be used in selecting the states that could qualify to participate in the programme. Using performance benchmarks as 'entry qualification' for the programme would in turn increase the attractiveness of the programme and lure the governors into striving harder to qualify to participate. Seen this way, lampooning Harvard, and almost accusing them of conniving to dupe the Nigerian state, seems overdone. As an academic institution, the JFK School of Government and the programmes within it such as PICCR, are there to provide training to those who meet their requirements, including customised training for those who need. It is not their duty to moralise to people who come to buy training about the sources of their funds or how they ought to use the funds under their care. Were these institutions to adopt such an approach, wouldn't we also accuse them of bias and discrimination? Obviously the excessive negative media attention that this attracted boxed PICCR into a corner, forcing its leader, Professor Robert Rotberg, into rather desperate explanations that were clearly aimed at not allowing the MOU deal to rubbish the image of Harvard.

If we accept we all have an innate desire to obtain our training (including our children's training) from the best institution we could afford, why should the governors be condemned for striving to obtain the training from one of the best providers available – even before we know the cost of the programme? The idea of criminalizing all public office holders is certainly one of the biggest disincentives to some credible people who would have otherwise made themselves available for public offices.

Three, power can have either a radicalising or de-radicalising effects on people. Among the Governors that reportedly travelled to the USA to sign the MOU with PICCR was 'Comrade' Adams Oshiomole. Though I am not necessarily against the MOU with PICCR, it is tempting to speculate on how Oshiomole would have reacted to the deal when he was the leader of the Nigerian Labour Congress? Has he sold out? Or was he really another opportunist who used the visibility provided by his leadership of the Nigerian Labour Congress to position himself to become governor of Edo state? Many people see Oshiomole as representing the constituency of the 'professional critics', (also known as the 'usual suspects') and they are eager to see what he does with the power that is now entrusted to him.

Daily Trust 23 February 2012

CHAPTER 92

REFLECTIONS ON THE ANAMBRA STATE ELECTIONS

he February 6, 2010 gubernatorial election in Anambra state has come and gone. Governor Peter Obi has been announced winner of the Telection. Several candidates in the election, while condemning the irregularities in the poll, indicated that they had no plans to challenge its outcome at the election tribunals. Chukwuma Soludo, the PDP candidate, was the first to congratulate Peter Obi, but later recanted. Chris Ngige, the AC candidate, has indicated he will challenge INEC's declaration of Obi as the winner, arguing that the APGA candidate did not fulfil the constitutional requirement that a candidate must secure 25 percent of the total votes cast in at least two-thirds of the local government areas in the state. Obi insisted that he did. As victory sinks in, and with it triumphalism and its repercussions, it is not clear whether others that had earlier accepted the announced outcome of the election will change their mind.

There are several observations about the election:

One, the conduct of the campaigns was issues-based, with little of the mudslinging, violence and the use of thugs, which appear to have become part of the country's political culture. This could in part be because of the quality and maturity of the candidates, and in part because all the candidates were conscious that too many eyes were on them. We must not forget the tolerance and civility that characterised much of the campaign – irrespective of any post election dispute that may arise.

Two, the election showed that many people, including this writer, may have grossly underestimated Peter Obi's political skills. For instance, some people are beginning to suspect that the persona Obi projects into the public space – that of a naïve administrator with little political skills- may be a deliberate mask to hide his shrewdness and goad his opponents into underestimating him. This could be akin to the way Obasanjo had for years successfully used his dour personality and temper to camouflage his smartness, extreme cunning and political calculations. His opponents who fell for the decoy have lived to regret it. In Obi's case, his projected public persona, accentuated by his simple dressing, funny voice, and reported tightfistedness, feeds into a narrative that he is not a traditional politician (he never wears the red cap or 'agbada' for instance), and by innuendo, more honest than other politicians. This public persona means that given the level of voter disenfranchisement at the election, only his emergence as the Governor from the exercise would have made the outcome acceptable because the general perception is that he is too morally-driven and too naïve to be involved in election manipulation.

Obi's public persona also means that, like Obasanjo, his opponents are sometimes unable to see the political plots in some of his moves. For instance when he made town unions the fourth tier of government early in the life of his regime, very few people foresaw that he was building a 'partnership' with the town unions, perhaps with an eye for his re-election campaign. It will not come as a surprise if the 'apolitical' Obi, who once indicated he would not seek re-election, and who remained unruffled at criticisms that he was doing nothing to build APGA as the party to beat in the state, uses his second term in office to plot for a higher political outing for himself.

Three, there were several reasons why, based on the announced results, the PDP performed as poorly as it did. Apart from the internal crisis in the party and its fallouts, the suspicion that Soludo was being prepared to run for the presidency which under the PDP's zoning arrangement, would be zoned to the South in 2015, was an invisible hurdle. It is suspected that many potential rivals from the same party, both from the South East and the South South, did every thing behind the scene to frustrate his candidacy while publicly pledging their support – pretty much the way NPN did in 1983 with Dim Ojukwu when he ran for the Senate. Yaradua's AWOL and the politics surrounding his failure to transmit a letter to the National Assembly to enable Jonathan assume the position of Acting President also fed into an already negative image of the PDP across the country. While Soludo's handlers sought to distinguish their platform by calling it the 'New PDP' this was apparently not sufficiently and convincingly marketed.

There were other strategic mistakes by Soludo's handlers. It was perhaps a mistake to market him on the basis of his brilliance instead of projecting him as a humble, down-to-earth and humane guy next door. Unlike companies, making a person's obvious personal attribute the person's unique selling point is often counter productive. A very pretty woman for instance enhances her perception of beauty by deliberately downplaying it rather than flaunting it. Similarly, Soludo's image as a technocrat would have been accentuated if he had avoided the regalia of traditional politicians, including the red cap (preferably showing up in campaigns with his sleeves rolled up). Additionally, his promise of turning Anambra state into African Dubai Taiwan could have connected more with the common people if it was simply presented as urban renewal, city redevelopment or even the development of new cities. No one doubts that Anambra state seriously yearns for a well-planned city.

Four, the election perhaps handed a world record, albeit a notorious one, to Anambra state. According to the International IDEA Voter Turnout Website, (www.idea.int/vt) which contains the most comprehensive global collection of voter turnout statistics available for presidential and parliamentary elections since 1945, Mali has the world record for the lowest voter turnout (the number of registered voters who came out to vote). Mali's average of 21.3% turnout in two elections since 1992 has now been worsted by the 17% 'turnout' in Anambra state. We will of course never know the actual voter turnout given the suspected high percentage of disenfranchisement (i.e. the number of voters who registered, turned out to vote but were unable to do so). It is germane to note that even in countries like USA where voter apathy has been a major source of concern (apart from the last Presidential election), turnout has always been over 40 percent (the global average turnout is above 60 percent). For instance 47% percent of the voting age population participated in the 1996 presidential election in the US, which had a remarkably low turnout. Out of this turnout, President Clinton received 49% of the votes – or 23% of the eligible voters – far more than the percentage of registered voters, which voted in the Anambra election.

Five, people calling on aggrieved candidates not to take their case to the election tribunal are not helping the course of our democracy. Our democracy can only be deepened if contentious aspects of it are subjected to legal challenge rather than people bottling up their grievances and unleashing violence through proxies. Besides, if part of Peter Obi's appeal to some people was based on the way he doggedly fought to reclaim his mandate at the courts, over three years; it will appear as blackmail to prevent similarly aggrieved candidates from seeking redress in the courts. Additionally, while disenfranchisement cannot be completely avoided in any election, it may well be worth a judicial pronouncement on whether there is a level of disenfranchisement that will render an election null and void.

Daily Trust 24 May 2012

CHAPTER 93

ANAMBRA STATE: SHAME OF THE NATION?

Anambra State has been very much in the national news even before the recent (ill-fated?) ward congress of the PDP to elect delegates for the party's primaries for the February 2010 gubernatorial election in the state. Like some states in the country such as Oyo, Anambra's political temperature, even in its former incarnation, has always been in treble digits. In the state, politicians are rarely accused of trying to 'overheat the polity' – because the polity appears to be constantly overheated. Besides being the unofficial kidnap capital of the country, some of the recent dramatic news from the state include the infamous abduction of a sitting governor and the ubiquity of godfathers and their antics. It is also perhaps only in Anambra state that over 40 candidates could each pay a whopping N5.25 million just to contest to become a party's governorship flag bearer while those who contested at the wards just for the right to vote at the primaries were made to part with N10, 000 each. It is doubtful whether these huge sums could have been imposed on candidates in other states of the federation without courting a mini revolution or at least a national outcry.

Gabriel Suswam, Governor of the neighbouring Benue State, who headed the Congress Committee that oversaw the ward election in the state, captured the perception of Anambra state in the popular imagination: "Is it not a shame that I had to bring 326 people from Benue State to conduct ward congresses here? It is a shame for any person from Anambra. It is a big shame."

But is Anambra state really the shame of the nation – despite the negative news flow? I beg to differ.

One, in many ways, Anambra state is the embodiment of the Igbo man's famed aggressive competitive spirit and extreme republicanism (these attributes reinforce each other). While these facilitate the production of geniuses and great achievers in businesses and the professions, they also unfortunately equally help in creating uniquely endowed felons that operate from the other side of the moral divide. For instance while ingenuity enabled some entrepreneurs at Onitsha to re-invent the home video industry (which had been existing for ages in other parts of the country) and took it to lofty heights as Nollywood, some elements from the state, in a twisted display of the same ingenuity, also copied the art of kidnapping from the Niger Delta, and characteristically took it to the next level. Anambra state is thus a reinforcement of the belief that genius and madness are often neighbours or two sides of the same coin. While this is no excuse for mayhem and lawlessness, the point is that it will be an incomplete portraiture to abstract an aspect of the state and elevate it to its defining characteristic.

Two, while the extreme republicanism of the people and their morbid distaste for dynasties, (including a distrust of any one trying to dominate the public space for too long) appear to make Anambra a Hobbesian state of nature - a place where every man appears to be for himself and God for all - paradoxically, the same traits are often the surest bulwarks against tyranny. Therefore while it may be true that the state is driven by machine politics, the burn- rate of the drivers of this machine (the so called godfathers) is very high. It is perhaps for these that the state has never given any of its governors a second term in office and rarely allowed any godfather to control the political machine for long. An interesting development in the state in recent times is the rapid increase in the number of rich individuals either trying to be part of the group controlling this political machine or to prevent their rivals from doing so. One of the consequences is that the godfathers are beginning to cancel themselves out, and as they do so, they unwittingly open up the political space both for robust debate and for increased participation in the political process. If this trend continues, it could signal the end of machine politics and godfatherism in the state as the cost of being a godfather will become prohibitive. In other words, being linked to any godfather, will, if this trend continues, turn out to be an albatross for any candidate.

Three, often overlooked in the portraiture of the state is that despite its apparent chaos and anarchy, the quality of leadership has increased dramatically since Chris Ngige. It is generally believed that it is unlikely that the system will throw up again the likes of Dr Mbadinuju who allowed schools to be closed for one year or owed workers several months' salary. Similarly, despite the apparent deification of wealth by the people and the fun poked at them as a nation of traders, the state has one of the highest literacy rates in the country and one of the highest number of JAMB candidates every year, suggesting that people in the state still appreciate the value of education. It also remains one of the richest states in the country. Anecdotal evidence in fact suggests that a majority of the Igbos owning choice property or businesses in places like Abuja, Lagos or Port Harcourt are from Anambra state. This raises an interesting question of whether the apparent anarchical tendencies of the people do in fact aid their individual successes.

Four, while their 'can-do' mentality has helped most people in the state to get basic education and avoid absolute poverty - despite the failure of the state over the years to fulfil its basic functions - it remains a matter of conjecture whether the people's political behaviour will change if the current improvement in the quality of political leadership in the state since Ngige is sustained for a long time.

Five, the long-term implications of the rapid blurring of the age-old dichotomy between 'Onitsha traders' and the professionals in the state remain unknown. Several years ago, OMATA (the umbrella body of Onitsha market traders) was a derogatory term used to describe Onitsha traders and anyone deemed as not being sufficiently educated or polished. The traders were stereotyped as being 'money miss roads' who liked to hug the limelight at the launch of community projects while the professionals and civil servants were stereotyped as 'polished but poor', who could at best only offer 'moral support' at such events. These days however there is evidence of an increasing convergence: many educated people are no longer content to parade a long list of their academic and professional achievements but are also into trading and other ventures that will shore up their economic base. Similarly, many of the 'traditional' traders are becoming very educated and 'polished', with many either having university degrees or pursuing higher education. It is tempting to speculate on the long-term effects of the blurring of this dichotomy on the political behaviour of the state.

In summary, Anambra is a complex state - simultaneously notorious and a leading light. While most people from the state agree there is a lot to be done, I have never met anyone who is ashamed to be from the state.

Daily Independent 10 September, 2009

CHAPTER 94

ANAMBRA STATE NEEDS LIBERATION

A nambra state has been in the news, often for the wrong reason, for much of the 4th Republic. It has in many ways become a microcosm of all that is wrong and right with the Igbo nation, even the Nigerian state. While the state has continued to produce new talents that excel to dizzying heights – the Philip Emeagwalis, Ngozi Chimamanda Adichies and the Onitsha entrepreneurs that reinvented home videos into Nollywood – it simultaneously appears to have reached a new level of notoriety by its apparent inability to organise itself or enthrone order and civility in the conduct of its affairs. Practices – for good or evil- that are prevalent in other states, once copied by elements from the state, get taken to a new level. Godfatherism and kidnapping here readily come to mind. Though neither of these originated from the state, today these two evils appear to have become the defining features of the state.

How did things get this bad?

Shortly after the inception of the 4th Republic in 1999, the 'godfather' of the time, 'Sir' Emeka Offor, reportedly handpicked and installed Dr Chinwoke Mbadinuju as the Governor of the state. But the 'godfather' quickly fell out with his 'godson', and for nearly one year, schools were closed because the state couldn't pay staff salaries after deploying much of its resources in fighting off Offor's antics. Mbadinuju was rightly denied a re-election. But rather than being an opportunity for a new beginning, a new 'godfather' Chris Uba, then still in his 30s, was thrown up, and was even more uncompromising in his insistence on total control of both the party and the government apparatuses in the state. Oaths of allegiance were allegedly sworn to him at the Okija shrine and when he felt his 'godson' Dr Chris Ngige was beginning to assert himself, he allegedly masterminded his kidnapping. Uba was later to confess that he rigged the election that brought Dr Ngige to power – a confession that was aimed more at ensuring that Ngige was pushed out of power than any genuine act of contrition.

Rather than punish a felon that openly confessed to rigging elections and allegedly masterminded the kidnapping of a state governor, Chris

Uba was rewarded with oil blocks, made a member of the party's Board of Trustees and handed over the party's structures in Anambra state. To this extent, the PDP - and by extension the federal government - cannot exculpate itself from the political chaos that Anambra has become. Is it coincidental that the urchins that have been elevated as godfathers in the state are usually of the same stock – limited education, no aversion to the use violence to achieve their aims, and no qualms in operating from the other side of the moral divide? Each godfather was also rewarded with oil blocks.

The recently botched PDP ward congress in the state was a chance for the party to redeem itself. It was alleged that more than half of the over 40 candidates who picked the nomination forms were sponsored by Chris Uba. In the ward congress to elect people that would in turn choose the party's gubernatorial candidate, the same Chris Uba was alleged to have sponsored and secured the loyalty of at least 600 of the over 900 delegates - ensuring that despite his inglorious past, only his anointed would emerge the party's flag bearer, and perhaps the Governor of the state. One would want to know why people would be made to pay N10,000 just to qualify to become electors of the party's governorship candidate? What was the subtext in this? Uba himself boasted of how much he had spent for the party in the state, including N800,000 in buying "brand new" Peugeot 406 cars for the party's executives in each of the 21 local government areas in the state. It may be germane to ask what a person who spends so much for a party in the state expects in return, and the implications of such for the democratic process.

For sure, federal government-created godfathers are not the only problems facing Anambra state. With ragamuffins who are elevated into godfathers deified by even the most educated, personalisation of politics and community life, a key feature of godfatherism, appears to have percolated into towns and villages in Igboland, but more especially in Anambra state. Thus in almost every town and village in the state, you find individuals who have suddenly come into wealth, and want to be treated as King Kongs. Like the federal government-backed godfathers in the state, the local 'godfathers' and godfather-wannabes brook no opposition, foment divisions and often engineer the ostracisation of those they consider enemies. Though these local champions may shower benevolence on needy families, such 'generosity' is often geared more to buy admiration and create a culture of dependence than any genuine act of charity. For an extremely republican people, 'selling' their support or admiration could be tactical, a rational, even if unacceptable, way of getting their own piece of the national cake. Often as soon as a local godfather stops 'topping up' his benevolence, (in a pay-as-you-go fashion) or a potentially new godfather with deeper pocket shows up, allegiances are readily switched. As happens at the state level where the godfather usually battles it out in a proxy war with other wealthy and powerful individuals, a sort of turf war also goes on in many towns and villages in the state among the local godfathers. In essence money and godfatherism appear to have corrupted the republicanist nature of many ordinary Anambra citizens. I believe there is a link between the current high crime rate in the state, including kidnapping, and a burning desire by some youths to cut corners to get loads of money and be deified as 'godfathers' either at the state level or in their towns or villages.

Anambra state appears to be a living paradox – genius and madness agreeing to co-exist in an ill-defined arrangement. While the people's republicanism ought to have been a bulwark against godfatherism and the politics it spurns, the people's love of money, (especially in a condition of extreme deprivation) on the other hand means that they 'tactically' accommodate and even encourage godfathers. As this plays out, the republicanism of the Igbos, expressed in their famed village democracy, mutates into a 'cash-and-carry politics' while loyalty becomes mostly based on 'pay-as-you-go'. Anambra state needs liberation from this brand of machine politics to be positioned for sustainable progress.

Daily Independent 19 May 2009

CHAPTER 95

BETWEEN ASUU, SOUTHEAST GOVERNORS AND COMMON SENSE

The strike embarked by the Southeast section of the Academic Staff Union of Universities (ASUU) since July 2, 2010, has generated headlines. At issue are grievances by the lecturers in the state universities in the zone that the Southeast governments have failed to honour the October 2, 2010 pact between ASUU and the Federal Government, which ended a prolonged nationwide strike that the union commenced on June 22, 2009. The institutions affected by the current strike in the Southeast include the Abia State University, ABSU, Evan Enwerem University (EEU), Anambra State University (ANSU), Ebonyi State University (EBSU) and Enugu State University (ESUT).

Both sides have their own arguments. Governor Peter of Anambra State was for instance quoted by the Vanguard (online) of November 7, 2003, as saying that the agreement between the Federal Government and the ASUU, is not binding on private and state universities. He was also reported as claiming that as a responsible government, states in the zone will not promise what they cannot afford to pay and that the lecturers had insisted on continuing with the strike, even after they were offered a 50 percent salary increase. ASUU, on its own, claims that the Southeast state governments are simply nonchalant towards education, and are more interested in the politics of self-succession and second term than the decay in the state universities. The lecturers further contend that the state governors do not mind having these universities closed forever because their children and wards do not study there.

The face-off between ASUU and the Southeast governors raise quite a number of issues:

One, both the southeast Governors and the lecturers appear more interested in grand-standing than in resolving the issue. While the state governors have a good case that they should not be blackmailed into promising what they cannot legitimately afford to pay, the moral ground on which this argument is predicated seems shaky. If actually the Governors meant well, what was the point of insisting at the October 17, 2010 meeting between the two parties that the negotiation must be conducted in Igbo language? Exactly what point did the Governors want to make? The insistence that the conduct of the negotiation must be in Igbo language, when proficiency in the language was not part of the conditions for employing the lecturers, raised legitimate concerns about a possible hidden agenda by the Governors.

The grand-standing by academics is also unhelpful. Accusing the Governors of being only interested in self-succession and second term is playing to the gallery, which could only make the resolution of the issue more difficult.

Two, the strike by the Southeast ASUU raises a fundamental question of whether lecturers in universities in the country really should be enjoying the same salaries and welfare benefits. It certainly is not the practice across the world for lecturers to have unified salary structure – whether they are working for big or smaller, federal or state universities. Similarly it does not make sense that Governors should be enjoying the same salary and emoluments despite their widely different revenue bases, revenue generating capacity and level of socio-economic development.

Three, the strike reflects very poorly on both the lecturers and the Governors – with both parties increasingly seen as mean and uncaring. It is particularly surprising that the Southeast Governors appear to have forgotten so soon how the closure of schools in Anambra state for nearly one year by the Mbadinuju administration –helped to account for the infamy that is today associated with Mbadinuju's name in the state. Just as there is apparent insincerity by the Governors in this negotiation, the persistent and knee jerk recourse to strike by the lecturers makes them part of the problems of our higher education.

Four, the analyses of the problems of the education sector, including the conditions of service of academics by ASUU, sometimes seem to forget, or deliberately ignore the fact that many of the identified problems are merely symptoms of an underdeveloped economy, and not problems that are unique to the education sector. It is for instance not only University lecturers that are underpaid and work in adverse conditions – virtually all workers in the public sector such as the police, the army, primary and secondary school teachers and doctors - face similar challenges. Therefore focusing exclusively on the problems in the education sector in isolation of the general challenges in the other sectors of the economy will only give a distorted picture of reality.

Take for instance the 2006 agreement between the federal government and ASUU, which required that 26 percent of annual budget (UNESCO's recommendation) be devoted to the education sector. How realistic is this in the face of competing demands for the country's dwindling revenue? It is instructive to note that the highest allocation to the education sector in modern times was the 11 percent allocated to it under General Abdulsalami Alhaji Abubakar's regime (June 9, 1998 –

May 29, 1999). This is however not to suggest that the current paltry allocations that hardly exceed an average of 2.5 percent is acceptable.

Five, rewards and obligations should go together. Just as the lecturers make legitimate demands on the government as their employers, the governments – federal and state- should concomitantly not be shy to insist that the lecturers should fulfil the obligations of their employment. There is for instance a need for the government to articulate the minimum obligations expected of the lecturers, including demonstrable teaching or research abilities and avoiding actions that could lead to disruptions of the school calendar. It may be wise for lecturers in each university to be balloted before a strike action such that if a minimum number of votes were not secured, the strike would be deemed illegal. The government should also take a firmer look at some of the contradictions within the ivory tower itself including corruption, sexual harassment and moonlighting. There is sometimes a suspicion that strikes serve the interest of the lecturers better because it not only affords them the luxury of receiving full pay for doing nothing, but also gives them more time to attend to their moonlighting ventures. We must also face the fact that many lecturers in our universities are barely literate or have become what political scientist Ali Mazrui would call 'ex intellectuals' (intellectuals, who have lost their ability to handle abstract ideas as a result of non-refurbishment of acquired skills).

In summary what is needed in this face-off is for common sense to prevail. Any resolution must not just be about meeting lecturers' demands but also the demands of the states as their employers, including sanctions for illegal disruption of the school calendar, sexual harassment, and soliciting or accepting bribes from students.

Daily Trust 10 November 2010

CHAPTER 96

ARE STATES REALLY ON THE VERGE OF BANKRUPTCY?

That most of the States in the country depend on the monthly allocations from the Federation Account for even their recurrent expenditures is an old story. This dependence sharpened as the number of states ballooned from 19 in 1976 to 21 states in 1987; 30 in 1991 and 36 in 1996. It therefore did not come as a surprise when Senator Olubunmi Adetunmbi, in a motion entitled 'Looming danger of bankruptcy in states: the need for fiscal evaluation', declared that most of the 36 states in the federation are in dire financial straits. The Senator said he based his conclusions on the Nigerian Governors' Forum's (NGF) Labour Policy Report 2011 which found that only Abia, Akwa Ibom, Anambra and Jigawa are in good financial health. The Report further categorised Kano, Sokoto, Niger, Zamfara and Osun as being in distress while Ekiti, Plateau, Benue, Edo, Borno, Adamawa, Cross Rivers, Enugu, Taraba, Ogun, Kogi, Yobe, Ebonyi, Ondo and Kaduna are classified as being in a critical state; Oyo, Bauchi, Bayelsa, Nasarawa, Gombe and Rivers are categorised as unhealthy while Kwara, Lagos, Imo, Kebbi and Delta are said to be in 'tolerable' state.

Several issues are raised by Senator Adetunmbi's motion:

One, while I have always believed that the current revenue allocation formula is unfair to the States, I feel that Senator Adetunmbi's motion smacks of PR work for the Governors who have always been agitating for more money from the Federation Account using every available opportunity such as the newly introduced Minimum Wage. There is of course nothing wrong in this. In fact in the definition of politics as the 'authoritative allocation of values', you do as much as you can to bring the most you can to your constituency. In this sense the Governors will be failing in part of their duties if they fail to fight to get the most for their States using every available argument.

The flipside to fighting to get as much as you can for your State however is that it opens you up for scrutiny on how you have managed the resources received. Here most of the Governors will fail the public perception test. In fact, going by Senator Adetunmbi's figures and the data from the Ministry of Finance on the net amount accruing to the States from the Federation Account in September 2011 (and shared in October 2011), the problem of the Governors does not appear to be money. For instance Rivers State which has the second largest receipt from the Federation Account after Akwa Ibom at N16,523,005,723.01

and Bayelsa which received a whopping N11,372,846,367.92 were among the States classified as unhealthy. On the other hand the four States said to be healthy - Abia, Akwa Ibom, Anambra and Jigawa, had net receipts of N2,874,893,833.59, N16,970,763,778.24, N3,594,187,407.11 and N3,858,431,759.41 respectively. Similarly Delta which received N15, 800,700,940.40 andLagoswhich by virtue of its location has a huge income from Internally Generated Revenues were classified as being in 'tolerable' financial state. Ironically of the 'rich oil States', only Akwa Ibom is certified to be in good health, while Jigawa which received about one-eighth of what Rivers and Delta received, made the list of States certified to be in good health. The conclusion from this therefore is that there is no correlation between the amount of money available to a State and its financial health. This therefore defeats the argument that increasing the allocation to the States will save them from the alleged threat of bankruptcy.

Two, the notion that the States are on the brink of 'bankruptcy' is a misnomer. 'Bankruptcy' simply denotes the legal status of a person or organisation which cannot repay the debts owed to its creditors. In most jurisdictions it is imposed by a court order, often initiated by the debtor. Nigerian States as units of the Nigerian federation are not bankrupt and cannot, technically speaking, be bankrupt since it is impossible to liquidate them or put them under administration as one can do with a company or an organisation. In fact their external debts are guaranteed by the federal government. The cash flows to the States are also guaranteed for as long as the Constitutional provision that empowers them to partake in the monthly sharing from the Federation Account subsists.

Three, a major argument against the current 36-state system is not over fear of bankruptcy but over their viability. Ideally States should be able to meet their recurrent expenditures from internally generated revenues while allocations from the Federation Account should be invested in capital projects. If this parameter is used to determine the viability of States, even the States said to be in good financial health by Senator Adetunmbi will fail the test because with the possible exception of two or three States, virtually all the other States use more than 70 percent of their total revenue (including the allocations from the Federation Account) for recurrent expenditures, leaving very little, if any, for investment in development projects. To put it in perspective, if we had just 18 States in the country, of the N177,666,426,671.65 shared to the 36 states and the FCT in September, at least half of this huge sum would be available for investment in development projects. And this huge sum is just for one month! Add to this what would be additionally saved from the reduction in the number of Senators, Members of House of Representatives and Ministers – because our Constitution demands that each state will have three Senators, a certain number of Members of the HOR and at least a Minister. Increasing allocations to the States will therefore, at best, be a palliative measure. A fundamental question remains on whether we really need 36 States.Indiawith a population of about 1.21 billion people has only 28 States.

Between Arik Air and British Airways

The recent spat between Arik Air and British Airways over landing slots, has dominated the headlines. According to the story – mostly the Arik version of it - under the Bilateral Air Services Agreement (BASA) betweenNigeriaandUK, each country was given 21 frequencies or landing slots a week. British Airways and Virgin Atlantic utilise the British slots, (British Airways uses seven slots each on both the Abuja and the Lagos routes) while Arik was allotted seven slots on the Lagos to London Heathrow route and five on the Abuja –London Heathrow route by the Nigerian authorities.

Arik claims that while the British Authorities allocated seven slots to it in the Lagos-London Heathrow route, it refused to issue slots in the Abuja-London Heathrow routes on the grounds that there were no more slots available. Arik further claims that it complained to the then Minister of Aviation Babatunde Omotoba on May 19 2009 who assured them that the issue would be resolved within six months and advised the company to lease slots temporarily from BMI, a subsidiary of Lufthansa, which it did at the cost of £60,000 per month. Arik Air claims that after the six months' lease, it again approachedUKauthorities for the allocation of slots but was told there were no more slots available. Meanwhile BMI from where it bought slots for six months increased the price of the slots from £60,000 to £90,000 a month before finally telling them that the slots were no longer available and that its current lease would cease to be effective from October 27, 2011, meaning that from that date it would no longer be able to fly from Abuja to London Heathrow.

Following the complaints from Arik, which suspected connivance betweenUKauthorities and rival British Airways, the federal government reduced the number of slots to British Airways on that route from seven to three. The Senate has since backed the decision. Nigeriaand theUKhave reportedly begun talks on how to resolve the impasse.

The government must be commended for patriotically and promptly coming out on the side of a local company. True, most of our airlines, including Arik Air, are hamstrung by debts, poor funding and relatively poor services. But these cannot obviate the fact that it is the duty of the government to help its companies involved in trans-border transactions to overcome barriers to entry into foreign markets – just as many Western governments use non-tariff barriers to shield their local companies from foreign competition. If our companies are helped to overcome the barriers to entering a foreign market, they will make more money, which will help them to improve both their competitiveness and the quality of services they provide – not to talk of the jobs they will create in the process.

Corrigenda

In my last week's piece, 'That Peace May reign in Jos' I erroneously stated that theKaduna crisis took place in 1998 rather than 2000. I also wrongly referred to former Governor Makarfi as a sitting Senator. The errors are regretted.

Daily Trust 10 November 2011

CHAPTER 97

DAVID MARK AND THE AGITATION FOR MORE STATES

The Senate President David Mark was recently quoted as saying that the demand for new states is "is right, legitimate and desirable" (Leadership online, 26 May 2010). The paper further quoted him as saying: "Creation of more states ostensibly to address the imbalances in the federal structures and ultimately meet the yearnings and aspirations of our citizens informed the needs by National Assembly to give the exercise a prime attention in the review of the 1999 Constitution." The Senate President, who reportedly made these remarks while playing host to separate delegations from agitators for Amana State (from present Adamawa State) and Savana State (from the present Borno State) was also said to have expressed optimism that barring any unforeseen circumstances the present National Assembly would create more states within the ambits of the constitution and the law.

There are a number of concerns with the Senate President's explicit endorsement of state agitations:

One, agitations for state creation, which was largely predicated on fears of domination by ethnic minorities in the 1950s, has led the country moving from three regions to four regions in 1963; to 12 states in 1967; 19 states in 1976; 21 states in 1987; 30 in 1991 and 36 in 1996. Despite these balkanisations, state creation has failed to allay fears of ethnic or cultural domination. On the contrary, each exercise has created new ethnic and cultural minorities, triggering in turn a fresh agitation for new states. Interestingly, no state creation exercise had been preceded by a referendum to determine the true feelings of the people to be affected. More often than not, new states are rewards to influential politicians with right connections, who champion the state creation exercise.

Two, none of the states created was preceded by a feasibility study about their financial viability. In fact of the current 36 states, no more than three can meet even the basic cost of administration without the monthly allocations from the federation account. That the National Assembly should therefore regard state creation as a priority at a time of extreme economic uncertainty raises grave concerns about our priorities as a nation. Not long ago several newspapers reported that the federal government withheld the N736.985 billion monthly allocations due to the three tiers of government for April 2010 because of distress in the Excess Crude Account (ECA). Minister of state for finance, Remi

Babalola, reportedly said that if the three tiers of government shared the amount due to them, the country would run out of money within the next three months. Babalola was also quoted as saying that if the country embarks on any form of financial profligacy, it would hinder the nation's ability to address its various fiscal challenges in the near future. Will state creation at this time therefore not be the height of financial irresponsibility? Just consider the cost of running a state: maintaining a Governor (including of course the infamous security vote), commissioners, state legislators, coterie of advisers, hangers-on, a new civil service etc. At the federal level, each state created will also add to the already bloated size of the federal government because section 14 of the 1979 Constitution makes states the basic units used in determining whether the government is 'reflecting the federal character' in its appointments, composition of the federal public service and dispensation of privileges or not. This means that with each new state, the number of ministers, special advisers will necessarily be increased to ensure balanced representation of the number of states in appointments. Similarly each new state will have three senators and a certain number of Members of the House of Representatives. And we know it is not cheap to maintain the legislators! It was for instance recently revealed that in addition to their salaries, each senator gets a quarterly allocation of N45m while each of the 360 members of the House of Representatives gets N27.9m every quarter, besides another N4.9bn (about N1.3m per legislator) as monthly salary. It was equally reported that some members of the HOR are pressurizing the House leadership to raise their quarterly allowance to N42 million each.

Three, one of the arguments for state creation is that 'it brings government nearer to the people'. The Senate President in fact rehashed this argument. "The essence of the [state creation] exercise is not necessarily because people (agitators) are oppressed but to bring government nearer to the people so that our citizens can feel the effects of governance", he was reported to have said (Leadership online, 26 May 2010). This line of argument is, with due respect, misleading. What exactly is meant by 'government being nearer to the people'? Is this synonymous with villagers and local people having the 'opportunity' to see the motorcades of His Excellency and other government functionaries? Does our own historical experience show that "government being nearer to the people" necessarily leads to their "feeling the effects of governance" in terms of the provision of infrastructure, jobs and physical and human security? What is the whole point of Local Government Areas of which the country currently has 774, which are constitutionally recognised as the third tiers of government?

Our experience will seem to suggest that contrary to the position of the Senate President, each time states are created, the ability of the new states and the federal government to make the citizens "feel the effects of governance" is compromised largely because each exercise increases the cost of governance and the opportunity for primitive accumulation, leaving very little for development projects. In this sense, state creation is anti-development and anti-people.

Four, state creation worsens the anarchical character of our politics. Section 126 (2-6) of the 1979 Constitution for instance demands that to be elected president a candidate must have no less than 25 percent of the votes cast at the election in each of at least two-thirds of all the states in the federation. This provision gives the number of states in each geopolitical zone a special political salience. Rival geopolitical or ethnic groups such as *North v South* or *Yorubas v Igbos* routinely overheat the polity with their politics of state creation to ensure that they either maintain their current power balance or get more states in its zone to redress a perceived imbalance. Of course elites who feel that new states will make them big fishes in small ponds do not help in this regard. In this sense, state creation and the politics it spawns, complicates the nation-building process.

Five, state creation is also inconsistent with the emerging consensus that the enthronement of true federalism in the country is a necessary condition for a meaningful fashioning of a nation from the agglomeration of nationalities that make up the country. Federalism – a system of government in which both the centre and the federating units are each, within a sphere co-ordinate and equal - cannot work when the units are dependent on the centre to meet even the cost of paying the salaries of its employees. What we currently have is a unitary system of government in federal clothing; and each state creation exercise worsens the situation.

Six, rather than create more states, the National Assembly should in fact find a way of consolidating the current 36 states into no more than six states to reduce the size of government, improve efficiency and save costs. Consolidating the current 36 states into about six, and giving a clear signal that state creation is off limits for a certain number of years, is also likely to reduce the jockeying and bickering for political influence by the various geopolitical zones, which the politics of state creation generates.

Daily Trust 6 March 2010

SECTION FIVE

BELIEF SYSTEM, IDEAS AND IDEATIONS

CHAPTER 98

NIGERIAN SCAMMERS: A CONTRARY VIEW

Nigerian scammers – a generic term I would use to cover 'Yahoo boys', 419ers, credit card fraudsters, putative hackers and others operating from the other side of the moral divide – have acquired a unique international notoriety. Globally, there appears to be a suspicion that every Nigerian carries a peculiar gene, which endows a certain twisted cleverness - a cleverness that is less oriented towards creating useful products for mankind than in figuring out how to circumvent what others have created. While Nigerians react differently to this labelling, what is often missing in the discussion is how the misdirected skills of our notorious scammers could be harnessed for the good of the society after they have been punished for their crimes.

Some Nigerians appear unduly concerned about the purported bad name this group of people give to the country – as if without them the country's international image would have been any different. We know it is only an irrational person that judges weather just by its inclementine side. To this extent, those who use the activities of the scammers to tar all Nigerians deserve our pity, not our apology. To hide our heads in shame is to give in to blackmail, for the same Nigeria that produces scammers, just like other countries, also has its fair share of geniuses in all walks of life. In any case, scamming did not originate from Nigeria. For instance, Nigeria's notorious Advance Fee Fraud (419) is a mere copycat version of the Spanish Prisoner, a confidence trick dating back to the 1900s, in which a conman tells his potential victim that he is in correspondence with a wealthy person imprisoned in Spain under a false identity, that the alleged prisoner cannot reveal his identity without serious repercussions to him and is therefore relying on the confidence trickster to raise money to secure his release. Like the Nigerian 419 scams, the Spanish conman would offer to let the potential victim supply some of the money in exchange for a generous reward once the purported wealthy prisoner is released.

Consider for instance how some of the countries that want to tar all Nigerians as fraudsters treat their own criminals who misapplied their talents.

Kevin Mitnick, who called himself "hacker poster boy," was once described by the Department of Justice as "the most wanted computer criminal in United States history." His 'breakthroughs' included exploiting the Los Angeles bus punch card system to get free rides and breaking into America's national defence warning systems. So notorious was Mitnick that his cybercrime exploits were detailed in two movies: *Freedom Downtime* and *Takedown*. He was eventually apprehended, and served five years in prison for his crimes. However, when he was released he was quickly rehabilitated and the society looked beyond his criminal past to the skills that aided his crime. He became a famous a computer security consultant, author and speaker. What would have happened to Kevin Mitnick if he was a Nigerian?

There is equally the case of Kevin Poulsen - also known as Dark Dante. US authorities began to pursue Poulsen after he hacked into a federal investigation database. And while he was being pursued, he further incensed the authorities by hacking into federal computers for wiretap information. He was eventually captured and sentenced to five years in prison. After serving his time, he was quickly rehabilitated in recognition of his special skills. He became a journalist and a senior editor for *Wired News*. One of his remarkable write-ups was on how he used his hacking skills to identify 744 sex offenders with MySpace profiles. What would have happened to Kevin if he was a Nigerian? In fact, in many countries, known computer hackers have been employed by software companies as 'white hats' to help them test their systems.

But it is not only among hackers that people who misused their talents are given a second chance in the West. Consider the case of Bernard "The Executioner" Hopkins who turned into crime early in life. At the age of 13, he was mugging people and was stabbed three times. At 17, Hopkins was sentenced to 18 years in prison for nine felonies. However after serving almost five years in prison, he was released and guided into boxing. Americans looked beyond his criminal past as he became the Middle Weight champion of the world, and reigned for a record ten years. A majority of America's distinguished boxers including Oliver McCall, James Toney, Mike Tyson, Jameel McCline and Riddick Bowe served time in prison before discovering boxing and channelling the aggression that defined their criminal past into the sport. The same is true of a number of the famous NBL players. Would these people have had a second chance if they were Nigerians?

Recently we read that Nigerian scammers have started hacking into people's email accounts, including the Hotmail account of the British Justice Secretary, Jack Straw, who was said to have been stranded in Lagos, and needed a 'soft loan' to help him settle his hotel bill and get back home. Looking beyond the crime, which must be condemned, there is also a certain glee that Nigerians are now beginning to join the technological revolution, that despite the rot in our education system some kids out there (if it was actually done by Nigerians) have quickly acquired the technical savvy to hack into email accounts. Then there is also the audacity of taking it to a British minister! Unfortunately much of the discussion has focused on the criminal aspects of the act, with nothing heard about harnessing the twisted talents of the fraudsters after they have been punished for their crime.

Is it not time we engaged in honest discussions about how the nation could utilise the skills of its notorious scammers, as other countries do, after they have been punished for their crimes? For instance as Nigerian banks begin to embrace a credit card culture, will they have job opportunities for some of those who had the twisted skills to perpetrate credit card frauds and who have been punished for their crimes? Is there any chance of gainful employment for some of the 419ers and Yahoo Boys? Or must we continue to throw away the baby with the bathwater?

Daily Independent 3 December 2009

CHAPTER 99

THE POLITICS OF 'GENERATION SHIFT'

The idea of power shift to the younger generation has moved up the agenda of political discussion since former military President Ibrahim Babangida, 69, allegedly claimed that Nigerian youths are incapable of giving the country a qualitative leadership. Though the Mina General, who was trying to justify his desire to contest for the presidency next year despite his age claimed he was quoted out of context, the purported statement appears to have renewed the politics of generation shift, raising in the process, a number of very interesting issues:

One, in politics, language could be used to frame discussion in a way that suggests an ethical divide between good and evil or between the good guys and the bad guys. For instance accusing a regime of being in possession of 'weapons of mass destruction' conjures the image of an impending Armageddon, which then justifies any action to remove that regime in order to save humanity. In the politics of generation shift, language is also cleverly deployed to mask motives. For instance those who want to have a dig on Babangida can conveniently lap onto his age to deliver a few jabs by using innuendos to suggest that his age is synonymous with such expressions as 'wasted generation', 'dead woods', 'recycled leaders' or 'old men who refuse to retire'. Of course Babangida's supporters could counter by presenting his age as the equivalent of 'experience' or 'maturity' rather than old, and implying that the younger generation are not experienced enough for the high office he is aspiring for. In a very brilliant piece in the *Daily Trust* of August 26, 2010, Modibo Kawu contends that those arguing for the handover of power in a 'generational shift' manner have often failed to "put across any meaningful radical ideas in the interest of independent national progress or the struggle against underdevelopment. Lurking under the call is a suspicious craving to be at the helm in order to be in control of lucre!"

It is in fact part of the ironies of history that Babangida, who championed a so-called New Breed politics during his tortuous political transition programme when he banned and unbanned 'old politicians' seems to be now on the receiving end of the politics of generation shift.

Two, the politics of generation shift is often based on a wrong notion of a linear progression from one generation to another. Frantz Fanon, in his over- quoted 'message to the youths of Africa', contributed to this misconception when he declared: "Every generation out of its relative obscurity discovers its mission, fulfils it or betrays it". The truth is that every generation embodies something from the preceding generation, something it wishes to do differently from its forebears and also nostalgia for some values it wishes it could recapture from the previous generation. In this sense, Wole Soyinka was probably too hard on his generation when he declared it a 'wasted generation' because despite its failures, it recorded achievements in a number of areas – in literature, the sciences and in consolidating the notion of Nigeria as a country on a journey to nationhood. Before that generation, the basis of the different nationalities that make up the country being together was more sharply contested.

Three, 'generation shift' is not a form of relay race between the old and the young, in which the old, out of exhaustion or impending exhaustion have to pass on the baton to the younger, and presumably more dynamic runners. In reality, 'generation gap' often denotes the dominant ideas and ways of doing things of an era, and subscribers to such new ways could be both the old and young even though certain age groups tend to be more closely allied with certain trends. A good example here is the networking websites like Facebook, which initially was a fad for the young but has since been embraced also by the not so young. In this sense it may be necessary to make a distinction between 'old young people' (people who may be relatively old in age but continue to feel young in their minds and who constantly ally themselves with modern trends and progressive ideas) and 'young old people' (young people who are resistant to change).

Four, the politics of generation shift is complicated by the fact that the notion of 'generation' remains contested. For instance while in the Bible a generation is roughly 40 years, in Generation X or Generation Y, it could be anywhere from 17 years to 30. A 'generation' could even be as low as ten years if it is defined in terms of people who have similar cultural experiences and political beliefs.

Five, the politics of generation shift could be a double edged sword for young people. Since young people appear to be taking responsibility at a much earlier age than their forebears, it could be argued that youth is no longer the future but that the future has indeed arrived for them. This means that young people are on the spot, and share responsibilities for the problems of the current era. Of course the formula for sharing blame between the young and old may not be clear-cut. If the President of a country is say 70 years old, while his cabinet, the civil service, bureaucracy and the private sector is dominated by young people, will the regime be said to be under an old guard or young people?

Six, the virtues ascribed to youth in the politics of generation shift may not always stand empirical tests. Babangida, Buhari, Gowon, Obasanjo (in his first coming) and Murtala ruled this country when they were relatively young. Similarly it is generally agreed that President Jonathon and Dimeji Bankole are young for the positions they occupy. Does the report card of these leaders and many of the young governors in the country justify the virtues ascribed to the youth in the politics of generation shift?

In sum, it will seem that a more rational approach to the politics of generation shift will be to find the right balance between the experience and maturity that often come with age and the vigour and idealism that are usually associated with the youth. It will also be necessary to separate the ideas needed to take the country to the next level from those purveying such ideas. All over the world chronological age is not what it used to be – people not only live longer but also healthier. Retirement age is being increased all over the world in recognition of this and there are people in their 60s and 70s who look better and healthier than some in their 30s and 40s.

Daily Trust 7 September 2010

CHAPTER 100

THE LURE OF PROTEST POLITICS

Why do candidates who know they have absolutely no chance of winning an election insist on contesting? Why do some repeatedly choose to punch above their natural political weight? Chris Okotie, who became a music icon while a law student in the 1980s before he discovered Christ and abandoned secular music to become a pastor, will contest for the presidency in the April 2011 polls under the banner of Fresh Democratic Party. It will be his third attempt. Sarah Jibril, the only female candidate in the last PDP presidential primaries received a standing ovation when one vote, her own vote, was eventually announced to her name. She has been a perennial candidate since 1992. Professor Pat Utomi, a very brilliant mind who got a PhD at 26, is the presidential candidate of the Social Democratic Mega Party. In the 2007 elections, he was also the presidential candidate of the African Democratic Congress. Dele Momodu, publisher of Ovation, a glossy that celebrates vanity, tried to run for President under the Labour Party, and when the party told him he did not have what it takes to run for such a high office, he went to an even smaller fringe party, the National Conscience Party, where he emerged as the party's presidential candidate. In fact among the 21 candidates cleared by INEC to run for the Presidency in the April polls, less than seven are likely to have any electoral impact even in their wards. So why are these people in the race? Several observations could be made:

One, protest politics – narrowly defined here to mean contesting for the presidency when you have absolutely no chance of impacting on the electoral outcome - must be distinguished from ideologically-driven movements and cause groups such as environmentalists or labour unions which contest in some countries often for the purpose of making the cause they espouse top of the political agenda. My personal opinion is that there are few, if any, ideologically-driven movements or cause groups in the country despite a tendency by some actors to sanctimoniously appropriate the label of 'progressives' to themselves.

Two, if the aim of the protest political gladiators is to acquire the epithet of 'former presidential candidate' or to use any improved visibility to negotiate for relevance or political appointment, it may be necessary to interrogate the cost. True, those who manage to make themselves heard will enrich the marketplace of our political ideas and probably get noticed by the mainstream politicians. However, in the current cacophony of our political marketplace, it is unlikely that most of the fringe candidates can shout loud enough to be heard. Additionally, when a candidate runs for the first time and makes a zero impact, a second run without a likelihood of making any impact will lead to the diminution, if not the crash of the candidate's political stock. This is why I am exceedingly saddened that Pat Utomi is contesting again, under the banner of a party that has neither the resources nor the organisation, money or structure to impact on the electoral outcome or even the political process. My fear is that the highly admirable Professor Utomi risks boxing himself into a corner such that moving down to his natural political weight and running for Governor or Senate may become difficult for him. Professor Utomi has name recognition and does not lack a platform for disseminating his ideas, raising the question of what he stands to gain from being a perennial protest candidate.

Three, are candidates who embrace protest politics the messiahs that the system purportedly never allow to come to our rescue? This is obviously a theoretical question because, as they say, you never really know a person until you have too much money or power thrust upon that person. A few indicative questions could however be posed: is there any fundamental difference in the espoused political visions of Nobel laureate Wole Soyinka, Professor Utomi, Dele Momodu, Femi Falana, Reverend Chris Okotie and a host of other 'progressives' that they must each have their own political party where they are entrenched either as life chairman/chairman of board of trustees or as presidential candidate? If the egos of the protest gladiators cannot allow them to bandy together to offer a credible challenge to the existing unacceptable order, how can they be trusted to forge the sort of national consensus required to accelerate our nation building project and rescue our economy from its current precipice? My personal opinion is that the whole political labelling and grandstanding, including among the major parties and politicians are mere masks over the real issue of contention, namely who will be in charge of the distribution of lucre?

Four, Sarah Jibril, who has been contesting for the presidency since 1993, and secured only her own vote in the last PDP presidential primaries on January 13, has been lionised by some people for her 'courage'. Ms Jibril herself was quoted as asking Nigerian women to 'search their consciences' for not supporting her candidacy. My personal opinion is that Sarah Jibril owes Nigerian women an apology - not the other way round - because there was nothing in her perennial candidacy to show she was serious. In fact her perennial candidacy makes mockery of the achievements of several women who have to work extremely hard for their successes. Is there really any evidence that Mrs Jibril worked hard to sell her candidacy? How much money did she raise for her campaigns because all over the world presidential contest is capital and labour intensive? How many people know the name of her campaign manager in any of her outings? I strongly feel that Sarah Jibril's reward for just putting down her name as a candidate – the media attention, sharing a podium with President Jonathan in the last PDP primaries and possibly being offered a political appointment in a future government of national unity if Jonathan wins – are very disproportionate to her dismal and half-hearted input.

Five, the effort to encourage female candidates by the various political parties is laudable. For instance in the last PDP primaries while the male candidates paid N11 million each for the expression of interest and nomination forms, Ms Jibril paid only N1 million. While this is a good step, a wrong impression is unfortunately created that gender is the primary and only hindrance to political participation. Apart from devaluing the achievements of some women who got to the top through a dint of hard work, this sort of affirmative action is prone to abuse as we have seen in the case of Sarah Jibril. What I would have loved to see is the broadening of the eligibility criteria for the affirmative action plan such that other weak and vulnerable groups – organised labour, students, farmers, the physically challenged and pauperised professionals could be empowered through positive discrimination. This means in essence that instead of gender being the sole source of the affirmative action, one's access to critical determinants of electoral outcomes – money, godfathers, and even 'election fixers' could come become part of the indices for determining eligibility for the affirmative action programme.

Daily Trust 24 February 2011

CHAPTER 101

LESSONS FROM THE TITANIC

I had actually wanted to publish this piece last week to commemorate the centenary of the sinking of the Titanic during its maiden voyage on April 14, 1912. I was conflicted on this. Why should I join the bandwagon of those commemorating other people's history when virtually nothing from our shores is deemed worthy of commemoration? I abandoned the piece perhaps as a protest - pretty much the same way I have refused to be strongly identified with the ethnicisation of European football league – despite having played football up to the University team level and living in Europe for 22 years. My standard answer to those who ask of the team (meaning of course the English football team) I support has always been: 'Rangers of Enugu'. Do I mind if they sneer behind my back and call me a yesterday's man? Not really.

I am returning to the Titanic story this week because it is really well documented in books and, most memorably, in that 1997 film of the same title written, directed and co-produced by James Cameron and starring Leonardo DiCaprio and Kate Winslet as members of different social classes who fell in love aboard the ill-fated ship.

The Titanic, built in Belfast Northern Ireland, was designed to be the epitome of comfort and luxury. One of three Olympic class ocean liners operated by the British company White Star Line, it had advanced safety features such as watertight compartments and remotely activated watertight doors and therefore thought to be unsinkable. It took three years to build and would cost about $400 million in today's US dollars. So impressed were its stakeholders that it was unveiled and promoted as the: 'Largest and finest steamer in the world'. Legend had it that some of those associated with the ship boasted that not even God could sink it – a blasphemy many historians say was never uttered in relation to the ship. What was not in dispute, however, was that it was built not only to be the safest and biggest ship of its time but also the last word on comfort and luxury. Yet tragedy struck on its maiden journey.

For its maiden voyage, the Titanic left Southampton on 10 April 1912, calling at Cherbourg in France and Queenstown (now Cobh) in Ireland before heading westwards towards New York. On April 14 1912 and with 2,235 people on board, it hit an iceberg some 400 miles off the coast of Newfoundland which caused its hull plates to buckle inwards in a number of locations on the side of its starboard, opening five of her sixteen watertight compartments to the sea. Within two hours and 40 minutes the 46,382-ton liner, with lifeboats for only 50 per cent of her passengers, sank, causing the death of 1,514 people in one of the deadliest peacetime maritime disasters in history. There were only 710 survivors.

As we celebrate the centenary of this tragedy, it is perhaps germane to reflect on some of the lessons that could be learnt from it:

One, sentiments aside, I ask myself the level of technological development in, say my village, Ozubulu, Anambra State, at about the time this supposedly sea goddess was constructed. Yes, I know that some great empires and civilisations existed in some parts of Africa even before the Whiteman came. I believe that at that time in most villages in the country, if the people had woken up and seen such a ship, their first impulse would have been to start worshipping it, wondering what the gods were trying to communicate to them. This is not a put down on our people. Rather it is to underline the progress we have made. These days we talk of 'catching up' with those who built the ship as quickly as possible, of Vision 20:2020 and becoming part of the developed world. Given where we were technologically when this ship was built, and where we are today in relation to them, it is obvious that we are really catching up, even if we still have a long way to go. This is really a challenge to the pervasive sense of Afro-pessimism that one sometimes feels around.

Two, an obvious lesson from the Titanic saga is the need to avoid hubris. For most people there is often a big temptation to be overconfident in whatever one believes one has become very experienced in doing or has acquired an unparalleled expertise in. The belief in the Titanic's 'unsinkability' was based on its pioneering new double hull and its series of watertight compartments separated by remote control sealing doors. The designers had figured that in a worst case scenario, the ship would be able to withstand the holing of four of the watertight compartments and still stay afloat. Unfortunately, the collision with the iceberg holed five compartments.

The lesson is that the moment we begin to believe our own hype or the hype of the sycophants around us, it should trigger an alarm bell in us that we have indeed become vulnerable. In fact so confident were the crew in the 'unsinkability' of the Titanic that they took less than half the number of lifeboats that was required for the number of passengers on board. Additionally, it was alleged that the lookouts had no binoculars because they were left behind at Southampton, where Titanic began her voyage – because it was thought unnecessary for such an 'unsinkable' ship. It has been suggested that with binoculars the lookouts would have spotted the iceberg much earlier and perhaps avoided the tragedy. As a young boy in Onitsha in the 1970s, I recall we used to go to the bank of the River Niger to watch a certain young boy who swam in the River Niger and performed several tricks. One day he dived into the water and never came up again. The lesson is that apart from God's guarantees, we are all vulnerable no matter what we believe makes us invincible.

Three, there is often a need to go beyond appearances and look deeper for the underlying causes of a phenomenon. This is common sense that often turns out not to be so common. On the Titanic, it was said that almost everyone, including the captain, was way too busy partying when young Fredrick Fleet, the junior watchman, spotted the iceberg on Sunday night at 11:35 pm. The night was said to be clear and free of fog, meaning there was really no reason to hit the iceberg at all. The iceberg that common eyes could see was only its tip, hence the upper structure of the ship that it damaged was very limited, so initially no one worried that much. The problem however is that two-thirds of the iceberg was below the surface, unseen, and it was this unseen part that ripped the deadly holes in the hull below the waterline and ultimately sank the ship. The lesson here is that the instinctive desire, especially in our type of society, to elevate the institutional manifestations of a phenomenon to its defining characteristic could mean that most of the time we end up dealing with the symptoms of a problem rather than its cause. We often see this in our approach to many issues – from Boko Haram to the problems in our education and health sectors. Often the problems persist or mutate because we refuse to accept that what is observed could have an underlying cause, especially when such underlying causes do not fit into the binoculars through which we filter the realities around us.

Four, the Titanic tragedy also calls to mind the class or primordial interest that the leadership of any country or organisation unconsciously projects or defends, especially when it matters most. Historians of the Titanic tragedy often note that the major death toll took place among the 'little people', essentially those in the Third Class cabin. Though women and children were prioritised in the rescue, the leadership of the ship has often been pilloried for this apparent discrimination against the 'little guys'. Some of the male survivors, notably the White Star Line's chairman, J Bruce Ismay, were accused of cowardice for leaving the ship while people were still on board and consequently socially ostracised. Wherever we are stationed in life, when it matters most, on whose side do we pitch our tents?

Five, the Titanic tragedy raises questions about fate and its ironies. When do we know when a particular discomfort is designed to save us from a bigger tragedy? For instance it was said that the Titanic just narrowly missed a collision with another ship SS New York when it was coming out of Southampton after New York's mooring cable snapped. It was said that sharp steering by the Titanic's captain saved the day as it avoided a collision by less than five feet. In retrospect, what seemed like a good fortune at that time turned out not to be so. The belief is that if the two ships had collided, the worst that could have happened would be that the Titanic's journey would have been delayed by several hours, possibly days. But that accident, had it happened, would perhaps have saved the ship from the greater tragedy of the iceberg. So how do we fathom out the irony of fate?

Daily Trust 26 April 2012

CHAPTER 102

BETWEEN OCTOPUS PAUL AND NIGERIAN JUJU MEN AND PASTORS

One of the celebrities thrown up by the just concluded World Cup tournament in South Africa is the German Octopus Paul. The two-year-old psychic cephalopod achieved global fame for correctly predicting all of Germany's World Cup matches, including their two defeats by Spain and Serbia. It also successfully tipped Spain to win the World Cup – predictions that reportedly led to the mollusc receiving death threats from Dutch fans as it did from German supporters in the two occasions it successfully predicted German defeats. Surprisingly the animal announced its retirement just a day after the conclusion of the World Cup.

There are a number of lessons from Octopus Paul.

One, belief in divination and other paranormal experiences is not an exclusively African thing, as is sometimes wrongly presented in the Western media. In addition to Octopus Paul, there are TV stations in Europe that are dedicated to broadcasting occult practices and paranormal experiences. Wives of some prominent politicians in the West have also been rumoured to be avid customers of those who claim to possess supernatural powers. In many African countries, even though the belief in occult and paranormal phenomena is pervasive, very few people want to be openly identified with them – for fear of being thought primitive. Will the open resort to divination in the West during the World Cup (as the case of Octopus showed) remove the stigma attached to such practices in Africa?

Two, the method used by Octopus Paul was transparent: it got the choice of picking food from two different transparent containers lowered into his tank - one with a German flag on it and one with the opponent 's flag. The container Paul opens first is regarded as his pick. Another creature that achieved a celebrity status during the World Cup, though less celebrated than Octopus Paul, was a parakeet, Mani, who in far away Singapore was said to have correctly predicted the results of the last five but one matches in the World Cup tournament. Mani's method was also transparent: the 13-year-old parakeet would grab a card in his beak bearing the flag of the country it was predicting to win.

It is tempting to speculate on what would have happened if Octopus Paul was owned by a Nigerian, and the animal correctly predicted the outcome of one or two matches during the World Cup. It is likely that the owner would paint his face and eye lashes with the weirdest chalk around, build a mysterious grove for the creature (and if possible let decomposing corpses litter the pathway to the shrine) and spend the better part of an hour chanting incantations whenever any customer showed up. Of course he would only enter the shrine with his back, and tell every customer that the octopus was a gift from his great grand father or from a benevolent Water Mermaid. Were Octopus Paul owned by a Nigerian, we would by now have had priests and worshippers of the poor creature! Additionally, unlike Octopus Paul whose psychic power was apparently limited to predicting football matches, the Nigerian owner would claim the octopus would predict any event, heal any disease and infirmity and even tell you the person 'blocking' your success in life.

Three, despite the successes of Octopus Paul, it is unlikely to convince most Europeans that the alleged psychic abilities of the mollusc is reliable. For instance though he had a 100 percent success rate at the World Cup, of the six predictions he made during the 2008 European championship, he got only four correct. Similarly Mani wrongly picked the Netherlands to defeat Spain at the finals of the World Cup. For many Europeans, yes, Octopus Paul has a high success rate, but he is unreliable.

Unlike Europeans, in Nigeria, the mere fact that the octopus achieved 100 percent success rate at the World Cup will mean that whatever he says (or is contrived to have said), will henceforth be taken as gospel truth – not mere prediction with a reasonable chance of error. How many diviners and pastors have created eternal enmity in families and communities by fingering people who are probably innocent, as the cause of other people's misfortunes? By forcing practitioners (including pastors who claim healing and miracle powers) to make their methods more transparent to encourage public interrogation of such claims, the people will be better served, and abuses and bogus claims checked.

Four, anything that has a name probably exists in one form or the other so I am not totally discountenancing the existence of esoteric phenomena and occult practices. But there is something that does not seem right the way these claims are bandied around in Nigeria. Tales of occult practices – of people who could make your manhood disappear simply by shaking your hands, of women who could use 'love potion' to ensnare you into marrying them or to do their wishes, of people turning into yam tubers simply from wearing Okada helmets – are a daily staple instilling fears, even paranoia in the hearts of many. Often opportunities to raise questions about the supposed powers of these 'forces' are missed. For instance even though many people tremble when some shrines like

Okija are mentioned, we do know that people like Dr Chris Ngige, former Governor of Anambra State, and Governor Theodore Orji of Abia State who apparently swore an oath of allegiance to their godfathers at the shrine fell out with these god fathers without anything apparently happening to them. Don't we deserve an explanation from the administrators or priests of the Okija shrine - to help other clients hedge their risks? In the same vein, the curse famously placed by the Oba of Benin on kidnappers in the state does not seem to have stopped the menace of the hoodlums in the state. Doesn't the public deserve to ask the Oba some questions about this curse, and why it doesn't seem to have worked? This point is important because there are many people who consult oracles and accept whatever they are thought to have said as gospel truth – without any question on the method they used to arrive at their conclusions or the level of error in their judgments. There remain to this day illiterate and poor villagers who are forced to swear to deities and to accept whatever judgment or punishment they purportedly hand out – even though they do not understand how such forces work. The same is also true of people who rely on the jurisprudence of their pastors as intermediaries between them and God.

Five, though Octopus Paul has retired, the celebrity status it acquired during the World Cup is likely to spur further research on the psychic abilities of molluscs. There will certainly be books on the invertebrate and its psychic powers. How many books have been written about such phenomena in our country to inform or encourage debate? But come to think of it: what is really the difference between what the Asians proudly package and market as yoga and some of our traditional religious practices? Is there any difference between those Asians market as 'gurus', 'earth masters', 'holy men' and our 'babalawos', 'dibias' and 'juju men'?

We can only tap into the positive aspects of psychic phenomena and occult practices by removing the stigmas that are attached to them and encouraging public scrutiny of claims.

Daily Trust 14 July 2010

CHAPTER 103

DO GHOSTS REALLY EXIST?

There is apparently more to the Dana Air crash than the loss of over 150 souls to the tragedy. Some residents of Iju-Ishaga, a suburb of Lagos where the Dana airline crashed into buildings on June 3 2012, have reacted negatively to proposals for the mass burial of unidentified victims in the area, fearing that the ghosts of the departed would come to torment them.

One Idayatu Ali, a 24-year-old unemployed resident of the area was quoted as saying: "This is no superstition; I have witnessed where a young man died in an accident and his ghost continued to cry at the scene for days until a sacrifice was performed." Ms Ali was further reported as saying that if the authorities went ahead with their plan for a mass burial of the unidentified victims in the area, many residents would be forced to relocate to another area. There is a strong suspicion that one of the grounds of opposition to the idea of mass burial is the traditional belief that if the dead are not properly buried with all the rituals and rites, their spirits may be wandering and seeking vengeance on the living.

The fear of ghosts occasioned by the Dana Air crash raises a fundamental question not only about whether ghosts really exist but also about our belief systems and their implications for the type of solutions we seek for the problems that confront us as a nation.

It must be clarified from the onset that belief in the manifestations of the spirit of the dead is widespread across climes and cultures. It is generally thought that certain practices such as funeral rites and exorcism are rituals designed to appease the spirit of the dead. The Chinese tradition of Ghost Festival involves the ritual feeding of the dead.

While the belief in the existence of ghosts, occult and other paranormal phenomena exists in all cultures, there is something untoward about the way this belief is expressed in Africa, which has led some to conclude that our belief systems are at least part of the reasons why the rest of the world have left us behind in political and economic underdevelopment. Perhaps the African cosmology, which is intensely spiritual, predisposes us to a pattern of belief that verges on the superstitious. Traditionally Africans believe that up above is the abode of God, the Creator and Supreme deity and that below the earth is the world of the ancestors - or the living-dead - who exercise some influence over the affairs of the living. They also believe that spirits – both good and malevolent inhabit the earth with humans and that each person is assigned a personal 'chi' (guardian angel), not only to help him/her ward off the perceived evil designs of the malevolent spirits but also to intercede on his/her behalf in the ancestral world and the world of the Supreme God. Perhaps this intensely spiritual nature of our cosmology is one of the reasons why many Nigerians find supernatural explanation for virtually every occurrence, creating in the process an avenue for brisk businesses by 'smart' pastors, Imams and babalawos.

How do the African belief in the supernatural and the occult differ from the way such beliefs are expressed in say the Western culture? Let me illustrate this with just two examples:

One of the celebrities thrown up by the 2010 World Cup in South Africa was the German Octopus Paul. The then two-year-old psychic cephalopod, now late, achieved global fame for correctly predicting all of Germany's World Cup matches, including their two defeats by Spain and Serbia. It also successfully tipped Spain to win the World Cup – predictions that reportedly led to the mollusc receiving death threats from Dutch fans as it did from German supporters in the two occasions it successfully predicted German defeats.

One significant thing about Octopus Paul's predictions was that his method was transparent: it got the choice of picking food from two different transparent containers lowered into his tank and the container he opened first was regarded as his pick. Were Octopus Paul owned by a Nigerian and the animal correctly predicted the outcome of one or two matches during the World Cup, it is most likely that the owner would paint his face and eye lashes with the weirdest chalk around, build a mysterious grove for the creature (and if possible let decomposing corpses litter the pathway to the shrine) and spend the better part of an hour chanting incantations whenever any customer showed up. There would of course be high priests and worshippers of the creature. Additionally, unlike Octopus Paul whose psychic power was apparently limited to predicting football matches, the Nigerian owner would definitely claim the octopus would predict any event, heal any disease and infirmity and even tell you the person 'blocking' your success in life. While Octopus Paul announced his retirement from predictions just a day after the World Cup, for a Nigerian owner, the proper deification of the creature and the associated lucre would start after the World Cup. While there was an official announcement about the death of the mollusc in its German aquarium on October 25 2010, a Nigerian owner would contrive immortality for the creature. While for most Westerners Octopus Paul was essentially part of the entertainment for the World Cup – the way the Vuvuzela was - were the octopus owned by a Nigerian, the little manifestation of psychic ability would have been defined as the 'main reality' of life, while our world of reason and critical inquiry would be presented as at best 'virtual reality'. Again while the psychic successes of Octopus Paul never led to a generalised belief in the West about the reliability of its predictions, were the creature owned by a Nigerian, the mere fact that the octopus achieved 100 percent success rate at the World Cup will mean that whatever he says (or is contrived to have said) in the future, would be taken as gospel truth – not mere prediction with a reasonable chance of error. Just imagine the number of diviners, imams and pastors who have created eternal enmity in families and communities by fingering people who are probably innocent, as the cause of other people's misfortunes.

Let's take another example of the difference in the way the Western culture expresses its belief in paranormal activities and the way we do as Africans.

In the UK in the 1950s, one 'Dr Carl Kuon Suo' was peddling a manuscript called Third Eye. Just before the manuscript was published by Secker & Warburg in 1956, its author changed his name to Tuesday Lobsang Rampa. In the book, which turned out to be an instant best seller globally, the author claimed to have been a lama in Tibet and narrated a purported experience of growing up in a monastery there from the age of seven. Dr Rampa also claimed that during that period a small hole was drilled into his forehead, which aroused his 'third' (or 'inner') eye, giving him very strong powers of clairvoyance.

The spirit of critical inquiry forced Heinrich Harrer, an Austrian mountaineer and Tibetologist, to hire a private detective, Clifford Burgess, to investigate Dr Rampa and his claims. The detective was able to unmask Dr Rampa as Cyril Henry Hoskin, an Englishman who was born in Devon, and whose father was a plumber. It was also found that contrary to claims in the book Mr Hoskin had never been to Tibet and spoke no Tibetan. Caught red-handed, Dr Rampa did not deny that he had been born as Cyril Hoskin but claimed that his body was now occupied by the spirit of Lobsang Rampa. Curiously as an undergraduate in Nigeria in the 1980s, Lobsang Rampa's Third Eye was a sort of fashion accessory to a certain category of students who claimed to be seeking spiritual enlightenment. And this was some thirty years after 'Lobsang Rampa' had been unmasked as a fraud in Europe!

Critical inquiry could also affirm the existence of certain paranormal practices as the case of David Seth Kotkin, a Jewish American magician and illusionist, better known as David Copperfield. David Copperfield's proven illusions include walking through the Great Wall of China, making the Statue of Liberty disappear and flying and levitating over the Grand Canyon.

So do ghosts exist? Anything that has a name probably exists in one form or another. Additionally what a person intensely believes in exists for that person. While I am not totally discountenancing the existence of esoteric phenomena, I feel there is something that does not seem right the way occult and esoteric tales are bandied around in the country – often without the opportunity to subject the numerous claims to public scrutiny. One of the consequences is that tales of paranormal and occult practices – of people who could make your manhood disappear simply by shaking your hands, of women who could use 'love potion' to ensnare you into marrying them or to do their wishes, of people turning into yam tubers simply from wearing Okada helmets – are a daily staple, instilling fears, even paranoia, in the hearts of many.

Daily Trust 14 June 2012

CHAPTER 104

ON LIFE AND DEATH

The news of the passing on of Michael Jackson, the 'king of pop', has sent shock waves across the world. Though death awaits everyone, Jackson's transition is the type that sharply reminds the living of their mortality - that life ultimately ends in death, or what Plato, the great Greek philosopher called freeing the soul from the "hateful" company of the body. Here was a major public figure, whose unique voice is well known through his music, who was known to be rehearsing for well publicised concerts in the UK that were to start about three weeks before he moved on. Known to be health conscious, and buoyant enough to buy quality medical care despite his reported financial troubles, the manner of his death, reportedly of cardiac arrest, despite having a cardiologist by his side, adds another intriguing dimension to the Jackson story. Jackson's multiple personas were such that at least one of these would embed itself into most people's consciousness. In this sense, he was more like any relative or dear one, always there in our subconscious even if we do not have active contacts with the person. Any news of the sudden transition of such a person often triggers powerful emotions - shock, regrets or anger. The emotions tend to be stronger if the death had not been preceded by a long illness that would somehow prepare the minds of the affected people of the ultimate inevitability.

Mignon McLaughlin, the late American journalist and author, tells us that the death of someone we know always reminds us that we are still alive – perhaps for some purpose, which we ought to re-examine. Any such re-examination however usually leads to the ageless philosophical questions about life and death. What is really life? Is it worth all the hassle? Where did we come from? Where are we going? Is there an afterlife? If yes, what type of existence takes place there?

For Western Christian religion, the nature of afterlife is simple: on death, our real self, the soul, leaves the body for heaven or hell. Seen from this perspective, the essence of life becomes to prepare for the afterlife so our choices and actions on earth ought to be geared towards avoiding eternal damnation in hell fire. Early European Christianity was filled with images of, and sermons about the need to fear the judgment that would come upon the time of death. Christianity pontificates that the road is narrow that leads to eternal life in heaven and those who enter by it are few while the road is very wide that leads to eternal hellfire and those who enter by it are many. It offers prescriptions, codified in the Ten Commandments, on how we can organize our life on earth so we can avoid this hellfire and ensure an eternal life in the hereafter.

Not everyone however believes that death means entrance to another world. The 19th and 20th century existentialists tried to humanize and individualize death as the last stage of life rather than the entrance into that which is beyond life. Jean Paul Sartre, the French existentialist philosopher, playwright and novelist, believes that when a child dies, he or she becomes frozen in time, and the child's experience of life ends. He argues that if the dead person was a coward while he was alive, then the image of that person as a coward becomes the way he will be remembered. Sartre, who is an atheist, believes that there is no divine being and therefore no heaven or an afterlife but that what survives of a dead person are only the memories of those aspects of the conscious choices the person made while alive.

If death is the ultimate end of life, then there is a related question of what kind of experience life is. If you believe that when you die, all your hopes, dreams and aspirations die with you, obviously life would appear to have a lot less meaning to you, and death would be something to fear because everything you have spent your life working for would be gone in a moment, and so would you.

Albert Camus, the French philosopher, journalist and winner of the 1957 Nobel Prize in Literature, argues that humans are creatures who spend their lives trying to convince themselves that their existence is not 'absurd'. Camus's philosophy of the absurd basically tells us that our efforts to find meaning in the universe will fail (hence are absurd) because such meaning simply does not exist, at least in relation to the individual. He contends that you will never live if you are looking for the meaning of life. For Friedrich Nietzsche, the German philosopher, life is worth living only if there are goals inspiring one to live.

While there are disagreements on whether death is the final terminus for life or merely opens the entrance to another life, what unites the two perspectives appears to be that the legacy we leave behind is what we will be remembered for on earth. This is perhaps what Abraham Lincoln, the 16th president of the United States meant when he posited that "it's not the years in your life that count. It's the life in your years." Albert Einstein, the Jewish, German-born theoretical physicist, seemed to concur when he declared: "Only a life lived for others is a life worthwhile."

Can we then infer from the above that the purpose of a meaningful life, which, irrespective of what we do will ultimately end in death, is in a selfless existence for others? If yes, where do we locate the pilfering and outright embezzlement of public resources by those entrusted to guard same, including by those, who by biological reckoning, should know that the end is not too far away? Why do so many people live as if there is no tomorrow and as if they are immortal? When you hear stories of public officials, including those nearing 70 years of age embezzling mind-boggling sums of public funds, am I the only one wondering what they need so much money for? Was the late American statesman James F Bymes after all right when he adumbrated: "Too many people are thinking of security instead of opportunity. They seem to be more afraid of life than death."

As we mourn Michael Jackson and other departed, while continuing our own life's journey - from the unknown to the unknown - it may help to moderate our behaviour if we can pause for five minutes everyday to reflect on how our family, friends and foes will remember us when our own inevitable apocalypse arrives.

Hollerafrica.com, 2 July 2009

CHAPTER 105

PROTECTING YOUR REPUTATION FROM NIGERIA'S 'INTERNET WARRIORS'

One of the numerous benefits of the internet is the democratisation of the publication of opinions. No matter what you want to put across to a wide audience, and the language in which such is couched, there will always be a website willing to publish you. In a worst case scenario, you can start your own blog at virtually no cost. In the days of yore, to get your opinion published, you needed to satisfy an elitist editor somewhere, that you really know what you are talking about, that the material is not libellous and that it is written in at least passable prose. In this sense the internet has helped to demystify the shenanigans of the literati.

A number of Nigeria-focused websites have emerged to provide a platform for Nigerians to exchange ideas about their country and ventilate their love for putting their opinions across. While some are clearly tabloids and driven by a certain political agenda or love for sensationalism, others like the Nigeria Village Square (www.nigeriavillagesquare.com) are truly non-ideological and will usually publish different perspectives on a given issue. However, as would be expected in any forum bringing together people from different academic, social, ethnic, religious and emotional intelligence backgrounds, the quality of the contributions could vary remarkably. It is possible to identify at least five broad categories of contributors on NVS:

The analysts: These are often contributors, who, from their writings, will leave you in no doubt that they know what they are talking about, and that their write-ups have benefited from some research and good proofreading. In their writings, they try as much as possible to be objective, interrogating various points of views in an argument before drawing a conclusion.

Informed commentators: While the informed commentators may not really tell you anything new, they tend to have good narrative skills – using very compelling prose or anecdotes to tell familiar stories. Many of the analysts and informed contributors who write for the NVS tend to have academic pedigree and also maintain regular column in established newspapers. Their contributions on NVS are often a republication of their weekly or periodic newspaper articles.

Privileged Contributors: Periodically some contributors with privileged information such as serving or former top government functionaries or respected Nigerians contribute articles that give information that may not have been previously available in the public domain.

Conscientious objectors: These contributors are usually not afraid to flow against the tide, consistently taking 'unpopular' positions either on principle or on ethnic or ideological convictions. Some of the conscientious objectors could fit into the category of informed contributors or even analysts

The Grandstanders or 'Internet Warriors': Though quite a few in this category can write reasonably well, their defining feature seems to be the use of caustic and abusive language to make up for their lack of writing or research skills. They are usually ubiquitous in forums, frequently throw adult tantrums to be noticed, mistake abusive and insulting language for courage, and often go by various aliases. I believe it is this set of people that Professor Pat Utomi had in mind when he labelled some contributors on websites as 'Internet Warriors'.The above classification is of course merely an ideal type, because in real life, the boundary between the categories could be quite fluid.

I believe that the activities of Internet Warriors worldwide have helped to re-enact the debate on the appropriate interface between a libertarian do - nothing course for the freedom offered by the internet and the need for an authoritarian censorship. In a recent book, *Free Speech v Reputation: Public Interest Defence in English and American Law of Defamation* (2010), I discussed the balancing acts in American and English jurisdictions between free speech interests (seen as the foundational block of democracy) and the need to protect people's reputation (universally seen as part of human dignity). While most traditional publishers in the Western world have the resources and the foresight to libel-read for their print editions, and strictly regulate commentaries on the online versions of their publications, many of the Nigerian news websites, understandably cannot afford this.

For many Nigerians, there are increasing concerns on how to prevent the Internet Warriors from damaging their hard-earned reputations. There are a number of available options:

One, is to approach one of the increasing number of companies in Europe and America that offer online reputation management. You could use Google to find some of these companies and then check them out before engaging them.

Two, it is now established that Internet Warriors could be successfully sued for defamatory remarks on the web. In fact as early as 2000, the UK internet Service Provider Demon Internet settled a libel case by agreeing to pay one Laurence Godfrey the sum of £15,000 pounds (plus legal costs) after defamatory postings about him appeared in news groups hosted by Demon. The case, which was the first of its kind to go before English courts, rested primarily on whether Demon could be treated as the publisher of the offensive material.

Three, though bringing defamatory proceedings are generally expensive and tortuous, in the UK, the extension in the use of CFAs (Conditional Fee Agreements) – also known as 'no-win, no fee' arrangements - between lawyers and their clients to defamation cases in 1999, could help people who wish to bring proceedings against Internet Warriors.

Four, contrary to some belief, you do not need to be a company or a 'big shot' to be sued for online libel. In 2006 for instance, a political argument that erupted in a remote corner of cyberspace descended into vicious name-calling. Michael Keith-Smith, a former Conservative party member in the UK successfully sued a college teacher with whom he was having an online debate on the merits of military action in Iraq after the woman variously labeled him a "lard brain" a "Nazi", a "racist bigot" and a "nonce". He was awarded £10,000 in damages and legal costs of £7,200. The case was one of the first of its kinds between two private individuals to go to court.

Five, given the cross border nature of the internet, you may actually pick and choose where you want to bring libel proceedings against an Internet Warrior. In 2002 for instance, an Australian court ruled that a Melbourne-based businessman, Joseph Gutnik, could sue an American website owned by Dow Jones in Australia because he read the offensive material in his native town. This means that you can choose to sue for online libel in the UK (if you read the material in the UK, which is regarded as the defamation capital of the world), with a chance of using the 'no win, no fee' lawyers - if they assess you have a reasonable chance of succeeding.

I am not, by the above, arguing for a return to the English Victorian era when many insulted nobles brought libel proceedings on matters as trite as being accused of cheating in a card game. While I believe that libels and threats of libel actions could undermine the democratic process by 'chilling' free speech, however free speech without the necessary self censorship would leave individuals and companies robbed of their hard earned reputation and dignity. As Shakespeare would put it in the play, Othelo:

'Who steals my purse steals trash;
'tis something, nothing...
But he that filches from me my good name
Robs me of that which not enriches him
And makes me poor indeed.'

I believe that the change we all desire can actually start with us: How about agreeing to disagree without making ourselves disagreeable?

Daily Trust 4 August 2010

CHAPTER 106

NAKED PROTEST IN PUBLIC SPACES

The right to naked protest in public places is one of the most contentious forms of freedom in many countries. In jurisdictions like the USA and the European Union, where political speech enjoys a high level of protection as a way of preserving their democracy, protesting naked often raises two issues: one is the issue of the protest itself, which is often respected as political speech or expressive conduct that is worthy of protection in order to safeguard democracy - provided permission is secured for the protest. The other aspect is being naked in the course of the protest. Nakedness itself could be a form of speech (i.e. you are expressing your political beliefs by going naked, which ideally means that your actions should also enjoy a level of political protection to safeguard democracy). The problem here however is that protesting nude, in as much as it could be regarded as political speech, could also conflict with obscenity or indecency laws in some jurisdictions. If there is a conflict between free speech interests and the need to protect public order and morality using relevant laws, which one should triumph? In the USA, the First and Fourteenth Amendments would ensure a triumph of free speech unless it is proven that such a triumph would pose a 'clear and imminent danger' to the country.

In Europe, the Strasbourg jurisprudence on human rights now clearly mirrors the First and Fourteenth Amendments in the USA. In a landmark case, *Handyside v UK, [1976]*, where the European Court of Human Rights had to decide whether the English obscenity law was a restriction on the freedom of expression, the court held that freedom of expression "constitutes one of the essential foundations of a democratic society, one of the basic conditions for its progress and for the development of every man… it is applicable not only to information or ideas that are favourably received or regarded as inoffensive but also to those that offend, shock or disturb the state or any other sector of the population."

Aside from the legal issues involved in naked protest, there has been a noticeable rise in the number of people taking off their clothes to make their point. In April 2002 for instance some prostitutes in Madagascar stripped naked to demand the lifting of roadblocks set up by supporters of the country's embattled president, Didier Ratsiraka, arguing that the roadblocks deprived them of clients and money. In 2001, some 300 Kenyan women stripped naked and stormed the site where the government was attempting to annex their lands to extend a nature reserve, forcing the scientists on the project to flee. In Mexico, naked protest first caused a stir in 1985 when sacked miners took to the streets wearing only their hats, boots and tool belts. In 2003, a peasant group from the state of Veracruz in the same country (called the Movement of the 400 Villages), invaded the capital, nude, for three weeks in protest against repression. Similarly, in the run-up to the Iraq war, many groups across the world protested naked in a bid to prevent the war. In California for instance, about 100 women used their bodies to spell out the word "Peace" on a local beach. In 2002-2003 Nigerian women invoked the curse of nakedness when they staged nude protests against ChevronTexaco. In the wake of the inconclusive election in Ekiti in April 2009, a group of women clad in white attires protested around Ado-Ekiti, half-dressed.But why do people need to protest naked ?

One, is that for some, especially in the West, the right to go naked is seen as a fundamental right, a demonstration of their right over their body, and a protest against an all-intrusive nanny state, which even has to tell people how to treat their own body. As the American nude activist, Terri Webb, puts it: "To be offended by the visual appearance of another person is prejudice, akin to racism. The right to exist, uncovered, should hold precedence over the right not to view this, for the objection is irrational."

Second, stripping naked grabs attention quicker than just carrying placards and chanting slogans. There is the fact of the courage to go naked in public, the unmasking of the mystique of the human genitalia, and the spectacle of naked human bodies in assorted shapes – from the inviting to the off-putting. In other words, going naked could be the easiest way of attracting human and media attention.

Third, stripping naked in many ways conveys a narrative of both desperation and transparency. On the one hand, it tells that the protesters are up against a mightier power, that they have been pushed to the wall, and that they could lay their lives for their belief. On the other hand, their nakedness communicates a narrative of transparency, that the protesters have nothing to hide, and nothing to lose.

Fourth, an essential power of naked protest lies in the vulnerability of the protesters. Someone naked is vulnerable to the weather and prying eyes. Nude protesters, by the fact of their nudity, symbolicaly communicate that they have no protection of any sort, and therefore defenceless. In this sense naked protest preys on the compassion normally reserved for the underdog, the weak, and children.

Critics of naked protest however have their own arguments, one of which is that baring naked bodies in public places where children might see such is immoral and indecent. It is also argued that protesting nude could lead to sexual violence and rape, especially from people who could not control themselves from seeing unclothed human bodies.

While the moralists and the legalists may never agree on the issue, what is obvious is that with the increasing tendency for nude protest in Nigeria, the country will have to take a closer look at its laws: is there any law in Nigeria prohibiting naked protest in public places? If so, does such law undermine the freedom of expression, and concomitantly abridge the country's democracy project? If there is a conflict between such law and freedom of expression (including from expressive conducts such as nude protests), how will the tension be resolved? It is instructive to note that in the UK and USA, it has been extremely difficult to secure conviction against nude protesters. Often the police tactic is to threaten to arrest the nude protesters 'unless they put on their clothes'. So far nude protesters appear to enjoy similar freedom in Nigeria.

Daily Independent 7 May 2009

CHAPTER 107

THE POLITICS OF SAME SEX MARRIAGE

The bill passed by the Senate on December 1 2011 banning same sex marriage has continued to generate furore. While some question whether such legislation merited to be an issue at all when there are apparently more pressing issues, I understand that the trigger for the bill was that two gay men went to a registry somewhere in Edo State to get married and were refused. The gay partners and their organisation were said to have threatened to sue the registrar for discrimination who then alerted the authorities that there were no laws in the land specifically banning same sex marriage. If this were true, then it is understandable why the Senators felt a bill against same sex marriage was indeed urgent.

The bill, if signed into law by the President, would punish individuals who engage in same sex marriage with 14 years imprisonment and a ten-year jail term for individuals or groups involved in the formalisation of such relationships in the country. The bill irked both Britain and Canada, with the British Prime Minister David Cameron reportedly threatening that his country would not give any financial assistance or aid to countries that were opposed to same sex marriage. The arguments of the British and Canadian authorities were that such a law would trample upon the fundamental human rights of homosexuals and gay people. It was also reported by Next (online) of December 6 2011 that following the passage of the bill, a group of about 15 Black and White people protested around the Nigeria House in New York.

My personal opinion is that the same sex marriage debate has been clouded by too much emotionalism, half truths, scaremongering and grandstanding by both the proponents and opponents. This has made it difficult for many people to grasp the real issues in the discourse.

I need to make a disclosure here. Personally I am very uncomfortable with the idea of same sex marriage but I also recognise that those pushing for the legalisation of such a marriage are also likely to be uncomfortable with my personal taste. I am equally conscious that my version of morality has no universal validity. The issue for me then is how to interrogate the issues in the debate dispassionately. What are really the issues? There are several of them.

Those who are vehemently opposed to the ban on same sex marriage often premise their position on the need to respect the civil liberties and human rights of minorities. They often equate discrimination against gays to the historic discriminations against Blacks, Jews and women, and argue that the campaign for same sex marriage should be seen as a continuation of the civil rights struggles for minorities and those historically discriminated against. In fact gay activists regard Lawrence *v Texas* (2003) - where the US Supreme Court declared that the sodomy laws in Texas were an unconstitutional breach of privacy - as their own version of *Brown v Board of Education* (1954). The latter was a landmark decision of the US Supreme Court, which declared state laws establishing separate public schools for Blacks and Whites unconstitutional. *Brown* paved the way for the civil rights movement and the integration of Blacks into the American mainstream.

Framing the same sex marriage discourse in this light often puts many politicians in countries like US and the UK in a quandary because few mainstream politicians want to be seen publicly as homophobic or intolerant of minorities. This has often led to many politicians speaking from both sides of their mouth on the issue. For instance while President Obama favours a 'civil union' for same sex couples in the US and regards the U.S. Defence of Marriage Act (DOMA) - a 1996 legislation which defined marriage solely as a union between a couple of the opposite sex for all federal purposes - as unconstitutional, he has not embraced same sex marriage. But typical of politicians, he seems to want to please all the critical constituencies on the issue by adding that his views on the subject were 'still evolving'.

But is a ban on same sex marriage really a breach of the fundamental human rights of gay people? In a key judgment issued on June 24 2010, the European Court of Human Rights (ECHR) held that there was no violation of the human rights of two homosexuals in Austria who were denied the right to marry by the government. The applicants, Schalk and Kopf, had complained both under Article 12 (right to marry), Article 14 (prohibition of discrimination) in conjunction with Article 8 (right to privacy and family life). While the court found no violation of the applicants' human rights, it was divided on the issue of discrimination. With four votes against three, it held that Austria did not discriminate against them.

Under the notion of 'protection of morals' the ECHR provides a lawful basis for signatories to the European Convention for the Protection of Human Rights and Fundamental Freedoms ('the Convention') to restrict particular rights and freedoms contained in the Convention. In this sense, David Cameron's argument that banning same sex marriage means abridging their civil liberties cannot wash because within the European Union member countries have rights to abridge such freedoms on grounds of 'protecting morals.' While Nigeria is not a member of the European Union, it must be seen as also having the rights to 'protect morals'.

Additionally, there is sometimes a big paradox in the use of human rights argument to push for the legalisation of same sex marriage. For instance while the proponents of legalisation accuse the 'refuseniks' of intolerance, they often display a similar intolerance to those who refuse to share their version of truth as we can see with David Cameron's threat to cut off financial aid to countries that pass laws prohibiting same sex marriage.

I have also issues with those who rely exclusively on religious arguments to oppose same sex marriage. For such people, same sex marriage is against God's design for marriage because God deliberately created Adam and Eve to signify that marriage should be between a man and a woman. The danger in relying on religious sentiments to oppose same sex marriage however is that that there are several injunctions in the Holy Books which appear to be observed only in the breach. What, one may ask, happened to those religious injunctions against adultery, fornication, taking God's name in vain or loving your neighbour as yourself? To single out the religious notion of marriage and insist on its strict observance will therefore seem hypocritical.

What I regard as a critical issue in the discourse is a non- recognition by both sides in the debate that attitudes do change - but at its own pace. For instance not long ago most countries in the world had laws against sodomy, which was punished harshly. Today attitudes have relaxed in the US and several European countries such that seeing a gay couple is no longer something that will make people cringe. However while people have become more tolerant of homosexuals in these countries, their attitudes do not seem to have changed sufficient enough to be comfortable with same sex marriage. This could be seen in the fact that the first legalisation of same sex marriage in the world took place only as recent as 2001 in the Netherlands. Again of the more than 190 countries in the world, only ten countries have legalised same sex marriage, and David Cameron's United Kingdom is not among these. Of the 50 States in the United States of America, same sex partners can legally marry only in six States (Connecticut, Iowa, Massachusetts, New Hampshire, New York, Vermont) and the District of Columbia.

The implication of the above therefore is that attitudinal change, even in countries that have accepted homosexuality, does not seem to have caught up with the quest by homosexuals to be allowed to marry. This means therefore that in countries like Nigeria where the idea of homosexuality has not even been accepted (and many continue to deny its existence in the society), asking people to accept gay marriages will simply be difficult - for now. This is the point I believe both Canada and the UK miss. And the manner they threw diplomacy to the wind and publicly took a position against a bill passed by a sovereign country, will only amount to campaigning against the very group they claim to be protecting.

Daily Trust 8 December 2011

CHAPTER 108

YELLOW SISI: REVISITING THE LIGHT SKIN/BLACK SKIN DIVIDE

The recent revelation that during the last US presidential election, Harry Reid, the current US Senate Majority Leader, in private conversation, described Barack Obama, as "light skinned" and "with no Negro dialect, unless he wanted to have one," made headlines across the world. Though Reid, whose off-the-cuff remarks are included in the book, *Game Change,* by Time Magazine's Mark Halperin and New York magazine's John Heilemann, has since apologised, the gaffe enraged much of Black America. It should be recalled that in 2007, Vice President Joe Biden, then one of the Democratic presidential candidates, also reportedly described Obama as "the first mainstream African-American who is articulate and bright and clean and a nice-looking guy... I mean, that's a storybook, man." The Delaware Senator's remark drew outrage and he quickly apologised. In accepting Biden's apology, Obama said: "I didn't take Sen. Biden's comments personally, but obviously they were historically inaccurate. African-American presidential candidates like Jesse Jackson, Shirley Chisholm, Carol Moseley Braun and Al Sharpton gave a voice to many important issues through their campaigns, and no one would call them inarticulate." Obama's answer was a delicate balancing act between the hurt feelings of his primary Black constituency and the need to play down the issue of race, which would not do him any good in the election. There are indications that since becoming the first African American President of the country, this has remained his strategy on issues of race. It was therefore not surprising that he accepted Reid's apologies and played down the issue.

But how has Reid's remarks played out in the wider Black America?

One of the fallouts appears to be a renewed focus on 'colourism' and the politics of hue among Blacks in America. Since the days of slavery, skin colour has been used as a tool of separation and preferential treatment within the Black community. This played out in the 'house Negro' versus 'field Negro' divide. The 'house' slaves, which were often products of a relationship between a master and a female slave, tended to have lighter skin and received the special favour of doing work inside the house, away from the scorching sun. Also because they worked in the house, they ate better, looked better and were often taught how to read and write. In contrast, the dark-skinned slaves, who worked in the fields, were rough-hewn - as some manual workers are wont to be. Understandably there was a lot of animosity and distrust between the 'house Negro' and the 'field Negro', which continued after the abolition of slavery. In other words, after slavery was abolished, 'colourism' continued, with one's skin hue and hair texture often influencing one's career prospects. One of the ways this happened was the "brown paper bag" test, in which Blacks whose skins were darker than the bag's colour were denied inclusion into social events or organisations. In fact, a 2006 study by University of Georgia doctoral candidate, Matthew Harrison, showed that skin hue played a significant role in the hiring of Blacks. In the study, psychology undergraduates, most of whom were White, were given fake photos and CVs to make hiring recommendations. It was found that lighter-skinned women applicants were preferred over those with darker complexions but equal credentials. Similarly, the study found that light-skinned Black men were also preferred over those with dark skin who had better credentials.

Curiously 'colourism', which favoured the light skinned also created identity problems for them in America: the lighter the skin, the better the acceptance by White America but the greater the problem of acceptance by the Black community – for not being black enough. The problem here is that under America's 'one-drop rule', you are classified as Black if there is a drop of Black blood in your gene. This means that many who are officially classified as Blacks such as people from mixed race relationships are viewed with suspicions and never fully accepted within the Black community.

If slavery could be used to explain the preference of light skin in the USA, how do we explain the phenomenon of many dark skinned Blacks from the Caribbean and Africa resorting to bleaching cream in a bid to be light skinned?

A documentary by ABC News on January 12, 2009 entitled "Senegal's Fashion Victims," found that in many African countries such as Senegal, trying to change one's skin colour was still seen as a way to get ahead. Again a study by Malangu Ntambwe and a team from the National School of Public Health at Medunsa, published in the online journal, Science in Africa, in March 2004, also found a widespread use of bleaching creams in Africa. In Bamako, Mali, the researchers calculated 25% prevalence, while in some studies in Dakar, Senegal, up to 52% prevalence was observed. A study in Pretoria, South Africa revealed up to 35% prevalence, while the most disturbing was a study in 2002 which showed up to 77% prevalence in Lagos, Nigeria. If the figures about Nigeria are correct, then the country has a potential public health time bomb – given the health concerns associated with bleaching creams. One would have thought that skin lightning declined after the late Afrobeat king, Fela Anikulapo Kuti, mocked those who indulged in the practice in his album Yellow Fever (1976), and street kids subsequently began making caricatures of 'bleachers' as people with 'Fanta Face but Coca-Cola Legs'.

Bleaching is also widespread among Blacks and Africans in the Diaspora, especially by women.

In a blog on 2 Feb 2009, entitled: "Bleached Skin Isn't The New Black", Folake Kuye Huntoon, reviewed a show by Tyra Banks in which the latter hosted some women who bleached their skin. Some of the women in the show confessed that they also bleached the skins of their children. According to Folake: "These folks, whom I pitied so much, claimed that light skinned women were more beautiful, got more attention and that they defined beauty in every sense of the word." Ms Huntoon posed a pertinent question: "Are these folks victims or do they really need to start taking responsibility for their actions and stop pointing fingers? I thought we had progressed from this and the media has somewhat embraced black beauty; have we not?"

The remarks by Senator Harry Reid may have refocused attention on the politics of colour hue among Blacks in the USA, but for Africans, both in the Continent and in the Diaspora, it is an opportunity to revisit the 'complexion complex' especially among women, and the resort to bleaching creams. Is bleaching cream not the clearest evidence of 'bleaching complex' – another name for self-hatred? What has happened to all those notions of 'black beauty' and 'black and proud'? Haba, Yellow Sisi! What coded message are you sending out to the wider world about your people by lightening your skin with dangerous creams that could cause you skin cancer?

Hollerafrica.com, 21 January 2010

CHAPTER 109

THE GOAT-MAN AND THE 'OTHER REALITY' IN NIGERIA

The story of the goat (or was it really a sheep?), which was arrested recently for being an armed robbery suspect, has continued to make headlines, with a certain slant that ridicules the apparent ignorance or superstition that informed the arrest. The BBC gave the story prominence on its website, with an innuendo suggestive of Africans being captive of weird beliefs.

Briefly the goat-man came into being when a local vigilante group gave two men, who were allegedly trying to steal a Mazda car in Kwara state, a hot pursuit. As the vigilantes came within reach of one of the hoodlums, he reportedly leaned his back against a wall and turned into a goat. Apparently the vigilantes caught the man in the said act of esoteric transformation and 'heroically' took it/him to a local police station, which dutifully effected an arrest, and authorised an investigation. The Kwara police later felt embarrassed and quickly recanted its earlier statement that the goat-man would remain under arrest while it investigated the matter. It also invoked an extant law to auction the goat-man.

The police recant under pressure and media ridicule is a mistake. The society would perhaps have been better served if investigation into the issue had continued, with the vigilantes who apprehended the goat-man asked to provide proof. The village where the goat/sheep was apprehended should also have been encouraged to look for a possible owner of such a sheep/goat, and if no owner showed up, the police would then take the matter further by calling upon those who claim to be versed in such things to come forward and prove that the goat is indeed 'human'. This approach would not only have given the story of the vigilantes a deserved benefit of the doubts but would also, even more importantly, provide a good opportunity for a national discussion of a phenomenon that seems to hold the life of many Nigerians hostage. What if such a feat was possible and the hoodlum did indeed turn into a goat? The manner in which this was treated with ridicule would in future discourage the police and vigilantes from arresting hoodlums who allegedly turn into funny objects such as mosquitoes or even a pair of old shoes.

In Nigeria, tales of occult practices are a daily staple, instilling fears in the hearts of many. There are unbelievable stories of people turning human beings into money-spitting zombies, of men having their manhood disappear just by shaking hands with some people, of charms which could protect people from machete cuts or even gun shots, and of women using 'love potion' to ensnare men into marrying them or to get them to do their wishes. None of these claims, I believe, has ever been subjected to critical public scrutiny, and the consequence is that they continue to feed into an already existing rich repertoir of alleged ubiquity of the esoterics in the Nigerian space dimension. Many Nigerians therefore live in fear, even paranoia, of these alleged forces without even being sure of their existence.

Consider a related story in the UK in the 1950s where one 'Dr Carl Kuon Suo' was peddling a manuscript called *Third Eye*. Just before the manuscript was published by Secker & Warburg in 1956, its author changed his name to Tuesday Lobsang Rampa. In the book, which turned out to be an instant best seller globally, the author claimed to have been a *lama* in Tibet and narrated a purported experience of growing up in a monastery there from the age of seven. Dr Rampa also claimed that during that period a small hole was drilled into his forehead, which aroused his 'third' (or 'inner') eye, giving him very stong powers of clairvoyance.

The spirit of critical inquiry forced Heinrich Harrer, an Austrian mountaineer and Tibetologist, to hire a private detective, Clifford Burgess, to investigate Dr Rampa and his claims. The detective was able to unmask Dr Rampa as Cyril Henry Hoskin, an Englishman who was born in Devon, and whose father was a plumber. It was also found that contrary to claims in the book Mr Hoskin had never been to Tibet and spoke no Tibetan. Caught red-handed, Dr Rampa did not deny that he had been born as Cyril Hoskin, but claimed that his body was now occupied by the spirit of Lobsang Rampa. Curiously as an undergraduate in Nigeria in the 1980s, Lobsang Rampa's *Third Eye* was a sort of fashion accessory to a certain category of students who claimed to be seeking spiritual enlightenment.

Critical inquiry could also affirm the existence of certain paranormal practices as the case of David Seth Kotkin, a Jewish American magician and illusionist, better known as David Copperfield, illustrates. David Copperfield's claims to magical powers had been subjected to rigorous scrutiny over the years. He was not only the youngest person ever admitted to the Society of American Magicians but his proven illusions include walking through the Great Wall of China, making the Statue of Liberty disappear, flying, and levitating over the Grand Canyon. Not only did he provide entertainment he also used his magical powers to good effect, when in 1982, he founded Project Magic, a rehabilitation programme aimed at using magical powers to help disabled patients regain lost or damaged dexterity skills. The programme has been accredited by the American Occupational Therapy Association, and is reportedly in use in over over 1100 hospitals in some 30 countries worldwide. Essentially the magic of David Copperfield is tested and proven and some public good have indeed come out of it.

The above two instances illustrate a certain probability of any paranormal claim being either a fraud or with some merit. It is only with critical public scrutinty that we will know whether the goat-man story was simply magic - a mere illussion - or a confirmation of what many Nigerians believe to be an ubiquity of the occult in the country, or simply nonsense.We should not allow the inanities of church militants or the shame of being thought 'primitive' to asyphyxiate the spirit of inquiry necessary for separating the credible from the creduluous and the charlatan from the serious.

Daily Trust 27 October 2011

CHAPTER 110

THE POLITICS OF LANGUAGE

I have a great deal of sympathy for Rod Blagojevich, the embattled Democratic Governor of the state of Illinois in the United States. I am not in support of what he was alleged to have done. But I have sympathy for him because he appears to be the proverbial unlucky fellow who, as the Igbo would say, gets water stuck between his teeth. His alleged crime of political horse-trading is actually believed to be the spice of politics.

Constitutionally Rod Blagovich has the right to appoint a successor to the Senate seat vacated by Barrack Obama following his election as the President of the country. The day after the elections, Blagojevich was taped telling an aide: "I've got this thing and it's fucking golden, and, uh, uh, I'm just not giving it up for fucking nothing. I'm not gonna do it." He was subsequently arrested by the FBI on suspicions that he was poised to 'sell' the seat to the highest bidder. Blago has vowed to fight on after the Illinois House of Representatives voted by 114 to one to start his impeachment process, clearing the way for a trial in the state senate which could result in his removal from office.

A crucial question is whether any other Governor in the USA would have just appointed whomsoever comes to his or her mind without doing any political and economic permutations of any sort? Quite unlikely.

Consider a case that is very similar to Blagovich's.

In New York State, Caroline Kennedy, the only surviving child of JFK Kennedy, is reportedly the favourite to be appointed by Governor David Paterson of New York as a replacement for Hillary Clinton's soon-to-be-vacated Senate seat. The argument here is that as a celebrity, she would be able to help the Democratic Party raise tons of money. In other words, Governor Paterson would benefit because Caroline Kennedy is expected to use her celebrity status and family brand name to raise loads of money for the 2010 elections in which he will also be on the ballot. So what is the actual difference between what Blagovich was alleged to have done and what Governor Paterson may end up doing? As Fromma Harrop noted ("Welcome to 'Nepotism Nation'", Realpolitics.com, December 28, 2008): "Would someone please draw a dark line of distinction between what we call a scandal in Illinois and business as usual in New York? Illinois Gov. Rod Blagojevich is accused of trying to sell a vacant Senate seat, while New York Gov. Paterson is expected to give a Senate seat to the woman whose family can raise lots of money for his benefit."

The different treatments given to the Blagovich and Kennedy cases amply illustrate the role of language, especially how language could be used to frame what is ethically acceptable and what is not, even if the same meaning is being conveyed. Blagojevich may have been guilty of being too direct, of veering off the 'normal' language code of horsetrading in American politics. You could find yourself on the other side of the moral divide, if not outrightly committing a crime, if you step outside the acceptable language code for expressing virtually the same thing in politics.

Language could also be used to frame international political discourses. For instance a word like 'dictatorship' implies a regime that represses its people, making 'mass revolt' against such a regime heroic since it implies a moral fight to throw off oppression. Given Americans' love of freedom, tagging any regime that America does not like a 'dictatorship' automatically justifies any state action against that regime in the eyes of many Americans. Similarly accusing any regime of possessing 'weapons of mass destruction' frames the discussion of an impending Armageddon, which then justifies any action to prevent it.

There is again the fine ethical line between the words 'lobbying' and 'bribery'.In the US, lobbying is estimated to be a 4- billion dollar industry. But what do lobbyists do? Put simply, lobbyists try to influence lawmakers to achieve a particular legislative outcome. Supporters of the lobbying industry contend that with the exponential growth in the power of the US federal government, it is not corruption, but self-government in action, for people to hire the services of professional lobbyists to put their own case strongly before those who make the laws. However, the problem here is that lobbying does not take place in a University seminar-style setting. It takes place in the real world where politics, power, influence and money mix, making it often difficult to draw the line between this and bribery. You could go to jail for bribery, but provided you use appropriate language and walk the fine line, lobbying is accepted.

It is however not only America or the West that uses language to frame political discourses. In Nigeria for instance, the late Alhaji Lamidi *Adedibu* has been rightly ridiculed for being a proponent of 'amala politics'. In one in interview, he reportedly vowed never to forgive a Governor he helped to put into office because the Governor refused to surrender to him 'just' ten percent of his security vote. Despite the justifiable moral outrage at what Adedibu was reported to have said, was he actually not being condemned for veering off the acceptable language code used to make such requests? Would there have been a moral outrage if the late Adedibu had accused the Governor of 'reneging on his promise to provide logistic support' for the 'popular project' of 'feeding the thousands of hungry people' that daily converged in his Molete residence?

In a recent newspaper interview, Chief Victor Umeh, leader of APGA, was reported as saying that he was pressing on Governor Peter Obi of Anambra state on the need to 'carry everyone along', especially those who contributed to his success during his court battles. Decoded, was Chief Umeh really not saying he was begging Governor Peter Obi to find 'something' for some of the party faithful and his own loyalists?

When 'Sir' Chris Uba accused his elder brother, Andy Uba, of stealing his 'structure' in Anambra state, what was he really talking about? Decoded, was he not simply talking of his thugs and others who supported his aspirations, including hangers-on on his payroll? What would have been the press's reaction if Uba had simply talked of his 'boys', or worse still his, of his 'thugs', which was what it was really all about?

Daily Trust 19 April 2012

SECTION SIX
NIGERIA AND THE WORLD

CHAPTER 111

DR ZUMA'S EMERGENCE AS CHAIRPERSON OF THE AU COMMISSION
JIDEOFOR ADIBE

The recent emergence of Dr Nkosazana Dlamini Zuma, South Africa's Minister of Home Affairs and former wife of the country's current President Jacob Zuma as the third chairperson of the African Union Commission has been generating angry reviews among many Nigerians who feel humiliated that for the umpteenth time the country's candidate for a key position in the continent was trounced. That defeat of Nigeria's official candidate is of course being deconstructed differently by several analysts. Nigeria supported Jean Ping, a mixed race Gabonese (his father was Chinese and mother Gabonese) who was running for re-election. There are several lessons from that election.

One, there is a need to make a clear distinction between the African Union Commission and the African union. The African Union Commission serves as the AU's administrative branch and as a secretariat of the Pan African Parliament. The Commission implements AU policies and coordinates the body's activities and meetings. The Chairperson of the Commission is elected to a four year term. Since the inception of that position in 2002, it has been monopolised by nationals of French-speaking countries. The Commission's first Chairman, Amara Essy of Côte d'Ivoire held the position in acting capacity for one year (July 9 2002 to September 16 2003). After Amara Essy we had Alpha Oumar Konare from Mali (September 16 2003 to April 28 2008) and Jean Ping from Gabon (April 28 2008 to July 15 2012).

Unlike the African Union Commission, Chairpersons of the African Union are elected for a one-year tenure and the person must be a serving Head of State or Government. The current chairman of AU is Yayi Boni from the Republic of Benin (whose tenure started on January 29 2012). Before him we had Theodoro Obiang Nguema Mbasogo from Equatorial Guinea, whose tenure lasted from January 31 2011 to January 29 2011. What is clear is that the English-speaking part of the continent has felt, to use a Nigerian expression, 'marginalised', and craved for the strategic positions in the continental body to reflect the continent's linguistic character.

Two, I believe that Nigeria's foreign policy strategists monitoring the politics around the election of a new Chairperson of the African Union Commission did not have their ears on the ground and therefore failed to pick up the muffled grumbling of the Anglophone part of the continent, especially members of the Southern African Development Commission (SADC). Had they done so, they would have dropped their support of Jean Ping after the January stalemated election and propped up an Anglophone candidate from one of the small countries in the SADC region, preferably a female candidate. Jean Ping has had a one term of four years and for organisations like the African Commission, it is actually unhealthy to allow its key officers, including the Chairman of the Commission, to have more than one term as such positions need to go round quickly among the different members to give every country what Nigerian politicians would call a 'sense of belonging'.

Three, there is no doubt that Zuma's emergence as the Commission's Chairperson is at variance with Nigeria's strategic interests. Nigeria, South Africa, Egypt and Ethiopia are all contenders for an African slot as a Permanent Member of the UN Security Council – if that slot becomes available. The fear therefore is not only that Dr Zuma could use her position to project South Africa's foreign policy positions but that she could also use it to subtly canvas for her country's candidacy for the envisaged African slot as a Permanent Member of the UN Security Council. These fears perhaps informed the opposition of Nigeria, Egypt and Ethiopia to Dr Zuma's candidacy. I think that given the threat posed by Dr Zuma's Chairmanship of the Commission to Nigeria's strategic interests, President Jonathan was misadvised about attending the conference. He – or at least the Vice President – ought to have been in Ethiopia to engage in the last minute horse-trading that often decides the outcome of such crucial elections.

Four, it is true that there is a convention that the Chairmanship of the AU Commission should be reserved for the smaller countries and that the five largest contributors to the AU– Nigeria, South Africa, Libya, Egypt and Algeria – are discouraged from contesting for that position. But that is only a convention, not a rule. South Africa not only tapped into the latent grumbling among the Anglophone countries by presenting a candidate, she also ensured that any loud grumbling against the violation of that convention would be muffled by presenting a woman because in the global politics of feminism, a woman is seen as a minority subordinated and dominated in a largely patriarchal world. Had Nigeria propped up a qualified female candidate from an English-speaking country, preferably from SADC, the issue of violating the convention would have been successfully played up.

Five, the election of Dr Zuma shows a failure of not just leadership but foreign policy formulation in Nigeria. In late December 2010, the National Economic Council (NEC) reportedly resolved that going forward, Nigeria would no longer play 'big brother' to countries in trouble without getting anything in return. It also proposed that the nation's foreign interventions and assistance would henceforth be guided by 'national interest'. At a seminar to 'review Nigeria's foreign policy' organised by the Presidential Advisory Council on International Relations (PAC-IR) in collaboration with the Ministry of Foreign Affairs at Abuja from August 1- 4 2011, this point was re-emphasised. In an address at the seminar, the Minister of Foreign Affairs, Ambassador Olugbenga Ashiru reportedly said that Nigerians must benefit maximally from the nation's foreign policy. In his speech while declaring the seminar open, President Jonathan reportedly noted that "although the country had played a leading role in the emancipation of the African continent from colonialism and racial discrimination, there is need to now focus on new priorities...." (Daily Trust August 11, 2011). The President's position re-echoes the sentiments expressed by Governor Babangida Aliyu of Niger State after the NEC meeting in December 2010 when he was quoted as saying that "...we are going to shed that belief that we are big brother where we go to help other people and we never get something in return...So, wherever we go or whoever we relate with, must be because it will help us develop, rather than, as we normally say, that we have gone to help these or that people without getting anything in return."

I regard these pronouncements and posturing as among the lowest points in our foreign policy formulations. Not only was 'national interest' wrongly conceived in very narrow mercantilist term of immediate economic gratification, they also declared that 'henceforth Africa would no longer be the centrepiece of the country's foreign policy'. Ironically the country's strategic importance to the rest of the world is largely because of its perceived leadership role in the continent. In essence, such inappropriate grandstanding in the name of reviewing our foreign policy was meant to discourage the sort of sociological investments in other African countries which usually translate into leverages in situations such as the election of Chairperson of the Commission of the African Union. We cannot eat our cake and have it. Countries are not respected because of their past benevolence but because of the leverages they can bring to the table at any given point in time.

Six, did Nigeria deliberately allow South Africa's Dr Zuma to triumph as a payback for the country's support of Dr Ngozi Iweala's bid for the presidency of the World Bank – as some people believe? While anything is possible in international politics, in the absence of hard evidence to support such a position, it must remain in the realm of speculation. What seems to be obvious is that the country needs to return to the drawing board in its foreign policy-making. We can still accomplish far more than we are doing now in our foreign policy – despite lingering domestic problems - if we get our foreign policies right and play smart politics. For a start, we do not need to announce to the whole world that we are reviewing our foreign policy as we misguidedly did last year. Foreign policies ought to be under constant review anyway because of the dynamic nature of the international system. It is the day job of the Minister of Foreign Affairs and think tanks such as the Nigerian Institute of International Affairs to constantly monitor developments in the international system for potential changes that will throw up opportunities or threats or affect the configuration of power and then devise appropriate responses. You do not need to advertise your weakness to the whole world by announcing that you are reviewing your foreign policy or that henceforth your foreign policy will be guided only by national interest because as Wole Soyinka would tell us 'a tiger never proclaims its tigeritude'.

Daily Trust 19 July 2012

CHAPTER 112

WHO IS AN AFRICAN?

Who is an African? At face value, the answer to this question seems obvious. Surely, everyone knows who the African is, it would seem. But the answer becomes less obvious once other probing qualifiers are added to the question. Are White South Africans really Africans? Are Moroccans, Egyptians and other Arab Africans as much Africans as say, Nigerians or Ghanaians? Is Barrack Obama an African? Do all categorised as African or as having an African pedigree perceive themselves as such? Are all who perceive themselves as Africans accepted as such? Are there levels of "African-ness", and are some more African than others? Who allots this African-ness, and why? How does African identity interface with other levels of identity and citizenship in Africa? In short, how is the African identity constructed in the face of the mosaic of identities that people of African ancestry living within and beyond the continent bear?

The above are some of the questions one confronts when trying to empirically delineate the African.

For some, the African is simply a racial category - a Black man with certain Bantu features. But this classificatory scheme often poses more questions than it answers. Let us for instance assume that a Caucasian English police officer described the scene of a crime thus: "At the scene of the crime were four Africans and four white boys." What kinds of images come to our mind to differentiate the four 'Africans' from the four White boys? If the same police officer changes the description to: "There were four Black men and four White boys at the scene of the crime", what sorts of imageries come to our mind? Or better put, what sorts of imageries do we think he is trying to convey?

It would seem that the use of 'African' is much narrower than the use of 'Black' because our hypothetical Caucasian police officer would most likely think of Africans as being different from Black Caribbean, Black Guyanese or African-Americans even though they are all generically called Blacks. This analogy suggests that while race does matter as an organising category in identifying the African, it would be inadequate in properly differentiating, in the Western imagination at least, who is an African from who is Black.

Again if we use race alone in the delineation of the African, a legitimate question is raised about non-Blacks with African citizenship, say, the White South Africans, who never knew any other country but South Africa. Are they Africans?

Some have tried to use territoriality to define the African. For those who adopt this perspective, all it takes will be to look at the map of the world and categorise all who were born in the continent of Africa or who hold the citizenship of one of the countries that make up the continent, or has ancestry in the continent, as African. This option however has equally a number of problems. For example, if we choose to call all who have 'African' ancestry Africans, how far back in time should we go? This perspective also wrongly assumes that all who are citizens of the countries that make up the continent of Africa accept that they are 'Africans'. Even within sub-Saharan Africa, sections of countries like Somalia, Mauritania, Niger and Sudan would prefer to be called Arabs, not Africans.

There are also those who believe that consciousness of being an African, or commitment to the cause of Africa should be the only or main criterion for delineating who the African is. This form of classification is quite popular with the remnants of the African ideological left and those eager to wear the toga of universalism and cosmopolitanism. One of the weaknesses of this classificatory scheme however is that it is so fluid that any one expressing any sort of interest in African affairs could, by this definition, legitimately claim to be an African. For instance is Tony Blair, who as Prime Minister of Britain, said that Africa was a scar on the consciousness of the world, and felt moved enough to set up the Commission for Africa, an African by this definition? Besides, using consciousness to delineate the African could end up de-Africanising a majority of the people who non-Africans will commonly identify as Africans. Does for instance the village Igbo or Yoruba or Hausa woman in Nigeria have any consciousness of being an African? If, as is commonly believed, such a consciousness is non-existent, or at best insipient, does that then imply that such people are not Africans?

Eminent African political scientist Professor Ali Mazrui made a distinction between "Africans of the blood and Africans of the soil". For him, Africans of the blood are defined in racial and genealogical terms. They are identified with the black race while Africans of the soil are defined in geographical terms. For Mazrui therefore, both territoriality and race should be used simultaneously in identifying the African. A major problem with this view however is that it seems to imply a hierarchy of Africans since someone who is both an African of the blood and an African of the soil could legitimately claim a higher ranking than those who have fewer attributes such as those who are only Africans of the soil or of the blood.

More than the controversial question of who is an African, are the implications of the contentious nature of African identity for the continent's unity project and development trajectory? Fortunately they are many who believe that despite these challenges, there are sufficient grounds for optimism. These grounds include the rise of new economic powers – Brazil, China, India and Russia- which are increasingly looking upon Africa as the next big destination, the apparent deepening of democratic ethos in the continent, which could lead to a weakening of the fissiparous tendencies that underlie the various notions of Africanity, and the emergence of Barrack Obama as the 44th President of the United States of America.

For many Africans Obama is both an African name they can relate to, and a metaphor expressing that anything is possible if you strive hard for it with the 'right attitude.' It is believed that this 'right attitude' is an attitude that is post-chauvinism, for it is only by being post-racial and a reconciler that a Blackman, with an African Muslim father, who was not born into privilege, could emerge president of the most powerful country in the world. This lesson is not lost on Africans and it is a powerful boost to the African unity project.

Daily Independent, 21 May 2009

CHAPTER 113

FROM ABROAD, WITH LOVE

O l guy please alert me of any opportunity while there."
"Of course, you can count on that", he re-assures.
I remind him that many returnees behave like politician friends. As soon as they get into office or secure appointments they commit 'class suicide' and develop an attitude towards old friends.

Okey swears he is not that type. A big private firm in Lagos had offered him a director-level position and matched his UK salary, plus other incentives such as paid holidays to see his family in the UK three times a year. It is the type of 'soft-landing' most people on 'Whingeland' abroad would regard as God-sent. Okey has recently returned to the UK from a one-month preliminary contact with his new employers. He has some concerns and of course new whinges: What if the company collapses or refuses to keep to the contract? Can he cope with his new boss's 'Nigerian Big Man's' mentality, which expects him to grovel and answer to his beck and call with 'Yes sir'? He felt embarrassed by the way his subordinates always answered 'yes sir, yes sir" to whatever he said, were they not just doing eye service? He has heard numerous stories about the use of *juju* in office politics, is that really true?

Like most people who have taken the bold step of returning home, Okey has suddenly become a celebrity among those itching to return home but are paralysed by fears of the unknown and reverse culture shock. People call him to hear how things are really there on the ground, how he got the job, how other returnees are faring, and any advice on how they should plot their own return.

We discuss the divorce rate in the UK, especially among black families, noting recent news report that Britain held its first ever divorce fair named "Starting Over Show" in the resort town of Brighton, Sunday, March 15, 2009. We review the experiences of some Africans unravelled by their family situations.

We talk about the loneliness and the alienation, which prevent most immigrants from integrating properly into the land of their sojourn irrespective of the type of job they have or how successful they are in business. In fact, most of those very eager to return home could be regarded as professionally accomplished.

I refer to a recent article about the flood of skilled immigrants leaving the US for the country of their birth. In the article research funded by the Kauffman Foundation tracked 1,200 Chinese and Indian immigrants who had returned home. It found 51% of the Chinese returnees had master's degrees and 41% had PhDs while 66% of the Indians had a master's and 12.1% had PhDs. The reasons given by the returnees included missing their family and friends at home, growing demand for their skills at home or the need to be near ageing parents. The research also found that those who returned had reverse culture shock: the Indians complained of traffic and congestion, lack of infrastructure, excessive bureaucracy, and pollution. The Chinese complained of pollution, reverse culture shock, inferior education for children, frustration with government bureaucracy, and the quality of health care. The returnees said they were generally making less money in absolute terms, but they also said they enjoyed a higher quality of life than in the USA. I ask if we can draw any lessons from the research about those planning to return home to Nigeria. We agree the research missed out some of the reasons many Africans, especially those who have been here for ten years or more seem to miss home terribly as the years go by. One, most African immigrants arrived abroad as adults, often in their 20s or even 30s, so their idea of 'home' is fixed as their country of birth. Two, many fear that if their children reach a certain age abroad, their notion of 'home' will be their (i.e. the children's) country of birth, not the country of birth of their parents. This means in essence a certain fear that when they are ready to return 'home', their children may refuse to tag along oraccept their definition of 'home'. Three, many African immigrants prioritize investments at 'home', to investments in their land of sojourn. However as the years pass by, and the contradiction in the notion of 'home' between them and their children sharpens, they suddenly realize that their children may not be bothered about fighting for whatever they may have in their home country, raising questions about why they bothered to work so hard all these years. For some therefore, one way out of this will be to plot to return 'home' with their children before they develop the 'wrong' notion that their 'home' is abroad, and not in Nigeria. Fourth, Nigerians believe their country is tough, and that one needs to return 'home' when there is still some fight left in one. Fifth, is the fear of growing old in a foreign country and being dumped into an Old People's Home. Africans take it for granted that children are sort of pension funds and care providers for their parents when they get old. African immigrants are not too sure that their children, if they grow up abroad, will properly imbibe that aspect of their culture.

Obviously for some, the project of returning home could be complicated. Kofi is a Ghanaian lawyer married to a white English woman, Susie. They had resolved the issue of 'home' by agreeing to work towards making Ghana their main home while the UK would be a

Jideofor Adibe

backup. All these however changed when they built a four-bedroom house in Kofi's village. Susie is irate that her husband allowed his mother and sister to live in the house "without paying rents".

My discussion with Okey has now stretched to nearly two hours. We talk regularly on the phone but have not really met up in the last two years. Suddenly there was a little panic in his voice. His wife has just driven in, he says. The home is in a mess and he needs to quickly tidy it up before she enters the house.

I ask him to give her my regards and chuckle with "London, na waooo", as the echo of his panicky breathing pierces through my telephone handset.

Daily Indepdendent 19 March 2009

CHAPTER 114

SHOULD AFRICA BE RE-COLONISED?

Afro-pessimism, which reached its crescendo in the late 1990s and early 2000s, seems to be creeping back. There are increasingly some mutterings and planted stories about the need to re-colonise Africa. Proponents of such a perspective point to the deplorable conditions in Africa – alarming poverty, debilitating corruption, incompetent leadership, failed states, epidemic of diseases, yawning illiteracy and pervasive superstition. In 2000 for instance, Gordon Frisch, a US political adventurist, who had spent many years in Africa as a geologist, lent the voice of an 'expert' to the discussion when he declared: "Black Africa now teeters on the edge of a yawning abyss, and at the bottom lies total anarchy and chaos. Many say it can't get much worse. We say: it can and it will." Though Frisch's animus was Mugabe's seizure of white-owned lands in Zimbabwe, he also reeled out other statistics to support his thesis of a hopeless continent. His panacea was the use of mercenaries to enthrone law and order in sub-Saharan Africa, after which, "African governments should invite former colonists back as partners in running their countries, developing their economies and educating their people. The 'politically correct' hacks of the world will bristle at these proposals, but millions of Africans are dying while the 'politically correct' civilized world looks on in ignorant smugness. When all ivory tower theories fail, try something that has proved workable." Like the ideology of earlier colonisation, which was premised on the need to 'civilise' Africans, Frisch also rationalised his call on a higher altruism – the need to save 'millions of dying Africans'.

Frisch's article, which had a disclaimer that it was not racist – as if such would obviate the fact that racial superiority is the underlying ideology of colonialism - reflected many of the views of the Afro pessimists. Though in recent times it appeared that Afro pessimism had become passé, the idea about re-colonising Africa got a fresh wind from developments in Mayote, an overseas collectivity of France, which is geographically part of the Comoro Islands, but has been politically separate since the 1970s. In a referendum on March 29 2009, the island of 190,000 inhabitants voted by 95.5 percent to become the 101st department of France – a move that alarmed many Africanists and re-ignited the debate about a possible re-colonisation of Africa.

Though it is understandable that many African elites and intellectuals would consider even a discussion of that topic an insult, we may be surprised at the number of ordinary Africans who will vote for re-colonisation, if given the opportunity – a clear indictment on African leaders and frustration with the snail pace of progress on many socio-economic indicators. A better approach perhaps would be to soberly subject the idea of re-colonisation to rigorous scrutiny in the marketplace of political ideas because it is only by so doing that some of the weaknesses in the internal logic of the argument could be laid bare, thus preventing it from becoming romantic ideas underground or in pubs and beer parlours.

There are many issues with the suggestions for Africa to be re-colonised:

First, is that the proponents of the idea focus only on the potential economic gains of re-colonisation. The belief is that the former colonial masters would bring their alleged superior administrative skills and would also be better able to attract and manage investments for the benefit of both Africa and the African poor. While this may or may not be true, it is often forgotten that one of the worst scars of earlier colonisations was psychological – self-hatred, inferiority complex and the natural tendency of the coloniser to look down on the colonised. The political independence achieved by many African countries was thus a long journey in healing the psychological trauma inflicted by colonisation. 'Colonial mentality' - the lingering aftereffect of that colonial subjugation - is still being addressed and progress is being made. If bread and butter issues and political stability would be sufficient to justify re-colonisation, then we would not have the phenomenon of accomplished African professionals in the West suddenly giving up their jobs and life styles to return home to Africa. Re-colonisation would therefore be a reversal of the gain made at political independence, which concretely defined Africa as the home of Africans.

Second, it is wrongly believed that re-colonisation would be benign as happened after the Berlin Conference of 1884-85. In an article on 19 April 2008 aptly captioned, 'The New Scramble for Africa begins', Times of London columnist Matthew Parris warned: "Fifty years ago the decolonisation of Africa began. The next half-century may see the continent recolonised. But the new imperialism will be less benign. Great powers aren't interested in administering wild places any more, still less in settling them: just raping them. Black gangster governments sponsored by self-interested Asian or Western powers could become the central story in 21st-century African history." If the botched plan in 2004 to use mercenaries to topple the government of President Teodoro Obiang Nguema of the oil-rich Equatorial Guinea was to be the template of this form of re-colonisation, then the failure of that plot, and the fate of the plotters, including Sir Denis Thatcher, son of former British Prime Minister Margaret Thatcher, could also be taken as an indication that such a move is unlikely to succeed in modern times.

Third, with the increase in the number of highly educated African immigrants in the West and Asia, and increasingly number of vocal domestic activists, it is doubtful that Western governments could broach domestic opposition for such a wild adventure. The protests against the Iraq war and its political fallouts will most likely caution against such a move – especially in this age of the internet and blogging, when activists could mobilise and pass information around quickly.

Fourth, the election of Barrack Obama as the 44th President of the United States of America seems to be a big filip in the healing of the psychologcal damage inflicted by years of slave trade and colonialism. For many Africans therefore, Obama is not simply an African name, but more importantly a metaphor, suggesting that with a 'can do' gusto and the right attitude, Africans could take their rightful place in the comity of nations. To bring back discussions of re-colonisation at this historical moment therefore appears to be a cruel joke.

There is no doubt that Africa could do better but progress is being made, even if slowly. There is a revolution going on in the minds of many Africans, which issue in increasing frustrations with their governments and the upping of the bar of expectations for their leaders. This is a big source of hope for the continent.

---

nigeriavillagesquare.com 1 May 2009

CHAPTER 115

PLAYING PRANKS WITH POPULATION

Jeffrey Sachs, respected economist and adviser to the United Nations' Secretary-General Ban Ki-moon was reported to have warnedNigeria against population explosion, saying the "current figure of 158 million could balloon to 730 million by 2100". Sachs was further quoted as saying: "I am really scared about population explosion inNigeria. It is not healthy.Nigeriashould work towards attaining a maximum of three children per family." (Daily Trust, May 25 2011).

I shall come back to Jeffrey Sachs later.

In July 2011, Family Watch International, a radical U.S-based non-governmental organisation, reportedly expressed concerns over the decline in world population. Sharon Slater, president of the organisation, reportedly said: "The developed countries are actually importing people from other countries because they don't have enough workers, they don't have enough people to support their social security system, to support the old people and run their economies." (Vanguard, July 18, 2011). The same paper said that Slater warnedAfricathat if it took "the advice to limit its population, it would eventually run into the same problem of lack of human capacity as the developed world was currently experiencing."

Slater and Jeffery Sachs represent discordant perspectives on the population discourse. But whose position most closely mirrors the realities of the Nigerian condition?

There is no doubt that Jeffrey Sachs brings an imposing resume to the table. Believed to be one of the youngest economics professors in the history of Harvard University, Sachs became famous (or infamous – depending on which side you are) for his role as an adviser to the Eastern European countries during their transition from communism to market-based economies and to African governments during the era of the IMF/World Bank-supported structural adjustment programmes that many believe helped to exacerbate the underdevelopment crisis in the continent. His books, *The End of Poverty* and *Common Wealth* were New York Times best sellers and he has also been named one of Time magazine's '100 Most influential people in the World'. His voice therefore carries considerable weight.

Despite his impressive resume, I believe that while Sachs who once predicted that Nigeria would join the New Economic Powers - often known by the acronym of BRICS (Brazil, Russia, India, China and South Africa so the acronym would become BRINCS), may have had the best intentions for the country in his latest outing, I am inclined to align myself with the conclusions of Sharon Slater on this. I do so however on a different set of explanations from the ones she offered. For instance Sachs' alarm onNigeria's population growth rate appears to re-echo the discredited Malthusian population nightmare. Critics have in fact argued that the basic premises of the population growth model formulated by Thomas Malthus, the British political economist, have been invalidated by rapid technological progress. It is for instance argued that in the technologically advanced countries, only a tiny fraction of the population produce the food that feeds the entire nation, meaning that technological progress has stretched to a point of being nearly inelastic the notion of 'carrying capacity' - the number of individuals that an area can support without sustaining damage. This means in my opinion that the problem with Nigeria is not population growth but crisis of underdevelopment because were Nigeria to be a developed economy less than 0.5 percent of its population would be engaged in farming and would produce enough to feed the country and for export. There is also sufficient landmass to accommodate even the projected population of 730 million by 2100. In this sense Sachs seems to be proffering answers to the wrong question.

The advice from Sachs also comes at a time when the reputation of the two Bretton Woods institution inAfricaremains damaged. Has the IMF and its sister institution the World Bank really succeeded with its advice and economic prognoses in any African country? In fact, the IMF/World Bank's supported structural adjustment programmes inAfricain the 1980s and early 1990s are generally believed to have exacerbated the underdevelopment crisis in the continent. Sachs' close association with these institutions therefore means that his advice, however well-intentioned, comes with credibility deficit by association. Alan Greenspan, the former Chairman of the US Federal Reserve once famously said he succeeded in his job by doing the opposite of the advice from the two Bretton Woods institutions.

There are also people who are deeply suspicious of the motives of those calling onNigeriato reduce or stem its population growth – when all the great nations of the world and those tipped to join that league are often countries with huge populations. Consider that the BRICS economies are all populous countries (with the exception ofSouth Africawhich has a population of just over 49 million). Some have in fact argued that the whole notion of regional integration inEurope(the European Union) was based on 'population envy'. Based on this, conspiracy theorists often argue that the preaching about stemming population growth inNigeriais to prevent the country from posing the sort of economic threat thatIndiaandChinatoday pose to the advanced economies of the West. It is instructive that the Scandinavian countries, which enjoy the highest standards of living in the world, are rarely regarded as significant players in world affairs largely because of their small populations.

There is also something that does not add up in the predictions of population catastrophe forNigeria. If, as official statistics suggest, the life expectancy is less than 50 years, how come thatNigeriais seen as facing a population Armageddon? Common sense will seem to suggest that the country may need a relatively healthy population growth rate to replenish and sustain current figures.

I am obviously not advocating that people should simply 'go and multiply' so that their 'descendant will be uncountable as the stars'. I am only against externally imposed population control measures. I do however believe that each family should know its 'carrying capacity' and plan accordingly. As individuals we are all enthralled by different values: one family may desire to have just one child so that they can travel round the world while another cares less about travelling round the world but derives maximum satisfaction from the number of children it has. Values are relative. What is therefore needed may be an enlightenment campaign for each family to decide on what is its own population carrying capacity, not a fiat limiting of family size.

National Identity Numbers: Forward to the past?

The recent announcement that the National Identity Management Commission will start issuing National Identity Numbers (NIN) from August 1 2011 raises a number of interesting issues. The thinking behind the project is obviously a noble one and the potential benefits are numerous – it could for instance help the governments to plan the provision of social services and improve the efficiency in tax and motor vehicle administrations as well as in fighting crimes. Our experiences have however shown that the road to many projects in this country are paved with good intentions. The intentions of a project are therefore not enough. Its operations on the ground are what matters. The National Identity Management Commission must convince Nigerians that NIN will not go the way of its progenitor, the National ID project, which started in 2003 and quickly became enmeshed in controversies and allegations of fraud and corruption. It must also assure Nigerians that the scheme will not intrude on people's privacy. Also with identity theft being a serious issue even in the advanced economies of the West, NIMC must convince Nigerians that the 'Nigerian factor' and the pervasive corruption it breeds will not lead to the NIN generating a black market on people's identities.

More importantly, with census being an ever contentious issue in the country (because population is linked to the voting strength of sections of the country), NIMC must equally allay any fears that the NIN scheme is a sort of census through the back door.

Daily Trust 21 July 2011

CHAPTER 116

LESSONS FROM THE COUP IN MALI

When on March 22, 2012, a group of junior soldiers in Mali led by Captain Amadou Sanogo announced the toppling of the democratically elected regime of Amadou Toumani Touré, a number of Africanists who thought that military consciousness had receded for good in the continent, had a rude awakening. The Afro-pessimism of the 1980s and 1990s has been gradually snowballing into Afro-optimism, even if grudgingly, despite resilient challenges. Analysts who believe that Africa is beginning to get its act together and that given the current conjuncture of local and global forces, only a buffoon of a soldier would embark on a coup project, waited with suspense to see how the whole impasse would play out.

There are several lessons from the coup and its aftermath.

One, credit must be given to ECOWAS for the way it resolutely rejected the coup. The regional grouping imposed diplomatic, economic and financial sanctions against the regime just as it rejected the unilateral declaration of independence by a Tuareg rebel group in the North. Though it cannot be ruled out that the fear of possible domino effect and therefore threat to their own power base could have been partly responsible for ECOWAS members' resistance to the coup, it still amounted to progress. For instance when in early August 2005, President Maaouiya Ould Sid Ahmed Taya of Mauritania was overthrown by the so-called Military Council for Justice and Democracy, international reaction to the coup, initially strongly hostile, including suspension from the African Union, quickly weakened. The AU, while formally condemning the coup also buckled and began to urge the new junta to quickly restore "constitutional order" - a euphemism indicating it would be alright for the junta to civilianise itself in a shambolic election with predictable outcome. The United States too, which initially called for Ould Taya to be restored to power, eventually backed down. In the case of the Mali coup, President Jonathan not only indicated that the coup would not be acceptable under any circumstance, the Nigerian Senate, even proposed the use of force to remove the coup makers. This must be commended. ECOWAS' strong resistance forced members of the junta to reach a face-saving deal whereby the junta surrendered power in exchange for amnesty from prosecution and the lifting of sanctions against the country. This is a very important victory for African diplomacy as it demonstrates that we may not always need foreign intervention to solve our own problems.

Two, the Mali coup shows that though democratic consciousness is growing in the continent, it equally reveals that the continent does not lack adventurist soldiers who may want to exploit popular discontent to supplant legitimately constituted authority. After decades of military rule, the rationalisations for the military's intervention in African politics no longer wash with people who are old enough to remember what it was really like under the military. In Nigeria, after the 'wahala' NADECO and other civil society groups gave Generals Babangida and Abacha, people may have relapsed into complacency that the soldiers will never have the courage to attempt the overthrow of a civilian regime again. The Mali coup in this sense is a call for vigilance and the need to protect our democracy – despite its shortcomings. The freedom of expression under our current democracy project remains infinitely better than the reign of fear and intimidation of the citizens that were the hallmarks of military dictatorships in the country.

Three, it is true that people thronged to welcome the coupists in Mali – as they invariably did each time there was martial music in Nigeria and elsewhere in the continent – it is wrong to use this as an index for measuring the popularity of a coup. A coup is not legitimated simply because people trooped out to welcome a change. In fact this has been a constant feature of any regime change in Africa, including change from one civilian regime to another, and from one military regime to another. The tendency of people thronging to the streets to welcome a regime change is rooted in common people's constant hope for salvation from their seemingly never-ending squalid conditions. As Africa's history however sadly shows, such joy and hope on regime change is usually short-lived because discontent and poverty seem to worsen with each change. In fact, if any lesson could be learnt from the years of military rule in Africa, it is that martial music is more of a threnody to any country; each time it is played, the affected country dies a little more.

Four, Mali, a landlocked country of 14.5 million people, is a reflection of the paradox that is Africa. While today, Africa, thought to be the original ancestry of all human beings has been left behind by others in all the development indices, Mali, once part of the three West African empires that controlled the highly lucrative trans-Saharan trade from the 8th until the 16th century (the other two were the Ghana Empire and the Songhai empire), is today one of the poorest countries in the world. Again while the University of Timbuktu, founded in the 11th century by the Tuareg Imashagan is generally thought to be the first university in the world with some 25,000 students in a city of about 100,000 people at its peak, today estimates of literacy rate in Mali are in the dismal ranges of 27–30% to 46.4%, with the rates significantly lower among women.

Five, though the declaration of a secessionist state of Azawad by the Tuaregs in the North of the country through their National Movement for the Liberation of Azawad (MNLA) has been roundly condemned by the African Union, ECOWAS and the 'international community' in line with the African Union's position on the sanctity of inherited colonial borders, there is a need to revisit the conditions under which nationalities in African states should be allowed to decide if they want to continue being part of their colonially constructed State. This should not by any means be construed to means favouring balkanization of African States but with countries like Eritrea and South Sudan achieving independence from Ethiopia and Sudan respectively after protracted armed struggle, there is a need to avoid giving the impression that prolonged military campaign is the only way to force the international community to respect a group's quest for self-determination. The Tuaregs, a Berber people with a traditionally nomadic pastoralist lifestyle, has been fighting for self-determination since Mali's independence in 1960. Since the 1990s, there has been a Tuareg ethnic revival with its own flag of red, white, and blue. I am not arguing for the so called Republic of Azawad to be recognised. The point is that with most African countries still unable to transit into proper nation- states after more than 100 years of forced statehood and with demands for a sovereign national conference to decide if the nationalities that make up Nigeria want to continue being together reaching a crescendo, there may be a need to evolve rigorous criteria for assessing the demand for self-determination by various nationalities that make up African States. This is especially so when the crisis in the nation-building project of most Africa countries feeds into the problems of underdevelopment to create a whole range of issues for these countries.

Though there are several successful cases of previously independent nationalities being welded together to form an 'imagined community' such as Germany, there are equally several instances of nationalities which divorced or are agitating for divorce after years or even centuries of being together. Mali for instance was once part of French Sudan, then known as the Sudanese Republic, which joined with Senegal in 1959 to achieve independence in 1960 as the Mali Federation. Shortly after however Senegal withdrew from the federation and the Sudanese Republic declared itself the Independent Republic of Mali. Similarly the Federation of Rhodesia and Nyasaland, which was created between

August 1 and October 23 1953 imploded on December 31 1963, giving birth to present day Zambia, Zimbabwe and Malawi. In the UK, Scottish and Irish resistance to being part of the United Kingdom continues despite centuries of being in the union. My personal opinion is that instead of insisting on the sanctity of colonial borders and selectively violating that doctrine the challenge should be to evolve rigorous conditions which nationalities that want to walk away from the colonially constructed nation-states should meet. The impression must not be given by default that self-determination could only be achieved through the shedding of blood that prolonged armed struggle often entails. After all Czechoslovakia was able to achieve democracy through a 'Velvet' or 'Gentle Revolution', which subsequently enabled a peaceful dissolution of the country in 1993, resulting in the birth of the Czech Republic and Slovakia.

Daily Trust 12 April 2012

CHAPTER 117

ARE REVOLUTIONS REALLY WORTH THE HASSLE?

The report by the *Vanguard* of July 8 2011that tens of thousands of Egyptians took to the streets to defend the 'revolution' that toppled President Hosni Mubarak inEgypt in February 2011 was very instructive. According to the report, the protesters directed their anger at the new military rulers over the slow pace of reforms. One protester was said to have carried a banner, which read: "We haven't felt any change. We removed Mubarak and got a field marshal." He was referring to Hussein Tantawi, the head of the Supreme Council of the Armed Forces, which took power in February. The armed forces, hailed as heroes at the start of the uprising for not siding with Mubarak, have come under fire from local and international rights groups for alleged abuses.

The speed with which the heroes of yesterdays have become the villains of today in Egypt raises the question of whether revolutions really accomplish anything, especially at a time when calls for revolution in our country has gone mainstream. While the goals of any revolution are usually lofty and populist – a desire to quickly change the society or its institutions for the better, the tendency for revolutionists to use a very simplistic approach for a highly complex problem also means that when the dust settles after the revolutionary flourish, so many unintended consequences usually beget the question of whether the entire effort is worth it. Apart from the recent demonstration inEgypt, consider also the following examples:

The American War of Independence (1775-1783) was spurred by a noble protest against taxation without representation. ThoughAmerica's victory helped to spread a belief in the principles of republicanism, it also sharply polarised the country and subsequently led to a bitter civil war. Some critics today argue that looking at howAmericahas shaped up since independence in terms of education, freedom of expression and quality of life, it is not substantially different fromCanada,AustraliaandNew Zealand, which did not follow such a revolutionary path. The cost of the war was also to bankruptFrance, without whose military and financial support,Americawould not have won the war.

There was also the French Revolution (1789–1799), fought primarily to overthrow absolute monarchy with its feudal privileges for the aristocracy and Catholic clergy. The revolution, fought under the noble ideals of 'freedom, equality and fraternity', quickly became a caricature under Robespierre and his Reign of Terror. Not only did the revolution fail to giveFrancea representative government by the people, or prevent a rapid return to autocratic rule, 'revolutionary'Francealso fought the most savage of all wars in the 1790s to preserve slavery inSanto Domingo(present-dayHaitiandDominican Republic). So much for freedom, equality and fraternity! In fact, some historians today regard the French Revolution as a terrible waste of time and blood because whatever positives came out of it were equally accomplished by many countries such as Britain with much less bloodshed.

Again consider the Russian Revolution - a collective term for the series of revolutions inRussia in 1917, which succeeded in destroying Tsarist autocracy and creating theSoviet Union. Today, the Soviet Union has since imploded andRussia is not more democratic or more economically advanced than most other European countries that did not embark on such a revolution. Many historians today question whether there was indeed any benefit from that revolution, which led to the loss of millions of lives and replaced Tsarist autocracy with other dictators – from Lenin and Stalin to Putin.

Consider equally the Iranian revolution that toppled the rule of Mohammed Reza Shah more than 30 years ago. The revolution ushered a period of unprecedented hostility to the West and helped to radicalise theMiddle East. Almost overnight, the West's most steadfast ally in the Muslim world became a violent and volatile enemy, where mass crowds raised their fists to chant "death toAmerica". Within months of the revolution however, the euphoria had evaporated as rival factions began a brutal battle for the control of the country, which ended with a repressive state that imprisoned and executed thousands of political prisoners – including many of the revolutionaries. Today some Iranians, including those who participated in the revolution, openly wonder whether it was worth it and what the country really achieved from it.

InNigeria, benefits from what could be called our own 'revolution' are also questionable. Consider this instance:

In 1966, Major Chukwuma Nzeogwu's Supreme Council of the Revolution of the Nigerian Armed Forces, which said it wanted to "establish a strong, united and prosperous nation, free from corruption and internal strife", ended up unleashing forces that culminated in a civil war. Today, more than forty years after Nzeogwu's 'revolution', Nigerians look with nostalgia to the society the young Majors riled against.

From the above, my personal opinion is that the system dynamics in most countries favour evolutionary social progress rather than a revolutionary one. While the philosophy of most revolutions has an emotional appeal, in reality, only few revolutions are successful or worth the effort. This for me should be a caution to those advocating for a revolution in the country. True, there is a justifiable anger at the direction that things are going in the country – palpable decadence, pervasive insecurity, endemic ethnic and religious strife and a country perpetually tethering on the brink of collapse and mediocrity – the solution may not be to destroy the house and rebuild it from scratch. We will still need the building to shield us from the elements while the reconstruction is going on.

I believe the most urgent challenge facing the country today is finding a strong and focused leader who will be a unifier, a healer of wounds which each and every constituent part of the Nigerian arrangement feels it has suffered. Our nation-building project has truly come unstuck. Without the cogs in this project being carefully removed, we will only be dancing in circles. At the moment we seem to haveNigeriawithout Nigerians – or at bestNigeriawith only half-hearted or episodic Nigerians. Unfortunately the process of de-Nigerianisation – many otherwise 'proud Nigerians' by birth consciously or unconsciously renouncing their Nigerianness or subordinating it to other primordial identities – appears to be increasing at an alarming rate. If Jonathan's presidency can resolve the crisis of the nation state, that will be an incremental progress that can be worth more than any revolution. If a succeeding regime fixes the electricity problem in a sustainable manner that too will be a remarkable piecemeal progress. The worst nightmare for Nigerians will be a regime that leaves no lasting legacy or squanders those he or she met on the ground.

UBA's self-inflicted PR disaster

A new rule at the United Bank for Africa increasing the minimum balance for savings and current accounts for customers of the bank to N25,000, has turned out a PR disaster for the bank. The new rule, which takes effect from September 1, 2011, led to a flurry of de-marketing text messages from the bank's justifiably angry small customers. The negative messages, which were also transmitted through the social network media sites like Facebook and Twitter claimed the new account balance regime in UBA was a means by the bank to cover a hole in its books. As if this was not enough, the Deputy Governor, Banking Operations of the Central Bank Tunde Lemo was reported as saying that the new minimum bank balance directive did not receive any approval from the banking sector regulator.

Despite UBA's explanations, I strongly believe that its new directive will seriously undermine current efforts to bring the un-banked and under-banked Nigerians into the banking system. It was pathetic the way most customers of the bank learnt of the new directive.

Daily Trust 14 July 2011

CHAPTER 118

HOW NOT TO FORMULATE FOREIGN POLICY

ate last year, the National Economic Council (NEC) reportedly resolved that going forward, Nigeria would no longer play 'big brother' to countries in trouble without getting anything in return. It also proposed that the nation's foreign interventions and assistance would henceforth be guided by 'national interest'. At a seminar to 'review Nigeria's foreign policy' organised by the Presidential Advisory Council on International Relations (PAC-IR) in collaboration with the Ministry of Foreign Affairs at Abuja from August 1- 4 2011, this point was re-emphasised. In an address at the seminar, the Minister of Foreign Affairs, Ambassador Olugbenga Ashiru reportedly said that Nigerians must benefit maximally from the nation's foreign policy. In his speech while declaring the seminar open, President Jonathan reportedly noted that 'although the country had played a leading role in the emancipation of the African continent from colonialism and racial discrimination, there is need to now focus on new priorities....' (Daily Trust August 11, 2011). The President's position re-echoes the sentiments expressed by Governor Babangida Aliyu of Niger State after the NEC meeting late last year when he was quoted as saying that "...we are going to shed that belief that we are big brother where we go to help other people and we never get something in return...So, wherever we go or whoever we relate with, must be because it will help us develop, rather than, as we normally say, that we have gone to help these or that people without getting anything in return." Foreign Minister Ashiru is reportedly a big supporter of a trade-driven foreign policy.

While it is true that national interest is at the heart of foreign policy, (in fact the French word 'raison d'état', - which means 'reason of the State' -vividly captures this), rarely is a country so rude as to stick it to the face of other international actors that its primary concern in its relations with them is the advancement of its 'national interest'. For instance though the colonisation of Africa was in the main undertaken because of the interest of the colonists to find raw materials, it was couched on the morally acceptable ideology of the 'need to civilise the natives'. In the same vein, former US President George W Bush justified the Iraq war on the moralistic need to find Saddam Hussein's Weapons of Mass Destruction – even though many people believed it was a camouflage for other interests. Even the Opium Wars (1839-1842, 1856-1860), one of the most mercantilist projections of 'national interest' in history was still given a morally acceptable justification. Though the wars were caused by the smuggling of opium by merchants from British India into China in defiance of Chinese prohibition laws, Britain's formal justification for the war was a need to stem China's balance of payment deficits. Those calling for a more explicit embedment of immediate economic gratification in our foreign policy are therefore not only throwing diplomatese to the winds but also advertising the country's weakness to the world. As Wole Soyinka would tell us, 'a tiger does not need to proclaim its tigeritude.'

I am also very uncomfortable with the idea of announcing to the whole world that there is a review of our foreign policy. Not only does this re-echo policy reversals and instabilities for which we have become infamous, my personal opinion is that you don't really need to have a Presidential Committee on Review of Nigeria's Foreign Policy to do this. How many times have we read about the US, Britain or Germany announcing a panel to review its foreign policy? My personal opinion is that this is the day job of the Ministry of Foreign Affairs and think-tanks such as the Nigerian Institute of International Affairs and other institutions that organise seminars and workshops on international affairs. Given the dynamic nature of international relations, a country through its Ministry of Foreign affairs, independent think-tanks and consultants is constantly reviewing its relations with different countries and institutions depending on changes in power configurations that create new opportunities or threaten its national interest. I have a feeling that people who grandstand about trade and economic-driven diplomacy or immediate financial gratification from any international engagement are mixing up the role of the economic/trade missions found in the country's various embassies with foreign policy.

I also feel that there is a little confusion about the meaning of 'national interest' – the totality of a country's goals and ambitions whether economic, cultural, military or otherwise. Contrary to the impression that 'national interest' is projected only when financial gains are expressly and immediately extracted from an interaction with other state and non-state actors, sometimes states invest in enhancing its influence in a country or region because of the leverage such influence could give it in the future (such as being allowed to station a military base in the country/region in the future or to avoid the influx of refugees that could overwhelm its social services). This too is projecting 'national interest'. I believe that contrary to popular belief, we have actually benefitted from the countries we helped in the past – South Africa, Liberia, Sierra Leone etc. I believe that we derived the intangible benefit of our international prestige rising as we 'helped' them. If we were not able to leverage on such intangible assets, it was more because of the failure of leadership, not foreign policy. Usually forgotten in the discussion of how 'ungrateful' countries we have helped in the past have become is that we often 'unleash' our human capital on them after 'helping' them. It certainly seems that the population of Nigerians in countries we 'helped' increased astronomically after our 'help'. It seems that the role of such Nigerians in the remittance economy is overlooked.

It is therefore misleading to assume that playing 'big brother' to other African countries means that the country's 'national interest' is not being projected. This is the whole notion of 'soft power' - winning over the minds of the people in the countries we play 'big brother' to. Converting this soft power to economic benefits will depend on the character of the country's political leadership.

Related to this is that a nation's respectability in international relations is not wholly contingent upon its past benevolence but often more on the current leverages it can bring to the table. Even in domestic politics, past benevolence seems to count for little as we have seen in the face-offs between political god-fathers and almost all the Governors that they installed in office. The bottom line therefore is that if Nigeria wants to command influence and respect, it must improve on its ability to bring leverages to the table. This is obviously where the interplay between domestic politics and foreign policy comes into play. As the Igbo would say, the goat follows the person who carries the palm fronds.

I am miffed at suggestions that Africa would no longer be the centre-piece of our foreign policy. My personal opinion is that Africa being the centre piece of our foreign policy does not mean that we would always take Afrocentric position on issues – but that we should strive to be a leader in the continent. It is not unusual for a country to once in a while have a more compelling national interest which would require taking positions that is contrary to the position of most of its immediate allies. For instance during the Thirty Years' War in Europe (1618-1648) – a largely religious conflict between Protestants and Catholics - France chose to intervene on the side of the Protestants despite its overwhelming Catholicism because the regime was apparently more interested at that time in blocking the growing power of the Holy Roman Emperor than in protecting its religious faith. Similarly though Europe could be called the centre-piece of British foreign policy, Britain sometimes disagrees with other European countries (such as during the Iraq War) but would often return to rebuild burnt bridges after such disagreements in other not to undermine its leadership role in the continent.

I am not suggesting that all is well with our foreign policies. But the problem, as I see it, is not in trying to find one sexy phrase to encapsulate our foreign policies – Africa as the centrepiece of our foreign policy, the notion of concentric circle, citizen diplomacy etc. My personal opinion is that the problems in our foreign policy are largely symptomatic of the crisis of underdevelopment weighing down the country and which in turn feeds on our stalled nation-building project.

Daily Trust 18 August 2011

CHAPTER 119

NIGERIA'S CALL FOR AU NOT TO INTERFERE IN ITS INTERNAL AFFAIRS

The recent report that the Nigerian government has cautioned the African Union, (AU), not to interfere in its internal matters, following calls by the Nigerian Bar Association (NBA) on the continental body to prevail on the Federal Government to prosecute perpetrators of the recent crisis in Jos, Plateau State, made an interesting reading. It should be recalled that the NBA had in its presentation at the 48th session of the African Commission on Human and Peoples Rights in Banjul, Gambia, called on the AU to press on the Nigerian Government to prosecute those behind the recent crisis in Jos in which many lives and property worth million of naira were lost. Pius Otey of the Ministry of Justice, who read Nigeria's reply, was reported by the Vanguard of November 15, 2010 as offering the warning.

The purported warning by Nigeria to the African Union raises a number of interesting issues.

One, the idea of 'non-interference' in the internal affairs of other countries is based on a certain notion of state sovereignty, in which each country's domestic affairs are said to be no one else's business. For a long time dictators and maximum rulers hid under the doctrine of 'non-interference' to ward off any criticisms of human rights abuses in their countries. However with the end of the Cold War and the increasing globalization of such values as democracy and human rights, there has been a shift in the traditional notion of state sovereignty with its emphasis on 'non-interference' in the internal affairs of other countries to the notion of sovereignty as a 'responsibility to protect citizens'.

In fact, the global pressure to re-think the notion of 'non-interference' gained special momentum during the 1994 Rwandan genocide and again in Kosovo in the late 1990s when NATO was compelled to intervene. Following NATO's intervention in Kosovo, the then United Nations Secretary General Kofi Annan challenged the international community to reconcile the two foundational aspects of legitimate statehood – sovereignty and the protection of fundamental human rights of peoples. The International Commission on Intervention and State Sovereignty (ICISS), which developed the notion of 'sovereignty as responsibility' argued that a state has the primary responsibility to protect its populations, and where it is unable or unwilling to do so, such a responsibility would be borne by the international community. ICISS also showed that the relationship between sovereignty and humanitarian intervention is complimentary rather than contradictory.

Two, even within the African Union, the idea of 'non-interference' has also evolved, with emphasis increasingly placed on 'non-indifference' in the affairs of Member States that will have deleterious consequences for human rights or democracy in the affected country. In fact, Article 4 (h) of the Constitutive Act of the African Union provides for the right of the Union, in certain cases, to intervene in the affairs of a member state on the recommendation of the Peace and Security Council while Article 4(j) provides for the right of Member States to request for such an intervention. The decision by the Assembly of Heads of State and Government of the OAU (which adopted the Constitutive Act of the African Union) to incorporate the right of intervention in that Act stemmed from concerns about OAU's failure to intervene in order to stop the gross and massive human rights violations witnessed in Africa in the past such as the excesses of Id Amin in Uganda, Bokassa in the Central African Republic in the 1970s and the genocide in Rwanda in 1994.

The evolution of the notion of 'non-interference' both globally and at the African continent will suggest that calling on African Union not to interfere in Nigeria's internal affairs, using the old doctrine of 'non-interference', amounts to the country making a fool of itself. In fact with the developments in the notions of state sovereignty, it has become rare for leaders to use 'non-interference' in its internal affairs to ward off external criticisms of its policies. As a rule, these days a country opens itself up for suspicion if it recourses to the use of 'non-interference' in its internal affairs as a defense against external audits of its policy options. Countries likely to hide under the old banner of 'non-interference' are those that are under intense international pressure for its human rights abuses. Nigeria is not in such a category of countries despite her numerous challenges.

Three, there is a distinction between 'non-interference' and 'non-intervention' in the affairs of a State. While both denote non-consensual involvement in the affairs of another country, intervention suggests action of a more aggressive and forceful nature. Nations do actually routinely 'interfere' in the internal affairs of others such as using diplomatic channels to offer advice or providing grants and loans to support defined projects. In this sense, if the report that Nigeria called on AU not to 'interfere in its internal affairs' were true, then the country failed to appreciate the difference between 'interference' and 'intervention'. It would actually seem from the *Vanguard* report that the NBA was merely lobbying African Union to apply diplomatic pressures on the Nigerian government so that the country will prosecute the perpetrators of the Jos crisis. I do not see anything wrong in it as it has not asked the AU to intervene in the country to twist the country's arms towards a given policy option.

Four, after carefully reading through the report in the *Vanguard*, it will seem that this purported embarrassing call was the result of wrong reporting rather than a gaffe by Mr Otey. I found nowhere in the report that corroborated the paper's headline suggestion that the federal government called on the African Union not to 'interfere' in its internal affairs. The closest statements that came to matching the headlines were these quotes attributed to Mr Otey: "We wish to state that there is no basis for the call by the NBA for the intervention of the AU in the resolution of the Jos crisis. Nigeria has already commenced the implementation of several peace building measures in its sovereign capacity and we are hopeful that the measure will achieve the desired result."

Certainly these statements do not amount to calling on the African Union not to interfere in the country's domestic affairs. Unfortunately the impression from that headline would be that Nigeria has become one of those 'banana republics' where the maximum rulers cannot brook any criticisms of its actions, and whose foreign policy formulators are so much behind the times that they cannot realize when a foreign policy concept has become anachronistic.

Daily Trust 17 November 2010

CHAPTER 120

NEC WAS WRONG ON NEW FOREIGN POLICY PROPOSAL

The recent report that the National Economic Council (NEC) has taken a decision that Nigeria will no longer play 'big brother' to countries in trouble without getting anything in return, and that henceforth the nation's foreign interventions and assistance will be guided by 'national interest', made headlines. Briefing journalists after the Council's meeting at Abuja, Governor Babangida Aliyu of Niger State was quoted as saying: "...we are going to shed that belief that we are big brother where we go to help other people and we never get something in return...So, wherever we go or whoever we relate with, must be because it will help us develop, rather than, as we normally say, that we have gone to help these or that people without getting anything in return."

The NEC's resurgent 'nationalism' raises a number of issues:

One, it is difficult to know the notion of 'national interest', which NEC was espousing, or how it came to the conclusion that the country's foreign policy has not been guided by 'national interest'. The truth is that the national interest of a country is often multifaceted and dynamic. For a country like Nigeria, the 'national interest' includes keeping Nigeria as one united and peaceful country, economic development, respect for human rights, protecting the country's democracy, internal peace and security, peaceful relations with the country's neighbours, commanding the respect of other African countries (both for our ego needs and to leverage such in our relations with the big powers), and ensuring political stability among the country's neighbours (to prevent potential influx of refugees).

It is germane to note that what one regime may prioritise as 'national interest' may be seen differently by another regime. For instance during the Thirty Years' War in Europe (1618-1648) – a largely religious conflict between Protestants and Catholics - France chose to intervene on the side of the Protestants despite its overwhelming Catholicism because the regime was apparently more interested in blocking the growing power of the Holy Roman Emperor. It is possible that another regime could have taken a different course of action, based on a different articulation of the 'national interest'.

Two, it is wrong to assume that playing 'big brother' to other African countries means that the country's 'national interest' is not being projected. Suggesting that any relations must bring immediate economic gratification is not only 'cowboyism' but also short-sighted. At a time when the notion of 'soft power' – commanding influence through co-option and attraction (or winning hearts and minds) – has become ascendant in the foreign policy thrust of the major powers, to nurse a nostalgia for the discredited mercantilist approach to foreign policy is an error of judgment.

Three, it is understandable that some Nigerians are frustrated that countries we helped in their times of need such as South Africa during its struggle against apartheid and Liberia and Sierra Leone during their civil wars, do not seem to show us the desired respect. However, the truth is that a nation's respectability in international relations is not wholly contingent upon its past benevolence but often more on the current leverages it could bring to the table. Additionally, a nation's standing in the comity of nations cannot be divorced from its domestic circumstances, including its performance in such critical indices as transparency of elections, human rights record, security, good governance, and poverty alleviation. Moreover, it is not exactly true that Nigeria has not benefited from playing 'big brother' because apart from the country's profile being raised during the acts, the number of Nigerians that moved to South Africa at the end of apartheid and to Liberia and Sierra Leone at the end of the wars also increased. So what does Nigeria really expect these countries to do? It is true that if America or Britain had played similar roles, they would have ensured that British and American companies would corner the bulk of the reconstruction contracts. If Nigeria was unable to leverage its contributions in Liberia and Sierra Leone to win reconstruction contracts for Nigerian companies, then we are talking of the failure of economic diplomacy, not of foreign policy. It is unrealistic to expect countries to come prostrating to us, or fail to defend their own 'national interest' in their relations with us simply because we rendered some help to them in the past.

Four, the decision to jettison the country's 'big brother' role is an indirect abandonment of the notion of Africa being the centrepiece of the nation's foreign policy. This is quite unfortunate because the afro-centric nature of our foreign policy has never precluded relations with other countries, multilateral agencies or other actors. In fact, it can be argued that the country's strategic political importance to the world is hinged on its influence in the continent – just as Egypt is regarded as a strategic partner of the West largely because of its ability to leverage the West's relations with the Arab world. It will therefore be wrong for Nigeria to abandon the source of its potential strength in the world – paradoxically at a time it is campaigning for a permanent seat in the Security Council of the United Nations using the leverage it has in Africa as a key argument. Additionally, even when Nigeria 'develops', it will discover, as South Africa has done, that other African countries, not the West or Asia, will be the major market for its goods, because such goods will for a long time be too weak to compete at the global level.

Five, it was a monumental error on the part of the NEC to openly declare that it would henceforth get involved with other countries only if there was specific economic benefit for the country. While national interest always guides foreign policy (the French expression 'raison d'État' - meaning 'reason of the State' captures this well), it is usually masked in morally acceptable language such as the need to 'civilize the natives' (used to justify colonialism) or the need to find and destroy Saddam Hussein's 'weapons of mass destruction' (used to justify the Iraq War). In fact, Britain still found a morally acceptable justification for the Opium Wars (1839-1842, 1856-1860) - one of the most mercantilist projections of 'national interest' in history. Though the wars were caused by the smuggling of opium by merchants from British India into China in defiance of Chinese prohibition laws, Britain's formal justification for the war was a need to stem China's balance of payment deficits. Even companies rarely tell customers they set up businesses to make profit – but to provide needed goods and services and create jobs. Now the NEC has chosen to throw diplomatese to the winds by impliedly announcing that the country will henceforth be guided by 'cowboyism' in its international relations. With all due respect, this is misplaced nationalism.

Daily Trust 3 November 2010

CHAPTER 121

OBAMA: WAITING ON THE BLACK PRESIDENT

I have deliberately called Barack Obama 'the' Black president, rather than 'a' Black president because no election of any Black president anywhere has been as historic as his election as the 44th president of the United States of America. Besides, any President of the USA, the only remaining super-power, is generally regarded as President of the world. In that sense Obama is the first Black president of the world.

As monumental an achievement as his election was, his regime, to be inaugurated on 20 January 2009, faces tremendous challenges.

Obviously one of the biggest challenges will be managing expectations. These expectations come from different constituencies: from African Americans who gave him an unprecedented support, perhaps hoping that his regime will at least lead to a change in the way the Black person is perceived, and from America's political left of the centre which had become disenchanted with the Reagan brand of market economics that coincidentally tanked during the presidential campaigns and helped to elect Obama president. In fact, expectations from Obama are as diverse as his constituencies of support across the globe. Even the geeks believe that Obama, who is said to love BlackBerry, and once collected comic books, would be the first geek-in-chief. Benjamin Nugent, author of the book *American Nerd: The Story of My People* (2008), was reported as saying that Obama is good at "repressing his inner geek, but you can tell it's there." That is regarded as a compliment rather than insult but still some expectation to live up to!

Obama has won kudos for the speed with which he has assembled his cabinet. Similarly by selecting familiar and experienced officials, mostly from the Clinton era - an era that evokes powerful memories of prosperity and peace - Obama may be subtly trying to appropriate some of the halo from that period. He could also be signalling that his regime would be a sort of extension of Clinton's, in style and substance. Bill Clinton remains popular across the world. The selection of experienced and familiar names also helps to assuage fears in some quarters of a Black president with little experience and a funny sounding name.

One of Obama's most praised moves as president- elect has been his selection of a 'Team of Rivals'. Inspired by another President from Illinois, Abraham Lincoln, who appointed not only his three rivals for the Republican nomination in 1860 (William H. Seward, Salmon P. Chase and Edwards Bates) to key wartime posts but also gave important jobs to three Democrats of renown (Gideon Welles, Montgomery Blair, and Edwin M. Stanton), Obama chose Joe Biden as his running mate and appointed Hillary Clinton to the powerful post of Secretary of State. Both Joe Biden and Hillary Clinton contested the Democratic presidential nomination against him. Additionally he retained Robert Gates, a Republican, as the Defence Secretary.

There are opportunities and threats in Obama's 'Team of Rivals'. On the plus side, some have argued that Obama's 'Team of Rivals' might be a clever long-term political planning rather than any attempt to imitate Lincoln whom he openly admires. It is for instance argued that by co-opting Hillary Clinton into his administration, Obama might be hoping to neutralise a potential challenger in 2012. The co-optation could also be aimed at checkmating her ubiquitous husband, Bill Clinton, who has a propensity for foreign policy freelancing, some of which could embarrass the new regime. It was in fact reported that part of the deal that paved the way for Hillary Clinton's appointment was an agreement by the former president to let the State Department review his future speeches and business activities. The 'Team of Rivals' could also help to re-assure Americans and the world financial markets that Obama, who was suspected of being a 'liberal' (a term more pejorative in the US than in other political climes) and even a socialist (remember the 'Joe the Plumber' jibe?), would indeed rule from the centre.

There are however flipsides to the idea of 'Team of Rivals'. While pundits have hailed Hillary Clinton's appointment as Secretary of State - arguably the most important cabinet post in the US - there is always a distinct possibility that she could use the job to define herself in preparation for a 2012 run. Members of this 'Team of Rivals', with their over-sized egos, could also find teamwork difficult. Similarly can Obama really count on the unalloyed support of these former rivals who had derided his experience during the primaries when the inevitable challenges, pummelling from the G.O.P and stumbles that every first term president must face, begin to happen?

Obama also faces a special challenge of managing expectations from the developing world, especially Africa. By America's one-drop rule, Obama is a Blackman. By the system of patriarchy dominant in Africa, he is seen by many Africans as an African. There is therefore a certain belief that Obama will be able to understand the problems of Africa better than any previous American president, and would be more compassionate when dealing with issues concerning the continent. The problem here is that American foreign policy, like the foreign policy of any nation, is fundamentally driven by national interest, not altruism. To that extent the difference between an Obama administration and any other American administration is likely to be more in style rather than in the substance of governance.

There is of course the daunting challenge of the economic meltdown, which arguably handed the presidency to Obama. With the dire economic outlook for 2009 and the coming years, can Obama deliver? This may be too early to predict. But with George Bush's massive 600- billion dollar bailout, Obama has been provided a well-needed cover to increase the bailout and provide other stimulus packages that perhaps could enable him to spend his way out of the recession. Without George Bush's massive state intervention to save capitalism from imploding, allegations that Obama was a socialist would have been more difficult to shake off had the bailout started under his watch.

Daily Independent, 4 June 2009

CHAPTER 122

ARE WE TRYING TO PULL DOWN BARRACK OBAMA?

Since Barrack Obama announced a visit to Africa, his relationship with Nigerian Internet bloggers seems to have soured. Initially, many Nigerians interpreted the choice of 'little' Ghana, over the 'oil-producing, giant of Africa' as Obama's subtle way of rebuking Nigeria's leadership for not getting its act together, and of rewarding Ghana for its assumed good governance and deepening democratic ethos.

Ghana has always had a sort of 'siblings rivalry' with Nigeria, from the time its national football side would routinely trounce the Nigerian Eagles. Despite the rivalry, Nigerians prefer to see Ghanaians as sort of younger siblings who nurse some ambitions of upstaging their older, stronger and richer brothers. It is possible that the new hostility towards Obama may be an unconscious frustration that the 44th American president appeared to have taken sides in the 'siblings rivalry' between Nigeria and Ghana. But the formal charge is that he 'talked down' to Africans, and tried to lecture them in that speech to the Ghanaian parliament on July 11, 2009. But did he actually do so? Apparently the offensive part of the transcribed version of the speech was:

> "In many places, the hope of my father's generation gave way to cynicism, even despair. Now, it's easy to point fingers and to pin the blame of these problems on others. Yes, a colonial map that made little sense helped to breed conflict. The West has often approached Africa as a patron or a source of resources rather than a partner. But the West is not responsible for the destruction of the Zimbabwean economy over the last decade, or wars in which children are enlisted as combatants. In my father's life, it was partly tribalism and patronage and nepotism in an independent Kenya that for a long stretch derailed his career, and we know that this kind of corruption is still a daily fact of life for far too many."

Critics of the speech however appear to have taken this passage out of context. In fact just after the above quoted passage, the next paragraph was:

> "Now, we know that's also not the whole story. Here in Ghana, you show us a face of Africa that is too often overlooked by a

world that sees only tragedy or a need for charity. The people of Ghana have worked hard to put democracy on a firmer footing, with repeated peaceful transfers of power even in the wake of closely contested elections. (Applause.) And by the way, can I say that for that the minority deserves as much credit as the majority. (Applause.) And with improved governance and an emerging civil society, Ghana's economy has shown impressive rates of growth. (Applause.)"

Obama also narrated how his grandfather who was a cook for the British in colonial Kenya was called a "boy" for much of his life by his employers, even though he was a respected elder in his village. In the concluding part of the speech, Obama said mutual responsibility would be the basis of America's partnership with Africa.

For a black president, it takes remarkable courage to do what Obama has done so far. He has not tried to deny his identity – as many of our compatriots in top international positions abroad too often do. But he has at all times also been conscious of the fact that he was elected to be President of the United States, and by implication leader of the world, rather than to pander to his primordial identities. It is a tough balancing act that requires wisdom and courage. Read his speech to the National Association for the Advancement of Couloured Peoples (N.A.A.C.P) on July 17, 2009 and his reaction to the arrest and handcuffing of Professor Henry Louis Gates, the black director of Harvard's African-American research centre by the police from Cambridge, Massachusetts. Now compare this with a Nigerian female ambassador to Sweden who once told Nigerians in another Scandinavian country, before the leaders of that country, that Nigerians were thieves and should not be trusted. Her classical display of bleaching complex is often what we have come to expect of our leaders in privileged positions, especially when abroad.

In most of his speeches, Obama has shown he is nuanced as he tries to take on board most of the arguments in any given issue, conscious of the fact that the target of any speech goes beyond the immediate audience. In my book, he has displayed uncommon wisdom and level-headedness, and so far appear to have silenced critics who questioned whether a black guy could be trusted with such a highly complex office as the US presidency. Whatever is said against Obama's visit or speech, the fact remains that he visited sub-Saharan Africa within six months of his presidency. No other American President ever visited sub-Saharan Africa during his first term in office.

Obama has also been criticised for an interview he granted to CNN's "Anderson Cooper: 360" in July, shortly after the Ghana trip. Obama had compared the legacy of slavery to the Holocaust, saying both are horrible parts of history and that their lessons must never be forgotten.

It is thought the assertion displeased some Jews and Africans in equal measure. For some Jews, comparing the holocaust to slavery diminishes the centrality of 'holocaust' in the mainstream narrative of victimhood and evil. They suspect that Obama wanted to smuggle in the 'long forgotten slavery', which is hardly mainstream, to share the spotlight with the holocaust. For some Africans, the comparison is an 'insult', not only because of the differences in the duration of the two 'evils' but also because of the unique effects and after effects of slavery such as the inferiorisation, discrimination and racism against black people that it spurned. Can a former slave masters ever see his former slave as equals, some Africans ask?

While I am not against subjecting Obama's policies and speeches to critical scrutiny (we will actually be helping to strengthen his presidency by doing so), the way some bloggers are taking it these days appears to re-echo the familiar 'pull him down' mentality so common with our people. This begs the question of what we really expect from an Obama presidency, and what he can realistically offer us given that any American president is often a captive of the system that throws him up? I believe Obama's greatest gift to black people would be to succeed as an American president for that would mean that yet another psychological barrier has been broken down for the entire race. Just as some people paved the way for blacks to be accepted in fields such as entertainment and sports, so will a successful Obama presidency perhaps also pave the way for future generation of blacks. Therefore, if we lead the battle cry to pull him down, or even lend hand in any effort that pulls him down, then of course the doubt in some quarters that a black person could operate successfully at such a level would be confirmed. And we would all be worse for it.

Daily Independent 30 July 2009

CHAPTER 123

WINNERS AND LOSERS FROM THE RISE (OR RECOVERY) OF CHINA

C hina is believed to be the oldest continuous civilization on earth. Unlike Egypt, its rival claimant to that 'honour, it has remained an empire (Kitissou, 2007:11). In this sense, it could be argued that China is not rising, but merely recovering. For decades after its 1949 revolution, it pursued a policy of communist economic development based primarily on the state control of the means of production, distribution and exchange. In 1979 it began an 'open door' policy, a sort of gradualist economic reforms, 'without any detailed "blue print" guiding the process' (Prasad, 2004). The reforms are generally believed to have been successful because they led to tremendous growth, and an expansion in international trade, with its imports and exports growing at an average rate of 15% each year since 1979 (Prasad, 2004). Economic growth stood at an average of nine percent per annum. But who are the winners and losers from the rise (or recovery) of China?

Goldman Sachs (2003) notes that those most likely to benefit from the rise of China include exporters of capital and resource-intensive products, while those that specialise in labour intensive exports similar to those of China will have to undergo a significant adjustment. Many corporations in the mature economies of the West now have a China strategy, sometimes including moving the manufacturing arm of their business to China to take advantage of the relatively cheap labour there. A 2003 study by the Institute for Management Development (IMD), one of the world's best-known business schools, confirmed not only that China was becoming the world's manufacturing centre but also that it was providing favourable policies for economic development, especially in the eastern coastal areas, which has a huge labour market of 737 million people.

The IMD report also found that China promotes globalisation. On one of the IMD's lists comparing the extent of its globalization, China moved up two notches in the ranking, indicating that the country has opened wider, and in a more efficient way, since it joined the World Trade Organization in 2001. The study equally found that China's extraordinary growth rate, combined with the fact that it is fast becoming the world's manufacturing centre, has made it a growth engine for the global economy. Sachs (2005) in fact argues that the fate of the global economic system hangs precariously on China's and Asian developments, with global growth in the coming decades being dependent to a large degree on continued Chinese expansion. Sachs notes that the single most imbalance in today's global economy is the USA's vast current account deficit, which must be balanced through capital inflows from the rest of the world. He notes that a large and rising share of the saving for this balancing comes from China, which as early as 2002, was already the second largest foreign holder of US long-term debt securities, accounting for $165 billion or 6.5 per cent of total foreign holdings (IMF 2004, cited in Sachs, 2005:51-52). It has therefore been argued in some quarters that the prospect for global peace hinges more on the willingness of America to accept the transfer of hegemony to Asia. As Sachs (2005:53) puts it, "the real cause for concern therefore is not China's quiet rise but America's noisy decline".

One of the downsides of China's rise however has been the country's increasing contribution to the problem of global warming. Bradsher (2003) has argued that China's rising energy consumption complicates diplomatic efforts to limit emissions of global warming gases. The International Energy Agency in Paris in fact predicts that in China the increase in greenhouse gas emissions from 2000 to 2030 will nearly equal the increase from the entire industrialised world. As a developing country, China is exempt from the Kyoto Plan on green gas emission, which president Bush had rejected in 2001, citing among other reasons, that the exemption of China from the plan was a serious law.

In terms of global influence, one of the likely losers from the rise of China is America. China's deepening integration into the world economy has for instance seen the country's influence expand in Africa. China's trade and investment in Africa have grown rapidly, with trade between Africa and China doubling to $18.5 billion between 2002 and 2003, reaching $39.7 billion in 2005. China is now Africa's third most important trading partner, behind the United States and France, sustained by trade agreements reached with 40 African countries (Reilly and Na, 2007:135). China's outward FDI also posted the highest growth of any region from 2003 to 2004 at 327 percent (Boardman 2007, cited in Reilly and Na 2007:135).

China's increasing engagement with Africa has heightened concerns in the United States that China's rise could challenge the US's traditional economic and security interests in the region. China, which has historically positioned itself as the leader of the Third World, is attractive to many African countries, especially its professed respect for each country's sovereignty and non-interference in each country's internal politics.

Copson (2007) has cautioned against any temptation by America to ignite a new "scramble" for Africa in a bid to contain China's rising influence in the region, warning that such could lead to a number of unpalatable consequences, including weapon proliferation. He proposes that any response to the threat from China by the US must be couched in such a way that the benefits of China's growing role in the world economy must be preserved at the same time as mitigating the negative consequences of such a rise.

There are also concerns that China's increasing engagement with Africa, especially its policy of non-interference in a country's internal politics, could be helping to prop up or sustain dictatorial regimes in Africa. For instance China invested heavily in oil exploration, extraction, transport and processing in many African countries, including Sudan and Angola, in order to "lock up barrels" at their source. To protect its investments, it usually refuses to ally itself with the 'international community' in condemning certain abhorrent actions such as efforts by the US to sanction the Sudanese government for encouraging ethnic cleansing in the country's Darfur region because Sudanese oil output accounts for a very significant portion of its total imports. Chinese arms sales in Africa have also been a source of concern and it has been alleged that China made more than one billion dollars from the war in Eritrea in the 1990s (Servant, 2005:61). Servant (2005) has also called for vigilance to ensure that what on the face value could appear to be a "win-win" situation between China and Africa, is not in reality naked neocolonialism disguised as South-South co-operation.

China's rise is also linked to the current hike in global energy prices. In 2003 for instance, China's import of oil increased by 30% over the 2002 level, taking global energy analysts by surprise. That year China surpassed Japan to become the second largest importer of petroleum after the United States (Thompson, 2005:25). While the rise in commodity prices may be bad news for some, especially in the developed countries, it has benefited many developing countries. Copson (2007) in fact believes that the boost in commodity prices, caused in part by China's demand, contributed to the positive GDP growth rates now being seen in many African countries.

Overall therefore, while China's rise (or recovery) benefits some, inducing glee and hilarity from such constituencies, there are those who are definitely threatened by such a rise. Global peace in the next 50 years may therefore depend less on the current politics of the "clash of civilisations", manifested mostly in the superstructures of religion, politics and culture, than on the more subtle but potentially more dangerous struggle between on the one hand, China's 'quite rise' and efforts to contain that rise in the West, and America's 'noisy decline', on the other.

www.hollerafrica.com, 1 February 2008

CHAPTER 124

COMMEMORATING THE INTERNATIONAL MIGRANTS DAY

Migration – the tendency for people to move from one place to another for sundry reasons that could include family re-union, running away from poverty, wars or political persecution – has been part of human history from earliest times. Figures from the International Organisation for Migration (IOM) show that there are some 200 million migrants today – if we define immigration strictly in terms of foreigners passing or coming into a country for permanent residence. Asia accounts for the largest number of migrant workers in the world while Europe accounts for the highest concentration of international migrants followed by North America. According to Eurostat some 47.3 million people who were born outside their resident country lived in the EU in 2010 - representing 9.4 percent of the total EU population.

In the last few decades, especially in periods of economic downturn, the treatment of migrants in host countries, both by governments, employers and original population, has been a topic of continual debate and criticism. The migrants are too often abused by right wing elements with their fundamental human rights not being always guaranteed or respected. This is the backdrop against which the United Nations General Assembly adopted on December 18 1990 the international convention on the protection of the rights of migrant workers and members of their families via resolution 45/158. On December 4 2000, the United Nations General Assembly officially designated December 18 as the International Migrants Day (IMD).

The UN proclamation of the International Migrants Day is meant to offer a rallying point for all who are concerned about the protection of the rights and dignity of migrants. It is also an opportunity to recognise and celebrate the contributions made by millions of immigrants across the world. This is important because too often the popular portrayal of immigrants in the media of the host countries is negative – usually as people who take jobs from the natives, commit crimes and pose a threat to the cultural identity of the 'host' societies.

True, there are immigrants who stick their 'immigrantness' to the face of the host communities, causing irritation. True, also, is that some immigrants commit crimes or engage in all manner of anti-social behaviours. But they are often a very negligible percentage of the immigrant community - just as a small percentage of the 'host societies' invariably become social deviants. In a depressing economy, it is all too easy to make the immigrant the scapegoat.

The truth is that the list of immigrants who have changed the course of their host communities, often for the better, is literally endless. Consider just these four examples:

Levi Strauss (February 26, 1829 – September 26, 1902). What will America or even the world be today without the blue jeans? Few people however know that the blue jeans was an invention of a 24-year old German immigrant, who had gone to San Francisco to open a small branch of his brother's dry goods business but discovered there was a demand for 'pants strong enough to last'. Levi Strauss and Nevada tailor David Jacobs co-patented the process of putting rivets in pants for strength. They received US Patent No.139, 121 on May 20, 1873 – a date which is now considered the official birthday of 'blue jeans'

Andrew Carnegie (November 25, 1835 – August 11, 1919) was born in Dunfermline, Scotland. After moving to the United States in 1848, he worked in a series of lowly paid railroad jobs before setting up a steel company. By 1889 his Carnegie Steel Corporation had become the largest of its kind in the world. In 1901 he sold the business for more than $200m and decided to dedicate his time to expanding his philanthropic work, which included the establishment of the Carnegie Institute of Technology in Pittsburgh, which later became the Carnegie-Mellon University in 1904. An avid reader despite having very little formal education, he had in 1901 donated approximately $5 million – a huge sum in those days- to the New York Public Library so that it could open several branches. He equally formed the Carnegie Endowment for International Peace in 1910 and made several other donations. It is estimated that more than 2,800 libraries were opened in the US with his support.

Barrack Hussein Obama Sr (18 June 1936– 24 November 1982) was a Kenyan senior government economist better known for being the father of the current U.S. President. In 1959, Obama Sr. received a scholarship in economics which enabled him to study at the University of Hawaii at Manoa in Honolulu as the university's first African foreign student. In September 1960, he met Stanley Ann Dunham in a basic Russian language course and married her on 2 February 1961. Though the marriage did not last and whatever we may think of Obama Sr, he gave America Barrack Obama, who was born on August 4 1961. Will

America have produced a 'Black' President the time it did if Barrack Hussein Obama Sr had not gone to the US?

James Ramsey John, a Scottish chemist, emigrated in 1935 to Ghana (then called Gold Coast) with his wife, Mary, to work for the United Africa Company (UAC). In about 1941 he started a secret relationship with one Victoria Agbotui who was a caterer at the State House. The relationship, which lasted for some six years, produced Jeremiah Rawlings John on June 22 1947. Though James Ramsey John continued to deny the paternity of the child till his death in 1982, many believe that the offspring of that illicit liaison, Jerry Rawlings, helped to lay the foundations of the current economic and political renaissance in Ghana – in spite of the obvious excesses of his regime as a military dictator in Ghana. Though an 'irresponsible immigrant' will the course of Ghana have been the same if James Ramsey John had not emigrated from Scotland?

As we commemorate the International Migrants' Day, we are offered a golden opportunity to also reflect on the conditions of Nigerians who toil under stressful and alienating conditions in other countries but manage to wire home some $20bn annually to help maintain parents or train relatives. As we condemn racism and xenophobia in many migrant host countries in the West, IMD is an occasion for us to also reflect on how we treat our own immigrants – both those from other countries and in particular fellow Nigerians who immigrated to our communities. With the indigene/settler dichotomy creating tensions and violence in many parts of the country - not just in Jos but also in several ethnically homogenous states - IMD offers a golden opportunity to ask ourselves whether we are really better than the 'bloody White racists' we like to rile against.

Just as IMD enables us to celebrate the achievements of international migrants, we should also reflect on how our own local migrants have been beneficial to our communities. Another way to approach this will be to ask ourselves a few soul-searching questions: How many of the indigenes of our host communities really have investments in that community that power the local economy and provide jobs? How many of us really grew up and made a career in the communities we were born? Are we not, in a sense, all migrants – even if it means we only migrated from our place of birth to the next city? Where do we truly stand in the indigene/settler dichotomy? If the 'bloody White racists' can give Nigerians and other immigrants naturalised citizenship after a few years of residence in their country but we cannot grant full rights enjoyed by the 'indigenes' of our local community to long-term immigrants in that community, what does that tell us about ourselves? What would have been the nature of our racism and xenophobia if we were to exchange places with the 'bloody White racists'?

I believe the intractable indigene/settler dichotomy is a powerful indictment on us as hypocrites. We like to pontificate and 'blow all the big grammar' about how unjust the international system is, the imperialists and White supremacists who dehumanise us and our brethrens abroad but fail to see that we hide under the 'indigene' canopy to pursue even worse forms of discriminatory policies. Paradoxically, many of the immigrants who complain of discrimination and marginalisation in their host societies find all manner of reasons why the same rights they clamour for should not be extended to immigrants in their own host communities. For them, what is good for the goose is not necessarily good for the gander. IMD should therefore be more than an occasion to reflect on the agonies and achievements of international migrant workers, including Nigerians in the Diaspora. More importantly it should enable us look inwards and goad us to remove the logs in our own eyes before complaining of the specks in others' eyes.

Daily Trust 22 December 2011

Index

F

G

H

I

www.ingramcontent.com/pod-product-compliance
Lightning Source LLC
Chambersburg PA
CBHW060129280326
41932CB00012B/1463

www.ingramcontent.com/pod-product-compliance
Lightning Source LLC
Chambersburg PA
CBHW060129280326
41932CB00012B/1463